JOBS WITH E

Jobs with Equality

LANE KENWORTHY

OXFORD
UNIVERSITY PRESS

OXFORD
UNIVERSITY PRESS

Great Clarendon Street, Oxford OX2 6DP

Oxford University Press is a department of the University of Oxford.
It furthers the University's objective of excellence in research, scholarship,
and education by publishing worldwide in

Oxford New York

Auckland Cape Town Dar es Salaam Hong Kong Karachi
Kuala Lumpur Madrid Melbourne Mexico City Nairobi
New Delhi Shanghai Taipei Toronto

With offices in

Argentina Austria Brazil Chile Czech Republic France Greece
Guatemala Hungary Italy Japan Poland Portugal Singapore
South Korea Switzerland Thailand Turkey Ukraine Vietnam

Oxford is a registered trade mark of Oxford University Press
in the UK and in certain other countries

Published in the United States
by Oxford University Press Inc., New York

British Library Cataloguing in Publication Data

Data available

Library of Congress Cataloging in Publication Data

Kenworthy, Lane.
Jobs with equality / Lane Kenworthy.
p. cm.
Includes bibliographical references and index.
ISBN 978–0–19–955060–9—ISBN 978–0–19–955059–3 1. Employment
(Economic theory) 2. Income distribution. 3. Equality. I. Title.
HD5701.K46 2008
331.2'153—dc22   2008015440

Typeset by SPI Publisher Services Ltd, Pondicherry, India
Printed in Great Britain
on acid-free paper by
CPI Antony Rowe, Chippenham, Wiltshire

ISBN 978–0–19–955059-3 (Hbk)
ISBN 978–0–19–955060-9 (Pbk)

1 3 5 7 9 10 8 6 4 2

For my children—Mia, Hannah, Noah, and Josh

Acknowledgments

For helpful comments and discussion, I owe thanks to Lucio Baccaro, Jean-Claude Barbier, Keith Bentele, Pablo Beramendi, Barbara Bergmann, Ron Breiger, John Campbell, Frank Castles, Mike Dixon, Daniel Duerr, Bernhard Ebbinghaus, Werner Eichorst, Scott Eliason, Jessica Epstein, Gøsta Esping-Andersen, Miriam Golden, Janet Gornick, Bjorn Hallerod, Bob Hancké, Anke Hassel, Kieran Healy, Anton Hemerijck, Andrea Herrmann, Alex Hicks, John Hills, Jonathan Hopkin, Laura Hunter, Torben Iversen, Christopher Jencks, Lars Bo Kaspersen, Bernhard Kittel, Martin Kohli, Walter Korpi, Greta Krippner, Ed Leamer, Jane Lewis, Rianne Mahon, Jim Mahoney, Michael Mann, Isabella Mares, Ive Marx, Ed Miliband, Joya Misra, Kimberly Morgan, John Myles, Ann Orloff, Joakim Palme, Ove Pedersen, Niels Ploug, Jonas Pontusson, Adam Przeworski, Charles Ragin, Martin Rhodes, Frances Rosenbluth, Louise Roth, Bill Roy, Stefano Sacchi, John Schmitt, Michael Shalev, Marco Simoni, John Stephens, Wolfgang Streeck, Robin Stryker, Kathy Thelen, Jelle Visser, Roger Waldinger, Michael Wallerstein, Anne Wren, Jane Zavisca, and Jonathan Zeitlin. Of course, none of these kind souls should be held responsible for whatever the book lacks in accuracy or insight.

Portions of the book were written while I was a visiting fellow at the European University Institute (EUI) in Florence, a visiting fellow at the Centre for Analysis of Social Exclusion (CASE) at the London School of Economics, and a resident fellow at the Udall Center for Public Policy Studies at the University of Arizona. I am grateful to several people for helping to make these opportunities possible: Colin Crouch, who at that time chaired the EUI's Department of Political and Social Sciences; John Hills, Director of CASE; and Steve Cornell, Director of the Udall Center. I also thank the Economic and Social Research Council, which funded my visit to CASE.

Warm thanks to Danny and Cherie Mannheim, owners of the Espresso Art café in Tucson, where I've spent considerable time reading, analyzing, writing, and discussing over the past several years.

I am grateful most of all to my family—Kim, Mia, Hannah, Noah, and Josh—for allowing me time to work on this project, and for giving me good reason not to spend *all* of my time on it.

Contents

1

Introduction

THE PROBLEM

From the end of World War II until the mid-1970s, a number of affluent countries achieved a feat that many now look back upon with considerable envy: they combined continuously rising living standards with declining income inequality. Since the mid-1970s these economies have continued to grow, but at a much slower pace. And in many of them, inequality has increased; incomes for those in the middle and at the low end of the distribution have grown less rapidly than for those at the high end.

For policy analysts and policy makers who care about inequality, this poses a challenge. One view is that developments during the postwar "golden age" were a historical fluke and cannot be repeated. In this perspective, countries in the contemporary economic environment must choose between growth and low inequality; they cannot have both. In theoretical terms, the relationship between inequality and growth is ambiguous. There are reasons why low inequality might inhibit growth and other reasons why it might promote growth. The question, therefore, can only be decided empirically. Among the affluent countries, it turns out that there is no association in either direction between income inequality and economic growth since the 1970s (Kenworthy 2004a: ch. 4, 2008a).

This book does not speak to the question of inequality's impact on economic growth. I assume that if countries with low inequality have been (on average) able to grow just as rapidly as their high-inequality counterparts in recent decades, they may be able to do so over the next few decades as well. The question that motivates the book is: How can affluent countries maintain or move toward low inequality?

By "inequality" I mean posttax-posttransfer income inequality among households. There is good reason to care about inequality in the labor market—that is, inequality of earnings among employed individuals. But earnings typically are pooled within households. Hence, the household is arguably the unit about which we should be most centrally concerned.

Low income inequality is an increasingly difficult goal. Inequality in the market distribution of income—that is, before taxes and government transfers are taken into account—has been rising since the 1970s in many of these countries (Kenworthy 2004*a*; Kenworthy and Pontusson 2005). The first chart in Figure 1.1 shows levels of pretax-pretransfer income inequality among households with working-age heads in twelve countries. The data are for two peak business cycle years, 1979 and 2000. The latter is the most recent year for which reliable comparative data are available. Inequality is measured using the Gini coefficient; it ranges from zero to one, with larger numbers indicating greater inequality. Market inequality rose in eleven of the twelve nations, in some cases quite substantially.

One reason for this is that employment shifts from manufacturing to services, union fragmentation, decentralization of wage setting, globalization, technological change, and other developments have contributed to wage stagnation at the low end of the distribution and growing earnings inequality among employed individuals. The rise in individual earnings inequality began earliest and has been most pronounced in the United States and the United Kingdom, but since the mid-1990s it has occurred in a number of affluent nations (see Chapter 3). This in turn has contributed to rising income inequality among households.

Several other developments have reinforced and accentuated the impact of heightened earnings inequality (Chapter 3). With delayed marriage and more frequent divorce, more households have only a single adult and therefore only one potential earner. At the same time, in households with two adults (whether married or cohabiting), it is increasingly the case that both have paying jobs. These contrasting developments tend to widen the income gap between households. In addition, women and men with high education are increasingly likely to couple with one another, and the same is true for those with low education. This phenomenon, referred to as "marital homogamy," tends to further increase interhousehold income differences.

Declining inequality in the market distribution of earnings and income was key to countries' success in achieving reduced inequality in the distribution of posttax-posttransfer income during the golden age. But redistribution via taxation and government transfers was also an essential element. Given rising market inequality in recent decades, we might expect policy makers with a preference for low inequality to respond by increasing redistribution. The second chart in Figure 1.1 shows that the amount of redistribution achieved via taxes and transfers did indeed rise in most of the countries where market inequality increased. The only exceptions are Italy and the United States.

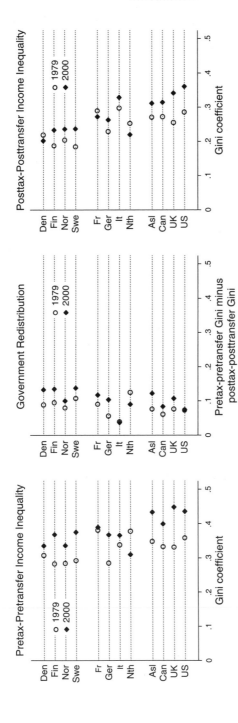

Figure 1.1. Market income inequality, government redistribution, and posttax-posttransfer income inequality, 1979 and 2000.

Note: The countries are ordered alphabetically within each group. The data are for households with working-age heads. Countries for which actual years are not 1979 and 2000: Australia 1981 and 2001, Canada 1981, Denmark 1987, Finland 1987, Germany 1981, Italy 1986, the Netherlands 1983 and 1999, Sweden 1981, United Kingdom 1999. For Italy and the United States, the level of government redistribution was the same in 2000 as in 1979. For data definitions and sources, see the appendix.

However, the third chart in the figure reveals that the rise in redistribution was not sufficient to offset the rise in market inequality. Posttax-posttransfer income inequality increased in nine of the twelve nations.

Countries also face new pressures and constraints on redistribution. One is population aging. Public pension systems in most affluent countries are financed on a "pay-as-you-go" basis: benefits for retirees come directly from current taxes. With low fertility rates and lengthening life spans, the cost of public pensions is rising relative to the tax base from which they are funded. Because pensions typically are the largest category of social expenditure aside from health care, this puts a strain on government finances. Pension systems can be adjusted—by raising the retirement age, reducing benefit levels, and/or taxing back the benefits of well-to-do retirees at steeper rates. But such changes are difficult to implement politically, and they may not yield enough cost savings in any case.

A second constraint is slower rates of productivity growth (growth of output per employed person). This owes to a variety of factors (Baumol, Blackmun, and Wolff 1989; Kenworthy 1995; Maddison 2001). Increased revenues produced by rapid growth of productivity could help to offset the fiscal pressures of population aging. But the past several decades have been characterized by slower, rather than faster, rates of increase in productivity, and there is no convincing evidence to suggest that this pattern will soon reverse.

Given the growing fiscal strain created by population aging and limited productivity growth, policy makers wishing to maintain or increase redistribution might be expected to raise tax rates. But that has been made more difficult by a third constraint: heightened capital mobility. Dire predictions of an all-out race to the bottom in tax rates have not been borne out, but in many countries rates have indeed been reduced, with revenues (as a share of GDP) holding constant only because the tax base has been broadened (Ganghof 2000; Genschel 2002).

A POSSIBLE SOLUTION

An increasingly common view, which I share, is that a key to limiting the growth of inequality in the face of these various pressures and constraints is to increase the employment rate (Esping-Andersen 1999; Ferrera, Hemerijck, and Rhodes 2000; Scharpf and Schmidt 2000; Esping-Andersen et al. 2002; Kok et al. 2003; Kenworthy 2004a; OECD 2005b, 2006b; Institute for Futures Studies 2006; Hemerijck 2007). Doing so is doubly beneficial for redistributive efforts: it yields an increase in tax revenues without an increase in tax rates; and to the extent it moves some current recipients of government benefits into the work force, it reduces welfare state costs.

While its chief benefit with respect to inequality reduction is via redistribution, employment can also reduce inequality in the distribution of market incomes across households. Half a century ago it was normal for many working-age adults to not be in the labor force. They were mainly women, and their husbands were employed. The fact that some adults were employed and others not had little impact on the distribution of earnings among households because inequality of employment occurred mainly within, rather than between, households. That is no longer the case. Women increasingly are in paid work, so inequality of employment occurs more and more between households. In other words, instead of having many households with one (usually male) earner and one (usually female) nonearner, a country with a low or moderate employment rate now is more likely to have many households with two earners and many with no earners (Gregg 1996; OECD 1998). This increases inequality of earnings and incomes between households (Chapter 3; Förster and Pearson 2002). To the extent it reduces the number of zero-earner households, high employment should help to counteract this development and thereby reduce market inequality.

Employment can also be justified on intrinsic grounds (Jahoda 1982; Wilson 1996; Phelps 1997: ch. 1). With heightened geographic mobility, later marriage, and increased divorce, neighborhood and family ties have dissipated somewhat. As a result, work is an increasingly important site of social interaction. Employment imposes regularity and discipline on people's lives. It can be a source of mental stimulation. It helps to fulfill the widespread desire to contribute to, and be integrated with, the larger society. For many individuals, work is inextricably bound up with identity and self-esteem.

What can affluent countries do to secure both low income inequality and high employment? In this book I examine the challenges such countries face, the strategies they have pursued in recent decades, and some options that might help them to do better.

OUTLINE OF THE BOOK

The book consists largely of empirical analysis of the experiences of rich democratic capitalist countries. Due mainly to data limitations but also in part to my desire to understand the institutional configurations and socioeconomic processes in individual countries in some detail, I focus on just twelve nations. Four are "Nordic" European countries: Denmark, Finland,

Norway, and Sweden. Four are "continental" European: France, Germany, Italy, and the Netherlands. The other four are "Anglo" (English-speaking): Australia, Canada, the United Kingdom, and the United States. I use this tripartite grouping of the twelve countries throughout the book. Its role, however, is purely heuristic; the aim is to facilitate the display of data and the exposition. I do not argue that membership in a particular group plays a causal role in determining either inequality or employment.

For the most part I concentrate on developments since the late 1970s. This too is due partly to data availability. But there is a substantive rationale as well. The late 1970s mark the beginning of a qualitatively distinct economic environment for these countries—one characterized by, among other things, slower economic growth, globalization, rapid technological change, labor movement fragmentation, and a rightward shift in politics.

In Chapter 2 I consider the question of why citizens and policy makers should want low inequality. Why should we object to inequality? Should we focus on equality of opportunity or equality of outcomes? Why not focus on poverty instead? Why emphasize incomes rather than wealth or material well-being? Do people in fact care about inequality?

In Chapter 3 I argue that in thinking about income inequality, our focus should be on the distribution of posttax-posttransfer income among households, rather than the distribution of earnings among individuals or the distribution of market income among households. I then explore the chief determinants of cross-country and over-time differences in posttax-posttransfer household income inequality. I examine the impact of individual earnings, employment patterns within and across households, household composition and structure, and government redistribution. Each of these has played a role in why some countries have more income inequality than others and in why inequality has increased in many nations. A key finding in Chapter 3 is that for the countries that have been most successful at limiting inequality, redistribution has been especially significant. I suggest that keeping individual earnings inequality in check is likely to be increasingly difficult and that household structure and composition are very difficult for policy makers to influence. Hence, redistribution may be even more important in the future.

Chapter 4 describes the way I conceptualize and measure employment performance. I argue that to assess employment performance since the late 1970s, the most useful measure is employment change. By this I mean change in the employment rate (sometimes referred to as the "employment-to-population ratio"), not change in the number of people employed. It would be helpful to adjust this for work hours, but data limitations prevent that and the best available data suggest that doing so would not change the story much in any event. Part of the cross-country variation in employment change is a product of the degree of job loss in manufacturing and agriculture, and that in turn was due largely to the share of employment in these two sectors at the beginning of the period. In assessing the impact of policies and institutions on employment change, I therefore focus on services.

Chapter 4 also outlines my strategy for analyzing the impact of equality-enhancing institutions and policies on employment performance. Most of the analysis in the book is macrocomparative. Countries are the unit of analysis, and inferences are based on comparison of employment change across countries. For both substantive and methodological reasons, much of the comparative analysis is relatively simple. This imposes some limits but also has some significant advantages. I supplement the macrocomparative analyses with examination of various types of within-country evidence, especially quantitative and qualitative data on over-time developments.

In Chapters 5 through 10 I examine a variety of institutions and policies that are likely to influence countries' success in pursuing low inequality with high employment: low-end wage levels, employment protection regulations, government benefits, taxes, skills, and "women-friendly" policies.

Chapters 5–8 examine ways in which institutions and policies at the heart of countries' efforts to reduce inequality—high wage floors, employment protection, generous government benefits, and high taxes—may or may not reduce employment. For the past decade conventional wisdom has held that affluent nations face a choice between two models. The "European model" features high wages, strong employment protection rules, generous benefits, and high taxes. It is thought to produce low inequality but also low employment. The "American model" features low wages, employer flexibility with respect to firing, stingy benefits, and low taxes. It is said to generate high inequality but also high employment. These images are to some degree caricatures of the continents and countries they are said to describe, but many critics of these stylized ideal-types too quickly and cursorily dismiss the possibility that there genuinely are tradeoffs.

In Chapter 5 I look at the effect of wage levels at the low end of the labor market on employment. The key concern here has to do with low-end service jobs. These have been a major source of employment growth in many of the countries that have achieved rising employment rates during the past several decades. Because productivity in these jobs tends to be low and difficult to increase, the question is whether relatively high wages will substantially reduce employer demand for labor. Within the United States, this has been the key question at issue in the recurring debate over whether, and to what degree, the statutory minimum wage should be increased. I focus on cross-country evidence. Are low wages really necessary in low-productivity service jobs? If so, how low do they need to be?

Strict employment protection rules are typically motivated by concern for fairness rather than equality, but they may nevertheless help to reduce inequality in earnings among the employed. The concern is that they may also reduce hiring, thereby inhibiting employment growth. What does the experience of affluent countries in recent decades suggest? I examine this issue in Chapter 6.

In Chapter 7 I turn to government benefits. Generous benefits are necessary for securing low inequality but, depending on the degree of generosity and the conditions of eligibility, they may discourage employment. Has that been the case in affluent countries in recent decades? After examining the comparative evidence, I turn to extended consideration of a particular type of transfer program: employment-conditional earnings subsidies, such as the Earned Income Tax Credit in the United States and the Working Tax Credit in the United Kingdom. This type of benefit has a variety of desirable features. Perhaps most important, it effectively targets transfers to households with low incomes while encouraging employment. What impact have such subsidies had in the countries where they have been tried? How, if at all, might they fit with the policy packages in other countries? What other types of benefits are needed for securing low income inequality in the twenty-first century?

Like benefit programs, tax rates and tax structures differ markedly across the rich countries. And like benefits, taxes play a key role in reducing inequality but may also reduce employment. Do taxes reduce inequality directly, or do they contribute to redistribution chiefly by providing the revenue for transfers? To what extent does globalization constrain governments' ability to maintain large and progressive tax systems? Have countries been moving toward more or less redistributive types of taxation? Do taxes in fact impede employment? If so, does the problem lie chiefly in the overall level of taxation or in the structure of the tax system? What is the magnitude of the effect? I examine these questions in Chapter 8.

Educational attainment is a good predictor of individuals' employment and earnings. In the standard view, this is because education is a useful measure of skills, which in turn are a key determinant of a person's productivity. In theory, equalizing skills could therefore lead to both high employment and a relatively equal distribution of earnings. In Chapter 9 I assess this supposition, drawing on both individual- and country-level data.

In countries that have employment deficits, the problem consists chiefly of a shortage of women in employment. For example, Germany's employment rate among men is almost as high as Sweden's, but the employment rate for women in the two countries differs by more than 10 percentage points. Italy's male employment rate is comparable to that in Finland, but its female employment rate is more than 20 percentage points lower. A critical task for low-employment countries, then, is to increase employment among women. In Chapter 10 I investigate the impact of "women-friendly" policies—funding or provision of childcare, paid maternity/home care leaves, public employment, promotion of part-time work, tax systems that do not penalize a second earner in a household, and antidiscrimination and affirmative action policies—on women's employment. I also consider the relationship between female employment levels and household income inequality.

In the concluding chapter, Chapter 11, I summarize the book's findings, recommend some strategies for combining low inequality with high employment, and consider some potential objections and alternatives.

A word for those who wish to read selectively: Readers concerned mainly with the equality–jobs tradeoff debate will be most interested in Chapters 5–8, but Chapter 4 should be read first. Those whose principal interest is equality and inequality will find Chapters 2 and 3 most directly relevant, but Chapters 5–10 also include useful information and discussion. A summary of the findings and my recommendations are in Chapter 11.

Part I

Equality

2

Why Should We Care About Inequality?

For many, the aim of limiting inequality needs some justification. There are several issues here. Why should we object to inequality? Should we focus on equality of opportunity or equality of outcomes? Why not focus on poverty instead? Why emphasize incomes rather than wealth or material well-being? Do people in fact care about inequality? I address each of these in turn.

Let me make clear at the outset that although I will frequently refer to "equality" in this book, I use this as a synonym for "low inequality." Few if any egalitarians favor perfect equality of outcomes. Complete equality would substantially reduce work incentives, thereby violating the principle of reciprocity (all who are able to contribute do so; see Bowles and Gintis 1998; Galston 2001; Rawls 2001; White 2004a) and undermining the other aim I advocate: high employment. Imagine a society in which the social product is divided into an equal consumption allowance for each citizen. If the population were 10 million, the effective marginal tax rate on additional income would be 99.99999%, and an average earner who abandoned paid employment would reduce the value of her own consumption share by a mere 0.00001%. Plainly, the incentive to opt out of employment would be quite strong.

WHY OBJECT TO INEQUALITY?

Objections to inequality tend to focus on considerations of fairness and on ways in which inequality may adversely affect other desirable outcomes.

Fairness

One reason to favor societal institutions and policies that reduce inequality has to do with the importance of luck in determining earnings and incomes (Rawls 1971; Jencks et al. 1972; Dworkin 1985; Roemer 1998; Miller 2003: ch. 4; Miller 2005). Much of what determines people's earnings and income—intelligence, creativity, physical and social skills, motivation, persistence, confidence, connections, inherited wealth, discrimination—is a product of genetics, parents' assets and traits, and the quality of one's childhood neighborhood and schools. With few exceptions, these things are not chosen; they are a matter of luck. A nontrivial portion of earnings inequality and income inequality is therefore undeserved.

Consequences of Inequality

Other arguments for low inequality focus on its consequences. A higher level of income inequality may result in slower economic growth, higher crime rates, poorer health, less educational attainment, heavier debt loads for the middle class, disproportionate political power wielded by the wealthy, and greater political polarization, among other societal ills. The extent to which it does so is an empirical question. It is a large question, and I will not attempt to answer it with empirical evidence here. Instead I will summarize recent arguments and findings.

Education. Higher levels of inequality may widen disparities in educational attainment. The main effect is likely to be on differences in college attendance. In the United States, even with substantial funds available for financial aid, many students from lower-income households are forced to pay a relatively large amount to attend college. A study by the U.S. Census Bureau (2002: table 6a) found that among students from families with incomes below $25,000, the average yearly cost of attending college as of the mid-1990s was $6,000. The average amount covered by financial aid was $3,000, leaving the remaining $3,000 to be paid by the student or her/his parents. Thomas Kane (2004) reports that in 1980, 55% of children from families in the top income quartile attended a four-year college, compared to 29% of those from families in the bottom quartile. By 1992, as income inequality increased, the difference had widened to 66% versus 28%. These quartile differences are smaller but still sizable when parents' education and student test scores and high school rank are controlled for (Kane 2004).

The effect of income inequality on inequality in college attendance is shaped by public policy. In the Nordic countries, access to college has been substantially enlarged in the past several decades by policies that fund such participation as a universal right of citizenship (OECD 2004e). Not surprisingly, the odds of a child with low-educated (and thus likely low-income) parents attending university are three to six times greater in Sweden, Denmark, and Norway than in the United States (Esping-Andersen 2007).

Health. Higher income inequality contributes to greater disparity of health outcomes (Mullahy, Robert, and Wolfe 2004). As with education, the size of the effect will be heavily influenced by government policy. But even in a system with universal health coverage, co-payments coupled with lesser knowledge will tend to reduce use of health services among the poor and higher income will enable the rich to purchase better treatment.

A number of studies have linked income inequality with lower average levels of health (Wilkinson 1996; Lynch and Kaplan 1997; Kawachi, Wilkinson, and Kennedy 1999). The mechanism commonly posited to account for this link is relative deprivation: having an income below one's reference group may increase stress and thereby worsen health, regardless of the person's absolute income. However, a variety of empirical studies have cast doubt on this link both across countries and within countries over time (Burtless and Jencks 2003; Deaton 2003; Beckfield 2004; Mullahy, Robert, and Wolfe 2004).

Crime. Inequality might increase crime via material incentives or via frustration. To the extent inequality is associated with limited job and income opportunities for young persons (especially males), it may encourage greater pursuit of illicit income-generating activities (Freeman 1996). High levels of inequality might also foster crime by breeding frustration. Perceived relative deprivation and blocked opportunity may contribute to greater criminal activity (Merton 1968).

Evidence on a link between inequality and crime is mixed (Burtless and Jencks 2003; Western, Kleykamp, and Rosenfeld 2004). At the individual level, the propensity to commit crime is higher among those with lower incomes. Cross-sectional studies across US states or localities have sometimes yielded findings of a positive association. The United States has higher income inequality than other affluent countries and a much higher rate of violent crime, but other types of crime that seem likely to be encouraged by inequality, such as theft, do not correlate with inequality across countries. And over time, the association between inequality and crime in the United States is not particularly strong.

Consumption and debt. Robert Frank (1999, 2005) argues persuasively that housing is a "positional" good. That is, people's happiness with their home depends more heavily on relative comparison with other nearby homes than is true for many other goods (such as toothpaste or vacation time). Consider a hypothetical scenario, Frank says, in which you must choose "between world A, in which you will live in a 4,000-square-foot house and others will live in 6,000-square-foot houses; and world B, in which you will live in a 3,000-square-foot house and others will live in 2,000-square-foot houses. Once you choose, your position on the local housing scale will persist. If only absolute consumption mattered, A would clearly be better. Yet most people say they would pick B, where their absolute house size is smaller but their relative house size is larger" (Frank 2005: 137). Frank suggests that rising income at the high end of the distribution in the United States (see below) has allowed the well-to-do to purchase increasingly large and elaborately equipped homes. Because housing satisfaction depends on relative comparison, middle-class homeowners have felt compelled to follow suit, leading to dramatic increases in home prices and housing expenditures. The result is reduced spending in other consumption areas, greater debt, and increased middle-class bankruptcy (Warren and Tyagi 2003; Mishel, Bernstein, and Allegretto 2007).

Economic growth. Although for a long time the conventional view held that income inequality is good for economic growth, in recent decades a contrary argument has emerged, suggesting that inequality may well impede growth. There are various mechanisms through which this effect might obtain (Lazear 1989; Akerlof and Yellen 1990; Levine 1991; Barr 1992; Alesina and Rodrik 1994; Persson and Tabellini 1994; Birdsall, Ross, and Sabot 1995; Kenworthy 1995: ch. 3; Bénabou 1996; Agell 1999; Gomez and Meltz 2001). One is reduced educational attainment, as discussed above. A second is that high levels of inequality may be viewed by those at the middle and bottom of the income distribution as excessively unfair, thereby reducing worker motivation and workplace cooperation. Third, the financial constraints and frustration generated by high levels of inequality may reduce trust, cooperation, civic engagement, and other growth-enhancing forms of social capital. Fourth, social insurance programs that reduce inequality may encourage human capital investment and employment by providing—more efficiently than private insurance markets—a cushion against risk of job loss, illness, and on-the-job injury. Fifth, income polarization may foster extralegal demands for economic and/or political reform. Rebellions, revolutions, and other forms of violent collective action diminish political stability, which may adversely affect growth. Sixth, higher levels of market inequality may generate popular demand for increased government spending, particularly on transfers, which might reduce growth. These latter two have limited applicability to affluent nations. In such countries, political stability has not been disrupted by violent collective action in recent decades, and higher levels of market inequality are not associated with higher levels of government transfers (see Chapters 3 and 7).

The empirical evidence on income inequality's effect on economic growth is mixed. A number of studies have found a negative cross-country and over-time association between inequality and growth in less-developed nations (Birdsall, Ross, and Sabot 1995; Clarke 1995; Perotti 1996). This is not surprising, as effects of inequality on education and political stability are likely to be sizeable in this type of context. In affluent countries there is much less consensus among scholars (Barro 2000; Forbes 2000; Burtless and Jencks 2003; Voitchovsky 2003). In my own recent analysis of rich countries, of the US states, and of over-time trends in the United States, I found no indication that income inequality either increases or reduces economic growth (Kenworthy 2004*a*: ch. 4).

Economic mobility. The notion that "a mobile society is better than an equal one" (*The Economist* 2007) probably strikes many as sensible. But what if high levels of inequality impede mobility? There are several mechanisms through which greater income inequality might reduce intergenerational mobility (Corcoran 1995, 2001; Meyers et al. 2004; Esping-Andersen 2007). The rich can pass their income on to their children directly via gifts and inheritance. Low parental income may inhibit opportunities for children via risk-averseness, greater stress, lesser access to quality childcare and preschool, inferior schools, limited health care, and more dangerous neighborhoods. The United States, which has the highest level of income inequality among rich countries, also has less intergenerational income mobility than most others (Corak 2004; Jäntti et al. 2006). The degree of mobility in the United States appears to have increased in the 1960s, when income inequality was declining, but then remained flat since the 1970s as inequality has risen (Harding et al. 2005).

Civic engagement. Involvement in community affairs and organizations is widely thought to be beneficial both for its own sake and for its effects on other desirable societal outcomes (Putnam 1993, 2000). In the United States at least, such engagement tends to be strongly stratified by income (Putnam 2000; Brady et al. 2003; Skocpol 2004). There is disagreement, however, about whether rising income inequality since the 1970s has widened the dispersion in civic engagement (Brady et al. 2000; Putnam 2000; Wuthnow 2002; Costa and Kahn 2003*a*, 2003*b*).

Political participation. Political participation includes activities such as voting, joining or contributing money or effort to a political organization or a campaign, and participating in community activities or protests. Differences in resources due to unequal incomes are most likely to produce inequality in monetary contribution. There is considerable evidence that they are associated with inequality in other kinds of political participation as well (Verba, Schlozman, and Brady 2004). On the other hand, it is not clear whether the degree of inequality in participation in the United States has risen in concert with income inequality over the past several decades (Brady 2004; Freeman 2004; Verba, Schlozman, and Brady 2004: 644–5).

Political influence. To the extent that private money affects elections and political decision-making, there is good reason to suspect greater income inequality will be associated with greater inequality in political influence. A task force commissioned by the American Political Science Association concluded recently that "Disparities of wealth, income, and access to opportunity

are growing more sharply than in other nations.... Progress toward realiz-
ing American ideals of democracy may have stalled, and in some arenas
reversed.... The privileged participate more than others and are increasingly
well organized to press their demands on government. Public officials, in turn,
are more responsive to the privileged than to average citizens and the least
affluent. Citizens with low or moderate incomes speak with a whisper that is
lost on the ears of inattentive government, while the advantaged roar with
a clarity and consistency that policy makers readily heed.... Our review of
research on inequality and political participation as well as other components
of American political life demonstrates an extraordinary association between
economic and political inequality" (Jacobs et al. 2004: 651, 655; see also
Phillips 2002; Verba, Schlozman, and Brady 2004; Krugman 2007).

Political polarization. Less obvious than its link with political inequality is
the fact that greater income inequality may contribute to political polarization.
In analyses of National Election Studies (NES) data, Nolan McCarty, Keith
Poole, and Howard Rosenthal (2006) find that party preference and voting in
the United States have become more closely correlated with income over time.
The positions of legislators from the two parties have moved further apart
since the 1970s, and over the course of the twentieth century the degree of
polarization tracks closely with the level of income inequality.

The study of income inequality's consequences is in some respects in its
infancy. Many of the hypotheses I have discussed here need further confirm-
ation. Perhaps the most important task for researchers is to better gauge
the magnitude of these effects. Are the adverse impacts of greater inequality
sizable? Or are they relatively minor compared to other determinants? We have
little in the way of answers to this question.

INEQUALITY OF OUTCOMES OR INEQUALITY
OF OPPORTUNITY?

For most Americans, and very likely for many people in other affluent countries, inequality of opportunity is much more objectionable than inequality
of outcomes. I share this view, but pursuing equal opportunity is not enough,
for two reasons. First, because parents' income affects children's capabilities,
true equality of opportunity would require something close to equalization
of assets and incomes, at least among households with children (Jencks
et al. 1972: 4; Duncan and Brooks-Gunn 1997; Bowles, Gintis, and Osborne
2004). Second, even if asset and income equalization were accomplished, truly
equal opportunities would remain unrealizable. Individuals' opportunities

are influenced by genetic endowments, parents and other adults, peers, and a variety of chance occurrences throughout childhood and adolescence. No liberal society—that is, one in which families and other institutions retain a sizable degree of autonomy—can ensure that its members reach adulthood with equal capacities for success. Institutions and policies that compensate for unequal opportunities by reducing inequality of outcomes are thus justifiable even for those who prioritize equality of opportunity.

INEQUALITY OR POVERTY?

Inequality should be distinguished from poverty. Inequality refers to the degree of dispersion in the distribution. Poverty refers to the incomes of those at the bottom of the distribution.

There are two broad approaches to thinking about poverty. The dominant one in Europe, and among researchers who study cross-country differences in poverty, conceptualizes poverty as relative. The poverty line, below which a household or person is defined as being poor, is set relative to the median income in the country. The most common choice is to set the poverty line at 40%, 50%, or 60% of the median. The poverty line therefore differs across countries and shifts over time, depending on the median. The principal rationale for thinking about poverty as relative is that people tend to assess their living standard by comparing it to that of others in their society. As Robert Goodin and his colleagues (1999: 28) put it: "People feel themselves to be poor, and think others to be poor, in ways that matter both sociologically and ultimately morally, if they have substantially less than what is commonplace among others in their society" (see also Sen 1983; Brady 2003; Iceland 2003; Rainwater and Smeeding 2003). Poverty, in this view, is relative deprivation.

If we conceptualize poverty in relative terms, there is little need to distinguish it from inequality. A relative measure of poverty *is* a measure of inequality. It differs from other measures in that it focuses only on the bottom half of the income distribution, but relative poverty in essence captures the degree of inequality between the median and those at the bottom of the distribution. For the twelve countries on which I focus in this book, the correlation between posttax-posttransfer household income inequality measured using the P50/P10 ratio and relative poverty with the poverty line set at 50% of the median is .98.

But what if we conceptualize poverty in an absolute sense—that is, focusing on the absolute income levels of those at the low end of the distribution? Societies with more inequality may also have more absolute poverty. But that is not inherently the case. A society could be highly unequal and yet have moderately high absolute incomes for those at the low end of the distribution. Conversely, an egalitarian society could have low absolute incomes at the bottom of the distribution. If these scenarios prevail, the distinction between inequality and poverty becomes potentially important for normative and policy debate.

Martin Feldstein (1999: 33) puts the issue in the following way:

According to official statistics, the distribution of income [in the United States] has become increasingly unequal during the past two decades. A common reaction in the popular press, in political debate, and in academic discussions is to regard the increased inequality as a problem that demands new redistributive policies. I disagree. I believe that inequality as such is not a problem and that it would be wrong to design policies to reduce it. What policy should address is not inequality but poverty.

The difference is not just semantics. It is about how we should think about the rise in incomes at the upper end of the income distribution. Imagine the following: Later today, a small magic bird appears and gives each *Public Interest* [the journal in which Feldstein's article was published] subscriber $1,000. We would all think that this is a good thing. And yet, since *Public Interest* subscribers undoubtedly have above-average incomes, that would also increase inequality in the nation. I think it would be wrong to consider those $1,000 windfalls morally suspect.

The argument is that as long as the poor are not made worse off, we should not object to a rise in inequality that is produced by growing incomes for those at the top of the distribution. The only reason for doing so, according to Feldstein (and others), is envy or spite.

One response is to focus on the consequences of inequality. If the incomes of the rich pull too far away from the rest of society, growing frustration may lead to rising crime, withdrawal from civic engagement, loss of social cohesion, and increasing political influence by the rich. As noted earlier, these are empirical questions, and not ones I will address here.

Let's return to normative considerations. The Feldstein-type challenge is consistent with a variety of other views about distributive justice, including that of John Rawls (1971). Rawls argued that the most reasonable way to decide upon a fair distributive principle is to imagine that you must make this decision knowing you will be born into the world but not knowing anything about what your assets and characteristics—intelligence, personality traits, parents, neighborhood, gender, skin color, etc.—will be. Rawls referred to this hypothetical scenario as the "original position." He suggested that in such a situation a rational person would choose a set of basic liberties coupled with a distributive principle requiring that any increase in inequality raise the income of those at the bottom. In Feldstein's example, according to the Rawlsian criterion the $1,000 windfall given to the well-to-do would only be justifiable if it was accompanied by some increase for those at the low end. In practical terms, one way to accomplish this would be to tax part of the $1,000 gain and redistribute it to the poor.

Rawls's distributive principle is a "maximin" one: whatever distribution maximizes the income of the poorest (and provides basic liberties) is to be preferred. As I suggested earlier, a system of perfectly equal (posttax-posttransfer) incomes would substantially reduce work incentives and thus reduce the average income (the "size of the pie"). It is therefore unlikely to maximize the income of the least well-off. It is an empirical question how unequal incomes would need to be in order to most effectively balance incentives for income-maximization with redistribution, but the point is that inequality is not objectionable per se in the Rawlsian view.

Some experimental evidence suggests that Rawls may have been wrong in his assumption about what distributive principle people in the original position would choose. In experiments in which five or so participants are placed in a situation approximating Rawls's original position, most do not tend to choose his distributive principle. Instead, they tend to choose a principle in which the average income is maximized with a floor under the incomes of those at the bottom (Frohlich, Oppenheimer, and Eavey 1987). In this view, as long as the poor have "adequate" incomes, an increase in the incomes of the rich need not benefit the poor to be considered just. The results of such experiments are consistent with Rawls, however, in suggesting that (absolute) poverty should be of greater concern than inequality.

Rawls reaches his conclusion about the preferability of a maximin principle by a priori ruling out envy as a legitimate motivation in thinking about distributive justice (1971: 143–4, 530–41). This resonates with the intuition many of us have when considering distributive issues. But does it make sense? Branko Milanovic (2003: 6) argues that what we think of as "envy" in this context actually is simply an expression of the view that the higher incomes of the best-off are undeserved: "What some people call envy is . . . not (the bad) envy but (the good) sense of justice." It is indeed envy, but it need not have the negative connotation we usually attach to it. If some people have higher incomes than others and that difference is undeserved, because it is due largely or entirely to luck, then we need not necessarily approve of it morally.

I am not arguing that low inequality is more desirable than low (absolute) poverty, but simply that low inequality does matter in and of itself. In my view, *both* should be taken into account in assessing distributive outcomes.

Consider the income distributions in Table 2.1. The table shows income levels and inequality in four hypothetical societies: A, B, C, and D. Each has three households: POOR, MIDDLE, and RICH. These societies can be thought of as representing different countries at the same point in time or the same

Table 2.1. Income distributions in four hypothetical societies.

	Household income			Average income	Gini coefficient
	Poor household	Middle household	Rich household		
Society A	20,000	40,000	75,000	45,000	.27
Society B	15,000	40,000	100,000	51,667	.37
Society C	25,000	40,000	200,000	88,333	.44
Society D	30,000	40,000	10,000,000	3,356,667	.66

country at different points in time. Household incomes are expressed in a common currency (dollars or euros, perhaps) and are adjusted for cost-of-living differences (over time or across countries). The incomes are posttax-posttransfer. The households are of equal size. Assume that incomes correlate perfectly with living standards, that is, there is no difference between the societies in household wealth or in publicly provided services. Assume also that these are recurring incomes; there is no upward or downward intra-generational mobility. The last column in the table shows a commonly used measure of inequality: the Gini coefficient. It ranges from zero to one, with larger numbers indicating more inequality.

First compare societies A and B. Which of these two should we prefer? The Rawlsian maximin criterion prefers A, because the income of POOR is higher in A than in B. The "maximize average income subject to a floor" criterion could prefer either A or B, depending on where the floor is set. If the floor is $18,000, A is preferred because in B the income of POOR is below the floor. If the floor is $15,000 or lower, society B is preferred, because POOR's income meets the floor and average income is higher than in A. Inequality is greater in B than in A, but perhaps the difference is not large enough for concern about inequality to trump concern about the income level of the poor or about the average income level.

Now compare A and B to C. Both Rawls and "maximize average income subject to a floor" prefer C to either A or B: Rawls because the income of POOR is highest in C, "maximize subject to a floor" because C has the highest average income of the three and if the income of POOR meets the floor in A or B it necessarily does so in C. Inequality is considerably greater in C than in A. But is the difference large enough that a "sensible egalitarian" would object?

Finally, consider society D. Here POOR has a higher income than in the other three societies, MIDDLE has the same, while RICH has an immensely higher income. Rawls and "maximize subject to a floor" would both prefer D to any of the other societies. But should we agree? There is much more inequality

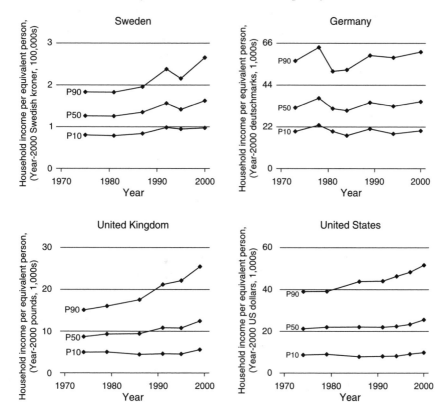

Figure 2.1. Changes in posttax-posttransfer household incomes at the 10th, 50th, and 90th percentiles, 1970–2000.

Note: Figures are in national currencies and thus permit only cross-country comparison of income changes, not of levels for data definitions and sources, see the appendix.

in D than in the other three societies. Suppose D's RICH household has an income of 10,000,000 because Feldstein's magic bird brings the money to it, or for some other reason that has to do largely with luck. Should we prefer society D on normative grounds? Though I am not certain how many readers will agree, I do not think we should.

The point of this exercise is to suggest that there is reason to be concerned about both poverty and inequality, rather than only about poverty.

Figure 2.1 offers another opportunity to assess the relative importance of poverty and inequality, this time using real data for four countries. The figure shows trends in inflation-adjusted posttax-posttransfer incomes per equivalent person (I explain what "per equivalent person" means in Chapter 3) for working-age households at the 10th, 50th (median), and 90th percentiles in

Sweden, Germany, the United Kingdom, and the United States. It includes all years for which Luxembourg Income Study data are available since the early 1970s. The incomes are shown in national currencies; the point is to compare income change over time, rather than income levels.

The incomes of the poor (proxied here by the 10th-percentile household) remained constant in each of the four countries during this period of two and a half decades, the only exception being Sweden, where there was a bit of an increase. Incomes at the top (proxied by the 90th percentile) increased in three of the four countries. They grew most rapidly in the United Kingdom, but as a result the UK had the sharpest increase in inequality. The United States was next in terms of the degree of increase in 90th-percentile income and in income inequality. Sweden followed. In Germany there was effectively no change in income at the bottom, middle, or top, and hence no rise in inequality.

Which of these countries had the most desirable performance, in terms of over-time developments? According to Rawls's maximin criterion, Sweden did best, since income at the bottom increased. According to "maximize average income subject to a floor," the United Kingdom performed best (if we assume that its minimum exceeded the floor). For someone who treats inequality as having the same weight in normative considerations as poverty, Germany might be judged to have had the best performance, since the trend for its poor was similar to that in other countries and it had the smallest increase in inequality.

For most readers, I suspect, there will be no simple or easy answer to the question. My inclination would not be to judge Germany's performance as best even though it had the least increase in inequality. I would probably conclude that Sweden's performance was the best among the four countries: incomes at the bottom increased somewhat, average incomes rose, and income inequality increased by less than in the United Kingdom or the United States.

Let me add one more illustration, again using real data. This time we will consider developments in the United States over a longer period—since the mid-1940s. Figure 2.2 shows trends in inflation-adjusted family incomes at the 20th, 40th, 60th, 80th, and 95th percentiles during this period (data for households, which is a more sensible unit to examine, are not available prior to the late 1960s). The data suggest that the principal difference between the "golden age" period from the mid-1940s to the mid-1970s and the ensuing period of rising inequality is the stagnation of incomes in the bottom half of the distribution (Kenworthy 2004*b*). Those at the high end have pulled away from the rest. But that is not because their income growth accelerated. Instead, it is because income growth slowed considerably for families in the bottom half.

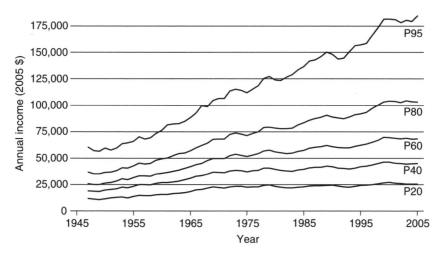

Figure 2.2. Family income trends in the United States at various percentiles, 1947ff.

Note: Pretax-posttransfer income.

Source: My calculations from U.S. Census Bureau data, www.census.gov/hhes/www/income/histinc/f01ar. html.

In my view, we should worry about this development mainly because despite growth of average income, poverty has not decreased. This is indicated by the lack of increase in real incomes at the 20th percentile, which we can treat as a proxy for poverty. It also is reflected in the lack of decline in the official government poverty rate, which was 11% in 1973, 11% in 2000, and 12% in 2006. This judgment of course presumes a counterfactual in which average income could have increased just as rapidly with a larger share going to those at the bottom.

There is more to the story. The Current Population Survey (CPS), which is the source for the income data in Figure 2.2, does not have useful information on the incomes of the richest Americans, as they are top-coded at $1 million ($300,000 prior to 1993). The best available time-series data on incomes for those at the very top of the distribution are from Thomas Piketty and Emmanuel Saez (2007b), who analyzed tax records back to 1913. Figure 2.3 shows the share of total household income going to the top 1% of taxpayers according to the Piketty and Saez calculations. The chart suggests a massive rise since the late 1970s, with the top 1%'s share of household income more than doubling.

Though available only since 1979, data from the Congressional Budget Office on the income levels of the top 1% tell a similar story. These are shown in Figure 2.4. They too suggest a substantial rise in incomes for the very rich since the 1970s.

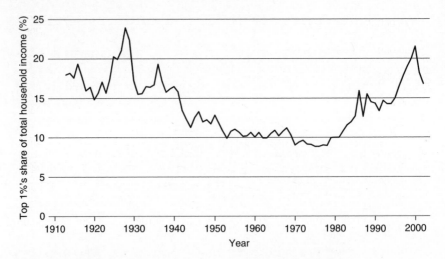

Figure 2.3. Income share of the top 1% in the United States, 1913ff.

Note: Taxpayer units. Pretax income. Includes capital gains, though the patterns are very similar if capital gains are excluded.

Source: Piketty and Saez (2007b: table 5A3).

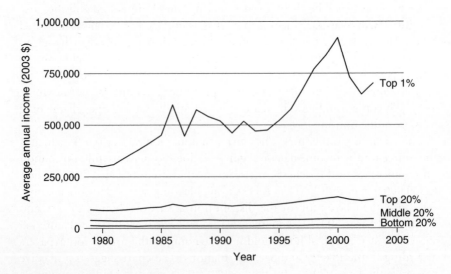

Figure 2.4. Income trends for the bottom 20%, middle 20%, top 20%, and top 1% of households in the United States, 1979ff.

Note: Posttax-posttransfer income.

Source: Unpublished calculations by Jared Bernstein from Congressional Budget Office data. See Mishel, Bernstein, and Allegretto (2007: 64–5).

In the view of Feldstein (and others), income developments in the United States in recent decades should not be cause for concern. Real income for households at the tenth and twentieth percentiles has been stagnant, while income for the top 1% has soared. From this perspective, the only reason to object to these developments is envy. I suspect many observers would disagree, both because some (perhaps much) of the huge increase for those at the very top is a product of luck of one kind or another—genetic inheritance of cognitive ability or work ethic, good parenting, attending the right schools, being in the right place or industry at the right time, and so on—and because it seems likely that average incomes could have increased no less rapidly had they done so with more going to those at the bottom.

What do I conclude from these reflections on poverty and inequality? I very much agree with the emphasis Rawls, Feldstein, and others place on the absolute income levels for those at the low end of the income distribution. Yet I do not find compelling the argument that concern about inequality should be dismissed. Because some or much of the higher incomes of those in the top portion of the income distribution may be a product of luck, because in many instances it is plausible to believe that a less unequal distribution would have yielded no loss in average income, because many people care as much or more about their relative position as about their absolute well-being, and because inequality may have undesirable effects on other aspects of society, I conclude that there is good reason to desire low inequality in and of itself—not instead of, but in addition to, high absolute incomes for those at the bottom.

WHY INCOME RATHER THAN WEALTH OR ACCESS TO BASIC MATERIAL NEEDS?

Arguably, income is a less useful indicator of material well-being than either wealth or access to basic material needs (Townsend 1979; Mayer and Jencks 1989; Wolff 2002). Unfortunately, comparative over-time data on wealth and material hardship are very limited. For better or worse, I therefore focus on income.

DOES MOBILITY OFFSET HIGH INEQUALITY?

Income inequality is measured with data from surveys that ask people about their income in a single year. It therefore captures the degree of dispersion at a particular point in time. What if the degree of income mobility—of upward and downward movement of households within the income distribution—differs across countries? Suppose two countries have the same amount of income inequality using the standard single-year measure, but country A has much more (intragenerational) mobility than country B. If households' income were measured over a period of multiple years, we would conclude that there is less inequality in A than in B.

To examine this possibility, we need data for the same households over multiple years. Although such data are scarce, the best available suggest that in fact there is relatively little cross-country difference in income mobility. Thus, measures of income inequality based on income in a single year are fairly accurate in gauging the true degree of inequality (Gangl 2005; Gangl, Palme, and Kenworthy 2008).

DO PEOPLE CARE ABOUT INEQUALITY?

Yes, they do. There is a great deal of evidence from experiments that suggests inequality matters to people, though it seldom is the dominant criterion (Konow 2003). For my purposes it is perhaps sufficient to point to some survey evidence. The best available comparative data come from the International Social Survey Programme (ISSP; for the United States see also Maxwell 2007; Pew Research Center for the People and the Press 2007). In 1999 the ISSP conducted a module specifically on social inequality.

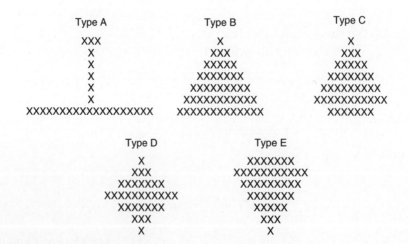

Figure 2.5. Income distributions in five hypothetical societies.
Source: ISSP (1999, questionnaire, variable: v 93).

One question asked whether respondents thought the difference in incomes between rich and poor in their country was currently "too large." The share saying they agreed or strongly agreed that the difference in their country was too large was 71% in Australia, 71% in Canada, 88% in France, 82% in Germany, 73% in Norway, 71% in Sweden, 82% in the United Kingdom, and 66% in the United States (ISSP 1999).

Another question offered respondents pictorial illustrations of various income distributions and asked "What do you think the distribution in your country ought to be like—which do you prefer?" The five choices were depicted as shown in Figure 2.5.

In each country some respondents did not answer and around 5% said they could not choose between the five types. Among those who did make a choice, a relatively small share said they preferred types A, B, or C: fewer than 2% chose A, fewer than 8% chose B, and fewer than 15% chose type C. The bulk of respondents selected either type D or type E.

Interestingly, in each of the countries included in the survey, a larger share of respondents chose type D than type E. D and E are identical in their population shares at the very bottom (the bottom two rows). The difference between the two is that D has a larger share in the middle, whereas E has a larger share at the top. E corresponds most closely to the "maximize average income subject to a floor" criterion, whereas the characteristic of D that differentiates it from the others is its lesser degree of inequality. Yet more respondents in the ISSP survey preferred D than preferred E: 55% versus 24% in Australia, 50% versus 35% in Canada, 46% versus 22% in France, 55% versus 20% in Germany, 57% versus 32% in Norway, 49% versus 34% in Sweden, and 47% versus 26% in the United States. This suggests strongly that people care about inequality in and of itself.

CONCLUSION

My aim in this chapter has been to suggest some reasons why citizens and policy makers in affluent countries should be interested in limiting income inequality. In the next chapter I consider the nature of the challenge they face.

3

Sources of Equality and Inequality: Wages, Jobs, Households, and Redistribution

It is helpful to think about inequality of earnings and income at three levels:

1. Inequality of earnings among employed individuals. This is frequently referred to as "earnings inequality," "pay inequality," or "wage inequality."

2. Inequality of earnings and investment income among households. This is often termed "pretax-pretransfer income inequality" or "market income inequality."

3. Inequality of income among households when government taxes and transfers are included. This is typically referred to as "posttax-posttransfer income inequality" or "disposable income inequality."

In my view, the most important of these is the third: posttax-posttransfer income inequality among households. Earnings are pooled (albeit not always equally) within households, and certainly the money available after taxes and transfers is of more relevance to households than their market income. If there is a level of inequality on which we should focus the most attention, this is it.

What are the principal sources of posttax-posttransfer inequality? To what extent do inequality of individual earnings, inequality of market household incomes, redistribution, and other factors influence the posttax-posttransfer income distribution? And what do the answers to these questions tell us about the best route to low posttax-posttransfer inequality?

WAGES

I begin with earnings inequality among employed individuals. Many things are likely to contribute to pay differentials. One candidate is the degree of inequality in skills and/or education. Greater skill dispersion should result in more inequality of pay levels. The distribution of skills also interacts with the level of demand for workers with high or low skills. If there are more less-skilled workers than employers want, there will be downward pressure on wage levels for such workers, which may result in greater pay inequality. Similarly, if there are fewer high-skilled employees than employers want, there will be upward pressure on pay levels for such employees, again generating higher pay inequality. Another factor is the sectoral composition of employment. Earnings are generally less unequal among those employed in the manufacturing sector than among those employed in services and agriculture. The larger the share in manufacturing, therefore, the less pay inequality there should be. Similarly, wages are normally more compressed in the public sector than in the private sector. The larger the share of the work force in public sector jobs, then, the less inequality we would expect to find. Government imposition of a minimum wage level sets a floor at the bottom of the pay distribution and may thereby reduce inequality. Unions often favor compression of pay levels. The stronger their position vis-à-vis employers, and the larger the segment of the work force they bargain for, the less pay inequality there is likely to be.

The best comparative data on earnings inequality among individuals are in a data set compiled by the OECD. The data are for weekly, monthly, or annual earnings at various percentiles of the distribution, such as the tenth, twentieth, fiftieth (median), and ninetieth. They cover only individuals who are employed full-time, which is sensible because part-time workers often earn less per week or month or year than full-time workers simply because they are working fewer hours.

A variety of "percentile ratio" measures of inequality can be constructed from the OECD earnings data set. The most common are "P90/P10" and "P50/P10" ratios. The former is calculated as the earnings level at the 90th percentile of the distribution divided by the earnings level at the 10th percentile. The latter is calculated as the 50th percentile divided by the 10th percentile. Although I will use the P50/P10 ratio in later chapters when the focus is on low-end wages, here I use the P90/P10 ratio, as it covers both the high end and the low end of the distribution. Figure 3.1 shows P90/P10 ratios for each of the twelve countries for all years in which they are available since 1979. For many of the countries the data are available for most of these years, but for a few—Norway, Italy, and Canada—they cover a much smaller portion of this period.

The Nordic countries have tended to have the lowest levels of individual earnings inequality, followed by the continental countries, with the English-speaking nations having the highest levels. Italy and Australia are exceptions. Italy's level of earnings inequality is similar to that in the Nordic countries (as of the late 1990s), and Australia's is similar to that in the continental countries.

The difference in levels of earnings inequality across countries is due first and foremost to union strength and the structure of the wage-setting process

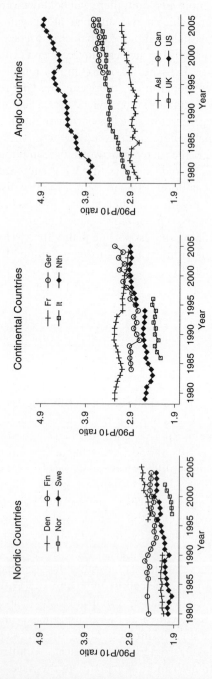

Figure 3.1. Earnings inequality among full-time employed individuals, 1979ff.

Note: Vertical axes of the charts are truncated (do not begin at one). The gaps for Denmark and the Netherlands represent a break in the time series for the former and a change in the data series for the latter. For data definitions and sources, see the appendix.

(Wallerstein 1999; Rueda and Pontusson 2000; Blau and Kahn 2002*b*; Devroye and Freeman 2002; OECD 2004*h*; EC 2005; Lucifora, McKnight, and Salverda 2005; Oskarsson 2005; Beramendi and Cusack 2007). In countries with higher levels of unionization or collective bargaining coverage and/or in which wages are bargained in more centralized fashion, unions' preference for wage compression tends to have more influence.

The United States is the only one of the twelve countries in which earnings inequality rose steadily and substantially through the two and a half decades. Inequality also increased rapidly in the United Kingdom, but only in the 1980s. In the other nations for which data are available throughout the time period, the overall pattern suggests limited change, though in most countries there has been some rise since the mid-1990s. (The apparent jump in the Netherlands in 1995 owes to a change in the data series.)

There is a wide-ranging debate over the determinants of the rise in earnings inequality in the United States (Katz and Autor 1999; Morris and Western 1999; Gottschalk and Danziger 2005; Mishel, Bernstein, and Allegretto 2007). Most research has focused on the effects of technological change and globalization. But other countries also experienced technological change and globalization—some in a more pronounced way than the United States—and yet had no comparable increase in earnings inequality, which casts some doubt on the causal importance of these two factors. A key element of earnings inequality in the United States has been stagnant real wages and earnings for those at the bottom of the distribution. Perhaps most important, then, is the fact that the United States has lacked effective institutions to prevent such stagnation. Unions have weakened considerably during this period: the unionized share of the work force dropped from 25% in 1979 to 13% in 2005. And the inflation-adjusted value of the statutory minimum wage declined from $7.80 per hour in 1979 to $5.15 per hour in 2005 (in 2005 dollars). In the other eleven countries, with the partial exception of the United Kingdom, unions have not declined to nearly the same extent and collective bargaining arrangements have continued to have considerable influence (European Commission 2004: ch. 1).

JOBS

The earnings inequality data shown in Figure 3.1 include only individuals who are employed full-time. This leaves out the fact that many people are not employed and therefore have zero earnings. And others work part-time rather than full-time.

Figure 3.2 show trends in employment rates—employed persons as a share of the working-age population—since the late 1970s. The Nordic countries have tended to have the highest levels of employment, though the rates in Sweden and especially Finland fell severely during their economic crises in the early 1990s and have yet to fully recover. The Anglo countries have the next highest levels. Employment rates in the four continental countries have tended to be lower, but there is considerable variation within this group. Employment in the Netherlands has increased dramatically since the mid-1980s and is now on par with the levels in Sweden and the Anglo nations. Germany's employment rate is similar to Finland's. France and particularly Italy have the lowest rates among the twelve countries.

The share of the working-age population that is not employed ranges from 20% in Denmark and Norway to 40% in Italy. Earnings inequality would be higher in all countries were we to include these individuals in the calculation, but including them would increase measured inequality to a much greater extent in Italy than in Denmark or Norway.

The same holds for part-time employment. Between 5% and 25% of the working-age population in these countries is employed part-time. Part-timers tend to earn less than those employed full-time, in part because their pay level per hour tends to be lower and in part because they work fewer hours. Including them would increase the degree of earnings inequality among individuals. Figure 3.3 shows over-time trends in the part-time employment rate, calculated as persons in part-time employment as a share of the working-age population. In Finland and Italy the share in part-time jobs has tended to be quite low, so their inclusion probably would not dramatically alter the level of measured inequality. In the Netherlands, where one-quarter of the working-age population is in part-time employment, inclusion would have a larger impact.

Individuals combine to form households, and they typically share their income among household (usually family) members. For this reason, households are, arguably, the unit we should care most about in thinking about inequality. A nonemployed individual or one who has a low-wage job may be cause for concern, but seemingly less so if his spouse has a moderate- or high-paying job that ensures the household a decent overall income.

If every household had one employed person, the distribution of earnings among households would be determined solely by the distribution of earnings among employed individuals. But that is not the case. Households vary in the number of employed persons they have. Some have one, some one-and-a-half (if we take into account part-time employment), others two, and some more than two.

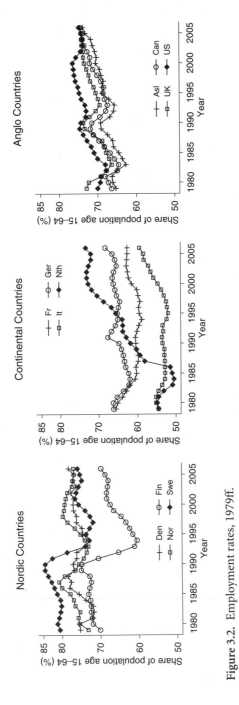

Figure 3.2. Employment rates, 1979ff.

Note: Vertical axes are truncated (do not begin at zero). For data definitions and sources, see the appendix.

Jobs with Equality

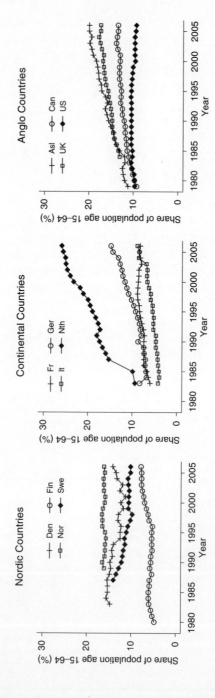

Figure 3.3. Part-time employment rates, 1979ff.

Note: For data definitions and sources, see the appendix.

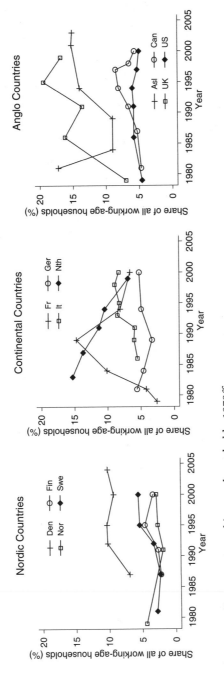

Figure 3.4. Zero-earner working-age households, 1979ff.

Note: For data definitions and sources, see the appendix.

Perhaps most important in terms of the distribution of employment among households is the distinction between households that have some earner(s) and those that have none. The larger the share of households that have zero earners, the greater the degree of inequality in household incomes is likely to be. Figure 3.4 shows trends in the share of households with zero earners in the twelve countries. With the exception of Denmark, the Nordic countries have tended to have a relatively small share of zero-earner households. Around 5% of working-age households in Finland, Norway, and Sweden have no earners. There is more variation within the continental and English-speaking groups. Germany has maintained a consistently small proportion. In France the share has tended to be relatively high, but with considerable fluctuation over time. In Italy the share of zero-earner households has increased steadily, while in the Netherlands it was quite high in the early 1980s but has fallen since then. Among the Anglo countries, the share has been consistently low in the United States. That is true of Canada too for most of the period. Since the early 1990s Australia and especially the United Kingdom have consistently had the largest share of households with zero earners among the twelve countries.

HOUSEHOLD COMPOSITION

A major contributor to the number of employed persons in a household is the number of adults in the household. Single-adult households by definition can have only one earner (assuming no employed children). Married or partnered couples may have one or two earners. And some households may have more than two adults who are employed.

An additional aspect of household composition that may affect income inequality has to do with earnings levels in households that have more than one earner. Some households have two low earners, others one low and one high earner, and others two high earners. Since there is a tendency for people with similar educational levels to couple, we typically find more low–low and high–high pairs than low–high pairs. This phenomenon is referred to as "marital homogamy." The degree of homogamy differs across countries. The larger the correlation between spouses' earnings in a country, the higher the degree of inequality among households is likely to be. As of 2000, the correlation between spouses' earnings in dual-earner couples ranged from .03 in the Netherlands to .32 in France and .33 in Italy (my calculations using LIS data).

EFFECTS OF WAGES, JOBS, AND HOUSEHOLD COMPOSITION ON PRETAX-PRETRANSFER HOUSEHOLD INCOME INEQUALITY

What impact do individual earnings inequality, employment, and household composition have on household income inequality? To find out, we need to examine inequality of households' market income.

Each of these three factors affects household earnings, and earnings are the main source of income for most households in affluent countries. Some households, though, have market income from sources other than earnings. The principal additional source is investment income—interest, dividends, and rental income. Because investment income tends to be concentrated among households with higher earnings, its inclusion increases the degree of measured inequality. It turns out, however, that investment income has very little impact on levels of household income inequality in the twelve countries and does not alter the variation across countries at all (Kenworthy 2004a: ch. 3).

In calculating household income inequality, I use data from the Luxembourg Income Study (LIS) database. This is the most reliable source for comparable cross-country data on household earnings and incomes in affluent nations (Atkinson and Brandolini 2001). The LIS data come from surveys or tax records collected in the individual countries, but considerable effort is made to harmonize the data sets so that they are truly comparable across nations. Extensive documentation of these efforts is available on the LIS website at www.lisproject.org. The LIS data are available in "waves." For each country there is an observation around 1985, 1990, and 1995, and for most there are ones around 1980 and 2000. For a handful of countries there also is an observation around 1975 and/or 2005. Because the LIS database consists of household-level data for each country, it is possible to calculate inequality measures with specifications chosen by the researcher.

Three additional points regarding measurement: First, I focus throughout the book on working-age households (including the children in them). The household income and inequality data I present refer to households with "heads" age 25 to 59. This excludes those most likely to be university students or retirees.

Second, households with differing numbers of persons presumably have different income needs. It is thus standard practice to adjust household income figures for household size. I do so using a conventional "equivalence scale": household income is divided by the square root of the number of persons in the household (Atkinson, Rainwater, and Smeeding 1995; Canberra

Group 2001). This presumes that larger households enjoy economies of scale in their use of income; for instance, a household of four is assumed to need only twice as much income as a household of one, rather than four times as much. Figures for household incomes and household income inequality reported throughout the book thus are for household income per "equivalent person."

Third, respondents to surveys may overestimate or underestimate their income. To minimize the effect of this, it is standard practice in analyses using the LIS data to top-code and bottom-code the country data sets in calculating income levels and income inequality. That is, an upper and lower limit for incomes is set based on some multiple and fraction of the median or mean. Any reported incomes above or below these figures are recoded as the limit figures. I follow the official LIS practice (see www.lisproject.org) of top-coding at 10 times the unequivalized median household income and bottom-coding at 1% of the equivalized mean. In other words, extremely high incomes are recoded as 10 times the median prior to adjustment for household size, and extremely low incomes are recoded as 1% of the mean after adjustment for household size. Households reporting a posttax-posttransfer income of zero are dropped.

Figure 3.5 shows levels of pretax-pretransfer household income inequality in the twelve countries since the late 1970s. Inequality is measured here using the Gini coefficient. The Gini coefficient ranges from zero to one, with larger numbers indicating more inequality. A Gini coefficient of zero indicates a perfectly equal distribution across households; it would equal one (1.0) if a single household had all of the income.

The Nordic countries and Germany began the 1980s with the lowest levels, but all experienced increases in the 1990s. Italy began with a moderate level which then increased in the 1990s. France and the Netherlands started with comparatively high levels. France stayed high, while market inequality in the Netherlands declined steadily. As of 2000 the level of pretax-pretransfer inequality in France, Germany, and Italy was roughly the same as in the Nordic countries. The Anglo countries entered the 1980s with levels similar to those in the continental nations, but each experienced sharp increases in the 1980s and 1990s. As of 2000 the Anglo countries had the highest levels among the twelve.

Figure 3.6 has a set of scatterplot charts showing the relationships across the twelve countries between pretax-pretransfer income inequality among working-age households (vertical axes) and earnings inequality among full-time employed individuals, three measures of employment, and two measures of household composition (horizontal axes). The data are for 2000. In each instance the pattern looks similar if we consider data for all available years, which run from the mid-1970s to 2000 (not shown).

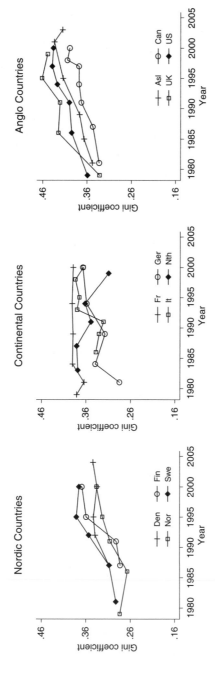

Figure 3.5. Pretax-pretransfer income inequality among working-age households, 1979ff.

Note: Vertical axes are truncated. Vertical axis scale is the same as for posttax-posttransfer inequality in Figure 3.11. For data definitions and sources, see the appendix.

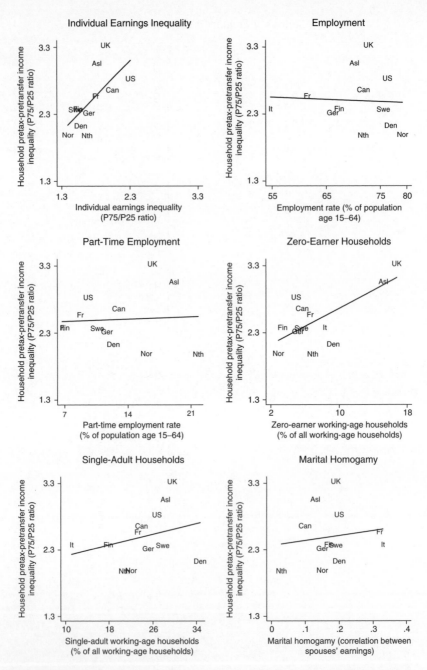

Figure 3.6. Pretax-pretransfer income inequality among working-age households by earnings inequality among full-time employed individuals, employment, and household composition, 2000.

Note: Some axes are truncated. Vertical axis scale is the same as that for individual earnings inequality (horizontal axis of the first chart in the figure). For data definitions and sources, see the appendix.

The first chart shows household pretax-pretransfer income inequality by individual earnings inequality. To best gauge the relationship between these two levels of inequality, it is helpful to use the same inequality measure for both. Unfortunately, it is not possible to calculate Gini coefficients from the OECD's percentile earnings data for employed individuals. An alternative is therefore to use the P90/P10 ratio, as in Figure 3.1. But for household pretax-pretransfer income the P90/P10 ratio turns out to be problematic. In some countries in certain years more than 10% of households had no earner. This means household pretax-pretransfer income at the 10th percentile of the distribution was either zero or only slightly above zero. As a result, the P90/P10 ratio is extremely large, rendering it effectively incomparable to those in other nations and to the P90/P10 ratios for earnings inequality among individuals. I therefore use the P75/P25 ratio. This measure incorporates less of the full range of the distribution than do the Gini coefficient and the P90/P10 ratio. But it nevertheless conveys a similar story: across the twelve countries, for earnings inequality among employed individuals the P75/P25 ratio correlates at .99 with the P90/P10 ratio, and for pretax-pretransfer household income inequality the P75/P25 ratio correlates at .95 with the Gini coefficient.

The fact that the data points are located in the upper-left portion of the chart indicates that in each of the countries there is considerably greater inequality of pretax-pretransfer income among households than of earnings among full-time employed individuals. That is not surprising; consistent with what I suggested earlier, it indicates that employment patterns and household composition increase the degree of inequality as we move from individuals to households.

There is a fairly strong positive association across the countries between the two levels of inequality. The countries with the highest levels of individual earnings inequality tend to have the highest levels of household market income inequality. There is some bunching of the low-inequality countries. As of 2000, Germany, the Netherlands, Denmark, Finland, Italy, and Sweden had similar levels of individual earnings inequality, whereas they differed a bit in inequality of household market income. Nevertheless, the relationship is relatively strong.

The second chart in Figure 3.6 shows market household income inequality by the employment rate. Here we see no relationship. Two of the countries with the highest employment rates, Denmark and Norway, had very low levels of pretax-pretransfer income inequality. Yet Germany and the Netherlands had low inequality despite only moderate employment. And the United States and United Kingdom had comparatively high employment together with very high levels of household inequality.

The same is true for part-time employment, shown in the third chart. Here too there is no apparent association across the twelve countries.

The fourth chart shows the share of working-age households that have no earner. Here we do observe a relatively strong relationship. Countries with more zero-earner households tended to have higher levels of inequality of pretax-pretransfer household income. The main exception to the pattern is the United States, which had very high inequality despite having relatively few zero-earner households. This suggests that market income inequality among US households may stem more from individual earnings inequality and/or household composition than is true for the other countries. The Netherlands is also somewhat of an exception, having a comparatively large share of zero-earner households but relatively low market inequality.

The last two charts in Figure 3.6 show pretax-pretransfer household income inequality by two measures of household composition: single-adult households and marital homogamy. The pattern suggests a weak positive association with the share of working-age households that have just one adult. This share is highest in Denmark, but it does not have particularly high inequality of market household income. In most of the countries the share of single-adult households is between 20% and 30%, but these countries have widely varying degrees of inequality, from Norway at the low end to Australia and the United Kingdom at the high end.

Marital homogamy appears to be associated in the expected positive direction with household inequality. Countries with a larger correlation among spouses' earnings tend to have higher levels of inequality. But the association is not terribly strong, as there are a number of exceptions.

To more thoroughly assess the relative import of these various factors, I estimated a variety of multivariate regressions with levels of pretax-pretransfer household income inequality as the dependent variable. Since there are only twelve countries and six independent variables, I tried all possible combinations of three or fewer of the independent variables. Figure 3.7 shows the results. The figure reports the results for each determinant of market inequality in a "box-and-whisker" plot (boxplot). The "whiskers" refer to the minimum and maximum coefficients. The edges of the box indicate the 25th- and 75th-percentile coefficients. The vertical white line is the median coefficient.

The results of these regressions are largely consistent with the patterns shown in the bivariate scatterplots. Individual earnings inequality and zero-earner households seem clearly to have an impact, and the same is likely true for single-adult households and marital homogamy.

Like the scatterplots, the regressions suggest no effect of either the employment rate or the part-time employment rate; the median coefficient for each is

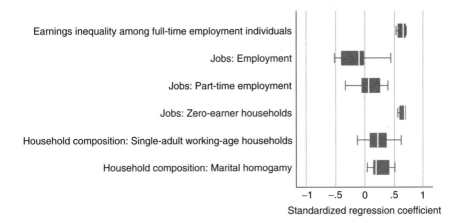

Figure 3.7. Regression results: Sources of cross-country variation in pretax-pretransfer income inequality among working-age households, 2000.

Note: Standardized coefficients from ordinary least squares (OLS) regressions using all possible combinations of three or fewer of the independent variables. Dependent variable is pretax-pretransfer income inequality among working-age households. $N = 12$. For data definitions and sources, see the appendix. The "whiskers" refer to the minimum and maximum coefficients. The edges of the box indicate the 25th- and 75th-percentile coefficients. The vertical white line is the median coefficient.

very close to zero. However, this is almost certainly not because employment and part-time employment have no impact on household income inequality. Instead, it is because these measures are too crude. What we really need is a measure of inequality of hours worked across households. Unfortunately, to my knowledge there are no cross-nationally comparable data from which such a measure could be calculated.

Figure 3.5 showed that the level of market income inequality among households has increased significantly in both Nordic and Anglo countries since the late 1970s. Individual earnings inequality seems unlikely to have been the main culprit, since Figure 3.1 indicates that individual earnings inequality increased substantially only in the United States and the United Kingdom during those two decades. In the United States the rise in earnings inequality among employed individuals does indeed seem to have been the main precipitant of the increase in household market income inequality, though increases in single-adult households and in marital homogamy also appear to have played a role (Burtless 1999; Reed and Cancian 2001). But in the other countries, particularly in Sweden and Finland, changes in employment were a key factor (Kenworthy 2004a: ch. 3; Kenworthy and Pontusson 2005). In these countries employment losses increased the share of households with only one earner or with no earners, and this affected already-low-earning households to a greater extent than households higher up in the distribution. As a result, pretax-pretransfer income declined for households at the bottom, which increased inequality. In the Netherlands the opposite occurred. Employment increases reduced the number of households with zero earners or just one earner, thereby raising household incomes at the low end of the distribution. Consequently, the Netherlands was the one country in which market income inequality among households decreased during the 1980s and 1990s.

REDISTRIBUTION

The final step in examining the various sources of inequality is to move from household pretax-pretransfer income inequality to household posttax-posttransfer income inequality. The difference between these is due to redistribution via government taxes and transfers. Figure 3.8 shows the relationship between household "pre" and "post" income inequality as of 2000. Here I use the Gini coefficient, though the charts look very similar if the P75/P25 ratio is used (not shown).

The cross-country association between these two levels of inequality is positive, indicating that countries with higher levels of pretax-pretransfer

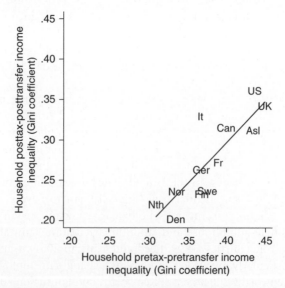

Figure 3.8. Posttax-posttransfer income inequality among working-age households by pretax-pretransfer income inequality among working-age households, 2000.

Note: Chart axes are truncated. For data definitions and sources, see the appendix.

income inequality also tend to have higher levels of posttax-posttransfer income inequality. That does not mean redistribution has no impact. I use the same range of values on both axes, and the data points are all located in the bottom-right portion of the chart. This indicates that inequality of posttax-posttransfer income (vertical axis) tends to be lower than inequality of pretax-pretransfer income (horizontal axis). Among the twelve countries government taxes and transfers reduced the degree of household income inequality by an average of 25% (calculated by subtracting the "post" Gini from the "pre" Gini and then dividing by the "pre" Gini). On the high end, redistribution reduced inequality by nearly 40% in Denmark, Finland, and Sweden. On the low end, it did so in Italy by just 10%.

Figures 3.9 and 3.10 show trends in two measures of redistribution in the twelve countries since the late 1970s. The first is government cash social expenditures on the working-age population. This measure is calculated as public spending on family benefits and benefits for unemployment, disability, occupational injury and disease, sickness, and "other contingencies" (mainly low income) as a share of GDP. The second is a measure of actual redistribution. It is calculated as the Gini coefficient for pretax-pretransfer household income minus the Gini coefficient for posttax-posttransfer household income. (Neither measure includes spending on public services such as education, health care, child care, job training, and so on.)

The two measures of redistribution tell a similar story. The four Nordic countries have the highest levels. And in each of these four nations redistribution increased significantly, though temporarily, in the early 1990s in response to the countries' economic crises. The continental and Anglo countries have had lower and roughly similar levels of redistribution. On the cash social expenditures measure the United States stands apart as the least redistributive country, while on the measure of actual redistribution Italy is at the low end. Both measures indicate a decline in redistribution in the Netherlands, which is a product of employment replacing the welfare state as the principal source of income for many households at the low end of the distribution.

POSTTAX-POSTTRANSFER HOUSEHOLD INCOME
INEQUALITY

Figure 3.10 shows inequality of posttax-posttransfer household income since the late 1970s. As already suggested in Figure 3.8, the Nordic countries have tended to have the lowest levels, followed by the continental countries, with the highest levels in the Anglo nations (see also Smeeding 2004; Förster

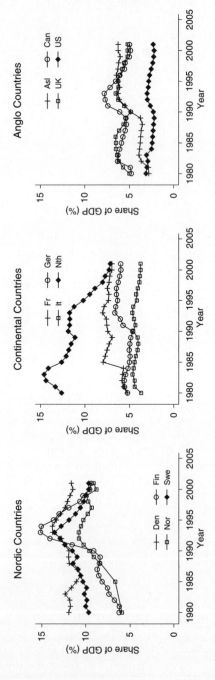

Figure 3.9. Redistribution: Government cash social expenditures on the working-age population, 1979ff.

Note: For data definitions and sources, see the appendix.

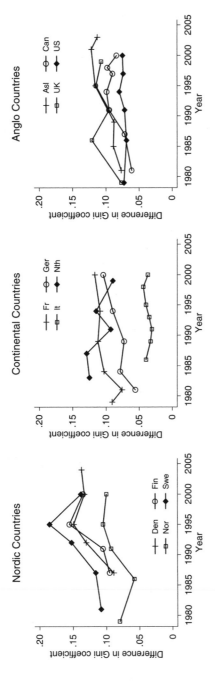

Figure 3.10. Redistribution: Pretax-pretransfer income inequality among working-age households minus posttax-posttransfer income inequality among working-age households, 1979ff.

Note: For data definitions and sources, see the appendix. For France and Italy, only information on redistribution via transfers (not taxes) is available.

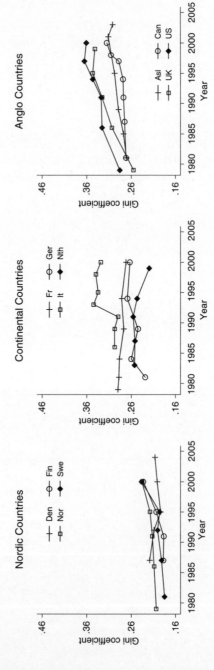

Figure 3.11. Posttax-posttransfer income inequality among working-age households, 1979ff.

Note: Vertical axes are truncated. Vertical axis scale is the same as for pretax-pretransfer inequality in Figure 3.5. For data definitions and sources, see the appendix.

and d'Ercole 2005). This rank ordering is not surprising. The Nordic countries have featured low-to-moderate market inequality and high redistribution. The continental countries have had moderate market inequality and moderate-to-low redistribution. And the Anglo countries have had moderate-to-high market inequality and moderate-to-low redistribution.

In the 1990s posttax-posttransfer inequality increased in three of the four Nordic countries—Finland, Norway, and Sweden. By 2000 these countries had levels similar to France and Germany, with Denmark and the Netherlands slightly lower. The level of inequality in Italy increased sharply in the early 1990s, putting it at the high end among the twelve nations along with the United Kingdom and United States. The Anglo countries diverged somewhat over the two decades. They began the 1980s with similar levels of posttax-posttransfer inequality, and inequality increased in all four, but it did so to a much greater extent in the United States and United Kingdom than in Australia and Canada.

Posttax-posttransfer income inequality increased most dramatically in the 1980s and 1990s in the United States, the United Kingdom, and Italy. This is not because they suffered the largest rise in market inequality (Figure 3.5). It is mainly because in these three countries there was little or no increase in redistribution to compensate for the increase in market inequality (Figure 3.10). In the Nordic countries, and particularly in Sweden and Finland, redistribution did increase in response to the rise in market inequality of the early 1990s. It did so not because social programs were made more generous by policy makers, but rather because unemployment insurance, social assistance, and other programs kicked in automatically as people lost jobs during the deep recessions in these countries (Kenworthy 2004*a*: ch. 3; Kenworthy and Pontusson 2005). The United States, United Kingdom, and Italy have less generous programs, and the rise in market inequality was less a function of job loss. Hence the "automatic compensation" effect of redistributive programs (Rhodes 1996) was weaker in those three countries.

At the end of the 1990s, on the other hand, posttax-posttransfer inequality increased in Finland, Norway, and Sweden. This happened despite the fact that market inequality rose less rapidly than it had earlier in the decade (Figure 3.5). It was due to declining redistribution (Figures 3.9 and 3.10), a product of reductions in the generosity of social programs that occurred during the early and mid-1990s. In each of these countries replacement rates were reduced and eligibility requirements stiffened (Ploug 1999; Huber and Stephens 2001; Pierson 2001; Swank 2002). The changes were relatively minor, and the Nordic countries' programs remain comparatively generous. But the cutbacks do appear to have had the effect of allowing posttax-posttransfer income inequality to rise.

Thus, while much of the cross-country variation in levels of posttax-posttransfer income inequality is a product of differences in levels of market inequality (Figure 3.8), redistribution is also important. And for understanding developments over time, redistribution is front and center (see also Kenworthy 2004*a*: ch. 3; Kenworthy and Pontusson 2005).

WHAT PATH TO LOW INEQUALITY?

Wages, jobs, households, and redistribution each play a role in influencing the degree of income inequality in a society. On which of these should countries focus in attempting to limit inequality of posttax-posttransfer household incomes? In my view, the focus ought to be chiefly on employment and redistribution, rather than on wage inequality and/or household composition.

As a practical matter, it is likely to be difficult to contain rising wage inequality in coming years. Unions have been weakening steadily in many affluent countries, and wage setting has tended to become more decentralized. The share of the work force covered by collective bargaining agreements has remained fairly stable, and in some countries temporary "pacts" between labor and employers associations, sometimes with government involvement, have had a recentralizing effect (European Commission 2004: ch. 1). Yet the trend toward increased autonomy for individual firms in determining wages is clear, and there is no compelling reason to think that this will be reversed. In addition, factors that may have already contributed to rising wage inequality, such as skill-biased technological change, globalization, and immigration, may generate further pressure in this direction (Nahuis and de Groot 2003). As of the mid-2000s earnings inequality among the full-time employed has risen to only a limited extent in most countries (Figure 3.1). But this shift seems likely to continue. Moreover, as I discuss in Chapter 5, there may be reason to *favor* greater individual-level earnings inequality. I do not mean to suggest that wage compression should be abandoned—merely that it should not be the centerpiece of a strategy for low inequality.

Of the four sources of inequality, household composition is probably the most difficult to change via policy. Policy makers are not impotent in this area, but in a liberal democratic society there are severe limits on the degree to which they can influence individuals' choices about forming partnerships (marital or otherwise) and remaining in them. And even if it were desirable to do so, it is not clear that policymakers could have much impact on the degree of marital homogamy.

To be sure, there also are limits on what can be done via redistribution. But those limits have mainly to do with resources. One way to increase the resources available for redistribution is to increase employment. When more people are employed, the tax base is larger; tax revenues are increased without an increase in tax rates. Higher employment is also likely to reduce the need for redistribution, as fewer individuals and households will have very low market incomes.

These considerations suggest an egalitarian path in which there may be a moderate degree of individual earnings inequality and a moderate or even high proportion of single-adult households, and in which inequality is held in check principally via high employment and redistribution. The key, then, is to figure out how to combine high employment with generously redistributive social policies.

Part II

Jobs

4

Measuring and Analyzing Employment Performance

In Part I of the book I argued that high employment is helpful for limiting income inequality. In Part II I consider the impact on employment of policies and institutions that are likely to contribute to low inequality: high low-end wages, employment protection regulations, generous government benefits, high taxes, skills, and women-friendly policies. But how should we conceptualize and measure employment performance? And what techniques are best suited for analyzing its determinants? This chapter addresses these questions.

MACROCOMPARATIVE ANALYSIS

Various analytical strategies can be pursued in attempting to answer a question such as what effect policies and institutions have on employment. One is to examine individual behavior (Moffitt 1992; Meyer 1995). Another is to consider patterns across firms or industries within countries (Galbraith 1998; Freeman and Schettkat 2000). A third is to look at developments over time in a single country or a small number of countries (Visser and Hemerijck 1997; Streeck and Trampusch 2005).

A fourth approach, which I follow in this book, is macrocomparative. Countries are the unit of analysis. The policies, institutions, and outcomes I examine are measured at the level of the nation. Analytical leverage is gained primarily by comparing across countries. In doing so one can contrast countries in terms of their levels of employment in a given year or during a particular period, or the focus can be on contrasting the countries in terms of their degree of change over time. I engage in both types of comparison, but for reasons outlined below much of the analysis in the book focuses on country differences in change over time. As noted in Chapter 1, due largely to data constraints I focus on twelve nations: Australia, Canada, Denmark,

Finland, France, Germany, Italy, the Netherlands, Norway, Sweden, the United Kingdom, and the United States.

Most of the comparative analysis in the book is quantitative. But quantitative analyses can only establish statistical associations. Even when macrocomparative data yield a strong and robust cross-country association, they need to be supplemented by within-country evidence, especially quantitative and qualitative data on over-time developments in particular countries. This type of information is critical for exploring hypothesized causal mechanisms (Mahoney 2000; Hall 2003; Collier, Brady, and Seawright 2004; George and Bennett 2004; Gerring 2004; Lieberman 2005). I examine such information throughout.

Even if done well, focusing on countries has notable limitations. Perhaps the most significant is that it ignores variation across regions within countries. Why employment patterns differ among the fifty American states or across regions in Germany or other countries is an important and interesting issue, but it is not my concern here. I analyze countries because many of the policies of interest are determined by national governments rather than local ones and because data for regions are much sparser.

PRIOR MACROCOMPARATIVE RESEARCH

Quantitative macrocomparative studies of employment performance have proliferated in the past decade. An incomplete but representative list includes the following:

- Layard, Nickell, and Jackman (1991); Nickell (1997); Nickell and Layard (1999); Nickell, Nunziata, and Ochel (2005)
- OECD (1994, 2006b)
- Elmeskov, Martin, and Scarpetta (1998)
- Iversen and Wren (1998)
- Belot and van Ours (2000)
- Blanchard and Wolfers (2000)
- Esping-Andersen (2000a, 2000b)
- Scharpf (2000)
- Blau and Kahn (2002a)
- Kenworthy (2002, 2004a)
- IMF (2003)
- Baker et al. (2005); Howell et al. (2006)
- Kemmerling (2005)

- Bassanini and Duval (2006)
- Baccaro and Rei (2007)
- Bradley and Stephens (2007)

Many of these studies include some or all of the policies and institutions on which I focus in Chapters 5–8: low-end wages (wage inequality), employment protection regulations, government benefits, and taxes. These are at the heart of debates about a possible equality–jobs tradeoff. What has this research found?

Virtually all of these studies have focused on unemployment. Baker et al. (2005) provide a thorough review of the literature up through 2005. They note that most studies have found an apparent adverse effect of taxes, unemployment benefit generosity, and employment protection on unemployment. Centralized wage bargaining, which typically boosts wages in low-end jobs, has frequently been found to be associated with lower unemployment. A more recent study by Andrea Bassanini and Romain Duval (2006), which provided the empirical basis for OECD's recent reassessment of its 1994 *Jobs Study* (OECD 2006*b*), yielded similar results, except for employment protection. They also find no association between wage inequality and unemployment.

Baker et al. (2005: 101) argue that "While this literature is widely viewed to provide strong evidence for the labor market rigidity view, a close reading of the leading papers suggests that the evidence is actually quite mixed, as several of the studies explicitly acknowledge." In their own analyses, Baker et al. (2005; Howell et al. 2006) find no robust association between employment protection, government benefit generosity, or tax levels and unemployment. Baccaro and Rei (2007) reach a similar conclusion in their recent analysis. Two recent surveys of this line of research by prominent labor economists have echoed the conclusion about the fragility of the comparative findings (Freeman 2005; Blanchard 2006*a*).

Far fewer studies have examined *em*ployment as the outcome of interest. Stephen Nickell and Richard Layard (1999: 3054) focused on unemployment but also analyzed cross-country variation in employment rates across twenty countries over two five-year periods, 1983–88 and 1989–94. They find evidence of an adverse effect of employment protection, government benefit generosity, and high taxes. Bassanini and Duval (2006) likewise concentrate on unemployment but also examine year-to-year changes in employment rates for twenty-one countries during the period 1982–2003. They find an adverse impact of benefit generosity and taxes, but not of employment protection regulations. They also find no effect of wage inequality. Torben Iversen and Anne Wren (1998) examine employment change in three-year periods between 1970 and 1990 for thirteen countries. They find a positive association between earnings inequality and employment growth. Gøsta Esping-Andersen (2000*a*) finds apparent adverse effects of employment protection and taxes on employment growth across twenty-one countries over the 1980s and early 1990s. Fritz Scharpf (2000) concludes that wage compression, employment protection, and especially payroll and consumption taxes are associated with lower employment rates as of the late 1990s. Achim Kemmerling (2005) explores the effect of payroll taxes on business-sector employment longitudinally for Germany, Sweden, and the United States and cross-sectionally for seventeen nations in the 1970s, 1980s, and 1990s. Both analyses suggest an employment-reducing effect of high payroll taxation. In an earlier analysis (Kenworthy 2004*a*: ch. 5), I examined employment change in fourteen countries between 1979 and 1995, finding a negative effect of taxes and a positive (but small) effect of earnings inequality.

WHAT IS NEW HERE?

In what ways do the analyses in the following chapters add to prior work? How might they improve our understanding? I summarize the key points in this section and elaborate on them in the rest of the chapter.

A central difference is in the operationalization and measurement of employment performance. Most of the existing research has analyzed unemployment, whereas I examine *employment*. Most previous studies, whether they focus on unemployment or employment, have either looked exclusively at cross-country differences in levels or have included variation in levels as a key component in pooled analyses. I believe it is more informative to focus on cross-country differences in employment *change*. A number of prior studies cover the period since 1960. Because the economic environment changed dramatically in the 1970s, I argue that it is more sensible to assess the impact of institutions and policies on employment by focusing on the period since the end of the 1970s. Most prior studies that have concentrated on over-time variation have examined short-run changes—either yearly or for five-year periods. In my view a longer-term focus is more appropriate. Most of the existing literature has examined overall unemployment or employment rates. But understanding comparative employment growth requires disaggregating by sector.

A second important difference is in my analytical approach. Much of the analysis in the book consists of examination of bivariate patterns in the data and multivariate single-period regressions that include a small number of variables. Compared to a pooled regression with 300 country-year observations, a dozen control variables, adjustments for country and/or year fixed effects, and a state-of-the-art technique for estimating standard errors, the analyses here may appear quite primitive. The simpler approach I pursue is dictated by the substantive and methodological considerations I discuss in this chapter, but it also has some advantages.

It has the benefit of encouraging close attention to underlying patterns in the data (Achen 2002; Kenworthy 2007b; Shalev 2007). Frequently in quantitative analyses these patterns are hidden behind an array of reduced-form regression coefficients. In macrocomparative research, theory often is vague; seldom is there strong theoretical rationale for preferring a particular model specification (Western 1996). It is therefore imperative that the analyst make clear the way in which the "final" or "preferred" multivariate regression coefficient for a variable of interest has emerged from the bivariate pattern— whether the sign and/or estimated magnitude of the association have changed, and if so why. I attempt to make the patterns in the data as transparent as possible.

In addition, because the number of nations is small, I am able to make use of a fair amount of country-specific knowledge. The more cases there are, the more information is required to have such case knowledge, and therefore the more difficult it is.

My approach also lends itself to careful consideration of the quality of the data and measures. David Howell and colleagues (2006: 7) have rightly observed that "While the literature [on employment performance] has been characterized by a steady increase in the sophistication of econometric techniques, remarkably little attention has been paid to the quality and consistency of the data."

A somewhat unusual feature of the book is that I display a great deal of data. Analysis always involves data reduction, but most quantitative macro-comparative research on affluent nations goes too far in this direction. In this type of research, which covers a relatively small number of countries, the cases are of substantial interest in and of themselves. Moreover, examining the raw data can aid in interpreting the findings of regression (or other multivariate) analysis. As William Cleveland (1994: 5) has noted: "Data display is critical to data analysis. Graphs allow us to explore data to see overall patterns and to see detailed behavior; no other approach can compete in revealing the structure of data so thoroughly." Data display also helps in identifying problematic measures or coding decisions, and it highlights the degree to which findings are influenced by a particular country or set of countries. With just twelve nations it is relatively easy to display most of the relevant data in graphical form, and I do so throughout. Those not interested can skip over these displays and focus on the text.

These advantages notwithstanding, I want to emphasize that the analyses here by no means offer a full and complete answer to the question of what impact equality-enhancing institutions and policies have had on employment—and certainly not the final word on the matter. My hope is simply that they push our understanding forward somewhat.

EMPLOYMENT OR UNEMPLOYMENT?

Should the focus be on employment rates or unemployment rates? The former is calculated as the number of people with a paying job divided by the working-age population (those age 15–64). The latter is the number of persons actively seeking a job but without one divided by the number of labor force participants (the employed plus the unemployed).

For more than half a century, beginning in the 1930s, unemployment was the standard measure of (bad) employment performance. As I noted in the previous section, a number of recent studies have continued to focus on it (Belot and van Ours 2000; Blanchard and Wolfers 2000; Esping-Andersen and Regini 2000; Bertola, Blau, and Kahn 2001; Blau and Kahn 2002*a*; Kenworthy 2002; IMF 2003; Baker et al. 2005; Nickell, Nunziata, and Ochel 2005; Bassanini and Duval 2006; Howell et al. 2006; OECD 2006*b*; Baccaro and Rei 2007). But unemployment rates can be misleading to the extent that joblessness is "hidden" by low levels of labor force participation or by various types of active labor market, early retirement, and other social-welfare policies. Thus, the employment rate is arguably a better barometer of a nation's labor market performance.

More important, as I suggested in Chapter 1, high employment is likely to be increasingly critical to the long-run financial viability of generous redistributive programs, and therefore to successful pursuit of low income inequality. A country with low unemployment but also low employment will be in a worse position in this respect than a country with low (or even moderate) unemployment but also high employment. For this reason, I focus on employment.

EMPLOYMENT LEVELS OR EMPLOYMENT CHANGE?

Here and throughout the book, "employment level" and "employment change" refer to the employment *rate*—employed divided by the working-age population—rather than the number of people employed. They are shorthand for "employment-rate level" and "employment-rate change."

The dominant approach in quantitative comparative research on employment performance—indeed, in quantitative macrocomparative research in general—is to use pooled cross-section time-series regression. Pooling data allows analyses to incorporate two aspects of variation: variation in levels across countries and variation over time within countries. Yet pooling can be problematic if there is causal heterogeneity across space and time—that is, if the determinants of variation in levels across countries differ from the determinants of variation over time within countries. Causal homogeneity is likely when an analysis covers a very long period, but less so for a period of just a few decades (Griffin et al. 1986; Kittel 1999; Kenworthy 2007*a*, 2007*b*; Shalev 2007).

The charts in Figure 4.1 show levels of employment in 1979 and 2000–06 and changes in employment over that period. Employment change is calculated by averaging employment rates over the years 2000–06 and then subtracting the rate in 1979. I use an average for 2000–06 as the ending point in order to balance business cycle considerations with a desire to include the most recent available employment data. For most of the twelve countries 1979 and 2000 were comparable points in the business cycle—both were business cycle peaks—and are therefore suitable for comparison. However, data on employment rates are available through 2006. As it turns out, using 2000 as the end point instead of 2000–06 would make relatively little difference, so I use the latter.

The charts in Figure 4.1 suggest that, for the period since the late 1970s, the determinants of variation in employment levels across the twelve countries are likely to have differed from those of employment change. The countries with the highest employment rates as of 2000–06 varied enormously in terms of employment change during the two decades. Norway and Denmark began with comparatively high levels and managed small-to-moderate increases. The United States, Canada, and Australia began moderately high and achieved sizable increases. Sweden started high but experienced a decline. The Netherlands began with the lowest level among the twelve countries and achieved a very substantial rise.

If pooling is not appropriate, should the focus be on variation in employment levels or variation in employment change? Because employment rates change only incrementally, employment levels during or at the end of this period will be heavily influenced by employment levels at the beginning. As I noted in Chapter 1, the economic environment for affluent countries changed fairly dramatically in the 1970s: firms faced heightened competition from both foreign and domestic sources, and technology changed in profound ways. These changes resulted in a decrease in employer demand for less-skilled labor. As a result, inequality-reducing institutions and policies that had no impact on

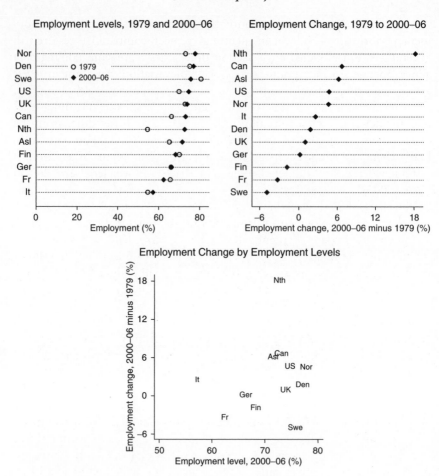

Figure 4.1. Employment levels and employment change.

Note: 2000–06 refers to an average over the seven years from 2000 to 2006. For data definitions and sources, see the appendix.

employment in the 1950s, 1960s, and 1970s may have become impediments since the 1970s.

If so, using employment levels as of 2000–06 as the indicator of employment performance may yield misleading conclusions. A country with a high employment rate in 1979 may still have had a comparatively high employment rate in 2000–06 even if its employment rate declined during the intervening years. Similarly, a country that started with a comparatively low employment rate but gained employment during the ensuing decades may still have had a comparatively low rate as of 2000–06. For this reason, the impact of institutions and policies since the 1970s is best assessed, in my view, using *change* in employment rates as the outcome. My analysis focuses on variation across the twelve countries in employment change.

Note that this does not imply that employment change should be the only consideration when assessing overall employment performance among these countries. "Which countries have had the best employment performance?" is a different question than "What has been the effect of inequality-reducing policies and institutions on employment?" Answering the latter question is the principal task of the coming chapters. I turn to the former question in the book's final chapter. To answer it we need to consider both employment growth and employment levels.

CHANGE → CHANGE OR LEVELS → CHANGE?

If the focus should be on changes in employment, is the hypothesis that such changes were produced by changes in the causal factors or by levels of the causal factors? Typically, we would expect the outcome to change only when the cause changes: change → change. One hypothesis about the rise in unemployment and its sustained high level in some European countries since the early 1980s is that it resulted from changes in institutions and policies—more generous and lengthy unemployment compensation, stricter employment protection, and perhaps others (Nickell, Nunziata, and Ochel 2005; Bassanini and Duval 2006).

The problem with this account is that, as I show in Chapters 6–9, there was little change in the key policies and institutions—low-end wage levels, employment protection, government benefit generosity, and tax levels. An alternative hypothesis, which guides my empirical analyses in those chapters, is the following: (*a*) The key change in the period since the late 1970s has been in the economic environment facing firms, workers, and policy makers. It features greater competition, greater uncertainty, and a decline in demand for less-skilled workers. (*b*) This shift may have had a particularly adverse impact on employment in countries with equality-enhancing institutions and policies, such as high wages at the low end of the distribution, generous government benefits, and high taxes. In this hypothesis, it is the levels of the institutions and/or policies that matter (Blanchard and Wolfers 2000). Hence, the appropriate specification for testing is levels → change.

SHORT-TERM OR LONG-TERM EMPLOYMENT CHANGE?

As I noted earlier, most quantitative macrocomparative analyses use pooled cross-section time-series regression. In such analyses the unit of analysis usually is the country-year—Australia 1980, Australia 1981 ... United States 2004, United States 2005 (e.g. Iversen and Wren 1998; Bassanini and Duval 2006). The benefit of using the country-year as the unit is that the number of observations increases substantially. If one has data for twelve countries over, say, twenty-five years, the number of observations becomes 12 × 25 = 300. This permits inclusion of a large number of independent variables in the regressions, thereby enhancing confidence that the analysis does not suffer from omitted variable bias.

But there is a cost. When the country-year is used as the unit, the analysis almost always presumes a short-run effect. It is possible to lag the independent variables, but that raises the question of what the correct lag is and whether it is safe to assume that it is the same for all countries. This problem is accentuated when one or more of the causal factors of interest changes little or not at all over time. As I show in later chapters, that is very much the case for a number of the institutions and policies I examine. Some analyses use five-year periods rather than single years (e.g. Nickell and Layard 1999; Blanchard and Wolfers 2000). This attenuates the problem, but only slightly.

I therefore prefer to analyze employment change over the full period.

ABSOLUTE CHANGE OR PERCENTAGE CHANGE?

The charts in Figure 4.1 measure employment change in absolute terms: the employment rate in the ending year minus the rate in the beginning year. But should change instead be measured in percentage terms—that is, as absolute change divided by the starting level (the rate in 1979)? The rationale for using a percentage measure is that there may be ceiling and/or catch-up effects. Countries beginning the period with high employment rates might find it difficult to increase employment further (ceiling), while countries beginning at low rates could have an easier time increasing employment (catch-up).

However, empirically, this turns out not to have been the case. The first chart in Figure 4.2 shows absolute employment change by 1979 employment rate. There is a negative association between the two, but it is entirely a function of the Netherlands and Sweden. Excluding those two countries, the association is only −.21. In other words, overall there is no indication that employment change in the since the late 1970s is a function of starting level.

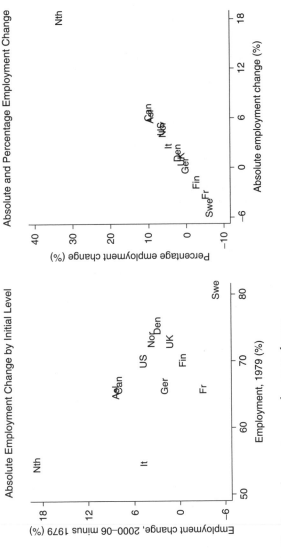

Figure 4.2. Absolute and percentage employment change.

Note: Horizontal axis in the first chart is truncated. For data definitions and sources, see the appendix.

The second chart in Figure 4.2 suggests that the choice of absolute versus percentage employment change makes no difference. Neither the rank ordering of countries nor the degree of variation among them differs between the two measures. Indeed, they correlate at .99.

IS EMPLOYMENT-RATE CHANGE A FUNCTION OF POPULATION CHANGE?

A concern about measuring employment change as change in the employment rate is that such change might be driven by developments in the denominator—the size of the working-age population. Suppose country A increases the number of people employed by only a small amount but has even less increase, or perhaps a decline, in the size of its working-age population. Its employment rate will go up. Country B, by contrast, experiences a dramatic rise in the number of employed but an even sharper increase in its working-age population. Its employment rate will go down. In this circumstance, the measure will mislead.

Figure 4.3 indicates that this concern turns out not to be relevant. Change in the employment rate is on the vertical axis, and change in the size of the

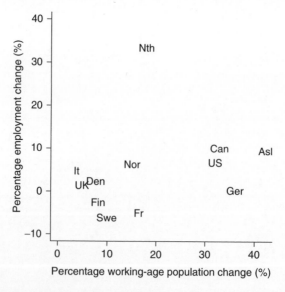

Figure 4.3. Employment change by working-age population change, 1979 to 2000–06.

Note: For data definitions and sources, see the appendix.

working-age population is on the horixontal axis. The latter needs to be mea-sured in percentage terms, so the former is as well. If countries with a smaller increase in the size of their working-age population had done better on the employment-rate change measure, the pattern of countries would slope down to the right. Instead, it is essentially flat. If anything, countries experiencing a smaller increase in the number of working-age persons tended to fare less well in terms of employment rate increases.

EMPLOYMENT ADJUSTED FOR WORK HOURS?

A limitation of the employment rate as a measure of employment performance is that it does not take into account the number of hours worked. A person employed for 40 hours per week is not distinguished from one employed for 10 hours. One concern is that part-time jobs may be more likely to be "bad" jobs—ones with lower hourly pay, fewer benefits, and less employment protection—and that people may be forced to take such jobs due to a short-age of available full-time positions. That is surely true for some individuals, though in a number of countries a large share of those working part-time say they do so by choice.

Of more direct concern here is that if a key rationale for promoting employ-ment is to enlarge the tax base in order to fund redistribution, then the num-ber of hours worked is potentially quite important. Tax revenues typically are based on earnings and income, which for those paid by the hour is a function not only of the wage rate but also of the number of hours worked. A society with an 80% employment rate but an average work week of 20 hours will raise much less revenue than one with a 75% employment rate and a 35-hour average work week.

Unfortunately, we lack reliable comparative data on working time. The OECD does have data, and for some countries they are available annually back to the early 1980s. But the OECD (2007*b*: 264) warns that these data "are intended for comparisons of trends over time; they are unsuitable for comparisons of the level of average annual hours of work for a given year, because of differences in their sources." Thus, although we can calculate a measure of change over time for work hours in each country, we can-not be confident that the resulting calculations are comparable across the countries.

Figure 4.4 shows the over-time trends for each of the twelve countries. The variation in over-time change is considerable. At one end, average work hours increased slightly in Sweden and declined only minimally in the United States.

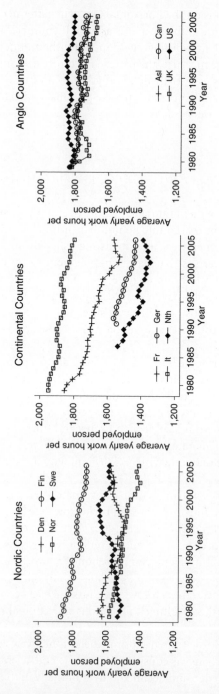

Figure 4.4. Average yearly work hours, 1979ff.

Note: Vertical axes are truncated. For data definitions and sources, see the appendix.

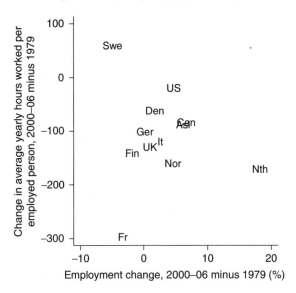

Figure 4.5. Work hours change by employment change, 1979 to 2000–06.

Note: For data definitions and sources, see the appendix.

At the other end, they fell by more than 150 hours in Norway, the Netherlands, and France.

How much might adjusting for work hours alter our assessment of employment performance? Figure 4.5 plots absolute change in average hours worked by absolute change in the employment rate. The years are 1979 to 2000–06, though for Germany and the Netherlands work hours data are available for only part of this period. The chart suggests two things. First, for most of the countries, changes in the employment rate and in hours worked are positively correlated. That is, countries experiencing a larger rise in their employment rate tended to experience a smaller decline in work hours. Thus, adjusting for hours worked would not substantially alter the assessment of employment performance.

Second, two of the countries, Sweden and the Netherlands, do not follow this pattern. Sweden suffered the largest decline in its employment rate but had an increase in average work hours. The Netherlands had the largest rise in employment rate (by far) but also experienced a large decline in average work hours. And the decline shown in the figure may be an underestimate, as the data on average work hours for the Netherlands begin only in 1987. As noted in Chapter 3, most of the employment growth in the Netherlands was in part-time jobs (Figure 3.3). Sweden, by contrast, was one of the few countries to experience a decline in part-time employment.

Because of the concern about cross-country comparability of the work hours data, I make no formal adjustment for working time in the measure of employment change I use throughout the book. Instead, I periodically call attention to the fact that taking work hours into account would likely improve Sweden's measured employment performance and weaken that of the Netherlands. For the other ten countries it might well make no difference.

EMPLOYMENT CHANGE BY SECTOR

Employment change has not been evenly distributed across sectors. The ISIC classification system (revision 2) groups employment into nine broad sectors:

ISIC 1. Agriculture
ISIC 2. Mining
ISIC 3. Manufacturing
ISIC 4. Electricity, gas, and water
ISIC 5. Construction
ISIC 6. Wholesale and retail trade, restaurants, and hotels
ISIC 7. Transport, storage, and communication
ISIC 8. Finance, insurance, real estate, and business services
ISIC 9. Community, social, and personal services

Figure 4.6 shows average employment levels for these sectors in 1979 and 2000–06 for eleven of the twelve countries. Sector-specific data are not available for France. Like the overall employment levels shown in previous figures, these are calculated as a share of the working-age population. In four of the nine sectors, employment rates were relatively low and stagnant: construction, transport/storage/communication, electricity/gas/water, and mining. On average these four sectors account for only 15% of total employment, and in each of them the employment rate has not changed since the late 1970s.

The bulk of employment, and all of the employment change since the late 1970s, is in five sectors: agriculture, manufacturing, finance/insurance/real estate/business services, wholesale and retail trade/restaurants/hotels, and community/social/personal services. Employment declined in agriculture and manufacturing, and it increased in the three service sectors. Understanding these developments and the way in which they differed across the countries is thus key to understanding the cross-country variation in overall employment changes.

It turns out that declines in employment in manufacturing and agriculture were largely a function of each country's starting point. All countries

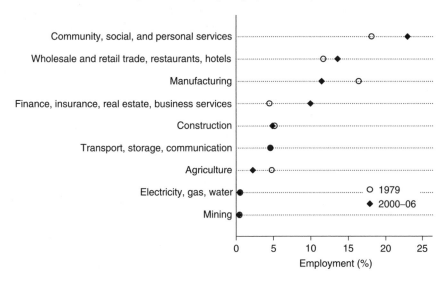

Figure 4.6. Employment by sector, 1979 and 2000–06.

Note: These figures are averages for eleven countries (data are not available for France). For data definitions and sources, see the appendix.

have deagriculturalized and deindustrialized since the 1960s, but they have done so at differing paces. Countries that have lost a significant amount of employment in these two sectors since the late 1970s had comparatively little left to lose. Those that began the process later had more to lose. The former countries have experienced relatively little decline, while the latter have tended to suffer much greater declines. The first chart in Figure 4.7 shows this pattern.

The other three sectors are usefully thought of as comprising two groups, which I will refer to as "high-end services" and "low-end services." The former consists of jobs in finance, insurance, real estate, and other business services (ISIC 8). These are mainly high-productivity jobs with relatively high pay. The latter includes jobs in wholesale and retail trade, restaurants, and hotels (ISIC 6) and in community, social, and personal services (ISIC 9). Productivity and pay in these jobs tend to be lower.

Have employment changes in these two groups also been largely a function of the starting point? The second and third charts in Figure 4.7 suggest not. It is on these two service sector groups, then, where the search for employment effects of institutions and policies should be concentrated. It would help to be able to separate private from public employment in these sectors, but unfortunately OECD data do not permit that beyond the mid-1990s.

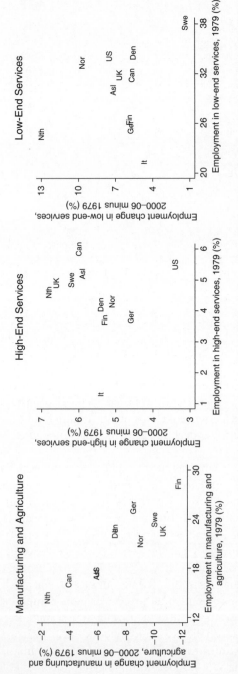

Figure 4.7. Employment change in manufacturing and agriculture, high-end services, and low-end services, 1979 to 2000–06, by initial employment level.

Note: Some axes are truncated. Data are not available for France. For data definitions and sources, see the appendix.

EMPLOYMENT CHANGE BY GENDER AND AGE GROUP

Patterns of employment change vary not only by sector but also by gender and age group. Male employment has remained largely unchanged in most countries. Women have accounted for most of the increase in employment in nations experiencing employment rises. Indeed, a considerable portion of the cross-country variation in employment change is among women who are at the young and old ends of the "working-age" spectrum—those age 15–24 and 55–64. I address this issue in Chapter 10.

POTENTIAL CONFOUNDING FACTORS

Given the small number of countries I include in the analyses and my choice to focus on longer-term effects, only a small number of control variables can be included in multivariate analyses. My strategy for dealing with this limitation is to estimate a series of regressions that include all possible combinations of three or fewer of the hypothesized causes, as I did in Chapter 3 (for further discussion, see Kenworthy 2004*a*: ch. 2).

The causal factors of interest are low-end wages, employment protection regulations, government benefits, taxes, skills, and women-friendly policies. Which controls should be included?

In the view of some analysts, macroeconomic policy is one of the most important determinants of employment (Dornbusch 1986; Ball 1999; Galbraith, Conceição, and Ferreira 1999; Martin 2004; Schettkat 2004, 2005; Howell 2005; Baccaro and Rei 2007). Stimulative macroeconomic policy increases demand for goods and services, which raises employer demand for workers. This leads to a rise in employment. The chief macroeconomic policy tool governments use to stimulate is monetary policy. Monetary policy principally involves setting interest rates. Low interest rates help to stimulate the economy by reducing the cost of borrowing money for firms and individuals. The best monetary policy indicator is real (inflation-adjusted) interest rates.

Globalization may hurt employment in a variety of ways. The two most prominent hypotheses have to do with trade, and specifically with imports. First, the more consumers purchase goods and services from abroad—that is, the higher the level of imports—the less need there may be for domestic employment. Second, when domestic employers face competition not only from other domestic firms but also from foreign companies, their profit rate is likely to be lower. This encourages employers to seek ways to cut costs, one of which may be to reduce employment levels. I measure imports here as a share of GDP.

Rapid increases in real unit labor costs—wages adjusted for inflation and for productivity—can reduce employer demand for workers and thereby impede employment growth. Some observers attribute cross-country varia- tion in employment performance since the 1970s in part to differences in wage behavior (OECD 1994; Visser and Hemerijck 1997; Hemerijck and Schludi 2000).

Strong product market regulations may affect employment growth (OECD 2002*a*; Alesina and Giavazzi 2006). Such regulations include barriers to entry, barriers to trade, price controls, government involvement in business oper- ations, public ownership, and market concentration. To the extent product market regulations reduce competition, they may stifle employment in several ways: by imposing deadweight costs, by deterring entry of new firms, by reduc- ing the supply of entrepreneurial talent, and by allowing higher wages that price some job-seekers out of the market. The OECD (2002*a*) has created a summary indicator—an index ranging from zero to six—based on regulation in seven industries. I use an updated version of these data from Bassanini and Duval (2006).

Figure 4.8 shows bivariate plots with employment change from 1979 to 2000–06 on the vertical axes and indicators of these four controls on the horizontal axes. The controls are measured as average levels over 1980 to the mid-2000s. The Netherlands is an outlier in each of these plots, and the regression lines are calculated with it omitted. The monetary policy chart suggests little or no association. The other three—those for imports, labor cost changes, and product market regulations—show the expected negative association. Of course, we should not thereby conclude that macroeconomic policy has played no role in cross-country differences in employment perfor- mance, nor that imports, labor cost changes, or product market regulations necessarily have played a role. Bivariate patterns can hide real relationships, and they can suggest ones that are in fact spurious.

The multivariate analyses in coming chapters will include each of these con- trols. However, in addition to the limits imposed by a small number of cases, multivariate analysis here faces an obstacle in multicollinearity. A number of the policies and institutions I examine covary strongly across countries. The correlations in Table 4.1 make this clear. Nations with higher low-end wages (less earnings inequality) tend to have stronger employment protection, more generous government benefits, higher tax levels, more trade, stronger prod- uct market regulations, higher measured cognitive skill, and more developed "women-friendly" policies. In this situation, multiple regression is a relatively blunt instrument for identifying the causal impact of any particular one of these factors. An alternative method for systematically analyzing relationships is qualitative comparative analysis (QCA). Unfortunately, QCA is no more

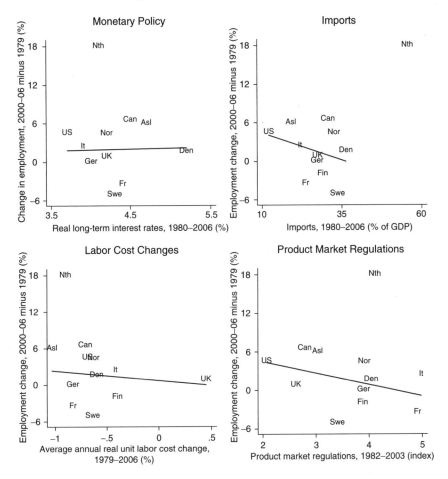

Figure 4.8. Employment change, 1979 to 2000–06, by measures of monetary policy, globalization, labor cost changes, and product market regulations.

Note: Horizontal axis is truncated. The regression lines are calculated with the Netherlands excluded. For data definitions and sources, see the appendix.

effective at handling highly correlated causal variables. In any event, QCA is designed to examine the effects of combinations of variables, rather than to isolate the impact of a particular variable (Ragin 1987, 2000; Epstein et al. 2008; Kenworthy and Hicks 2008).

In some instances data are available for additional countries, and this helps to alleviate the multicollinearity problem somewhat (Chapters 5–8). Nevertheless, in the face of these limitations I refrain from drawing inferences from the regression results about the precise magnitude of associations between the

Table 4.1. Correlations among potential determinants of employment performance.

	1	2	3	4	5	6	7	8	9
1. Earnings inequality									
2. Employment protection regulations	−.80								
3. Government benefit generosity	−.75[b]	.61[b]							
4. Payroll and consumption taxes	−.63	.85	.66[b]						
5. Real long-term interest rates	−.25[a]	−.08[a]	.45[c]	−.18[a]					
6. Imports	−.36	.37	.78[b]	.51	.22[a]				
7. Labor cost changes	.04	−.25	.08[b]	−.04	−.13[a]	−.09			
8. Product market regulations	−.71	.88	.69[b]	.72	.10[a]	.30	−.21		
9. Literacy	−.84[b]	.86[b]	.71[b]	.74[b]	.28[c]	.53[b]	−.26[b]	.74[b]	
10. Public child care expenditures	−.75[a]	.54[a]	.70[b]	.42[a]	.50[b]	.26[a]	.03[a]	.53[a]	.78[b]

Note: $N = 12$ except where otherwise noted. "Government benefit generosity" is referred to in Chapter 7 as "benefit employment disincentives." For data definitions and sources, see the appendix.

[a] $N = 11$

[b] $N = 10$

[c] $N = 9$

policies and institutions of interest and employment performance. Instead, I aim for upper-bound and lower-bound estimates. While this may seem frustratingly imprecise to some readers, it is, in my view, an accurate reflection of the degree of uncertainty inherent in attempting to draw conclusions from this type of data.

STATISTICAL SIGNIFICANCE?

To what extent can the findings from the book's analyses be generalized? In a strict sense, not at all. The twelve countries are not a representative sample drawn from a larger population. They are a "convenience sample," based on data availability. The population of affluent democratic countries includes twenty to twenty-five nations. In addition to the countries I examine, it includes Austria, Belgium, Ireland, Israel, Japan, New Zealand, Portugal, Spain, and Switzerland, and perhaps also Iceland, Luxembourg, and a few others. There is no reason to presume that findings for the twelve nations on which I focus will necessarily shed light on processes and outcomes in any—much less all—of these other countries. We can hope that they do, but the twelve countries are not a representative sample, so there are no grounds for assuming that they will. For this reason, I present no information about statistical inference—"statistical significance"—in the book (Berk 2004).

Nor can we treat observations from the period since the late 1970s as a representative sample of years for these twelve countries. Instead, they constitute the population of recent years (or periods). We thus cannot safely presume that findings for what has happened in these twelve counties since the late 1970s will provide a useful guide to developments in these countries in coming years. Then again, even if there can be little certainty, recent developments do offer the best information we have about what is likely to hold in the future. This is the principal rationale for studying them.

THE CHAPTERS TO COME

My aim in this second part of the book is to assess the impact on employment of inequality-reducing policies and institutions. Chapters 5–8 examine four that are commonly presumed to impede employment: high low-end wages, strict employment protection regulations, generous government benefits, and high taxes. Chapters 9 and 10 look at two that are often thought to boost employment: skills and women-friendly policies.

5

Low-End Wages

Higher wages for those at the low end of the labor market frequently are a key component of the egalitarian strategies of union leaders and progressive citizens and political parties. Should this goal be abandoned, or at least relaxed?

An argument for doing so goes as follows: In jobs where productivity is low and difficult to increase, employers can afford to pay only minimal wages. If forced to pay more, they will hire fewer people. Hence, policy makers and unions face a choice: allow low wages in such jobs and thereby get higher employment, or mandate higher wages and thereby get lower employment. This view has been around for a long time in economic debates about the impact of minimum wages, but its prominence was heightened by a series of reports issued by the OECD in the mid-1990s (OECD 1994, 1996b). Since then it has held considerable sway among scholars and in the business press (Wessel and Benjamin 1994; Bertola and Ichino 1995; Becker 1996; Krugman 1996; Samuelson 1996; *The Economist* 1997; Siebert 1997; Iversen and Wren 1998; Esping-Andersen 1999, 2000a; Blanchard and Wolfers 2000; Blau and Kahn 2002a; Iversen 2005).

I suggested in Chapter 1 that high employment is likely to be increasingly important for sustaining a generous level of government redistribution. If that is true, and if high low-end wages impede employment, egalitarians must decide which is the preferable route to low inequality: wage compression or redistribution.

The former route is, in my view, a risky one. Countries with low individual earnings inequality do tend to have low posttax-posttransfer household income inequality. But that is mainly because they also tend to have extensive redistribution. Figure 5.1 makes this clear. It shows P75/P25 ratios for individual earnings, pretax-pretransfer household income, and posttax-posttransfer household income for the twelve countries in 2000 (or the closest available year). I use the P75/P25 ratio to measure inequality here because it is the best measure that is available for all three of these levels (see Chapter 3). It is reasonable to assume that, across countries, earnings inequality among individuals will correlate closely with pretax-pretransfer income inequality

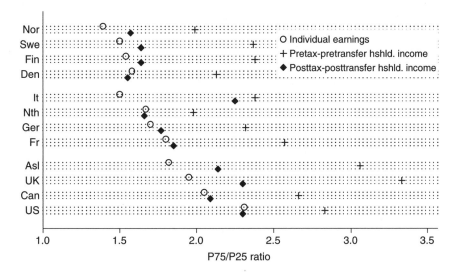

Figure 5.1. Inequality of individual earnings, pretax-pretransfer household income, and posttax-posttransfer household income, 2000.

Note: Actual year is 1999 for the Netherlands and the United Kingdom and 2001 for Australia. For data definitions and sources, see the appendix.

among households. But empirically there is considerable slippage between these. That is because while individual earnings inequality does affect household income inequality, so too do other factors such as household composition and employment patterns within households (Chapter 3; Kenworthy 2004*a*: ch. 3). As of 2000 the Nordic countries had the lowest levels of individual earnings inequality, and for Norway that was also true for inequality of pretax-pretransfer household income. But in Denmark, Sweden, and Finland pretax-pretransfer income inequality was higher than in the Netherlands and Germany and only slightly lower than in Italy and Canada. The reason why posttax-posttransfer income inequality in Denmark, Sweden, and Finland was lower than in these other nations is redistribution.

A compressed distribution of earnings among individuals does not guarantee a similarly compressed distribution of pretax-pretransfer income among households. And there is relatively little governments can do to affect household composition. What this suggests is that if there is in fact a tradeoff between wages and jobs, with countries forced to choose between wage compression and redistribution as their chief route to low income inequality, they might be advised to opt for the latter.

But is there in fact a tradeoff between wages and jobs? That is the question I address in this chapter.

Jobs with Equality

ALTERNATIVES TO THE TRADEOFF VIEW

I begin by outlining some reasons why there might be little or no trade-off between wages and jobs. There are four principal reasons why high pay levels might not necessarily reduce demand for labor in low-end consumer-service jobs. They have to do with productivity, employee turnover, consumer demand, and employers' desired and actual profit margins.

Virtually everyone agrees that there is some point at which wages in low-productivity jobs will discourage employment (e.g. Card and Krueger 1995: 13; Herzenberg, Alic, and Wial 1998: 153). But there is considerable uncertainty about where that point is. The question can only be answered empirically. What does the evidence tell us? To what extent can productivity improvements, reduced employee turnover, and higher consumer demand offset high labor costs? If forced to pay higher wages, will employers do so without reducing employment? I examine various types of empirical evidence, including studies of firms and some nation-specific macro-level patterns. Much of this evidence comes from studies of the United States. In a later section I turn to macrocomparative evidence.

Productivity

Although productivity in low-end service jobs tends to be low and difficult to increase, there almost certainly is some room for improvement. Stephen Herzenberg, John Alic, and Howard Wial (1998) have offered a thoughtful discussion of this issue. They categorize service-sector jobs into four types: high-skill autonomous, semiautonomous, unrationalized labor intensive, and tightly constrained. They ask whether productivity in these jobs can be improved, which would allow wages to rise without reducing employers' profits.

They begin by considering what contribution technological advance in the form of automation can potentially make. They conclude as follows:

Outside tightly constrained and pockets of semiautonomous work, technological change has had less dramatic effects. The lack of standardization of unrationalized labor-intensive work, the variability of most semiautonomous jobs, and the complexity of much high-skill autonomous work mean that technology—the janitor's backpack vacuum, the trucker's on-board telephone, the financial analyst's spreadsheet—is generally a supplemental tool with incremental rather than transforming effects. In such cases, technological change typically has only modest potential to improve performance or alter job quality....In the near future, as in the past, technological change will likely have its most pervasive impacts on tightly constrained service jobs; automation is easiest where people already perform machinelike tasks. Elevator operators have disappeared; computerized voice-recognition systems promise to make telephone operators all but obsolete. Although technological change plays some role in the evolution of all work systems, for most high-skill autonomous and unrationalized labor-intensive jobs that role is incremental.... The likely inability to rationalize large parts of the service sector in traditional ways means that we cannot count on widespread and sustained improvements in economic performance through rationalization and automation. (1998: 57–8, 78)

What about work reorganization as a means of raising productivity in services? The chief forms of work reorganization in manufacturing in recent decades have been statistical process control, total quality management, just-in-time production, and quality circles and self-managed work groups. In the view of Herzenberg and his colleagues (1998: ch. 5), these are of limited relevance to most service jobs. They are most helpful for tightly constrained jobs, which are a small share of service jobs. "We cannot improve service sector performance by using the methods that worked in mass manufacturing. In too much of the service sector there is too little scope for standardizing and rationalizing production" (p. 149). The main reason for this has to do with a distinction between what they call the "engineering model" and the "interpretive model":

[In most manufacturing] the output is a tangible product with well-defined attributes.... Manufacture, therefore, can be viewed as the solution of a technical or engineering problem, one that has unambiguous objectives (functional performance, cost, quality).... In much of the service sector, though, the engineering model applies poorly or not at all (or to only part of the production process). Intangible service outputs—health, a legal brief, even a clean hotel room—are, to begin with, difficult to define and measure in ways that would enable production to be viewed purely in engineering terms.... A second problem in applying the engineering model is that the attributes of service products may be partly or wholly inseparable from the process of production, as illustrated by table service in a restaurant.... A third problem arises when the customer takes part in the provision of the service but does not know, or knows only vaguely, what she wants.... Finally, some services (including child care, education, and much of health care) vary too much with the situation to permit application of the engineering model. (1988: 85–7)

Increasing productivity in services, they argue, requires an "interpretive" model: "In the interpretive model, workers develop skills in understanding customer wants and needs. They then translate those wants and needs into the services they provide. If the worker finds that the service and method of provision he has initially chosen are not producing the intended or desired effects, he modifies the service or method of delivery or his interpretation of what the customer wants or needs. The worker continues to adjust his interpretation of customer needs until he perceives that they match the customer's expectations" (p. 87).

The key question, in their view, is: Can productivity be improved substantially in unrationalized labor-intensive service positions such as childcare worker, hotel room cleaner, waitress/waiter, low-level health care provider (e.g. nursing aide), mail deliverer, trash collector, and others? These are low-end service-sector jobs that cannot be automated out of existence. Herzenberg, Alic, and Wial contend that there are two chief routes: "economies of depth," which refers to learning/skilling, and "economies of coordination," which refers to coordination and cooperation among employees (pp. 90–3). Unfortunately, Herzenberg and his colleagues discuss ways to raise productivity in only two types of unrationalized labor-intensive service work: home health aides and hotel housekeepers. And for both of these they merely suggest, without offering specific examples or referring to any evidence, that training workers to develop interpretive capacities and thereby resolve patients'/clients' problems in a thoughtful, problem-solving manner rather than in a rote, by-the-book fashion can yield productivity gains (pp. 99–101, 135). Although they pose the question of productivity improvements in low-end services in a very useful fashion, then, Herzenberg, Alic, and Wial leave us with considerable ambiguity as to the answer.

Room cleaning in hotels is a quintessential low-end consumer-service job. Seemingly there is little scope for productivity improvement. But a study of German and British hotels in the late 1980s suggests otherwise (Prais, Jarvis, and Wagner 1989). The authors compared hotels of similar size and quality in the two countries and found that productivity in room-cleaning operations was approximately 1.5–2 times higher, on average, in the German hotels. This was due to several factors. One is that the German hotels had introduced more labor-saving improvements in rooms, such as tiling of bathrooms, bed-bases down to the floor to reduce dust collecting underneath, curved joints between walls and floors to avoid dust traps, and wash basins molded into a large table surface to avoid dirt accumulating at joints. German hotels also were more likely to have provided room cleaners with special-purpose trolleys loaded with linen, towels, soaps, guest supplies (hotel guides, information leaflets), and cleaning tools and materials. This reduced the time cleaners spent transporting things between supply closets and guest rooms. Also, because cleaners were more effective and efficient in Germany, their supervisors were able to spend more time on organizational tasks such as work-scheduling for the staff, stock control, purchasing, and organizing external laundry work. British supervisors, by contrast, spent much more time on detailed checking of the cleaning and redoing or finishing off imperfect cleaning work.

These types of innovations may by now have been adopted at most hotels in affluent countries, leaving little opportunity for further increases in efficiency. But this example suggests that productivity improvements may be possible even in jobs where on the surface there would seem to be little prospect for them.

Differences in skills, work organization, and mechanization are the most common sources of differences in productivity levels. But in consumer-service jobs a potentially more important source is worker effort and commitment. In one view, employee effort and commitment are a function of pay levels (Akerlof and Yellen 1986). Low-productivity service jobs are among the most likely to be characterized by low employee commitment. Employers may therefore find it profitable to pay higher wages to the extent that doing so helps to alleviate this problem. In this context, higher relative pay levels at the bottom of the labor market would not deter employment.

The contrast between two of America's retail giants—Sam's Club, which is owned by Wal-Mart, and Costco—offers an instructive comparison (see Holmes and Zellner 2004; O'Toole and Lawler 2006: 160–1). As of 2003 Sam's Club had 102,000 employees, whereas Costco had just 68,000. Yet the two companies, which are direct competitors, generated virtually identical revenues: $35 billion for Sam's Club, $34 billion for Costco. The average productivity level was thus much higher among Costco's employees than among Sam's Club's. This allowed Costco to pay higher wages: the average hourly wage in 2003 was $15.97 for Costco employees, compared to $11.52 for Sam's Club workers. In addition, a larger share of Costco employees than Sam's Club employees were covered by company benefits: 82% versus 42% for health care and 91% versus 64% for retirement.

There are various possible reasons for the higher productivity of Costco's work force. One is that Costco's product line is slightly more upscale. But the better pay and benefits may produce greater work effort, idea sharing, and employee commitment, rendering higher pay levels (and more generous benefits) as much a cause as a consequence of higher productivity.

Employee Turnover

Employee turnover can be costly for firms. Expenses associated with search, hiring, and training increase overall labor costs (Gregg 2000; Manning 2003). If higher wages reduce employee turnover, they may not increase firms' overall labor costs.

A useful recent study on this issue examined food service workers in twelve US hospitals in 2001 (Appelbaum et al. 2003). The researchers found that higher pay was associated with lower turnover, controlling for job type, education, training, employment protection, union membership, age, gender, and race. Part of the reason Costco can afford to pay considerably higher wages than its competitor Sam's Club is lower turnover: just 6% of Costco employees leave within the first year, compared to 21% of Sam's Club workers (Holmes and Zellner 2004).

Consumer Demand

A third reason why high pay levels might not reduce employment in low-end services has to do with consumer demand. Job creation in consumer-oriented services depends not only on wages and productivity but also on the level of consumer demand. Higher demand can enable firms to raise prices while holding output constant, thereby permitting higher wages, or to expand output, thereby allowing for increased employment. In addition, greater sales volume increases a firm's ability to exploit economies of scale in various aspects of its business, which raises productivity.

A variety of things affect the level of demand for consumer services. One is the general level of consumer affluence. If people's preference for travel and for purchasing personal services such as cooking and cleaning rises with income, higher levels of disposable income will increase demand for hotels, restaurants, home cleaners, clothes cleaners, and related services. Another is tourism by foreigners, which heightens demand for hotel, restaurant, and other consumer services. The rate of female labor force participation also is likely to be important. The more women are in the paid labor force, the greater will be the need to outsource household tasks (Esping-Andersen 1999). Demand for consumer services may also be affected by consumer preferences. Where home-cooking and -cleaning are more institutionalized, demand for restaurants and housecleaning services may be lower (Freeman and Schettkat 2000).

Two recent studies have examined the impact of levels and changes in consumer demand on employment in France, Germany, the Netherlands, the United Kingdom, and the United States. One, by Andrew Glyn and colleagues (2005), focuses on employment in retail trade. They conclude that the most important factor accounting for the higher employment rate in this sector in the United States compared to the four European countries is America's higher GDP per capita, which contributes to greater per capita consumption of retail goods. In France and the Netherlands employment growth in retail trade also appears to be constrained by the mix of consumer demand, which is less oriented to goods consumption than in the United States. The other study, by Mary Gregory and Giovanni Russo (2004), concludes similarly that a key reason behind the more rapid increase of employment in the United States compared to the four European nations has been the greater increase in demand in the former.

Employers May Accept Lower Profits if Forced to Do So

Suppose you are an employer and you are asked or required to pay higher wages. No further improvements in productivity are available via mechanization, work reorganization, economies of depth, economies of coordination, or greater worker effort. Employee turnover is low and unlikely to decline. There is no reasonable prospect of heightened demand for your goods or services in the near future. Competition prevents you from raising your prices to offset the higher wage costs. Will you respond to the increased wage rate by reducing the size of your work force? The answer depends on whether your chief concern is your profit *rate* or your profit *volume*. If you get rid of some employees without any improvement in the productivity of those who remain, you may maintain the same profit rate as before but at the cost of a substantial reduction in the volume of your profits. If you continue with the same number of employees as before, you will suffer a reduced profit rate and a reduced profit volume (same revenues as before but greater wage costs), but the decline in profit volume will likely be less than if you fire some employees.

The point is that if forced to pay higher wages, employers may do so without reducing employment (Galbraith 1998; Shulman 2003; Meyerson 2004). For many firms a wage increase will reduce profits, but not to zero. As long as firms make some profit, they will accept this state of affairs rather than move elsewhere or go out of business.

This is particularly likely for consumer-service firms because of their geographic immobility. Unlike manufacturing plants, retail stores, hotels, and restaurants need to be located where the customers are. An employer cannot easily move to a rural area or a developing country to take advantage of cheaper labor. As Harold Meyerson (2004) has put it with respect to unions' likely influence on wages and employment: "In a globalized economy, even high levels of unionization in manufacturing industries such as auto and steel have been unable to protect workers from seeing their jobs shipped abroad and having to take lower-paying jobs in their stead. But with the continuing shift to a service-sector economy, the number of workers whose jobs cannot be exported—from sales clerks and cashiers to janitors, servers, and housekeepers—continues to grow." Because employers are trapped geographically, governments and/or strong unions may be able to impose high wages without sacrificing employment.

Some employers may even *increase* the size of their work force in response to a rise in the wage rate. Doing so may make it possible to maintain profit volume: the larger number of employees offsets the lower profit rate per employee. This only makes sense, however, if the employer is confident that the firm will be able to increase sales. If the market is already saturated, it does not make sense to increase the number of employees.

A helpful analogy is individuals' response to an increase in tax rates. Some people may respond by cutting back on work hours, because a larger portion of each dollar or euro or kroner that they earn is taken away by the government. Others may increase their work hours in order to maintain their prior level of net earnings. Others will respond by making no change in their work hours. The response depends on individuals' preferences and circumstances. The same holds for employers with respect to a wage increase.

There are various companies, industries, or localities in the United States in which wages for consumer-service workers are comparatively high or have been increased without adverse employment consequences. I noted earlier that Costco pays its employees about 50% more on average than its retail competitor Sam's Club. This is no doubt partly a function of higher productivity and less employee turnover. But it also stems to some degree from the fact that part of Costco's work force is unionized whereas Sam's Club is union-free.

Another example is hotel workers in Las Vegas. Harold Meyerson (2004) describes the situation as follows:

The median hourly wage of the American hotel dishwasher in 2000 was $7.45, a little better than the housekeeper's $7.09. Even luxury hotels seldom pay their low-end employees much more than the minimum wage. And while wages have stagnated, hours have declined, from 40 a week for low-end hotel workers in 1960 to 31 in 2000. [In contrast, Sylvester Garcia's] hourly wage at the Luxor [the Las Vegas hotel where he is employed] is $11.86—$4 higher than the industry average. He is paid for 40 hours every week, even if the company actually needs him for fewer. He has family health insurance paid for entirely by his employer. He has a defined-benefit pension. He has three weeks of vacation every year.... Housekeepers in Las Vegas make $11.40 hourly; tipped hotel employees have a $9.60 base wage, the highest in the land.

How is this possible? According to Meyerson, it is a product of efforts by the Las Vegas local of the Hotel Employees and Restaurant Employees International Union (HERE). A series of intense strike battles since the late 1980s, led by committed union leaders and made possible through the resolve of union members, both forced employers to accept higher wages and bolstered union membership and strength.

Then again, Las Vegas hotels are somewhat unique in their industry. Their profits come mainly from gambling, which generates unusually large revenues and thus renders these hotels better able to afford high wages and generous benefits. In addition, they reap substantial benefits from their location in a city to which many people are willing to travel. They are thus much more constrained in locational terms than other hotels, and hence are more vulnerable to the demands of well-organized workers. In short, the generalizability of this example is questionable.

Beth Shulman (2003: 140–2) describes two other examples: home health-care workers and janitors.

The Service Employees International Union (SEIU) health-care campaign in California is a telling example of how unions are improving the quality of today's lower-wage jobs. SEIU, in collaboration with disability and senior citizens groups, pressured counties throughout California to engage in collective bargaining with its home health-care workers after it helped to enact legislation that gave these counties collective bargaining authority. The SEIU then went door-to-door to sign up workers—with success that has been nothing short of astounding. Out of the approximately 200,000 home care workers in the State of California In-Home Supportive Services system, the SEIU today represents about 130,000 of these workers—75,000 in Los Angeles alone. As a result of the organizing campaign, home care workers in the Bay area, who in 1995 made $4.25 an hour with few if any benefits, make $10.00 an hour. They have employer-provided medical, dental, and vision coverage, and paid time off through a vacation fund....

In the past ten years, the SEIU's Justice for Janitors Campaign has organized over 75,000 janitors. In northern New Jersey, for example, janitors moved from $5.50 to $11.00 an hour over the three-year life of the contract and are now provided health insurance. Just as important, part-time jobs have been changed to full time, giving workers needed hours. Certainly, not all the gains have been that dramatic, but they have been substantial. To ensure that unionized janitorial contractors are not at a competitive disadvantage, the union attempts to organize an entire labor market in a city or region. When this is achieved, janitorial employers cannot use low wages as a tool for winning contracts from building owners. Because many of the real estate owners and building-service contractors have a nationwide scope, the union uses the power of its membership in one area to help organize another. Janitorial jobs that largely were poorly paid and lacking benefits have been changed for the better through this approach.

These four cases—Costco employees, hotel workers in Las Vegas, home care workers in California's Bay area, and janitors in northern New Jersey—suggest reason for optimism about possibilities for raising wage levels in low-productivity jobs without provoking employment reductions.

A source of more systematic evidence is statutory minimum wages in the United States. The most influential set of studies on this issue are of employment in fast-food restaurants by David Card and Alan Krueger (1995). Card and Krueger summarize their analyses and findings as follows:

Both studies use detailed data on individual fast-food restaurants that we collected to study the effects of the minimum wage. The choice of fast-food restaurants is deliberate: as suggested by the "McJobs" cliché, fast-food chains are the quintessential minimum-wage employers in today's labor market. Indeed, jobs in the fast-food industry account for a substantial fraction of all minimum-wage jobs in the U.S. economy.

The first case study focuses on the "natural experiment" generated by the April 1992 increase in the New Jersey minimum wage, from $4.25 to $5.05 per hour. Prior to the effective data of the new law, we surveyed 410 fast-food restaurants in New Jersey and eastern Pennsylvania [two neighboring and economically similar states]. We resurveyed the restaurants roughly ten months later, to determine how employment had responded to the hike in the minimum wage. Comparisons between restaurants in New Jersey and those in Pennsylvania, where the minimum wage remained fixed at $4.25 per hour, provide direct estimates of the effect of the new minimum wage. A second set of comparisons, between restaurants in New Jersey that had been paying $5.00 or more per hour before the law took effect and lower-wage New Jersey restaurants, which had to increase their pay rates in order to comply with the law, provides a further contrast for studying the effect of the minimum. Remarkably, regardless of the comparison used, the estimated employment effects of the minimum wage are virtually identical. Contrary to the stark prediction of competitive-demand theory, we find that the rise in the New Jersey minimum wage seems to have increased employment at restaurants that were forced to raise pay to comply with the law. [Actually, employment in the surveyed Pennsylvania restaurants declined on average while employment in the New Jersey restaurants remained constant.]

The second case study uses the natural experiment generated by the April 1991 increase in the federal minimum wage, from $3.80 to $4.25 per hour. In collaboration with Lawrence Katz, one of us (Krueger) conducted a survey of fast-food restaurants in Texas, in December 1990. We then conducted a second survey in July and August 1991, about four or five months after the increase in the federal minimum wage. More than 100 restaurants were interviewed in both surveys, permitting us to conduct a longitudinal analysis similar to the one conducted in the New Jersey-Pennsylvania study. Although the Texas analysis relies exclusively on the comparison between higher- and lower-wage restaurants within the same state to measure the effects of the minimum-wage hike, the results are similar to the results in the New Jersey-Pennsylvania study. Fast-food restaurants in Texas that were forced to increase pay to meet the new federal minimum-wage standard had faster employment growth than did those that already were paying $4.25 per hour or more. Again, the results seem to directly contradict the predictions of competitive-demand theory. (1995: 20–1)

These findings directly contradict the prior conventional wisdom, which suggested that an increase in the statutory minimum would likely reduce employment.

The Card–Krueger findings have spurred reanalysis of the Pennsylvania–New Jersey developments using different data. David Neumark and William Wascher (2000) used data from a survey of (a smaller number of) restaurants and found a negative effect of the New Jersey minimum wage increase on employment in fast-food restaurants. However, those data are of questionable reliability, as the survey was conducted after the Card–Krueger findings had received considerable media attention (see Card and Krueger 2000). Card and Krueger later gained access to employment records collected by state governments for the unemployment compensation program. These suggested no impact of New Jersey's minimum wage increase in either direction (Card and Krueger 2000).

Card and Krueger (1995) also examined the effect of different minimum wage levels on the propensity of new fast-food restaurants to open—rather than on changes in employment levels at already-existing restaurants—and found no impact.

Researchers also have analyzed the effect of increases in the federal minimum wage in 1990, 1991, 1996, and 1997 on employment and the impact of cross-state differences in minimum wage levels on overall employment and teenage employment (Card and Krueger 1995; Bernstein and Schmitt 1998; Chapman 2004). These studies suggest no observable adverse effect. By contrast, a recent examination of data from the Current Population Survey covering the years 1979 through 1997 finds that increases in the federal minimum wage have tended to raise wage levels but reduce employment and hours worked among those at or near the prior minimum (Neumark, Schweitzer, and Wascher 2004). This holds both for teenagers and for adults. The bulk of this effect shows up with a time lag of a year of more after the increase in the minimum wage. The overall impact, according to the authors, is to reduce earnings for low income workers. A state-level analysis of minimum wage increases in the years 1977–95 finds indication of an employment-reducing effect (Keil, Robertson, and Symons 2001).

Since the mid-1990s more than a hundred American city governments have passed "living wage" ordinances, which require businesses that contract with the city government to pay their employees a minimum wage of between $7 and $12 per hour, depending on the city (Living Wage Resource Center 2006). The most thorough study of these ordinances finds a small employment-reducing impact (Neumark 2002).

Given the discrepancy in findings from these recent studies, it is difficult to draw any firm conclusions regarding the impact of cross-state and over-time differences in statutory minimum wages on employment in the United States. And the relevance for other countries of such nation-specific findings is of course questionable in any case.

COUNTRY-LEVEL EVIDENCE

The theoretical considerations and empirical findings detailed in the previous section suggest some reason to think countries can in fact combine moderate-to-high wages and high employment. What do we find when we turn to macro-level comparative patterns?

Comparative studies of the impact of wages on employment often use earnings inequality rather than earnings levels as the key measure. A common measure is the ratio of earnings at the 50th percentile (median) to earnings at the 10th percentile (P50/P10 ratio). That is because low-end services in most countries remain heavily domestic. In manufacturing there is extensive cross-country trade, so employers in that sector may use wage levels in other countries as the principal benchmark in making decisions about hiring. But in low-end services, where there is little or no trade, the frame of reference for employers is more likely to be the median wage in the domestic economy rather than, say, the 10th-percentile wage level in other nations.

Comparative Patterns

Skeptics of the notion that there is a tradeoff between high low-end wages and employment frequently emphasize the fact that, across affluent countries, there is no apparent association between wage inequality and employment or unemployment rates (Bazen 2000; Bradley 2002: ch. 3; Howell 2002; Howell and Huebler 2005). The first chart in Figure 5.2 shows this pattern for the twelve countries as of 2000–06. The employment rate is on the vertical axis, and P50/P10 earnings inequality averaged over the years 1979–2006 is on the horizontal axis. There is no association to speak of. The regression line is calculated with Italy excluded, as it is a clear statistical outlier.

As I noted in Chapter 4, the problem with this approach to examining the cross-country evidence is that most analysts agree there was little or no trade-off prior to the late 1970s. In the 1960s and early 1970s most western European countries had both less earnings inequality and higher employment than the Anglo nations. The argument is that changes in the economic environment—skill-biased technological change, globalization, and heightened competition within domestic service industries—have created the tradeoff. Most important, these developments have reduced profit margins for firms, encouraging them to be more attentive to labor costs. If there was no tradeoff prior to the late 1970s, recent tradeoff pressures might not yet be apparent in cross-country data on levels of earnings inequality and employment. The

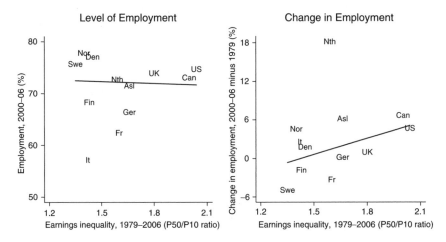

Figure 5.2. Employment levels and employment changes by earnings inequality.

Note: Some chart axes are truncated. The regression line in the first chart is calculated with Italy excluded; the line in the second chart is calculated with the Netherlands excluded. For data definitions and sources, see the appendix.

appropriate evidence to consider, then, is *changes* in employment since the late 1970s.

The second chart in Figure 5.2 has change in employment on the vertical axis, with change calculated as the employment rate in 2000–06 minus the employment rate in 1979. Earnings inequality averaged over 1979–2006 is again on the horizontal axis. The Netherlands plainly is an outlier, so I exclude it from this and subsequent analyses (the regression line is calculated based on the other eleven countries). Here we observe a pattern consistent with the tradeoff view: countries with lower levels of earnings inequality experienced slower employment growth, and in some cases outright decline.

The magnitude of earnings inequality's effect appears to be fairly large. A regression of change in employment on earnings inequality (with the Netherlands left out) yields a coefficient of 8.3. Earnings inequality measured using the P50/P10 ratio ranges from a low of 1.3 in Sweden to a high of 2.0 in the United States. This coefficient thus suggests that the payoff from moving all the way from the low end to the high end on earnings inequality would have been about 6 percentage points (0.7 × 8.3) in additional employment since the late 1970s.

High wages are expected to have an adverse employment effect chiefly by impeding employment growth in low-productivity consumer services. Figure 5.3 shows three scatterplots, each with earnings inequality on the horizontal axis and change in employment between 1979 and 2000–06 in a

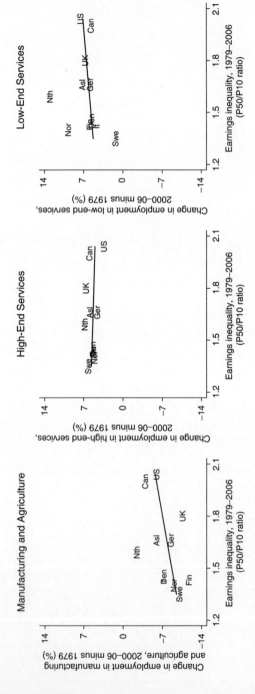

Figure 5.3. Change in employment in various sectors, 1979 to 2000–06, by earnings inequality.

Note: Horizontal axes are truncated. "High-end services" include finance, insurance, real estate, and other business services (ISIC 8). "Low-end services" include wholesale and retail trade, restaurants, and hotels (ISIC 6) and community, social, and personal services (ISIC 9). France is not included due to lack of data on employment by sector. Change in employment is calculated as the 2000–06 employment rate minus the 1979 employment rate. The regression lines are calculated with the Netherlands excluded. For data definitions and sources, see the appendix.

particular sector (or group of sectors) on the vertical axis. The sectors are manufacturing plus agriculture, high-end services (finance, insurance, real estate, and other business services), and low-end services (wholesale and retail trade, restaurants, hotels, and community, social, and personal services).

Surprisingly, the strongest association is with employment change in manufacturing and agriculture, which are not the sectors that analysts who suggest an employment-reducing impact of high wages typically have in mind. Moreover, this association is very likely spurious: as I noted in Chapter 4, employment trends in manufacturing and agriculture were determined largely by how much of a country's employment was in these two sectors at the start of the period. Employment change in manufacturing and agriculture from 1979 to 2000–06 correlates at −.86 with the level of employment in these two sectors in 1979. A regression of employment change in manufacturing and agriculture over 1979 to 2000–06 on earnings inequality yields a coefficient of 5.5. If the 1979 employment rate in manufacturing and agriculture is added to the regression, the coefficient for earnings inequality shrinks to 0.3, suggesting virtually no impact.

What does this imply for the association between earnings inequality and employment growth? As noted earlier, a regression of change in total employment from 1979 to 2000–06 on earnings inequality yields a coefficient of 8.3. In a similar regression with change in employment outside of manufacturing and agriculture as the dependent variable, the coefficient is 2.7. This suggests a considerably weaker adverse impact of low earnings inequality. And this is likely an upper-bound estimate, as no other determinants of employment change have been controlled for.

Finance, insurance, real estate, and other business services are the service jobs least likely to be affected by high low-end wages. It is thus not surprising to find, in the second chart in Figure 5.3, no cross-country association between P50/P10 earnings inequality and employment change in this sector.

The third chart in the figure shows the two service sectors most commonly expected to be hurt by high wage levels: wholesale and retail trade, restaurants, and hotels (ISIC 6) and community, social, and personal services (ISIC 9). Productivity in these sectors tends to be low and difficult to increase, and consumption of these services tends to be relatively price-sensitive. It would help to be able to separate private from public employment in these sectors, but unfortunately OECD data do not permit that beyond the mid-1990s.

There is a positive association between earnings inequality and change in employment in low-end services. But the association is weaker than might have been expected. With the Netherlands excluded, a regression of change in employment in these sectors on average earnings inequality produces a

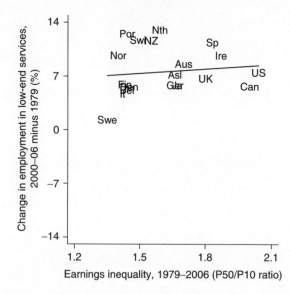

Figure 5.4. Change in employment in low-end services, 1979 to 2000–06, by earnings inequality—19 countries.

Note: The regression line is calculated with the Netherlands excluded. France is not included due to lack of data on employment by sector. For data definitions and sources, see the appendix.

coefficient of 2.5. If accurate, this suggests that the difference in employment growth in low-end services between a country at the high end of the earnings inequality distribution and a country at the low end would have been about 1.75 percentage points (0.7 × 2.5) since the late 1970s.

Data are available for both earnings inequality and employment change in low-end services for eight other affluent countries: Austria, Belgium, Ireland, Japan, New Zealand, Portugal, Spain, and Switzerland. Figure 5.4 replicates the third chart in Figure 5.3 with these eight countries added. The addition of these countries does virtually nothing to alter the pattern. Ireland and Spain had comparatively high levels of earnings inequality and experienced relatively rapid employment growth in low-end services. Belgium had comparatively low earnings inequality and little growth in low-end service employment. Austria and Japan were in the middle of the pack on both. These five countries thus reinforce the apparent positive association. New Zealand, Portugal, and Switzerland had moderate-to-low levels of earnings inequality and experienced rapid employment growth in low-end services. They are thus inconsistent with the general pattern. As noted earlier, a regression of employment change in low-end services on earnings inequality for our eleven countries (omitting the Netherlands, and with France missing due to lack of

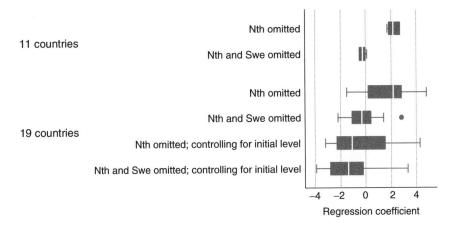

11 countries

19 countries

Figure 5.5. Regression results: Estimated effect of earnings inequality (P50/P10 ratio) on employment change in low-end services, 1979 to 2000–06.

Note: Unstandardized coefficients for the earnings inequality variable from ordinary least squares (OLS) regressions using all possible combinations of earnings inequality and one or two of the following additional independent variables: employment protection regulations (index), government benefit generosity (cash social expenditures on the working-age population as % of GDP), payroll and consumption taxes (% of GDP), real long-term interest rates (%), imports (% of GDP), real unit labor cost changes (%), and product market regulations (index). The third and fourth sets of regressions for 19 countries include a variable representing the level of employment in low-end services in 1979 to control for "catch-up" effects. The dependent variable is absolute change in the employment rate in low-end services: the employment rate in 2000–06 minus the rate in 1979. For data definitions and sources, see the appendix. France is not included due to lack of data on employment by sector. Finland is missing from regressions that include the real interest rate variable. With 11 countries, there are 6 regressions. For this group of countries the employment protection regulations, government benefit generosity, payroll and consumption taxes, and product market regulations variables cannot be included due to multicollinearity. With 19 countries, there are 26 regressions. The "whiskers" refer to the minimum and maximum coefficients. The edges of the box indicate the 25th- and 75th-percentile coefficients. The vertical white line is the median coefficient. Separate dots indicate "outliers"—coefficients that are substantially larger or smaller than the others in that set.

sector-specific employment data) yields a coefficient of 2.5. For the nineteen countries shown in Figure 5.4 (again excepting the Netherlands), the coefficient is 1.9.

This is without controlling for other determinants of employment growth. Figure 5.5 shows the coefficients for P50/P10 earnings inequality from a variety of regressions with employment change since 1979 in low-end services as the dependent variable. The regressions include the earnings inequality variable along with all possible combinations of several additional variables highlighted in Chapters 4, 6–8: employment protection regulations, government benefit generosity, payroll and consumption taxation, real long-term interest rates (monetary policy), imports (globalization), change in real unit labor costs (wage restraint), and product market regulations. Due to the small number of observations, no more than three independent variables are included in any regression. Because earnings inequality is very strongly correlated across countries with employment protection regulations, government benefit generosity, and product market regulations, the latter can be included only in regressions with the larger set of countries. Among the larger group of countries (not for the smaller group, as Figure 4.7 shows), there has been a "catch-up" effect for employment in low-end services: growth over 1979 to 2000–06 is negatively associated with the level in 1979. I therefore estimate an additional set of regressions for the larger group with a control for the 1979 level.

As in Chapter 3, the figure reports the results for the earnings inequality variable in each set of regressions in "box-and-whisker" plots (boxplots). The "whiskers" refer to the minimum and maximum coefficients. The edges of the box indicate the 25th- and 75th-percentile coefficients. The vertical white line is the median coefficient. Separate dots indicate "outliers"—coefficients that are substantially larger or smaller than the others in that set.

The coefficients vary fairly substantially. Some are around 2.0, which is roughly the magnitude of the coefficient in the bivariate regression. However, many are quite small and quite a few are negatively signed. This is especially true if Sweden is omitted. As Figures 5.3 and 5.4 suggest, the association between earnings inequality and change in low-end service employment is heavily influenced by Sweden's poor performance. In Sweden much of the employment in these sectors is public rather than private. The decline in employment for the period as a whole was as much or more a function of political decisions made during the severe economic crisis of the early 1990s as of choices made by private employers in response to wage levels (see below). Also, recall that relative to the other countries Sweden's employment performance is excessively penalized by the fact that it is not possible to adjust the employment measure for work hours (Chapter 4). When Sweden is dropped from the regressions, the coefficient for the earnings inequality variable tends to be negatively signed. The same is true when the 1979 employment level in low-end services is controlled for.

Examining employment performance in specific sectors, then, suggests reason for skepticism about the impact of low-end wages on employment. There is reason to suspect that higher wages reduce employer demand for labor in low-productivity service jobs. But in practice they may not reduce it by very much, and perhaps not at all.

More comparative evidence on the employment impact of wages in low-end services comes from a study of Germany and the United States by Richard Freeman and Ronald Schettkat (2000). Freeman and Schettkat found that low-wage services—eating, drinking, and care facilities, retail trade, and so on—account for a large portion of the difference in aggregate employ-ment rates between these two countries. Yet they also found that although Germany's overall pay structure is more egalitarian than that of the United States, the ratio of wages in the lowest-paying service sectors to average wages is approximately the same in the two countries. Because Germany does not have a statutory minimum wage and many of these jobs are outside of the collective bargaining system, German employers in low-end private services do not have to pay higher relative wages than American employers. This suggests reason for doubt about the role of wages in contributing to the two countries' different employment rates.

More recently, Andrew Glyn and colleagues (2005) have performed the same exercise for wages and employment in retail trade. They examined not only Germany and the United States but also France, the Netherlands, and the United Kingdom. They reach a similar conclusion: relative to average wage levels, wages for the lowest paid in this industry are approximately the same in each of these countries. Glyn et al. also found that productivity levels are similar across the countries—if anything, they are higher in the European countries. This suggests that wages have not been the main impediment to employment in retail trade.

Country Experiences

The comparative analysis in the previous section offers little or no support for the hypothesized adverse effect of low levels of earnings inequality on employment growth. Examining over-time developments within countries may yield additional insight.

Figure 5.6 shows over-time trends in earnings, earnings inequality, and employment in individual countries. Reasonably lengthy and continuous time-series data on earnings and sector-specific employment growth are avail-able for the period since 1979 for only eight of the twelve countries. I focus on six of them: the United States, the United Kingdom, Australia, Sweden, Germany, and the Netherlands. The earnings and inequality data are for the full-time employed. I show earnings at three points in the distribution: the 10th, 50th, and 90th percentiles. The earnings figures are in national curren-cies but adjusted for inflation. Inequality is again measured using the P50/P10 ratio. I show employment rates both overall and in low-end services.

United States

The United States plays an important role in the story that ties low wages and high earnings inequality to rapid employment growth. The United States has

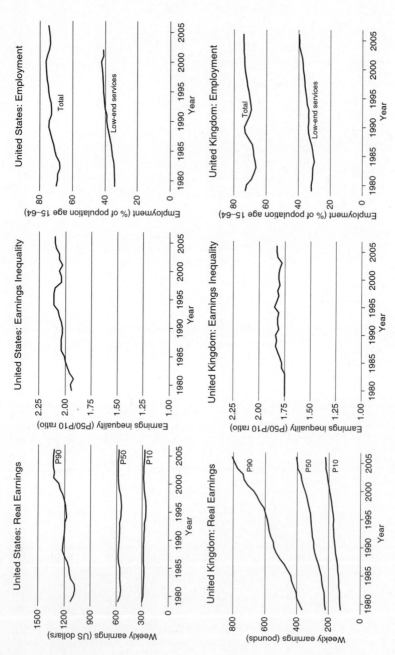

Figure 5.6. Earnings levels, earnings inequality, and employment, 1979ff.

Note: Real earnings and earnings inequality are for full-time employed individuals. Real earnings are expressed in (year-2000) national currencies, so levels cannot be compared across the countries. The breaks in the lines for real earnings and earnings inequality for the Netherlands are due to a change in the data series. Last year for low-end-services employment data for the United States is 2002. For data definitions and sources, see the appendix.

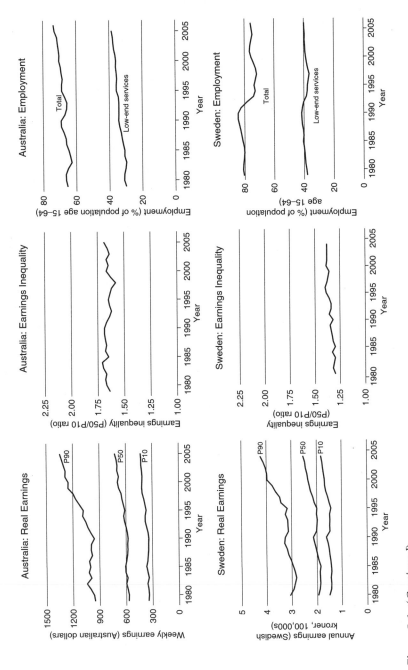

Figure 5.6. (*Continued*)

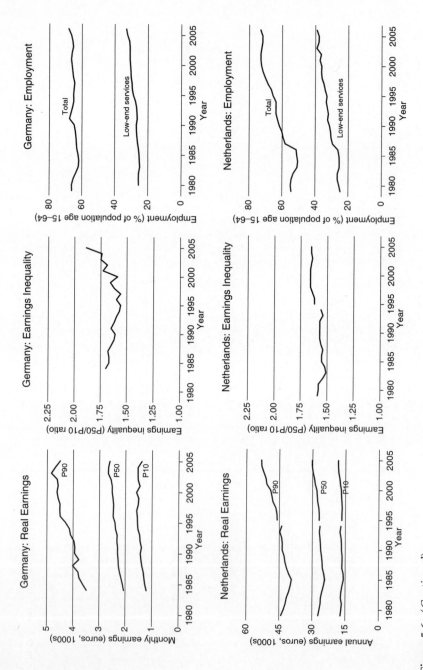

Figure 5.6. (*Continued*)

the most unequal distribution of earnings among the twelve countries, and the degree of inequality has increased sharply since the late 1970s. At the same time the country's employment rate has jumped sharply, both overall and in low-end services. It seems quite sensible to presume that low and stagnant wage levels among employees at the bottom of the earnings distribution make it more attractive for American employers to hire large numbers of people than would be the case if wages were higher. But several caveats are in order.

First, as noted earlier in the chapter, most of the research on the employment impact of statutory minimum wages in the United States suggests fairly small effects, if any. And various case studies reviewed earlier suggest that wages sometimes can be increased without any cutbacks in employment. Thus, even if we acknowledge that comparatively low wages have helped to boost US employment, it is by no means clear that the relationship is linear. It could be that an increase in the minimum wage of, say, $2 per hour would have no employment-reducing impact at all, whereas an increase of an additional $2 per hour beyond that would have a rather large impact.

Second, even if the US economy creates a comparatively large number of low-wage jobs, it is not clear that it creates enough of them. Much of the comparative discussion of the American model versus the European model over the past decade has implicitly presumed that the United States has "solved" the jobs problem and that its deficit lies in low wages and high earnings inequality. But some analysts of the American economy, most prominently William Julius Wilson (1987, 1996), contest this conclusion. They suggest that the US economy in fact suffers from a relatively large deficit of employment— particularly in decent-paying jobs but more broadly in any kind of jobs. In Wilson's argument this is partly a problem for the country as a whole but mainly a problem for inner cities. Other analysts, such as Timothy Bartik (2001), contend that the American employment deficit is generic and not confined to central cities. Bartik estimates that "the employment rates of lower-income groups in the United States, compared either to the past or to the earnings needs of these groups, are low enough to suggest a need for three to nine million additional jobs" (pp. 287–8).

Third, as the third chart for the United States in Figure 5.6 indicates, although the United States enjoyed a comparatively healthy rate of employment growth during the 1980s and 1990s, the period since 2000 has been less encouraging (Freeman and Rodgers 2005). The US employment rate increased from 68% in 1979 to 76% in 2000. Not only was this second to the Netherlands in terms of over-time change, but it put the United States near the top in its level of employment. But since 2000 America's employment rate has declined. As of 2006 it was 75%. The employment rate in low-end services has been largely stagnant. This recent employment trend in the United States is important to consider, particularly because it has persisted during several years of reasonably strong economic growth. As the first and second charts for the United States in Figure 5.6 indicate, this trend in the employment rate cannot be blamed on a jump in low-end wage levels or a decline in earnings inequality. Neither of these things occurred in the early 2000s.

United Kingdom

The United Kingdom also is commonly invoked as a country with comparatively low wages at the bottom of the distribution and high inequality. Its employment growth has been reasonably strong since the late 1970s. Interestingly, however, that growth was by no means exceptional in low-end services, which is precisely where the conventional wisdom would predict it to have been strongest. As the third chart in Figure 5.3 shows, employment growth in low-end services over 1979 to 2000–06 was no greater in the United Kingdom than in Denmark, Finland, Germany, and Italy.

Over-time developments in the United Kingdom have been particularly interesting, because a statutory minimum wage was introduced in 1999. It began at £3.60 for employees age 22 and above and £3.20 for those age 18 to 21. Since then it has been incresed each year roughly in line with average earnings. As of early 2008 the minimum will be £5.52 for those 22 and above and £4.60 for 18-to-21s.

In the run-up to passage of the minimum wage legislation, the usual predictions about potentially dire effects on job creation were made by those opposed to the law. However, the Low Pay Commission, a group of researchers charged with evaluating the level of the minimum wage and its impact, concluded in its most recent assessment that seven years on there is no indication of any such adverse effect (Low Pay Commission 2006; see also Draka, Dickens, and Vaitilingam 2005). Employment in low-end services increased from 31.8% of the working-age population in 1979 to 35.4% in 1999. By 2003, the last year for which sectoral employment data are available, it had jumped further to 37.8%. The increase over the 20 years prior to introduction of the minimum wage, in other words, was 3.6 percentage points, versus 2.4 percentage points in the four years after its introduction.

Australia

The Australian experience is interesting because it is a case of high employment growth, both overall and in low-end services, despite a moderate level of earnings inequality. Indeed, the P50/P10 ratio in Australia is approximately the same as in Germany. Moreover, unlike in the United States and the United Kingdom, the level of earnings inequality in Australia has not increased. It has remained virtually constant since the late 1970s. This suggests that even in a relatively liberal economy, low wages and/or rising wage inequality are not a necessary condition for successful employment performance.

Sweden

The second chart in Figure 5.2 and the third chart in Figure 5.3 portray Sweden as an employment failure. In terms of aggregate employment change, Sweden's performance since the late 1970s has been the worst among the twelve countries. The Swedish employment rate declined by 5 percentage points between 1979 and 2000–06. What caused this? And what lessons can we draw from the Swedish experience regarding the impact of earnings inequality on employment?

The place to start is Sweden's high employment *level*. In 1979 Sweden's employment rate was 79%, which was the highest among the twelve countries by several percentage points. It is thus not surprising that Sweden's performance with respect to employment *growth* has not been especially strong. Moreover, despite that disappointing performance, Sweden remains near the top of the pack in its employment rate, as shown in the first chart in Figure 5.2.

Still, given Sweden's high initial starting level, we might have expected mediocre employment growth. Instead, the employment rate dropped rather substantially. What happened? The answer has two parts.

The first is manufacturing and agriculture. In 1979, 24% of Swedish employment was in these two sectors. That was the second highest total among the twelve countries (Finland had the highest). As I emphasized in Chapter 4, by far the best predictor of a country's employment change in manufacturing and agriculture since 1979 is its level in 1979. None of these twelve countries has escaped deindustrialization. What has differed has mainly been the timing. Countries that deindustrialized earlier have been spared dramatic losses in ensuing years. Sweden was not an early deindustrializer, and it paid the price in those two decades: like other late deindustrializers such as Finland, Germany, and the United Kingdom, it experienced a decline in manufacturing and agricultural employment of more than 8 percentage points between 1979 and 2000–06.

The second part of the answer is the economic crisis of the early 1990s. Not only did the crisis accelerate the loss of manufacturing and agricultural jobs; it also produced significant loss of jobs in low-end services, as the third chart for Sweden in Figure 5.6 shows. There are various explanations for the crisis, but few attribute it to high wages in low-end service sector jobs. Instead, many observers attribute the economic crisis of the early 1990s mainly to policy choices (Benner and Vad 2000: 426–8; Furåker 2002; Scharpf 2000: 90; Palme et al. 2002: 162–4; Wilensky 2002: 111). Of particular importance was the decision to tie Sweden's currency, the kronor, to the European currency unit (ECU) in May 1991, which put the Swedish economy at the mercy of the German Bundesbank's hardcore monetarism. Then, in the midst of the recession the Swedish government raised taxes and reduced government expenditures (along with public employment), electing to focus on price stability and a balanced budget rather than on stimulation of the economy.

Sweden's comparatively poor record of employment growth since the late 1970s, then, appears to be almost fully explicable in terms of three factors—high starting level, late deindustrialization, and an exogenous economic crisis—that have nothing to do with high wages in low-productivity service sector jobs. Furthermore, to the extent labor market institutions and policies have contributed to poor Swedish employment performance, low earnings inequality is not the only potential culprit. Most notably, employment protection regulations are comparatively stiff (Chapter 6). Government benefits available to the nonemployed—via unemployment insurance, sickness insurance, disability insurance, social assistance, and retirement pension—are quite generous (Chapter 7). And taxes—particularly those on payroll and consumption, which are the kind most frequently linked to employment difficulties—are relatively high (Chapter 8).

Germany

To an even greater extent than Sweden, Germany is commonly viewed as a case of poor employment performance in recent decades. There was no significant decline in Germany's employment rate, but it failed to achieve any increase despite starting from a comparatively low level. Germany's employment rate in 1979 was 66%, which was below the rates of all four Nordic countries plus the United Kingdom and United States and about the same as the rates in Australia, Canada, and France. Only Italy and the Netherlands began the 1980s with appreciably lower employment levels.

However, as with Sweden, there is reason for skepticism about the role of high low-end wages, or of low earnings inequality, in contributing to Germany's disappointing employment performance. First and foremost, there is unification with the East. Most manufacturing firms in the East were uncompetitive in a market environment, so following unification many had to be shut down or at least substantially, reduce their work force. This left a large number of formerly employed East Germans without jobs. Then again, as the third chart for Germany in Figure 5.6 indicates, unification did not produce a massive decline in the German employment rate. Indeed, the degree of decline in the early 1990s was similar to that experienced by most affluent countries during those recession years.

Second, like Sweden, Germany began the 1980s with a comparatively large share of its employment in manufacturing and agriculture. Employment losses in these two sectors during the 1980s and 1990s totaled about 8 percentage points.

Third, a variety of labor market policies and institutions may have contributed to Germany's stalled employment rate. As discussed in Chapter 10, there are numerous disincentives for women to enter or remain in the labor force: half-day schooling, a shortage of childcare spaces, a three-year parental leave, family-based (rather than individualized) pensions, and joint taxation with steep marginal tax rates for a second earner. Employment protection regulations are comparatively strict. Until very recently, unemployment benefits were both generous and available for a lengthy period. And employer payroll taxes are steep, adding 21% to labor costs (employee contributions also are 21%).

Fourth, Germany's employment performance may have suffered from excessively tight monetary policy since the 1970s. The Bundesbank was perhaps the most zealously anti-inflationary of the affluent countries' central banks in recent decades. On the other hand, several countries tied their monetary policy to Germany's and others tended to follow the Bundesbank's lead more informally, which suggests that German monetary policy may not in fact have been more restrictive than that of many other European nations. Ronald Schettkat (2005) argues that the problem has not been tight monetary policy per se, but the lack of coordination of macroeconomic policy, which allowed an employment-impeding combination of tight monetary policy, loose fiscal policy, and rising real labor costs.

Finally, Germany's level of earnings inequality has been in the middle of the pack among the twelve countries since the 1970s. Figure 5.2 shows that earnings inequality is significantly lower than in the United States, Canada, and the United Kingdom, but significantly higher than in the four Nordic countries and Italy. More directly relevant is Freeman and Schettkat's finding (2000), mentioned earlier, that German employers in low-end services pay wages that are no higher compared to countrywide average wages than do their American counterparts. This suggests that to the extent labor costs are relevant in accounting for the difference in low-end service employment between Germany and the United States, it is likely the difference in payroll taxes (nonwage labor costs) that is the key explanatory factor (Chapter 8).

As the middle chart in Figure 5.6 indicates, since 2000 earnings inequality in the bottom half of the distribution has increased dramatically in Germany. Real median earnings have risen, whereas those at the 10th percentile have declined slightly. To the extent this widening dispersion is sustained, it will offer a useful test of the hypothesis that low wages are conducive to employment growth in low-end services. But as of this writing (January 2008), it is too soon to tell.

The Netherlands

As of the late 1970s, the Netherlands had the lowest employment rate among the twelve countries. By 2006 it had one of the highest. Was this due to low wages and high earnings inequality?

That does not seem likely. As Figure 5.2 makes clear, earnings inequality in the Netherlands is about average among the twelve countries. And the first two charts for the Netherlands in Figure 5.6 indicate that there has been no significant decline in low-end wage levels or increase in P50/P10 earnings inequality since the 1970s. As noted earlier, the apparent change in the mid-1990s is a product of a shift in the data series. In any event, much of the employment increase had already occurred by then.

One influential account of the Netherlands' employment success assigns a key role to wage restraint beginning in the early 1980s (Visser and Hemerijck 1997; see also Hemerijck, Unger, and Visser 2000; Gorter 2000; Schettkat 2005). The trends for P10 and P50 earnings among full-time employed individuals, shown in the first chart for the Netherlands in Figure 5.6, are consistent with this story. Aside from the United States, the Netherlands is the only country among the twelve in which inflation-adjusted earnings in the bottom half of the distribution were stagnant throughout the 1980s and 1990s. Yet that does not mean wages in the Netherlands were low, as the nation began the 1980s as a comparatively high-wage country (Visser and Hemerijck 1997). And its level of P50/P10 earnings inequality remains comparable to that of Germany, well below those of the United States and United Kingdom.

Skepticism about the role of low-end wage levels and earnings inequality levels is buttressed by the sectoral distribution of employment growth in the Netherlands. As the charts in Figure 5.3 indicate, part of the Netherlands' employment success owes to limited losses in manufacturing and agriculture. Deindustrialization was already quite advanced by the late 1970s. The country did experience rapid employment growth in the two low-end services sectors—wholesale and retail trade, restaurants, and hotels and community, social, and personal services. Employment growth in the former was particularly strong. But the Dutch economy also experienced more employment growth than any of the other eleven countries in high-end business services such as finance, insurance, and real estate. In a careful examination of Dutch employment growth in various industries between 1987 and 1995, Joop Hartog (1999) concluded that "employment growth is really across the board of the entire wage distribution, with neither support for a marked dualization nor for a concentration of employment growth in low-wage pockets."

As noted in Chapter 3, most of the new employment in the Netherlands has been part-time. Part-time jobs accounted for two-thirds to three-quarters of total job growth in the 1980s and 1990s, depending on the estimate (Salverda 1998; Hartog 1999; Visser 2002). Part-time employment jumped from 18% to 36% of total employment between 1983 (the first year for which data are available) and 2006. Yet part-time employment is not necessarily low-paid employment. Strikingly, for Dutch women, who account for most part-time employment, the median hourly earnings of part-time employees were 93% of those for full-time employees as of 1995 (OECD 1999*b*: 24; Visser 2002: 33).

As in the United States, United Kingdom, Australia, Sweden, and Germany, then, low-end wage levels and earnings inequality in the Netherlands appear to have played only a limited role in influencing employment developments in recent decades.

WAGES AND JOBS: WHAT TO DO?

There *is* a tradeoff between wages and jobs in low-end services. Productivity can be increased, but only up to a point. Demand can increase and employers will accept lower profits if forced to, but here too there are limits. There obviously is some point at which wages become an impediment to employment.

However, the macro-level empirical evidence suggests that wages probably have not been a sizable impediment in these twelve countries in recent decades. The cross-country association between earnings inequality and changes in employment rates since the late 1970s (second chart in Figure 5.2) is the piece of evidence most suggestive of an adverse impact. But as we have seen, part of that association is spurious: it is mainly a product of faster decline of manufacturing and agricultural employment in countries with low earnings inequality, and that decline owes chiefly to the comparatively high levels of manufacturing and agricultural employment at the beginning of the 1980s in

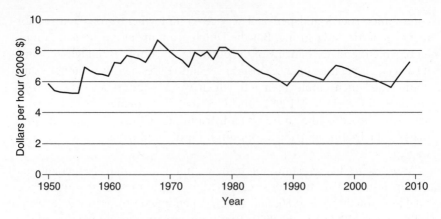

Figure 5.7. Real value of the US federal minimum wage.

Note: Author's calculations using US Bureau of labor statistics data. Inflation adjustment is the CPI-U-RS. Values for 2008 and 2009 assume an inflation rate of 3.0%.

these countries rather than to their low earnings inequality. The cross-country association between earnings inequality and employment changes in low-end services—wholesale and retail trade, restaurants, hotels, and community, social, and personal services—is rather weak, and there are a host of other labor market institutions and policies that may account for part or all of it. Most damning is the fact that in at least a few European countries, wages in low-end services are not in fact lower relative to average wages than they are in the United States (Freeman and Schettkat 2000; Glyn et al. 2005).

What are the implications for wages and employment in these countries? Let's begin with the United States. The main policy lever the US government has with respect to wages is the statutory minimum wage. The federal minimum is currently $5.15. With the increase approved in May 2007, it is scheduled to rise to $7.25 per hour in 2009. Figure 5.7 shows the evolution of US federal minimum wage since 1950. The late-2000s increase will bring it back to its late-1990s level, but still well below its peak in the late 1960s when it reached $8 per hour in 2006 dollars.

It seems very likely that the statutory minimum wage could be higher with little adverse employment impact in low-end services. But how much higher? Recent initiatives by state and city governments to set a higher minimum wage might be a useful guide. Table 5.1 lists these levels as of 2006, when the federal minimum was $5.15 per hour.

Cross-country comparison might also be informative. Suppose policy makers wished to reduce earnings inequality between the middle and the low end in the United States to something like the level in Sweden or Germany.

Table 5.1. State and city minimum wages in the United States.

	Statutory minimum wage, 2006 ($ per hour)
States	
Washington	7.63
Oregon	7.50
Connecticut	7.40
Vermont	7.25
Alaska	7.15
New Jersey	7.15
Rhode Island	7.10
California	6.75
Hawaii	6.75
Massachusetts	6.75
New York	6.75
Illinois	6.50
Maine	6.50
Wisconsin	6.50
Florida	6.40
Minnesota (large employers)	6.25
Delaware	6.15
Maryland	6.15
Cities	
Santa Fe, NM	9.50
San Francisco, CA	8.62
Washington, DC	7.50

Note: Federal minimum wage was $5.15 in 2006.

Sources: U.S. Department of Labor (2006) and Living Wage Resource Center (2006).

Sweden has one of the lowest levels of earnings inequality among the twelve countries: as of the mid-2000s its P50/P10 ratio for full-time employed individuals was approximately 1.4. Germany is roughly in the middle of the pack, with a P50/P10 ratio of about 1.7. In the United States the ratio in 2004 was 2.1.

The 10th-percentile wage level for the full-time employed in the United States was approximately $7.50 per hour in 2004, and the 50th-percentile wage level was about $15.50 per hour. In hypothetical 2009 dollars, using an inflation rate of 3.0%, the 10th-percentile level is $8.70 and the median is $18. For simplicity, assume no change in the median (P50) wage: it remains at $18 per hour in 2009 dollars. To get to a Swedish P50/P10 ratio of approximately 1.4, the 10th-percentile wage level in the United States would need to rise to $12.85 per hour. That implies an increase in the minimum wage to something like $10 per hour. To get to a German P50/P10 ratio of about 1.7, the 10th-percentile wage level would need to rise to $11.25 per hour in 2009 dollars. That implies a minimum wage of perhaps $8 per hour. Increasing the minimum to $10 per hour might have some adverse employment effect. But raising it to $8, rather than the currently scheduled $7.25, might well not.

A minimum wage of $8 per hour by 2009 would bring the absolute level in the United States closer to that in the other countries that have a statutory minimum. (Denmark, Finland, Italy, Germany, Norway, and Sweden do not; see Eyraud and Saget 2005.) As of 2006, minimum wage annual earnings levels—assuming a 40-hour week and 52-week year, and with currencies converted into US dollars using purchasing power parities—were approximately $19,200 in Australia, $12,900 in Canada (Ontario), $18,500 in France, $17,000 in the Netherlands, and $16,800 in the United Kingdom, compared to just $10,700 in the United States. At $8 per hour, the US figure would increase to $16,600.

Even if the US minimum wage were increased to $8, the country would still feature a large number of jobs that would accurately be described as "low-wage." Should egalitarians, then, favor a larger hike in the statutory minimum—say, to $10 per hour?

If that would indeed reduce employment in low-end service jobs, the question becomes: Is it better to have a smaller number of moderate-pay jobs or a larger number of low-pay jobs? My view is that a generation or two ago the former was probably preferable, because many couples were reasonably happy to have one person stay at home. But two things have changed. First, more women want to be employed. Second, as I argued in Chapter 1 and suggested at the beginning of this chapter, countries need more people employed in order to fund pension commitments and redistributive programs. The instinct of many egalitarians with respect to low-end service jobs typically is to favor either higher wages or the outright elimination of such jobs. But it may be possible to address some of the objectionable features of "bad" jobs—low household incomes, undesirable working conditions, inflexible hours, and limited opportunity for upward mobility—without having to substantially increase hourly wages. A sensible strategy might be to favor a moderate increase in the statutory minimum wage, to perhaps $8 (and then tied to inflation), an increase in the Earned Income Tax Credit to supplement the incomes of low-earning households, and improvements in working conditions and work-time flexibility.

What should European countries do with respect to wages and employment? From a scientific standpoint (if not a normative one), it would be helpful to have a few countries in which low-end wages began at a fairly high level (relative to the country median) but then decreased appreciably during the period of interest. This would help in assessing the likely impact of a fall in low-end wages. The closest approximation to this scenario is the Netherlands, where real earnings at the 10th percentile have been stagnant since the late 1970s. Earnings inequality has not risen because earnings have been stagnant at the median as well. The exceptional employment growth in the Netherlands seemingly argues in favor of such wage developments, though there is, as I suggested in the previous section, reason for skepticism.

One possible strategy for European countries would be to allow wages in low-end service jobs to drop a bit in order to spur employment and then use redistribution to mitigate the impact of the consequent rise in individual earnings inequality (see also Ferrera, Hemerijck, and Rhodes 2000; Kok et al. 2003; Kenworthy 2004*a*: ch. 8).

There are reasonable arguments against such an approach. One is that allowing (indeed encouraging) the development of a low-wage segment of the labor force is likely to weaken the labor movement, which is the chief political base of support for generous redistributive programs (Hall 2005). Another is that in most European countries policy makers have no direct control over the wage floor. Instead, low-end wage levels are determined mainly via collective bargaining between unions and employers, and the former are unlikely to permit, much less favor, any such decline (Kenworthy 2004*a*: 149).

A more relevant point may be that even if policy makers—social democratic or otherwise—in many European countries favored this approach, there is no indication that they would need to take any action. The findings of Freeman and Schettkat (2000) and Glyn et al. (2005) suggest that wages in low-end services in France, Germany, the Netherlands, and the United Kingdom already are at about the same level relative to average wages as in the United States. Given this, coupled with the fact that the aggregate evidence reviewed in this chapter suggests little if any adverse employment impact of earnings levels and earnings inequality in the these countries, there is little reason to think wages need to be lowered in order to stimulate more job creation in low-end services. Perhaps it might be helpful in other countries, such as Sweden or Denmark, for which (to my knowledge) comparable studies have not yet been done.

If the ratio of wages in low-end services to average wages is about the same in France, Germany, and the Netherlands as in the United States and the United Kingdom, why is there less overall earnings inequality in the former group of countries—and in other European nations as well—than in the latter? Partly, it would seem, because the former have fewer people employed in such jobs than do the latter. This raises a paradox: To stimulate growth of low-end service employment, the key may be not reducing wage levels but rather increasing consumer demand, reducing taxes, loosening restrictions on store hours, cutting certain government benefits, easing employment protection regulations, and so on. But suppose this succeeds in increasing employment in low-end services. The result may be the very increase in earnings inequality that (at least some) policy makers hoped to avoid in the first place.

Some will favor raising low-end wages in order to prevent such a development. But it might make more sense to embrace the development and focus on minimizing inequality among households via redistribution.

6

Employment Protection Regulations

Employment protection regulations restrict employers' freedom to fire and hire. They can be instituted by the government as legal rules or negotiated by unions and employers in collective bargaining. For regular ("permanent") employees, regulations govern the justification employers are required to provide for dismissal, approval they may be required to secure from employee representatives, the length of notice they must give, the type and extent of compensation employees receive if dismissed, and the length of the trial period before employees are protected. For fixed-term ("temporary") employees, regulations limit the circumstances or tasks for which fixed-term contracts can be issued, the number of times or length of time a worker can be hired on such a contract, and the types of work for which temporary work agencies can be utilized.

Affluent nations differ in the prominence and strength of employment protection regulations (Bertola, Boeri, and Cazes 1999; OECD 1999b, 2004 f). A comparison of Germany, Italy, Denmark, and the United States helps to illustrate the range of variation. In some countries an employer is permitted to fire a worker if the particular job is no longer deemed necessary or if the skill requirements for it have changed. This is the case, for example, in the United States and in Denmark. In Germany, by contrast, in this circumstance an employer is required to retrain the worker and if necessary shift her to a new position prior to dismissal. In the United States, Denmark, and Italy, an employer need only provide verbal or written notification of termination to the worker or to a works council. In Germany the procedure is more restrictive: the firm's works council must be notified, and often the employer must secure the works council's approval.

For most firings in the United States, the employer is not required to give any advance notice. In Denmark, Italy, and Germany, employees must be notified one to seven months in advance, depending on how long the worker has been employed. In most countries employers are not required to provide severance pay for dismissals deemed fair or justified, but for unjustified dismissals they typically are. In the United States this is largely irrelevant, as there is little recourse for fired employees except via a private lawsuit. In

Denmark, average compensation for unjust dismissal is approximately nine months of pay. In Italy it is fifteen months' pay, in Germany eighteen months'. The employer may also be forced to rehire the worker.

In Italy the "trial" period—the period before which these various protections apply—is less than one month on the job for a typical employee. In Germany the trial period averages six months. In Denmark protections do not take effect until after ten months. In the United States there are no protections to speak of, so the notion of a trial period is moot.

Prior to the late 1990s fixed-term employment was severely restricted in Italy. It was permissible only in a limited set of circumstances, the number of renewals of such contracts was tightly circumscribed, and use of temporary agencies was prohibited. Temp agencies were allowed beginning in 1997, and regulations on other conditions of fixed-term employment also have been eased somewhat. Germany and Denmark have lesser limitations, and both of these countries also loosened them in the late 1990s. In the United States there was virtually no restriction on firms' use of fixed-term employment throughout the 1980s and 1990s.

To what degree have employment protection regulations contributed to low inequality? What impact have they had on employment?

MEASURING EMPLOYMENT PROTECTION

The OECD (1999*b*, 2004*f*) has compiled extensive information on various aspects of employment protection regulations and has created an index representing their overall strictness. Originally available for only two time points in the eighties and nineties (the late 1980s and late 1990s), the index has recently been extended by Andrea Bassanini and Romain Duval (2006) to an annual time series beginning in 1982.

Over-time trends in employment protection regulations are shown in Figure 6.1. The scale ranges from zero to six, with larger numbers indicating greater strictness. Regulations have tended to be strictest in the continental countries, though the degree of strictness in Italy and Germany decreased in the 1990s. The Nordic countries are a bit more mixed. Norway and Sweden had comparatively stringent regulations through the 1980s, while Finland and Denmark had more moderate levels. Regulatory strictness decreased in all four Nordic nations in the 1990s, though in Finland, Sweden, and especially Norway it remains on par with that in the four continental countries. Since the mid-1990s Denmark has had the least restrictive regulations among the Nordic and continental countries. Three of the four continental countries also

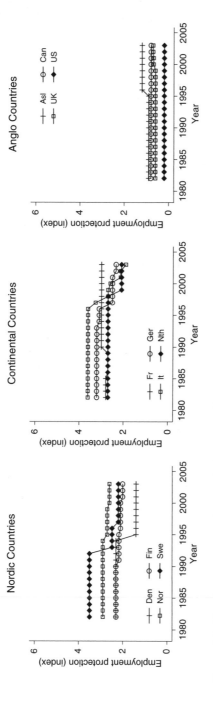

Figure 6.1. Employment protection regulations, 1982ff.

Note: Larger numbers on the index indicate stricter employment protection regulations. 1982 is the earliest year for which the data are available. For data definitions and sources, see the appendix.

relaxed their employment protection rules in the late 1980s. Employment protection was weakest throughout the two decades in the four Anglo countries, especially the United States.

Figures 6.2 and 6.3 show trends in employment protection regulations for regular contracts and fixed-term (temporary) contracts, respectively. Two things are particularly noteworthy. One is that the Nordic and continental countries differ little in strictness of employment protection for regular contracts. It is rules regarding fixed-term employment that separate these two groups of countries. Second, the reduction in strictness in some of the Nordic and continental countries beginning in the mid-1990s pertained solely to fixed-term contracts. None of the twelve countries altered its regulations for regular employees to any appreciable extent.

EMPLOYMENT PROTECTION AND INEQUALITY

Employment protection regulations are usually justified in terms of their contribution to fair treatment of workers, rather than to earnings or income equality. But employment protection might potentially reduce individual earnings inequality (Howell and Huebler 2005: 59). If it does, it should be mainly regulations on fixed-term employment that matter. Temporary employees tend to get paid less and work fewer hours than regular employees. Thus, their weekly, monthly, and annual earnings should tend to be lower. If employment protection rules for fixed-term employees discourage hiring, earnings dispersion among the employed should thus tend to be narrower.

The first chart in Figure 6.4 plots individual earnings inequality among employed individuals by employment protection strictness for fixed-term employees. Both are averaged over the 1980s and 1990s. There is a negative association; countries with more restrictive employment protection tend to have lower levels of earnings inequality. And it is quite strong.

Is it real? That is, is the relationship genuinely causal, or is it perhaps spurious? As I noted in Chapter 3, a key determinant of cross-country variation in earnings inequality is wage-setting arrangements. Countries in which a larger share of the work force has wages determined by union bargaining and countries in which wages are set in more centralized fashion tend to have lower levels of earnings inequality. The second and third charts in Figure 6.4 show the association between wage-setting arrangements and earnings inequality. Both charts have earnings inequality on the vertical axis. The second has on its horizontal axis the share of employees whose wages are determined by collective bargaining—either directly or because of extension practices, whereby

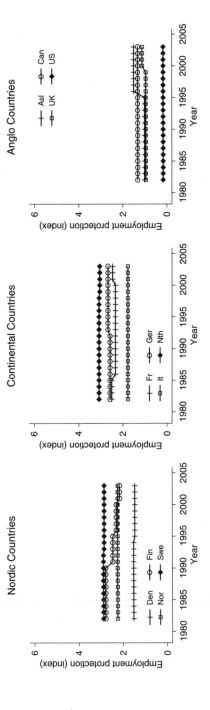

Figure 6.2. Employment protection regulations, regular contracts, 1982ff.

Note: Larger numbers on the index indicate stricter employment protection regulations. The values for Denmark and Finland are the same from 1982 to 1990. 1982 is the earliest year for which the data are available. For data definitions and sources, see the appendix.

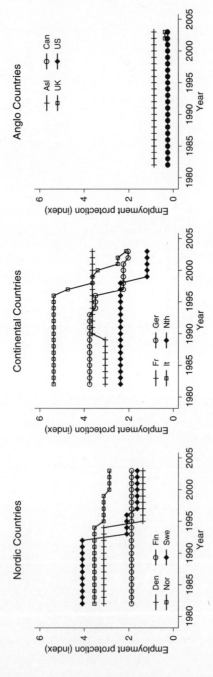

Figure 6.3. Employment protection regulations, fixed-term ("temporary") contracts, 1982ff.

Note: Larger numbers on the index indicate stricter employment protection regulations. The values for Canada, the United Kingdom, and the United States are the same in each year. 1982 is the earliest year for which the data are available. For data definitions and sources, see the appendix.

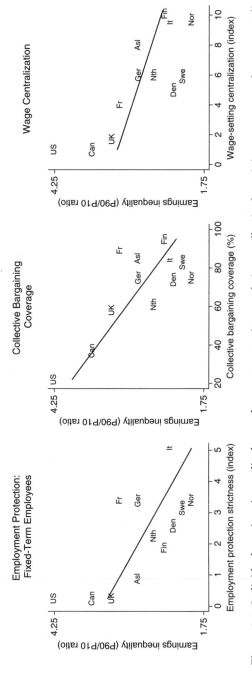

Figure 6.4. Individual earnings inequality by employment protection regulations, collective bargaining coverage, and wage centralization, 1979–2000.

Note: Some of the chart axes are truncated. All variables are measured as averages over the period 1979–2000. For data definitions and sources, see the appendix.

union-negotiated wages are extended by law or convention to nonunionized firms. The third has a measure of wage-bargaining centralization on the horizontal axis. Both charts suggest a strong cross-country correlation.

Across the twelve countries, employment protection for fixed-term employees correlates at .69 with collective bargaining coverage and at .65 with wage centralization. This suggests that part or all of the apparent inequality-reducing effect of employment protection might in fact be a product of wage-setting arrangements. A regression controlling for either collective bargaining coverage or wage centralization reduces the magnitude of the association suggested in the first chart in Figure 6.4 by about half. Yet a negative association does remain.

Suppose stricter employment protection for fixed-term contracts does in fact contribute to a lower level of individual earnings inequality. As we saw in Chapter 3, this is likely to contribute to lower levels of market inequality of income among households. But individual earnings inequality is only one among several things that contribute to inequality of market income across households. And inequality of posttax-posttransfer income across households is determined not only by the level of market inequality but also by redistribution. Thus, the impact of employment protection on posttax-posttransfer household income inequality is likely to be modest.

Perhaps more important, in the causal story hypothesized here employment protection regulations reduce inequality by excluding some low earners from jobs. That suggests an adverse effect on employment, which I have argued (Chapters 1 and 3) is critical for the long-run sustainability of inequality-reducing redistributive programs.

Does employment protection reduce employment? I examine this issue in the next section.

EMPLOYMENT PROTECTION AND EMPLOYMENT

Strong employment protection regulations make it more difficult and/or costly for employers to fire employees. They may have little or no impact on unemployment, because they may reduce both hiring and firing (OECD 1999b, 2004 f). Indeed, empirical studies have found mixed results on the relationship between employment protection and unemployment. Some find an association, while others find no such evidence (OECD 1994, 1999b, 2004 f, 2006b; Nickell 1997; Elmeskov, Martin, and Scarpetta 1998; Nickell and Layard 1999; Blanchard and Wolfers 2000; Esping-Andersen 2000a, 2000b; IMF 2003; Baker et al. 2005; Nickell, Nunziata, and Ochel 2005;

Bassanini and Duval 2006; Howell et al. 2006; Baccaro and Rei 2007). Even if they do not affect the unemployment rate, to the extent they reduce employer demand for new workers employment protection regulations may reduce growth of the *em*ployment rate.

Few comparative studies have looked at the impact of employment protection on employment. Layard and Nickell (1999), Esping-Andersen (2000*a*), and Scharpf (2000) find a negative cross-country association between employment protection and employment levels or growth during the 1980s and early 1990s. Bassanini and Duval (2006) find no robust association between employment protection and year-to-year changes in employment over the period 1982–2003.

I begin with macrocomparative evidence and then turn to individual country experiences.

Comparative Patterns

The first chart in Figure 6.5 shows that there is no association between average levels of (overall) employment protection during the 1980s and 1990s and employment rates as of the early-to-mid 2000s. The second chart, however, suggests an adverse impact on employment growth, if we exclude the Netherlands. A regression of employment change from 1979 to 2000–06 on the employment protection index yields a coefficient of −2.0. This implies that the average difference in employment change between a country at the low end on the employment protection index (0.2) and one at the high end (3.4) was 6.4 percentage points. That is quite a large difference. There were exceptions to the pattern: the Netherlands and Norway did well despite strict regulations, while the United Kingdom did not do particularly well despite lenient ones. But the overall pattern is suggestive of an adverse effect.

As in Chapter 5, it is helpful to disaggregate by sector. Recall that for low-end wage levels in Chapter 5 the prediction was that an adverse impact on employment would be strongest in low-end services, as those types of jobs tend to have the lowest productivity and the most limited opportunity for productivity improvement. That is not the case for employment protection regulations. The main effect of such regulations is to reduce employer flexibility rather than to increase labor costs. Thus, if they do discourage hiring, that effect should be visible in all sectors, not just in low-end services.

Figure 6.6 plots employment change in three sector groups— manufacturing and agriculture, high-end services, and low-end services—by the employment protection index. The patterns suggest reason for skepticism

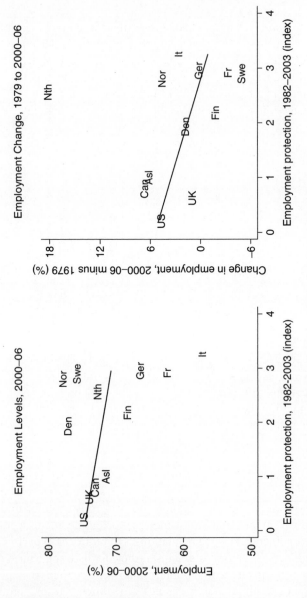

Figure 6.5. Employment levels and employment change by employment protection regulations.

Note: Vertical axis of the first chart is truncated. The regression line in the first chart is calculated with Italy excluded; the line in the second chart is calculated with the Netherlands excluded. For data definitions and sources, see the appendix.

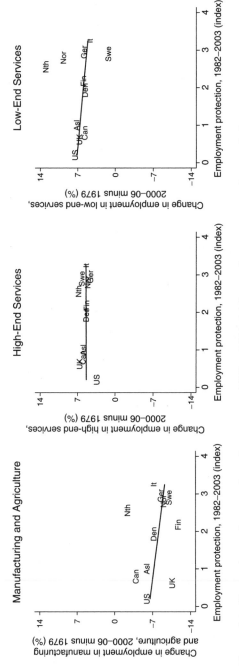

Figure 6.6. Change in employment in various sectors, 1979 to 2000–06, by employment protection regulations.

Note: "High-end services" include finance, insurance, real estate, and other business services (ISIC 8). "Low-end services" include wholesale and retail trade, restaurants, and hotels (ISIC 6) and community, social, and personal services (ISIC 9). France is not included due to lack of data on employment by sector. Change in employment is calculated as the 2000–06 employment rate minus the 1979 employment rate. Employment protection is measured as an average over the years 1982–2003. The regression lines are calculated with the Netherlands excluded. For data definitions and sources, see the appendix.

about the hypothesized adverse effect of employment protection on employment growth.

There is a negative association for employment change in manufacturing and agriculture. But in Chapter 4 I pointed out that virtually all of the cross-country variation in employment growth in these two sectors owes to the timing of deindustrialization and deagriculturalization. Countries that entered the 1980s with heavy employment in manufacturing and agriculture tended to experience the largest losses, while those that had already lost a lot of employment in these sectors have suffered smaller declines since then. A regression of employment change in manufacturing and agriculture on the average level of employment protection yields a coefficient of −1.1. If the level of employment in manufacturing and agriculture in 1979 is added to the regression, the coefficient for employment protection falls to zero.

In high-end services—finance, insurance, real estate, and other business services—there is no association between employment change and employment protection. This is similar to what we observed in Chapter 5. But again, in Chapter 5 this was to be expected. The level of wages at the low end of the distribution is not predicted to have an impact on employment growth in relatively high-productivity, high-profit service sectors. But stiff employment protection regulations should. If they impede employment growth, they should do so largely irrespective of productivity levels and profit margins. The lack of any correlation between employment protection rules and employment change in high-end services is therefore somewhat surprising.

In low-end services—wholesale and retail trade, hotels, restaurants, and community/social/personal services—the cross-country pattern does suggest a possible negative association. But it does not appear to be a particularly strong one. A regression of employment growth in these sectors on employment protection produces a coefficient of −0.7. This suggests that the difference in employment growth in low-end services between a country at the low end of employment protection strictness and a country at the high end has been approximately 2.25 percentage points since the late 1970s.

The apparent negative association in low-end services is heavily influenced by the Swedish case. I noted in Chapter 4 that Sweden's poor employment growth record owes partly to the inability to adjust for average work hours. It also owes to the deep economic crisis Sweden experienced in the early 1990s and to policy decisions during that period to reduce public employment in community and social services such as health, education, and childcare. Since it seems unlikely that stiff employment protection regulations contributed to that economic crisis, Sweden's influence on the cross-country pattern should perhaps be discounted, either partially or fully. If so, the magnitude of the

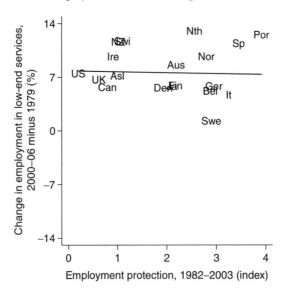

Figure 6.7. Change in employment in low-end services, 1979 to 2000–06, by employment protection regulations—19 countries.

Note: The regression line is calculated with the Netherlands excluded. France is not included due to lack of data on employment by sector. For data definitions and sources, see the appendix.

apparent negative impact of employment protection on employment change shrinks further. If Sweden is omitted, the regression coefficient drops to just −0.2.

Data for employment growth in low-end services and for employment protection are available for eight additional affluent countries: Austria, Belgium, Ireland, Japan, New Zealand, Portugal, Spain, and Switzerland. Figure 6.7 shows the bivariate pattern with these countries added. The additional countries produce no alteration in the pattern; it looks similar to that in the third chart in Figure 6.6. The slope of the regression line is −0.1.

Across countries, employment protection is strongly correlated with some of the key institutions and policies commonly believed to affect employment performance, particularly taxes and product market regulations (Table 4.1). This makes it impossible to control for these in multivariate analyses. It is, however, possible to control for earnings inequality (low-end wages), government benefit generosity, monetary policy, imports (globalization), and labor cost changes.

Figure 6.8 shows coefficients for the employment regulations variable in regressions that include all possible combinations of three or fewer of these variables. As in Chapter 5, the figure reports the results for the employment

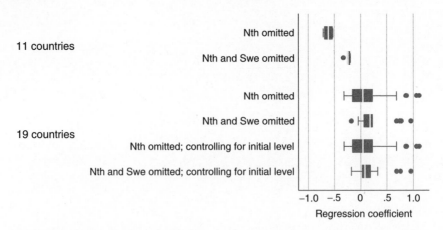

Figure 6.8. Regression results: Estimated effect of employment protection regulations on employment change in low-end services, 1979 to 2000–06.

Note: Unstandardized coefficients for the employment protection regulations variable from ordinary least squares (OLS) regressions using all possible combinations of employment protection and one or two of the following additional independent variables: earnings inequality (P50/P10 ratio), government benefit generosity (cash social expenditures on the working-age population as % of GDP), real long-term interest rates (%), imports (% of GDP), and real unit labor cost changes (%). Payroll and consumption taxes and product market regulations are not included in any of the regressions due to multicollinearity. The third and fourth sets of regressions for 19 countries also include a variable representing the level of employment in low-end services in 1979 to control for "catch-up" effects. The dependent variable is absolute change in the employment rate in low-end services: the employment rate in 2000–06 minus the rate in 1979. For data definitions and sources, see the appendix. France is not included due to lack of data on employment by sector. Finland is missing from regressions that include the real interest rate variable. With 11 countries, there are 6 regressions. For this group of countries the earnings inequality and government benefit generosity cannot be included due to multicollinearity. With 19 countries, there are 21 regressions. The "whiskers" refer to the minimum and maximum coefficients. The edges of the box indicate the 25th- and 75th-percentile coefficients. The vertical white line is the median coefficient. Separate dots indicate "outliers"—coefficients that are substantially larger or smaller than the others in that set.

protection variable in each set of regressions in boxplots. The dependent variable is change from 1979 to 2000–06 in employment in low-end services. In the regressions with the smaller group of countries, earnings inequality and government benefit generosity are not included due to multicollinearity. For the larger group of countries I control for the "catch-up" effect by estimating an additional set of regressions that include a variable representing the 1979 employment level in low-end services.

In some of the regressions the coefficient is negative, but usually small in magnitude. More often than not the coefficient is zero or positive, though still small. On the whole, these results suggest no cross-country association between employment protection regulations and employment growth in low-end services.

Country Experiences

Are there particular country experiences that may be helpful in assessing the impact of employment protection regulations on employment growth? If so, which countries are likely to be informative?

One type is countries that are exceptions to the strong cross-country correlation between employment protection and other inequality-reducing policies and institutions—high low-end wages, generous government benefits, and high taxes. Figure 6.9 shows three scatterplots. The employment protection measure is on the vertical axis in each. On the horizontal axes are earnings inequality, government benefit generosity, and payroll and consumption taxes, respectively (see Chapters 5, 7, and 8).

In two of the three charts—those for low-end wages and government benefits—Denmark lies below the regression line, indicating lower-than-predicted employment protection. Figure 6.1 above shows that until the mid-1990s Denmark's overall level of employment protection strictness, as measured by the OECD and Bassanini and Duval (2006), was similar to Finland's and lower than that of Sweden and Norway. Since 1995 Denmark's restrictiveness has been lower than in the other three Nordic countries. Figure 6.2 indicates that the lower level in Denmark was due mainly to its comparatively low level of employment protection for regular workers. Danish restrictions on fixed-term workers, shown in Figure 6.3, were similar to those in Norway and a bit below those in Sweden. Beginning in 1995 these were relaxed considerably, bringing Denmark down to near the Anglo level of protection for fixed-term employees.

Modest employment protection is a key piece of Denmark's "flexicurity" package, which in recent years has been hailed as a potentially successful approach for combining low inequality with a dynamic economy (Madsen 2001, 2006; Egger and Sengenberger 2003; Kenworthy 2003; OECD 2004 *f*, 2006*b*; EC 2006; Campbell and Pedersen 2007; Cohn 2007). Following Madsen (2001, 2006), a recent European Commission report (EC 2006: 78–9) describes the Danish model as a "golden triangle":

The sides of the triangle consist of (1) relatively loose legislation for employment protection; (2) generous social safety net for the unemployed; (3) high (intensity) spending (per unemployed) on ALMPs. [The result is a] high degree of mobility in and out of employment and between jobs. On average, close to a quarter of all workers pass through unemployment every year at least once. However, the transition rate to employment is relatively high for the vast majority of unemployed, reflecting the overall dynamism of the Danish labour market. After a certain period, the unemployed who are unable to find a job can benefit from Public Employment Services (PES) referral to one of a comprehensive set of ALMPs [active labor

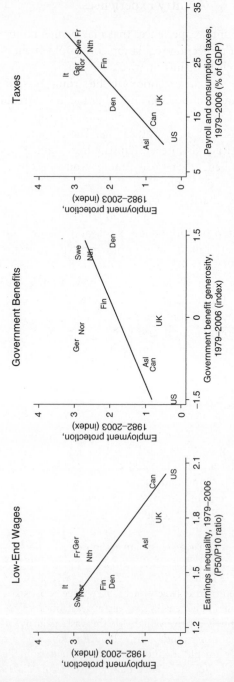

Figure 6.9. Employment protection regulations by other inequality-reducing institutions and policies, 1979–2006.

Note: Some axes are truncated. Government benefit generosity measure is a "benefit employment disincentives index"; see Chapter 7. For data definitions and sources, see the appendix.

market programs], which aim to upgrade skills or to facilitate adaptation to economic change, thereby supporting individual transitions and career development. This is also supported by an efficient education and training system, which includes well-developed schemes for continuous training of the workforce and life long learning. In particular, Danish employees have the opportunity to regularly improve their skills and competences through participation in adult vocational training programmes.

Among the Nordic countries, Sweden is the best with which to compare Denmark. Until the early 1990s Sweden had stricter employment regulations for fixed-term employees than Denmark, but after that the two countries moved in sync. Sweden's level of employment regulations for regular employees has been significantly higher than Denmark's throughout the period. These two countries are quite similar in many other important respects, including government benefit generosity and low-end wage levels (Figure 6.9; Chapters 5 and 7).

According to data for 2003 from the European Commission's Labor Force Survey (EC 2006: 84–6), employee job tenure and turnover patterns for these two countries are consistent with the expectation that employment protection regulations matter. Average job tenure as of 2003 was 8.5 years in Denmark and 11 years in Sweden. Approximately 30% of Danish workers had been with their current employer more than ten years, versus 40% of Swedish workers. Labor turnover is measured as the number of hires, layoffs (firings), and quits during a year divided by the number of people employed. The Danish rate was double that in Sweden: .38 compared to .18.

Does this make a difference for the employment rate? Figure 6.10 shows employment trends in the two countries since 1979. Sweden's employment rate dropped precipitously during the country's early 1990s economic crisis. Since then, however, it has kept pace with Denmark's. Given the severity of the crisis, it is no surprise that Sweden's employment rate still lags a bit behind Denmark's. What *is* surprising if stiff employment protection impedes employment growth, is how similar employment patterns in the two countries have been since the mid-1990s.

Are there other indicators that suggest Denmark's more lenient employment protection rules have boosted its employment performance relative to Sweden? One might be long-term unemployment. If stiff employment protection regulations discourage employers from hiring, we would expect the unemployed in Sweden to have a more difficult time finding a new job—particularly since the generosity of benefits for those out of work and the commitment to active labor market policy are quite similar in the two countries (Chapter 7). Yet in the 2000s the long-term unemployment rates for the two

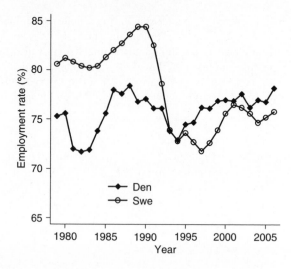

Figure 6.10. Employment trends in Denmark and Sweden, 1979ff.

Note: Vertical axis is truncated. For data definitions and sources, see the appendix.

countries have been virtually identical, at 15–20% of the total unemployed (OECD 2007: table G).

The Denmark–Sweden comparison thus yields ambiguous results regarding the impact of employment protection. Danish workers switch employers more frequently than their Swedish counterparts, but it is not clear that this contributes to lower long-term joblessness or to a higher employment rate.

The United Kingdom has weaker-than-predicted employment protection regulations in all three charts in Figure 6.9; it lies below the regression line in each. Germany has stronger-than-predicted regulations; it lies above the regression line in each chart. However, unlike Denmark, which differs from other Nordic countries in its employment protection regulations, the UK and Germany are very similar in employment regulation strictness to other members of their group. The level of employment protection in the United Kingdom is about the same as in the other three Anglo countries. The same is true for Germany relative to the other three continental nations. Hence there is little analytical leverage to be gained by focusing on either of these two countries.

A second set of countries whose individual experiences may be of analytical utility is those that have substantially altered their degree of employment protection over time. As I noted in Chapter 4, most of the policies and institutions I examine in this book have been fairly stable since the late 1970s. That was the case also of employment protection rules for regular employees in all of these nations. However, for fixed-term employees, several countries relaxed the degree of protection to a nontrivial extent in the 1990s. The most relevant are Sweden and Denmark. Germany, Italy, and the Netherlands also did so, but the changes in these countries came so late in the 1990s that there is as yet insufficient data to assess their impact (Figure 6.3).

The question is whether the sharp reduction in the strictness of rules governing fixed-term employment contracts in Sweden and Denmark had a noticeable impact on employment growth. The answer appears to be no. Figure 6.10 shows that the employment rate did rise in these two countries in the second half of the 1990s. But Figure 3.2 in Chapter 3 shows that it did so in virtually every other country as well. The magnitude of the increase was similar in other nations, and larger in a few.

CONCLUSION

Strong employment protection regulations may or may not promote equality. Across countries, there is a strong negative association between employment protection strictness and earnings inequality among employed individuals. But employment protection is correlated with several other institutions known to reduce earnings inequality: collective bargaining coverage and wage-setting centralization (Figure 6.4). It may be these rather than employment protection that lies behind the apparent association. Moreover, individual earnings dispersion is only one among a number of factors that affect posttax-posttransfer household income inequality.

To the extent employment protection does contribute to lower levels of inequality, it most likely does so by excluding some workers from jobs. This raises a concern about its impact on employment.

Cross-country patterns and the experiences of particular countries suggest reason for skepticism about the conventional view of the impact of employment protection on employment performance. The evidence supporting the hypothesized adverse effect is weak and fragile.

This suggests that policy makers and other actors who wish to secure low inequality and high employment may not need to be concerned about the strictness of employment protection regulations. In my view, however, it may nevertheless be wise for countries that currently have relatively strict regulations to relax them. Their contribution to household income inequality is probably nil. And if it is beneficial, it is beneficial in a bad way—via exclusion of some people from jobs. The best guess from the comparative evidence is that the impact of employment protection on employment performance also is nil. But there is sufficient uncertainty that, if there are no substantial benefits stemming from strong employment protection, it makes sense to weaken it.

Are there substantial benefits? For employees, the principal benefit is stability and fairness. But as Denmark and Sweden show us, there is an attractive alternative: active supports to retrain and place job losers into new positions coupled with generous benefits to ensure little or no financial loss during the period of joblessness. The Anglo countries, and particularly the United States, tend to do it differently. Benefits are less generous and supports for re-employment less extensive. This produces better performance in terms of low long-term unemployment, but at a nontrivial cost to the individual worker. Not surprisingly, data indicate that although most Americans who get fired from a job find a new one relatively soon, the new job often pays less and/or features less desirable working conditions (Osterman 1999; Uchitelle 2006). In a country such as Italy, which has long relied on jobs for life for male workers as a key component of the overall social protection regime, there is a sizable danger in contemplating a reduction of employment protection. If such a move is not accompanied by similar reforms in active labor market policy and government benefits, it may boost the aggregate employment rate but at substantial cost to some individuals.

Employment protection can also have beneficial effects for firms. In providing employees job security it likely heightens cooperation between labor and management, which can contribute to higher productivity (Brown, Stern, and Ulman 1993; Buechtemann 1993; Levine and Parkin 1994; Hicks and Kenworthy 1998). It also encourages investments by both employers and employees in firm- or industry-specific skills (Estevez-Abe, Iversen, and Soskice 2001; Hall and Soskice 2001).

Concern about losing these beneficial effects is likely to be especially pronounced for manufacturing firms in some European countries, which rely on employees with specialized training to produce quality-competitive (as opposed to price-competitive) products. Many of these firms continue to be highly successful in domestic and international markets. If easing employment protection regulations has the effect of disrupting this system, the drawbacks might outweigh the benefits.

One strategy, then, is to pursue what Torben Iversen (2005: 257–68) has termed "selective and shielded deregulation." Employment protection rules can be loosened mainly for part-time and temporary employees. As Figure 6.3 shows, that is what many countries in fact have done since the late 1990s.

While this seems a reasonable strategy from the point of view of attempting to enhance flexibility without disrupting arrangements in specific-skills manufacturing firms, it may be of only limited help in low-end services. The Dutch case is sometimes invoked as a success story in this regard, but the rise in part-time employment in the Netherlands began prior to the policy changes and did not accelerate after those changes (Chapter 10; Visser 2002). And though it is perhaps too soon to judge, as the reductions have occurred only within the past decade, there is little indication that partial deregulation has improved employment performance in other countries. The main result seems to have been to shift employment from permanent to fixed-term contracts, rather than to increase employment (Baker et al. 2005; DiPrete 2005; DiPrete et al. 2006; OECD 2006*b*).

Institutional arrangements in Japan may hold a potential lesson here. Japanese manufacturing firms also rely heavily on industry- and firm-specific skills. But formal employment protection regulations in Japan traditionally have been moderate, similar to the level in Denmark, and considerably less restrictive than those in most of the continental and Nordic countries (OECD 2004 *f*). Like in Europe, this system has worked effectively in Japan in part because employees and employers have confidence that the employment relationship will be a lengthy one. Both parties view the investment in such skills as rational, because both are able to take a long-term perspective regarding the payoff. But in Japan this confidence has stemmed largely from an implicit bargain, rather than from formal rules (Dore 1986, 1987; Aoki 1988). If formal employment protection rules were eased in European economies, the long practice of quasi-lifetime employment in large manufacturing firms, and the recognition by both management and labor of the payoffs to that practice, might well allow it to continue even in the absence of the formal regulations. This could also have the benefit of stimulating hiring in low-end services, where employers have greater need for flexibility in staffing.

7

Government Benefits

Redistribution is one of the principal mechanisms through which countries secure low income inequality. As I argued in Chapter 3 and in greater detail in Chapter 5, maintaining moderately high wage levels at the low end of the distribution may be increasingly difficult and perhaps even counter-productive from an egalitarian perspective. If so, redistribution is likely to become even more critical. Redistribution can be achieved through the tax system, via government transfers, or both. As we will see in Chapter 8, in practice very little redistribution is accomplished via taxation, and a shift toward greater use of taxes to achieve redistributive ends is unlikely. Benefits, therefore, may be the key to successful pursuit of low inequality for affluent countries.

But generous benefits can create employment disincentives. This produces a bind for policy makers. Generous benefits secure the redistribution countries need to get low inequality. Because of aging and capital mobility, a high employment rate is needed to finance those benefits, as I suggested in Chapter 1. But if benefits are generous, they may reduce the employment rate. Is there a way out of this dilemma?

I begin this chapter by examining the relationship between government benefits and inequality and between benefits and employment. In doing so, I utilize a new approach to measuring comparative benefit generosity.

I then outline a policy package that can potentially provide gener-ous benefits to working-age individuals and households who need them without creating excessive employment disincentives. The package features generous transfers to those unable to work due to involuntary job loss, sickness, disability, or family responsibilities. However, benefits provided on a temporary basis should be of relatively short duration, and eligi-bility criteria for those provided on a permanent basis should be fairly strict. In exchange for this strictness, extensive support should be pro-vided for those entering or returning to the work force, in the form of training, job placement, public employment, and childcare. A key com-ponent of the benefit package is an employment-conditional earnings subsidy.

MEASURING BENEFIT GENEROSITY

Let me begin with a brief summary of different types of social policy. Given my concern with employment, it is useful to distinguish between programs in terms of the work incentives and disincentives they create (see also Björklund and Freeman 1997).

A first type consists of benefits to individuals or households that have low earnings or incomes. Typically these benefits are means-tested, in that eligibility is conditional on low household income and limited assets. Eligibility is not conditional on prior employment. The benefit is reduced or lost altogether if the recipient becomes employed or increases earnings. In most countries the principal program of this type is called social assistance. Housing benefits and energy assistance also often take this form, as does Food Stamps in the United States. Such programs tend to discourage employment, though the severity of the effect depends greatly on program details and other factors such as the minimum wage level and the availability of jobs and affordable childcare.

At the opposite end of the spectrum are employment-conditional earnings subsidies. This type of benefit also goes primarily to individuals or households with low earnings or incomes. But typically it is not means-tested. The benefit is conditional on employment and increases with earnings, thereby encouraging rather than discouraging employment. At a certain earnings level the benefit peaks and then declines gradually. The principal examples of this type of program are the Earned Income Tax Credit in the United States and the Working Tax Credit in the United Kingdom.

A third type is social insurance programs that provide benefits to individuals who are not employed but who have previously been employed. Examples include unemployment compensation, sickness compensation, work injury compensation, disability compensation, pensions, and paid parental leave. In theoretical terms, the impact of these programs on employment is ambiguous. On the one hand, because benefit eligibility is conditional on prior employment, they create a pro-employment incentive. On the other hand, the existence of such programs encourages people to make use of them once eligible and to then remain on them rather than return to work.

A fourth type consists of government service programs that create positive work incentives. The best example is public provision or subsidization of childcare, which facilitates parents' entry into and continuity in employment.

A fifth type is transfers and government services that have no direct effect of either encouraging or discouraging employment. Employment, earnings, and income have no impact on eligibility, benefit or service levels, and duration of receipt. Schooling, medical care, and child allowances are prominent examples.

How should we measure the generosity of government benefits? Until very recently virtually all comparative research on the causes and consequences of such benefits relied on a crude proxy measure: government transfers as a share of GDP. One problem with this measure is that a considerable portion of the money transferred by governments does not go to households or individuals with low incomes. Another is that this type of measure fuses what might be termed the "intended generosity" of benefits with the need for benefits. The former refers to the level of generosity policy makers have in mind in constructing and altering benefit programs; for most analysts, this is the concept of interest. The latter is determined by the size of the elderly, unemployed, sick, disabled, and low income populations. A country with a relatively large elderly population or a comparatively high level of unemployment may score high on the transfers-as-percentage-of-GDP measure even if its benefit programs are not particularly generous in their structure.

In the past decade the OECD has created a new database of government expenditures on social programs (OECD 2004g). These data are available beginning in 1980. They include expenditures on cash benefit programs such as pensions, unemployment insurance, sickness insurance, disability benefits, and various means-tested transfers as well as on services such as health care and job training. These data get closer to a measure of the generosity of benefits, but they nonetheless suffer from the same problems as the government transfers measure.

In his 1990 book *The Three Worlds of Welfare Capitalism*, Gøsta Esping-Andersen urged comparative researchers to turn their attention from expenditure totals to program characteristics. Esping-Andersen combined information about eligibility criteria, benefit levels, and benefit duration to create a measure of "decommodification" for three types of benefits: pensions, unemployment insurance, and sickness insurance. This was an important step forward. It moved measurement closer to the "intended generosity" of social programs. However, the restricted set of programs included in the measure and the fact that it was available for only a single year, 1980, limited its utility. Recently Lyle Scruggs (2004) has addressed the latter problem by creating country scores for each aspect of these three programs, from eligibility to benefit level to duration, in each year from 1971 to 2002. Scruggs (2005a, 2005b) also has reexamined Esping-Andersen's decommodification measure, made some adjustments, and made the resulting scores available for each of these years. However, like Esping-Andersen's, the Scruggs data do not include several important programs such as social assistance, disability compensation, and others.

Since the mid-1990s the OECD has been assembling information on bene-fit packages—specifically, net replacement rates—available to households of various size and composition in each country (OECD 2004*a*). These too are useful data, and the country publications provide a wealth of information on country-specific program details (e.g. OECD 2004*b*, 2004*c*, 2004*d*). However, the focus is largely on unemployment insurance, and these data are available for only a limited number of years. In addition, it is not clear how, if at all, these various program details can be combined into a summary measure suitable for macrocomparative analysis.

An alternative to the expenditures and program details approaches to mea-suring benefit generosity is to examine the empirical distribution of gov-ernment benefits. In recent years several researchers have used Luxembourg Income Study (LIS) data to create a direct measure of redistribution (Bradley et al. 2003; Kenworthy 2004*a*; Kenworthy and Pontusson 2005; Mahler and Jesuit 2006). This approach, which follows the lead of some earlier schol-ars (Hicks and Swank 1984; Mitchell 1991), subtracts the Gini coefficient for posttax-posttransfer household income from that for pretax-pretransfer household income. (This also can be divided by the pretax-pretransfer Gini to create a percentage, rather than absolute, measure of redistribution.) However, while this is a very useful measure of redistribution, it is only an indirect measure of benefit generosity.

I make use of a new measure here, based on LIS data. It too draws on the empirical distribution of transfers and taxes. But it focuses directly on that dis-tribution, rather than on the degree of inequality reduction achieved. I meas-ure comparative benefit generosity by examining the posttax-posttransfer (disposable) incomes of households with low pretax-pretransfer (market) incomes.

I begin by looking at the relationship between pretax-pretransfer income and posttax-posttransfer income for low-income households of a particu-lar size and structure—for example, a single working-age adult with no children—in a particular country in a particular year. "Low income" is defined here as pretax-pretransfer household income less than 50% of the country's median household income. Some such households have pretax-pretransfer income of zero. Others have some but not very much market income. Others have market incomes close to 50% of the median. The dif-ference between pretax-pretransfer and posttax-posttransfer income is "net government benefits"—cash and near-cash transfers received minus tax pay-ments.

Table 7.1 lists the types of benefits and taxes included and not included in the measures I use throughout this chapter. They include the main cash and near-cash transfer programs in these countries. Because I focus on households

Table 7.1. Types of transfers and taxes included in benefit generosity measures in this chapter.

	Included	Not included

Transfers	Unemployment compensation
	Sickness, accident, and disability
	  compensation
	Pension
	Child/family allowance
	Maternity/parental benefit
	Military/veteran/war benefit
	Social assistance
	Near-cash benefits (e.g. food, housing,
	  energy assistance)
	Employment-conditional earnings
	  subsidies (EITC, WTC)
		Value of government services (e.g.
		  medical care, childcare)

Taxes	Income Payroll	Consumption

Note: All information is from the Luxembourg Income Study database.

with working-age heads, pension benefits, though included, are far less important than would be the case if I were examining households of all ages. Tax payments include those for income and payroll taxes. The LIS data do not include information on the value of services such as medical care, nor on consumption tax payments. These are therefore not included in my benefit generosity measures.

Among those with a particular level of pretax-pretransfer income, the amount received in benefits and the amount paid in taxes will vary somewhat. Typically, net benefits vary inversely with pretax-pretransfer income; that is, households with less market income tend to receive more in benefits and pay less in taxes than do those with more market income. Two pieces of information that can be gleaned from these data are helpful in measuring the generosity of government benefits. One is the average posttax-posttransfer income when pretax-pretransfer income is zero. This can be thought of as the country's (average) minimum income. The other is the average amount that posttax-posttransfer income increases per unit (dollar, euro, pound, kronor) increase in market income. This represents the (average) payoff to additional earnings. We would expect this payoff to be less than 1.0, since households with more earnings typically receive less in government transfers and pay more in taxes than those with less earnings.

Figure 7.1 shows this information as of 2000 for four countries: Sweden, Germany, the Netherlands, and the United States. In each chart

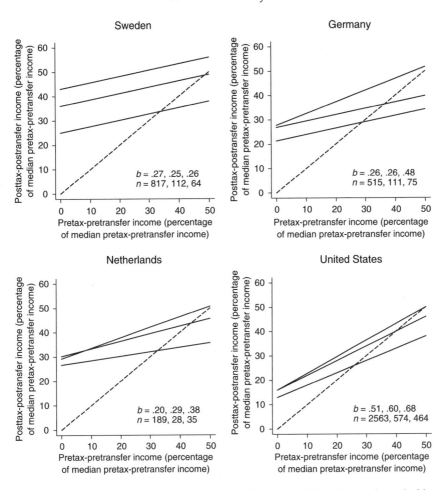

Figure 7.1. Government benefit generosity for three types of low-income households, 2000.

Note: Actual year is 1999 for the Netherlands. Included are households with a "head" age 25 to 59 and a market income less than 50% of the national median. From lowest to highest solid line and from left to right in the legend, the household types are: one adult with no children, one adult with one child, and one adult with two children. The solid lines are regression lines. The dotted line shows posttax-posttransfer income equal to pretax-pretransfer income. "*b*" is the coefficient from a regression of posttax-posttransfer income on pretax-pretransfer income. "*n*" is the number of observations. For data definitions and sources, see the appendix.

pretax-pretransfer income is on the horizontal axis and posttax-posttransfer household income is on the vertical axis. Both are expressed as a percentage of the country's median household income. The dotted line is a "45°" line; it shows posttax-posttransfer income equal to pretax-pretransfer income, which obtains if net government benefits are zero. There are three solid lines in each chart. They are regression lines describing the pattern of posttax-posttransfer income by pretax-pretransfer income for three types of households with working-age "heads": one adult with no children, one adult with one child, and one adult with two children.

The charts provide us with the two pieces of information mentioned above: the (average) minimum posttax-posttransfer income and the (average) payoff to additional earnings. These are represented by, respectively, the y-intercepts and the slopes of the regression lines. For instance, in Sweden in 2000 the y-intercept for the lowest solid line is 25. This indicates that households with one working-age adult and no children and zero market income had an average posttax-posttransfer income equal to 25% of Sweden's median pretax-pretransfer household income. The slope of that solid line is .27, indicating an average gain in posttax-posttransfer income of 27 kroner for each additional 100 kroner of market income. The earnings payoff was similar for the other two types of household, but the minimum incomes were higher, as we would expect given the greater number of children (and thus larger government benefits). For example, among households with one adult and two children and no market income, the average posttax-posttransfer income was nearly 45% of the median pretax-pretransfer income.

Note that the regression lines for households with no children and those with one child cross the 45° line. At that point such households begin, on average, to pay more in taxes than they receive in government benefits (their posttax-posttransfer income is less than their pretax-pretransfer income). Households with a single adult and two children continue to receive more in benefits than they pay in taxes until some point beyond market income of 50% of the median.

Why do I express benefits and posttax-posttransfer incomes relative to the country median, rather than with an absolute measure? The main reason is that one of my goals here is to examine the impact of benefit generosity on employment. What is likely to matter to a person considering whether to work or live off government benefits is how generous benefits are relative to wages and incomes in that country at that particular point in time, rather than how generous they are relative to benefits in other countries or to those in their own country at some point in the past.

How do the other three countries compare to Sweden? In Germany, average posttax-posttransfer incomes for each of the three household types were lower than in Sweden (relative to the country median). For instance, among those with zero market income, average posttax-posttransfer income was 25%, 38%, and 43% of the median in Sweden, compared to 22%, 28%, and 29% in Germany. The same was true for those with market income at half of the median, though incomes for single-adult households with two children were a little closer to those in Sweden.

In the Netherlands, the average posttax-posttransfer income for the three household types tended to be higher than in Germany but lower than in Sweden.

The United States differs sharply from the other three countries in having lower minimum incomes and higher earnings payoffs. For example, the average posttax-posttransfer income for households with one adult and two children and no market income was more than twice as high in Sweden (43% of the Swedish median) as in the United States (17% of the US median), and the earnings payoff for this type of household in Sweden (.26) was less than half that in the United States (.68). As a result, posttax-posttransfer incomes among those with very low market incomes were strikingly lower (relative to the median) in the United States than in the other three countries, whereas posttax-posttransfer incomes among households with market incomes closer to half of the median in the United States were comparable to those in the other countries.

One limitation of this measure is that it is based only on single-adult households. That is because for some countries the sample sizes of two-adult households with low market income are too small to permit reliable estimates.

Another limitation of this measure is that it does not distinguish between the types of benefits received by various households. Consider, for example, the group of one adult-one child households with zero pretax-pretransfer income in a particular country in a given year. Suppose the average posttax-posttransfer income among such households is approximately one-third of the median household income. All of the income for such households comes from government benefits. But those benefits may consist largely or entirely of social assistance for some of the households, of unemployment insurance or disability compensation for others, and of some combination of these and other types of benefits for others. And the mix of benefits will differ across countries and over time within countries.

Do changes in the mix of benefits result in noteworthy within-country shifts in this measure of benefit generosity over time? Figure 7.2 shows the average minimum income for each country in each year since 1979 for which there are available data in the LIS database. Figure 7.1 showed regression lines, indicating the average income throughout the set of low-income households—that is, among those with pretax-pretransfer incomes ranging from 0 up to 50% of the median. In order to convey changes over time in a manageable way, Figure 7.2 employs two types of data reduction. First, the charts show

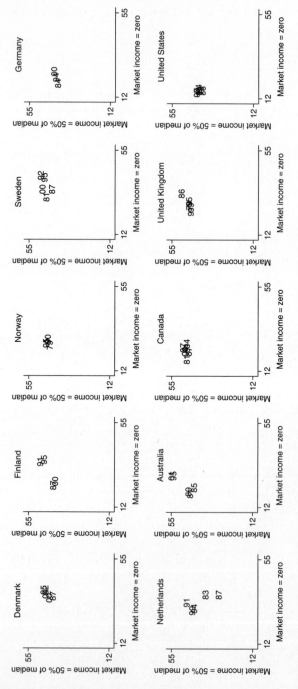

Figure 7.2. Government benefit generosity for three types of low-income households, 1979ff.

Note: Chart axes are truncated. The data are for average posttax-posttransfer household income when pretax-pretransfer household income is zero (horizontal axis) and when it is 50% of the country median (vertical axis). The figures are averaged for the three types of single-adult households featured in Figure 7.1. Numbers in the charts represent years; for instance, "00" refers to the year 2000. Two data sets for Germany (1981 and 1989) and one for Norway (1986) are omitted because sample sizes for some household types are too small. France and Italy are not included due to lack of data on pretax-pretransfer income. For data definitions and sources, see the appendix.

average posttax-posttransfer income at only two points in the distribution of low-income households: for those with pretax-pretransfer income of zero (horizontal axis) and for those with pretax-pretransfer income equal to 50% of the median (vertical axis). Second, I average the figures for the three types of households. The numbers in the charts refer to years; for instance, "00" refers to the year 2000. France and Italy are not included in the charts because data for pretax income are not available for these two countries in the LIS database.

These charts can be used to assess cross-country differences in the degree of benefit generosity. For example, in most years Sweden is in the upper-right corner, indicating relatively generous benefits both for households with no market income and for households with market income at half the country median. The United States, by contrast, is to the left on the horizontal axis and lower than most other countries on the vertical axis, indicating relatively stingy benefits.

With respect to changes over time, the key point to note is that in most of the countries the degree of benefit generosity has been quite stable.

There are three main exceptions to this constancy: Finland in 1991 and 1995, Sweden in 1992 and 1995, and the Netherlands in 1983 and 1987. In Sweden and Finland this owes to the fact that households with zero market income received more in benefits (as a share of median household income) in those two years. This was a product of the deep economic crises these two countries experienced in the first half of the 1990s. The main way in which the crisis affected benefit generosity as measured here is by increasing unemployment. In Finland, the unemployment rate jumped from 3% in 1990 to 15% in 1995; in Sweden, it rose from 2% to 9%. As a result, in these years a larger share of households with little or no market income were receiving unemployment compensation, which typically pays more than social assistance (my calculations; see also OECD 2005*b*: 111). A second impact of the crisis was that median household income dropped in both countries. I measure benefit generosity using posttax-posttransfer income as a percentage of median income (for a given level of pretax-pretransfer income). Thus, if the median declines while benefit levels remain the same, benefit generosity will increase somewhat.

The apparent shift between the late 1980s and the early 1990s in the Netherlands owes to the fact that the Dutch data set used in the Luxembourg Income Study database was switched after the 1980s. The data for 1983 and 1987 are from the Public Services Survey. Beginning in the 1990s the data are from the Dutch Socio-Economic Panel.

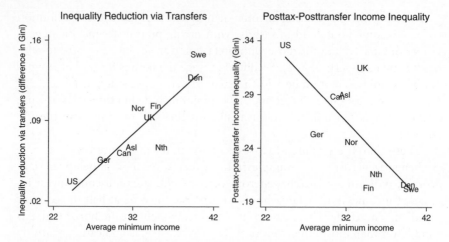

Figure 7.3. Inequality reduction via transfers and posttax-posttransfer income inequality by government benefit generosity, 1979–2006.

Note: Chart axes are truncated. All of the measures are averaged over all available 1979–2006 LIS years, though for most countries the most recent available LIS data set as of this writing (January 2008) is for the year 2000. "Average minimum income" is a measure of government benefit generosity; it is calculated as described in the text and also in the appendix. "Inequality reduction via transfers" is calculated as the Gini coefficient for household pretax-pretransfer income minus the Gini for household pretax-posttransfer income. France and Italy are not included due to lack of data on pretax-pretransfer income. For data definitions and sources, see the appendix.

BENEFIT GENEROSITY AND INEQUALITY

Do generous government benefits help to reduce income inequality? Yes, they do. Figure 7.3 shows this in two ways. The first chart in the figure plots "inequality reduction via transfers" by "average minimum income."

Inequality reduction via transfers is calculated as the Gini coefficient for pretax-pretransfer income minus the Gini for pretax-posttransfer income (for households with heads age 25–59). It is the amount by which income inequality among working-age households is reduced by government transfers.

"Average minimum income" is a measure of government benefit generosity. It is computed for each country by averaging the scores along the horizontal axis in Figure 7.2, multiplying the result by two, adding the average of the scores along the vertical axis, and dividing that sum by three. Let me elaborate. The measure is an average for three types of households: single adult with no children, single adult with one child, and single adult with two children. It is based on average posttax-posttransfer income (as a percentage of the country median) for households at two points in the income distribution: those with pretax-pretransfer income of zero and those with pretax-pretransfer income equal to 50% of the country median. Whereas Figure 7.2 showed these two data separately, in Figure 7.3 I have combined them to create a single indicator for each country. The measure is a weighted average of the two: posttax-posttransfer income for those with zero market income is multiplied by two and then added to posttax-posttransfer income for those with market income at half the median; the resulting sum is then divided by three. A measure of benefit generosity surely should weight benefits to households with lower incomes more heavily than benefits to those with higher incomes. The choice here to weight the former twice as heavily as the latter is arbitrary. We might just as well weight them three times as heavily, or four times, or more. But doing so has little impact on the cross-country variation in the measure. The measure in Figure 7.3 also differs from that in Figure 7.2 in that rather than show each LIS year separately, I have averaged the scores for each country across all 1979–2006 LIS years.

As the first chart in Figure 7.3 indicates, benefit generosity measured in this way is very closely correlated with inequality reduction via transfers ($r = .89$). Although unsurprising, this is not true by definition. Suppose a country offered very generous benefits to households with no market income and even more generous benefits to those with market incomes around half of the median. In Figure 7.1, the country's regression lines would have large y-intercepts and steep slopes. Such a country would score high on the measure of benefit generosity but would accomplish relatively little inequality reduction via transfers. In the first scatterplot in Figure 7.3, it would be in the lower-right corner.

The second chart in Figure 7.3 shows posttax-posttransfer income inequality by government benefit generosity. Inequality of disposable income is heavily influenced by inequality of market income (Chapter 3), so the correlation is not quite as strong as with inequality reduction. Even so, it *is* rather strong ($r = -.77$).

BENEFIT GENEROSITY AND EMPLOYMENT

Many empirical studies have concluded that generous government benefits contribute to poor employment performance (Murray 1984; OECD 1994, 2006*b*; Siebert 1997; Elmeskov, Martin, and Scarpetta 1998; Nickell and Layard 1999; Krueger and Meyer 2002; Peter 2004; Nickell, Nunziata, and Ochel 2005; Bassanini and Duval 2006). The concern with respect to wages in Chapter 5 was largely a demand-side one: if wages are too high in low-productivity jobs, employers will be reluctant to hire. The worry here is a supply-side one: if benefits are too generous, individuals at the low end of the labor market will be reluctant to enter or return to employment.

There is no doubt that at some level of generosity benefits will indeed have the effect of discouraging employment. A number of individual-level studies confirm this (Moffitt 1992; Meyer 1995). The question is: Is the impact large enough to matter for aggregate employment rates? And if so, how large is it?

Comparative Patterns

I focus here exclusively on cross-country variation in employment perform-ance. I use a measure of government benefit generosity slightly different from that in the previous section. It is based on the same data: those for posttax-posttransfer income among three types of low-income households. However, instead of averaging posttax-posttransfer income at various levels of pretax-pretransfer income, I use two indicators. The first is average—for three household types and over all available LIS years between 1979 and 2006—posttax-posttransfer income among households with zero market income. This is, in effect, the (average) income floor. It is the average y-intercept of the regression lines shown in Figure 7.1. The second is the average slope of the regression lines in Figure 7.1. This I refer to as the "earnings payoff." It repre-sents the average amount by which posttax-posttransfer income increases for each additional unit (dollars, euros, pounds, kroner, etc.) of market income.

My aim is for a measure of work disincentives created by government benefits. Work disincentives are greater the higher the income floor and the smaller the earnings payoff. To illustrate, let's return to Figure 7.1 and com-pare Sweden with the United States. In Sweden the income floor (posttax-posttransfer income when market income is zero) is larger (relative to the country median) for each type of household than in the United States; Sweden's y-intercepts are greater. All else equal, this creates stronger work disincentives in Sweden. The earnings payoff is smaller in Sweden than in the United States; Sweden's regression lines have flatter slopes. This too creates stronger work disincentives in Sweden. Although these two indicators coincide in comparing Sweden with the United States—that is, both imply greater work disincentives in Sweden—it is possible for a country to have a higher income floor but also a larger earnings payoff. I therefore combine these two indicators into a composite measure of "benefit employment disincentives." The measure is calculated by first standardizing both the income floor and earnings payoff measures. I then reverse the sign for the earnings payoff standardized scores, so that higher scores represent a smaller earnings payoff. I then average the two standardized scores for each country. This yields a measure of benefit

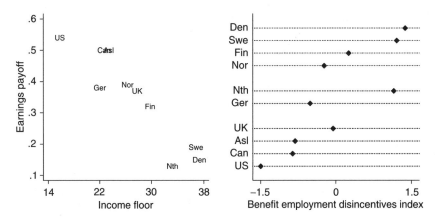

Figure 7.4. Government benefit generosity and employment disincentives.

Note: Axes in the first chart are truncated. The data are averaged across all available LIS years between 1979 and 2006, though for most countries the most recent available LIS data set as of this writing (January 2008) is for the year 2000. "Income floor," "earnings payoff," and "benefit employment disincentives index" are measures of government benefit generosity; they are calculated as described in the text (and in the appendix). France and Italy are not included due to lack of data on pretax-pretransfer income. For data definitions and sources, see the appendix.

employment disincentives that ranges from approximately −1.5 to +1.5, with positive values indicating stronger work disincentives.

The first chart in Figure 7.4 shows the average earnings payoff by the average income floor for each country. Both indicators are averaged for all available years between 1979 and 2006. As it turns out, the employment disincentives created by these two indicators are relatively consistent across countries. In other words, countries with a more generous income floor tend to also have a smaller earnings payoff. The second chart shows the combined measure of benefit employment disincentives. Benefit systems in Denmark, Sweden, and the Netherlands create the strongest work disincentives, whereas those in the United States create the weakest. In Denmark during the 1980s and 1990s working-age single-adult households with zero, one, or two children and no market income ended up with posttax-posttransfer incomes of, on average, nearly 40% of the Danish median pretax-pretransfer household income. Their American counterparts ended up with average posttax-posttransfer incomes just 15% of the US median. For American single-adult households with market incomes less than half the national median, the average payoff from an increase in market income was 55%. In other words, on average an increase in market income of $10,000 resulted in an increase in posttax-posttransfer income of $5,500. For their Danish counterparts, the average earnings payoff was just 15%.

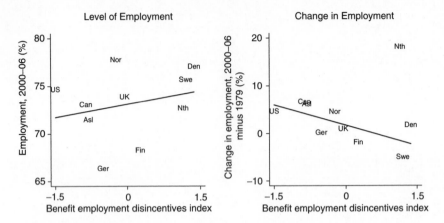

Figure 7.5. Employment levels and employment changes by benefit-generated employment disincentives.

Note: Vertical axis in the first chart is truncated. The regression line in the second chart is calculated with the Netherlands excluded. "Benefit employment disincentives index" is a measure of government benefit generosity; it is calculated as described in the text (and in the appendix). The benefit employment disincentives index is an average for all available LIS years between 1979 and 2006, though for most countries the most recent available LIS data set as of this writing (January 2008) is for the year 2000. France and Italy are not included due to lack of data. For data definitions and sources, see the appendix.

Have the employment disincentives created by government benefits affected employment performance? Figure 7.5 shows two relevant charts. The first plots employment rates as of 2000–06 by the benefit employment disincentives measure. To the extent there is a relationship evident, it is in the "wrong" direction; stronger employment disincentives are associated with higher employment.

However, as I noted in Chapter 4, it is more useful to examine *changes* in employment during these years, as few suggest there was any noteworthy tradeoff between benefit generosity and employment prior to the late 1970s. The second chart replaces employment levels on vertical axis with employment change, measured as the employment rate in 2000–06 minus the rate in 1979. Here, if we set aside the Netherlands, we see a pattern consistent with the conventional expectation. Countries with stronger benefit employment disincentives tended to experience employment decline or relatively little growth, while those with weaker employment disincentives experienced more rapid employment growth.

As in prior chapters, however, we need to disaggregate employment growth by sector. I do so in Figure 7.6. The three charts show employment change from 1979 to 2000–06 in, respectively, manufacturing and agriculture, high-end services, and low-end services. "High-end" services include finance,

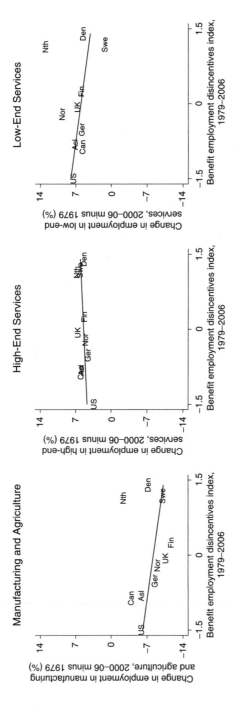

Figure 7.6. Change in employment in various sectors, 1979 to 2000–06, by benefit employment disincentives.

Note: "High-end services" include finance, insurance, real estate, and other business services (ISIC 8). "Low-end services" include wholesale and retail trade, restaurants, and hotels (ISIC 6) and community, social, and personal services (ISIC 9). "Benefit employment disincentives index" is a measure of government benefit generosity; it is calculated as described in the text (and in the appendix). The benefit employment disincentives index is an average for all available LIS years between 1979 and 2006, though for most countries the most recent available LIS data set as of this writing (January 2008) is for the year 2000. France and Italy are not included due to lack of data. Change in employment is calculated as the 2000–06 employment rate minus the 1979 employment rate. The regression lines are calculated with the Netherlands excluded. For data definitions and sources, see the appendix.

insurance, real estate, and other business services (ISIC 8). "Low-end" services include wholesale and retail trade, restaurants, and hotels (ISIC 6) and community, social, and personal services (ISIC 9). Because of its outlier status with respect to employment growth, the Netherlands is not included in calculating the regression lines in these charts.

The first chart suggests that part of the association between benefit-generated work disincentives and employment change is due to manufacturing and agriculture. In Chapter 4 I noted that employment trends in manufacturing and agriculture are explained almost entirely by the level of employment in these two sectors at the beginning of the period. All of these countries experienced job loss in manufacturing and agriculture, and the degree of loss was directly proportional to the level of manufacturing and agricultural employment in 1979. It is possible that the generosity of government benefits played some role in employment developments in these sectors, but if so that role is likely to have been fairly minor.

There is no association between the benefit employment disincentives index and employment change in high-end services. That is not surprising. Jobs in this sector tend to pay relatively well, so for most people even relatively generous benefits will not discourage employment.

It is in low-end services that we would expect to observe the strongest impact of benefit generosity. With the Netherlands excluded, there is indeed a negative association between the benefit employment disincentives index and employment growth in low-end services. For total employment, shown in the second chart in Figure 7.5, a regression of employment change on the employment disincentives index yields a coefficient of -2.8. This suggests that a country with a score at the low end of the index (around -1.5) would have enjoyed about 8.4 percentage points more employment growth than a country at the high end (around 1.5). For low-end services, the coefficient is only half as large: -1.3. And note that the pattern is heavily influenced by the Swedish case. If Sweden is omitted, the regression coefficient drops to -0.5.

Data are available for other countries for a substitute measure of government benefit generosity: cash social expenditures directed toward the working-age population, measured as a share of GDP. As I suggested above, this is a crude measure of benefit generosity. However, for the ten countries for which the benefit employment disincentives index can be calculated, the two measures (with each calculated as an average over all available years) are very closely correlated: $r = .94$. The cash social expenditures measure is thus likely to be a useful substitute.

Figure 7.7 replicates the third chart in Figure 7.6 with eight additional countries: Austria, Belgium, Ireland, Italy, Japan, New Zealand, Portugal, Spain, and Switzerland. The association is again negative, and similar in magnitude.

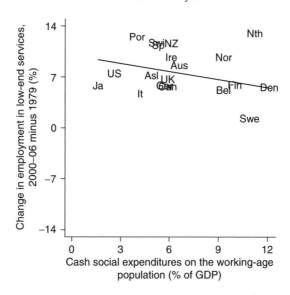

Figure 7.7. Change in employment in low-end services, 1979 to 2000–06, by cash social expenditures on the working-age population—19 countries.

Note: The regression line is calculated with the Netherlands excluded. Cash social expenditures on the working-age population is an alternative measure of government benefit generosity; it is used here because it allows inclusion of more countries. France is not included due to lack of data on employment by sector. For data definitions and sources, see the appendix.

With the cash social expenditures measure of benefit generosity used, the coefficient for regression line in the third chart of Figure 7.6, with 10 countries, is −.27. For the nineteen countries in Figure 7.7, the coefficient is −.37. (The Netherlands is excluded from both calculations.) The difference between the low-end country and the high-end country on the cash social expenditures measure is approximately 10 percentage points. Thus, if −.37 is the true effect of government benefit generosity, a country at the low end has experienced nearly 4 percentage points less growth in low-end service employment since the late 1970s than a country at the high end.

This, however, is without controlling for other determinants of employment growth. Figure 7.8 shows coefficients for government benefit generosity from a variety of regressions with employment change over 1979 to 2000–06 in low-end services as the dependent variable. As in Chapters 5 and 6, the figure reports the results for the government benefit generosity variable in each set of regressions in boxplots. I use the cash social expenditures on the working-age population measure of benefit generosity, as it is available for more countries than the employment benefit disincentives measure. The regressions include all possible combinations of the cash social expenditures variable and one

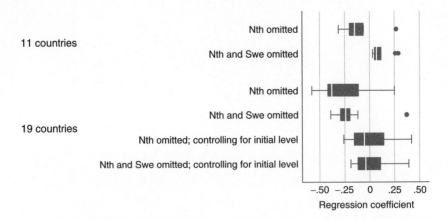

Figure 7.8. Regression results: Estimated effect of government benefit generosity on employment change in low-end services, 1979 to 2000–06.

Note: Unstandardized coefficients for government benefit generosity—measured as cash social expenditures on the working-age population variable as a share of GDP—from ordinary least squares (OLS) regressions using all possible combinations of government benefit generosity and one or two of the following additional independent variables: earnings inequality (P50/P10 ratio), employment protection regulations (index), payroll and consumption taxes (% of GDP), real long-term interest rates (%), imports (% of GDP), real unit labor cost changes (%), and product market regulations (index). Finland is missing from regressions that include the real interest rate variable. The third and fourth sets of regressions for 19 countries also include a variable representing the level of employment in low-end services in 1979 to control for "catch-up" effects. The dependent variable is absolute change in the employment rate in low-end services: the employment rate in 2000–06 minus the rate in 1979. For data definitions and sources, see the appendix. France is not included due to lack of data on employment by sector. Finland is missing from regressions that include the real interest rate variable. With 11 countries, there are 13 regressions. For this group of countries the earnings inequality and imports variables are not included due to multicollinearity. With 19 countries, there are 26 regressions. The "whiskers" refer to the minimum and maximum coefficients. The edges of the box indicate the 25th- and 75th-percentile coefficients. The vertical white line is the median coefficient. Separate dots indicate "outliers"—coefficients that are substantially larger or smaller than the others in that set.

or two of the other variables highlighted in Chapters 4, 5, 6, and 8: earnings inequality (low-end wages), employment protection regulations, payroll and consumption taxes, real long-term interest rates, imports, change in real unit labor costs, and product market regulations. For the smaller group of countries, earnings inequality and imports are too closely correlated with government benefit generosity to be included in the regressions. For the larger group of countries I control for the "catch-up" effect by estimating an additional set of regressions that include a variable representing the 1979 employment level in low-end services.

The coefficients for the government benefit generosity variable vary widely depending on the model specification and the countries included. For several of the sets of regressions, particularly those with Sweden excluded, the median coefficient is close to zero. For example, for the larger group with Sweden excluded and a control for 1979 employment in low-end services, the median coefficient is −.04. If that is the true effect of government benefit generosity on employment growth in low-end services, a country at the high end has experienced less than half a percentage point less growth since the late 1970s than a country at the high end. If that were to continue for 100 years, it would amount to a noteworthy difference. But in the medium run, it is not particularly large.

Country Experiences

Given the ambiguity of the cross-country comparative evidence, it would be helpful for analytical purposes to have a country or two in which government benefit generosity decreased substantially over time. If employment in low-end services subsequently increased, this would provide stronger support for a conclusion that benefit generosity is an important determinant of employment outcomes. Most affluent countries have reformed their social policy programs in one way or another during the past several decades (Hicks 1999; Huber and Stephens 2001; Pierson 2001; Swank 2002; Korpi and Palme 2003; Scruggs 2004; Hicks and Zorn 2005). Yet the charts in Figure 7.2 above indicate that degree of benefit generosity for low-earning working-age households has not shifted appreciably in any of the countries since the late 1970s.

A GENEROUS AND EMPLOYMENT-FRIENDLY
BENEFIT PACKAGE

Even if their impact on employment growth has not been large, generous benefits do create employment disincentives. One way to reduce such disincentives is to reduce the generosity of benefits. But for those interested in achieving both high employment and low inequality, that is not a desirable strategy. Are there other options? A policy strategy that includes generous benefits but also is conducive to high employment would be to couple a number of elements of the "social democratic approach" pursued in the Nordic countries with a type of benefit originating in the United Kingdom and the United States.

The Social Democratic Approach

The Nordic countries do many things right with respect to employment-friendly social policy. Cash and near-cash benefit programs tend to be comprehensive (they cover most types of social risk) and generous, and they are effective at reducing income inequality and poverty (Esping-Andersen 1990; Björklund and Freeman 1997; Björklund 1998; Korpi and Palme 1998; Kenworthy 1999, 2004*a*; Huber and Stephens 2001; Hicks and Kenworthy 2003; DeFina and Thanawala 2004; Smeeding 2004; OECD 2005*b*: ch. 6; Pontusson 2005, 2007; Scruggs and Allan 2005; Abrahamson 2006). Let me illustrate with reference to programs in Denmark and Sweden.

Unemployment and sickness insurance programs in these two countries are among the world's most generous (Scruggs 2004). The first two charts in Figure 7.9 show a measure of decommodification for these two policies. The decommodification score is an index based largely on the share of the labor force that is eligible for the program and on the average replacement rate— that is, the share of former income that the program benefit replaces. During the 1980s and 1990s, more than 70% (in the 1990s more than 80%) of the labor force was eligible for unemployment compensation in both countries. The net replacement rate—the amount of benefit after taxes relative to the worker's former wage or salary—was about 65% in Denmark and 75–80% in Sweden. More than 95% of the labor force in both countries was eligible for sickness compensation, and the replacement rate averaged around 65% in Denmark and 75–85% in Sweden.

Social assistance and disability compensation also are comparatively generous in these two countries. This is indicated perhaps most clearly by the high average posttax-posttransfer income (relative to the median) for single-adult households with no market income. These figures, which were used in Figure 7.3 above, are reproduced here in the third chart in Figure 7.9.

Sweden and Denmark also offer extensive provision of public services such as health care. Services are not included in measures of income, so public service provision has no direct impact on the measured degree of income inequality. But provision of high-quality public services clearly has an equalizing effect in practice. Service provision is equivalent to offering a flat-rate cash benefit to all households, which is redistributive as long as service consumption is relatively equal throughout the income distribution and the tax system is not structured too regressively. The fourth chart in Figure 7.9 shows that Denmark and Sweden devote a larger share of GDP to public expenditures on health care than do other countries.

What do these countries do to encourage and support employment? One way to do so is via eligibility rules and duration of benefit receipt. Here Sweden and Denmark have had mixed success. In both countries there is a "productivist" orientation toward work and welfare; with some exceptions, nondisabled working-age adults are expected to work. Yet this has been partially offset by some of the characteristics of benefit programs.

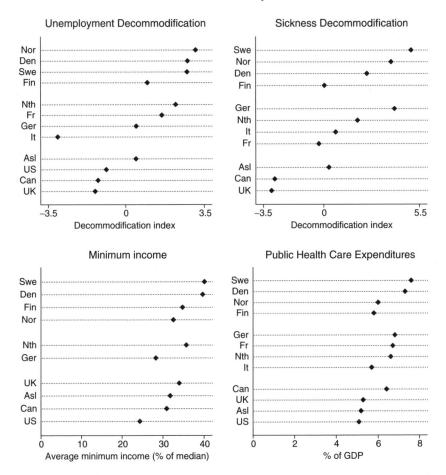

Figure 7.9. Key types of benefit generosity in the social democratic approach, 1979ff.

Note: Data are 1979ff period averages. Ending year is 2002 for the two decommodification indexes, 2006 for minimum income, and 2001 for public health care expenditures. "Average minimum income" is a measure of government benefit generosity; it is calculated as described in the text (and in the appendix). France and Italy are not included in the "minimum income" chart due to lack of data on pretax income. The United States has no public sickness insurance program. For data definitions and sources, see the appendix.

In Sweden, to qualify for unemployment insurance a person must have been employed for a full year and (except for 1988–92) there is a five-day waiting period before eligibility for the benefit commences. For a typical worker the maximum duration of benefit receipt is 60 months. These are reasonably stringent criteria. For sickness insurance, by contrast, there is no prior-length-of-employment stipulation for eligibility, the waiting period is just one day, and there is no formal limit on the duration of receipt. As a result, the sickness leave program has almost certainly encouraged abuse. As Jonas Agell (1996: 1767) notes: "According to the rules in place by the end of the 1980s, employees were entitled to a 90% compensation level from the first day of reporting sick. Due to supplementary insurance agreements in the labour market, however, many employees had a compensation level of 100%. For the first seven days of sickness leave, a physician's certificate was not required. If individuals ever respond to economic incentives, work absenteeism ought to have been widespread in Sweden. The increase in the average number of sickness days per insured employee from 13 days in 1963 to 25 days in 1988 can hardly be attributed to a deteriorating health status of the population."

In Denmark, work disincentives have been produced mainly by the unemployment insurance program. Since the early 1980s individuals have been eligible for sickness benefits for only two years, and more recently just one year. Unemployment benefits, by contrast, had no de facto duration limit prior to the mid-1990s. At that point duration was reduced to five years. This remains a comparatively long period for benefit eligibility, but the change appears to have had a beneficial impact on job-seeking and employment (Benner and Vad 2000; Björklund 2000; Goul Andersen 2002).

Sweden and Denmark have used active labor market programs such as retraining and job placement assistance to help improve the efficiency of the private-sector labor market and public employment to increase demand for labor (Ginsburg 1983; Rehn 1985; Björklund and Freeman 1997; Benner and Vad 2000; Björklund 2000; Martin 2000; Goul Andersen 2002; Kvist and Ploug 2003; OECD 2003a: 202–14; Madsen 2006). As Figure 7.10 shows, Denmark and especially Sweden have tended to commit a larger share of GDP to such programs than other countries. Sweden has long been at the forefront in use of active labor market policy. Swedish firms must notify their local board in advance when employees are to be laid off and when they have job openings that have lasted more than ten days. Workers who are displaced or who leave their job by choice can receive subsidized training through the employment service. Officials in local labor market boards keep in close communication with firms and with officials in other areas regarding trends in skill needs. The training programs are full-time and range in duration from two weeks to more than a year. The service then helps to place workers in new positions. If necessary, an employer subsidy may be used to encourage a private-sector employer to hire, or a public-sector job may be created. Denmark increased pursuit of active labor market programs in the mid-1990s, with apparently beneficial effects.

Figure 7.10 shows average levels of public employment as a share of the working-age population since the late 1970s. In these two countries the

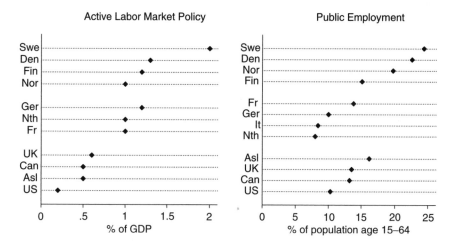

Figure 7.10. Policies to boost employment in the social democratic approach, 1979ff.

Note: Data are 1979–2001 period average for active labor market policy and 1979–97 period average for public employment. Data on active labor market policy expenditures are not available for Italy. For data definitions and sources, see the appendix.

government employs more than one in five working-age persons, compared to fewer than one in ten in a number of the other nations.

As detailed in Chapter 10, these two countries have been in the vanguard in introducing and expanding a variety of "women-friendly" policies that both encourage women to enter the labor market and facilitate their continuation in employment despite family needs. The most notable such policies are affordable childcare, paid maternity leave, public employment, supports for part-time work, and tax systems that do not discourage a second earner within households. Both countries provide very extensive provision of and generous support for high-quality child care and preschool, and both offer a generous but not-too-lengthy paid parental leave (see Figures 7.5–7.7).

Employment-Conditional Earnings Subsidies

The social democratic approach to benefits has two important drawbacks. One is that it is expensive (Björklund and Freeman 1997; Esping-Andersen 1999; Scharpf 2000; Andersen 2004; Iversen 2005). Part of the apparent cost is artificial. The Nordic countries provide generous benefits but then tax back a portion of them (Ferrarini and Nelson 2003). The measured level of expenditure and taxation is therefore exaggerated. But a substantial portion of the expense is real. As Figure 7.2 above indicates, these countries, and particularly Denmark and Sweden, offer comparatively generous net benefits to households with low market income. Sustaining the tax levels necessary for such transfers poses a significant political challenge.

The second drawback is that the generosity of the benefits creates employment disincentives. One way to alleviate this problem is to establish stringent eligibility criteria and keep the duration of benefit receipt relatively short (OECD 1994, 2005b: ch. 7; Layard and Nickell 2003). Although sensible in principle, this approach may not be so easy to implement in practice. If any countries are in position to pursue this approach, Sweden and Denmark fit the bill. As noted earlier, both have a "productivist" culture that values employment. And the governments in both countries offer an array of supports for employment, from job training and placement assistance to public-sector jobs to quality child care. These supports are likely to make stringent eligibility criteria for benefits more politically palatable. Yet both countries have struggled to some degree with what may be excessively lenient eligibility rules and/or excessively lengthy duration of particular types of benefits—Sweden with sickness compensation and Denmark with unemployment compensation.

An alternative approach is to offset the employment disincentives stemming from generous benefits by setting the wage floor at a relatively high level. As discussed in Chapter 5, however, doing so can create employment disincentives on the demand (employer) side. That is, more people may be encouraged to work by the high wages, but because wages are high employers may be unable or unwilling to hire them, at least in low-productivity positions.

A potentially effective tool for addressing this seeming impasse is an employment-conditional earnings subsidy. Such a subsidy permits lower wages at the low end of the distribution without excessive loss of household income. It also creates an employment incentive. And to the extent it promotes greater employment, it reduces expenditures on various types of benefits.

There are two main types of employment-conditional earnings subsidies (OECD 1999a, 2003b, 2004a, 2005c; Pearson and Scarpetta 2000). The Earned Income Tax Credit (EITC) in the United States and the Working Tax Credit (WTC) in the United Kingdom are examples of subsidies that are paid in the form of cash benefits—actually, refundable tax credits—to households, with the amount of the subsidy determined by household income. France, Germany, and the Netherlands, by contrast, have subsidies that take the form of a payroll-tax reduction for employees and are targeted to individuals rather than households.

The United Kingdom was the first country to introduce an employment-conditional earnings subsidy (Blundell et al. 2000; Dilnot and McCrae 2000; Brewer 2001; HM Treasury 2002). The Family Income Supplement, created in 1971, provided a means-tested benefit to adults working 24 hours or more per week with a dependent child. In 1988 the program name was changed to Family Credit. In the early 1990s the hours requirement was reduced to 16 per week, and a childcare disregard was added. In 1999 the Labour government replaced the Family Credit with the Working Families Tax Credit, substantially easing eligibility criteria and increasing the generosity of the benefit. These changes had large effects on program use and generosity. Within four years the average benefit level increased by nearly half and the number of recipients doubled (Leigh 2005: 6). In 2003 the credit was extended to childless households and the program name was changed to Working Tax Credit.

I will focus on the Earned Income Tax Credit (EITC) in the United States. The EITC was created in 1975. As of 2006, it provided a tax credit to households with at least one working adult and a pretax household income up to $36,000. The amount of the credit depends on household size and income. Figure 7.11 shows the benefit levels in 2006 for a couple with two or more children, a single adult with one child, and a single adult with no children. For a household with two or more children, the EITC provided a 40% earnings subsidy for those with earnings up to $11,000, a flat subsidy of $4,536 to those with earnings between $11,000 and $14,500, and a subsidy of $4,536 minus 21% of earnings above $14,500 for those with earnings between $14,500 and $36,000. The current level of the credit, which was established in 1993 and adjusted for inflation each year since then, is designed to ensure that a family of four with one full-time year-round minimum wage worker has an income

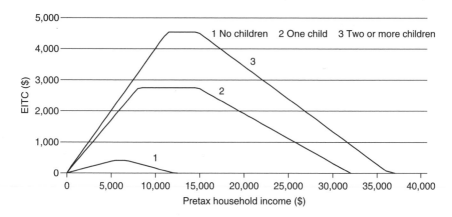

Figure 7.11. US Earned Income Tax Credit, 2006.

Note: The households are assumed here to have nonmarried adult(s); at certain pretax income levels, the benefit is slightly higher for a married couple.

Source: Center on Budget and Policy Priorities (2006).

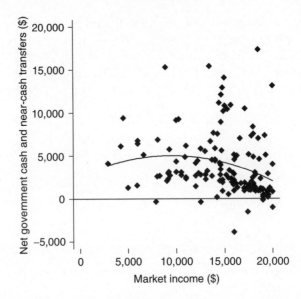

Figure 7.12. Net government transfers by market income for four-person families with two working-age employed adults and two children, United States, 2000.

Note: Dots represent households. "Net government transfers" refers to total government cash and near-cash transfers received by the household minus payroll and income taxes paid. These data are approximations, as the Luxembourg Income Study does not permit researchers to obtain data for individual households. For data definitions and sources, see the appendix.

at or above the official US poverty line through a combination of earnings, the EITC, and Food Stamps (Ellwood 1996). The EITC is refundable, which means that if it amounts to more than the household owes in federal income taxes, as is often the case, the household receives the difference as a cash refund. It therefore functions like a cash benefit.

Figure 7.12 illustrates the impact of the EITC on incomes for low-earning households. Using LIS data, it plots net government transfers (benefits minus taxes) by pretax-pretransfer income for US households with two employed adults and two children and market income of less than $20,000 in the year 2000. The dots in the chart represent households. (They are approximations, as LIS confidentiality rules prohibit researchers from accessing information about individual households.) There is considerable variation in the amount of net benefits received by such households at any given level of market income. This is to be expected, as these households may have received various types of transfers, including unemployment insurance, Temporary Assistance for Needy Families (TANF), Food Stamps, Supplemental Security Income (SSI), the Earned Income Tax Credit, and others. Still, the overall pattern is heavily influenced by the structure of the EITC.

The Earned Income Tax Credit is an effective program in several respects. First, it directly boosts the incomes of low-earning households. The EITC has been found to be more effective at increasing the incomes of low-earning households than employer hiring subsidies and the minimum wage (Dickert-Conlin and Holtz-Eakin 2000; Hotz and Scholz 2000; Neumark and Wascher 2000). This is largely because it is targeted to households rather than individuals. An employment-conditional earnings subsidy can, alternatively, be directed to individual low-wage workers (Haveman 1997). But a low-earning individual may or may not be part of a low-earning household. Since earnings tend to be pooled within households, *households* are, arguably, the unit to which subsidies should be provided (Blank 2000; Kenworthy 2004*a*). Second, studies consistently find that the EITC tends to encourage labor market participation (Blank, Card, and Robbins 2000; Hotz and Scholz 2000, 2004; Meyer and Rosenbaum 2002; Blank 2003: 1140; Hoffman and Seidman 2003). Third, the EITC is relatively inexpensive to administer. It has far lower administrative costs than more bureaucratic American programs such as AFDC-TANF and Food Stamps (Hotz and Scholz 2000). Fourth, because the EITC is implemented through the tax system, recipients avoid the discomfort and stigma associated with going to a public office to apply for assistance.

Table 7.2 offers some comparative insight into how the Earned Income Tax Credit can help to pull up incomes of low-wage workers. It compares the earnings and disposable incomes of low-wage workers in Denmark and the United States. The wage rates are representative for a hotel room cleaner as of 2006. The hourly wage in Denmark is three times that in the United States: $16.36 per hour versus $5.15. But in Denmark income taxes take a significant chunk (see Chapter 8). In the United States income taxes on earnings this low are collected only by state governments, and they are relatively small. Payroll taxes (Social Security and Medicare) also reduce net income, but again by a fairly small amount. For a household with two children (assumed here), the EITC payment significantly boosts the household's income. In the end the two households have similar disposable incomes despite the stark difference in wages.

There are important caveats. One is that if the household has only one child the EITC benefit is reduced by more than $2,000, and with no children it drops to virtually nothing. Second, the high tax payments in Denmark fund government services such as health care and childcare/preschool, which substantially boost living standards for low-income (and other) households. Third, in Denmark employees receive paid vacation equivalent to 15% of their gross earnings, which means the Danish worker receives earnings equivalent to 2,000 hours of work but in fact only has to work 1,740 hours. The point of this

Table 7.2. Earnings and posttax-posttransfer income for a hotel room cleaner in Denmark and the United States, 2006.

Denmark		
Earnings	$ 32,744	$16.36 per hour × 1,740 hours, + 15% (260 hours vacation pay)
Unemployment insurance contribution	−1, 273	
Income tax	−10, 891	
Wage subsidy (tax credit)	+120	
Subtotal	20,700	
Consumption tax	−5, 175	25% on two-thirds of net income ($20,680 × .25)
Total	$ 15,505	
United States		
Earnings	$ 10,300	$5.15 per hour × 2,000 hours
Social Security and Medicare tax	−800	7.65%
Federal income tax	−0	
State income tax	−1, 000	Estimate
Earned Income Tax Credit	+4,210	Assuming two children ($2,750 if one child; $250 if no children)
Child tax credit	+0	Kicks in at income of $12,000
Food Stamps	+2,570	Average monthly benefit as of 2006 = $214 ($214 × 12)
Subtotal	15,280	
Consumption tax	−520	5% on two-thirds of net income ($10,370 × .05)
Total	$ 14,760	

Note: Assumes two children. Conversion rate: 5.5 Danish kroner = US$1.

Source: Author's calculations with help from Niels Westergaard-Nielsen.

comparison is simply to illustrate how helpful an employment-conditional earnings subsidy can be in a low-wage context.

The EITC is now by far the most widely used cash or near-cash transfer program for working-age Americans; approximately 20% of the population receive EITC benefits (Kenworthy 2004*a*: 157). While the share of AFDC-TANF and Food Stamp recipients has dropped steadily since the mid-1990s, EITC use has remained high. This is a function of increased labor market participation among those with low skills and a 1993 expansion of eligibility criteria. As of the mid-2000s, approximately $36 billion was spent on the EITC, compared to $16 billion on TANF.

With respect to the goals of high employment and low inequality, it is clearly on the latter that the United States fares worst in comparative terms. Given the EITC's success at boosting incomes while simultaneously encouraging employment, one policy strategy for moving toward jobs with equality in the United States might center on increasing the generosity of the EITC. This would need to be complemented by an increase in the minimum wage.

Suppose we believe a minimally decent income for a family of one adult and two children is $22,000 after taxes and transfers. As of 2006, the official poverty line for a household of this size and composition was approximately $16,000, which is almost certainly far too low. A decade earlier, in 1996, the median response of Americans to a Gallup Poll asking "How much income do you feel your family would need just to get by?" was $30,000 (cited in Schiller 2001: 18). A 2001 study of the cost of living in metropolitan and rural areas throughout the United States concluded that the amount of money required to meet a "basic family budget" is two to three times the official US poverty line (Boushey et al. 2001: 11). This implies somewhere between $30,000 and $45,000. So let's use $22,000 as a very conservative estimate of a minimum acceptable income for a family of three.

How can this family get to $22,000? Suppose the adult works full-time year-round at a minimum wage job. She or he earns $10,712 ($5.15 per hour, the 2006 minimum wage level, multiplied by 2,080 hours per year). Payroll (Social Security and Medicare) taxes will reduce this by about $700, leaving approximately $10,000. Let's assume no federal or state income taxes are owed. Food Stamps would add approximately $2,000 (Stoker and Wilson 2006: 92). This yields roughly $12,000. To get to $22,000, the family needs an additional $10,000. As of 2006, this family would receive $4,200 from the EITC. Thus, the EITC benefit level would need to be more than doubled in order for this family to reach $22,000 in posttax-posttransfer income.

EITC payouts total approximately $36 billion. At first glance, then, doubling the benefit level presumably would cost approximately twice this much. Government cash social expenditures on the working-age population in the United States totaled about $240 billion (and a great deal more is spent on Social Security and Medicare), so doubling the EITC would represent an addition to social spending on this segment of the population of about 15%. That is certainly affordable. And it would not be unprecedented: the 1993 expansion of the EITC doubled the value of the credit for most households.

But a doubling of the benefit level would likely cost substantially more than this. The reason has to do with the phase-out range of the credit. Suppose that the maximum value of the credit for a family of four continued to kick in at a pretax income of $11,500 and that the phaseout continued to begin at $14,500. If the credit continued to decrease to zero at a pretax income of $36,000, the phase-out rate—the slope of the line on the right side of Figure 7.11—would increase sharply. This might create nontrivial work disincentives. That is especially true for two-adult households: because the level of the EITC benefit is based on total household income, it can potentially deter labor market entry for a spouse when her/his partner has a paying job with earnings at some point in the phase-out region (OECD 2003*b*: 118–19). At the current phase-out rate, this disincentive appears to have relatively little impact (Wasow 2000).

If the EITC benefit level were doubled, the credit would have to extend to households farther up the income distribution in order to keep the phase-out rate the same as it is now. To be precise, the credit would reach zero for families of three (one adult and two children) with a pretax income of approximately $58,000. That is almost exactly the median for a household of this size and type. Because the income distribution is roughly bell-shaped (though with a pronounced skew at high income levels), there are many households in the middle of the distribution. Thus, making those in the middle of the distribution eligible for the EITC would dramatically increase the number of recipients. While this would enlarge the base of political support for the program, it also would substantially increase its cost. The latter could prove to be a sizable political problem.

An alternative way to achieve the desired end would be to combine an increase in the EITC benefit level with an increase in the minimum wage (Blank 2001; Sawhill and Thomas 2001). Suppose, for instance, that the minimum wage were increased to $7.50 per hour. Now annual earnings in a minimum wage job would be approximately $15,600. Payroll taxes would subtract $1,200, and Food Stamps would again add about $1,600. This leaves $16,000, so our three-person family needs $6,000 to reach $22,000. At this earnings level the family currently would receive about $4,000 from the EITC. Now, in other words, the EITC would need to be increased by approximately 1.5 times, rather than doubled.

This calculation applies to only one type of household, of course. But it illustrates the point that it would be difficult to rely on the Earned Income Tax Credit alone to pull single-adult families up to even a fairly low income. An additional reason for combining an increase in the EITC with an increase in the minimum wage, rather than relying solely on the EITC, is to ensure that both taxpayers and employers, rather than the former alone, bear the cost of ensuring decent incomes for those at the low end of the distribution.

Aside from the potentially large financial cost of a substantial increase in its generosity, are there other reasons to be less than fully enthusiastic about using the Earned Income Tax Credit as the centerpiece of a jobs-with-equality strategy for the United States? The policy does have some limitations and drawbacks.

One limitation is that, as Figure 7.11 indicates, the EITC benefit for households with no children is very low. It should be increased.

A second is underutilization, which results from the fact that a household cannot receive the credit without filing a federal income tax return. An estimated 15–20% of those eligible fail to claim the credit (Center on Budget and Policy Priorities 2002).

A third drawback is fraud. A study of 1999 filings by the Internal Revenue Service found that claims for the EITC exceeded the amount to which filers were actually eligible by approximately 30% (Hotz and Scholz 2002: 13). However, this seems likely to have been an overestimate, and new compliance measures enacted in subsequent years have almost certainly reduced this (Greenstein 2003). For purposes of comparison, data on overall US tax compliance suggest that approximately 15–20% of total taxes owed are not paid.

Fourth, a generous EITC could potentially allow employers to keep wages artificially low or even reduce them. We have little information on the extent to which this has occurred thus far. Prior to 1993 the EITC benefit was almost certainly too low to have had any such impact. The real value of the benefit was effectively doubled in the years immediately after 1993. Yet from 1995 to 2000, real wages and earnings at the low end of the American labor market increased for the first time in more than two decades (Mishel, Bernstein, and Allegretto 2007). This seemingly contradicts the expectation that employers might use a generous earnings subsidy to freeze or reduce wages. But the mid-to-late 1990s was a boom period for the American economy, with a tight labor market. It is impossible to know what would have happened in the counterfactual scenario of an expanded EITC without an economic boom. Hence we have little evidence to help us assess the effect of a generous EITC on wage levels and trends.

A fifth concern has to do with the impact of the EITC on the underlying structure of the labor market. Subsidizing low-wage jobs means forgoing the opportunity to force employers to improve productivity (Bertola 2000). It reduces the incentive for individuals in low-wage jobs to upgrade their skills in order to advance up the earnings ladder. More fundamentally, it signals a commitment by citizens and policy makers to a low-wage economy. For some, this is the wrong choice to make. Instead, affluent countries should seek to upgrade the occupational and earnings structure so that a progressively larger share of the population is employed in jobs requiring moderate-to-high skills and paying moderate-to-high wages. Although this is an appealing vision, I am skeptical. As societies increase in affluence, citizens tend to spend a larger share of discretionary income on consumer and personal services: medical care, childcare, restaurants, hotels, and cleaning. People become more willing to pay someone to keep them healthy, to help take care of their children, to prepare and serve them meals, to keep their home and yard and clothes clean.

These jobs expand in numbers, seemingly inexorably. That is not a bad thing in and of itself. It provides opportunity for more people to be employed. The problem, as discussed in Chapter 5, is that productivity levels in these jobs are relatively low and difficult to increase. Hence there are limits to pay levels. Should we try to reduce the number of such jobs? Or should we accept them, even embrace them, and find a way to ensure decent incomes for those who work in them? My inclination is that the latter is the more sensible choice.

Finally, one of the chief appeals of the Earned Income Tax Credit is that it can potentially contribute to low inequality by increasing employment and thereby helping to finance a generous welfare state in a context of population aging and constraints on taxation. But if the policy consists of government payments to low-income households, will it really add to government revenues? Or might it actually cost more (Dickens and Ellwood 2001; Iversen 2005: 254, 256)? It is difficult to be sure about this, but there are several reasons for optimism. First, subsidizing low earnings is cheaper than paying full support (e.g. social assistance) to such people. Second, those who are employed and therefore eligible for the EITC pay payroll taxes. (Indeed, the EITC was initially conceived of by policy makers not as a transfer, but rather as a refund for the payroll taxes paid by low earners.) Third, those who become employed in order to qualify for the EITC will increase their work experience and perhaps other forms of human capital. At least some will later rise in the earnings ladder and thus no longer be recipients of the credit. A fourth consideration has to do with the EITC's direct impact on income inequality—that is, apart from its effect on government revenues. The EITC reduces household income inequality directly, by lowering the number of households that have no earners.

Would an employment-conditional earnings subsidy in the form of a cash payment or tax credit for low-income households be a useful policy tool for the Nordic and/or continental European countries? Three of these nations, Finland, France, and the Netherlands, have adopted one, but in all three cases the level of the benefit is quite small. The "Earned Income Allowance" in Finland is a tax deduction; it reduces the amount of income tax owed. The "*prime pour l'emploi*" (PPE) in France is a refundable tax credit like the EITC and WTC. The "Combination Tax Credit" in the Netherlands is a nonrefundable tax credit. The maximum value of the benefit is less than 3% of the country's average production worker wage in France, less than 2% in Finland, and less than 1% in the Netherlands (OECD 2005c: 141–4). For the US Earned Income Tax Credit and the UK Working Tax Credit, the corresponding figures are 13% and 35%, respectively.

Instead, France, Germany, and the Netherlands have prioritized a different form of employment-conditional subsidy: a reduction or elimination of payroll taxes paid by employees with low earnings and/or in particular types of low-paying jobs.

There are several reasons why the continental countries have preferred to offer the subsidy as a payroll-tax reduction rather than as a cash subsidy or tax credit to households. The most important is that payroll taxes are heavy in these countries (see Chapter 8). In Germany, for example, employees pay 21% of their earnings in payroll taxes. Elimination of the tax thus amounts to a 21% earnings subsidy.

Second, key political parties, unions, and many citizens in these countries do not want to embrace a US-style labor market with a sizable low-wage segment. Adoption of an EITC-style earnings subsidy is viewed as a movement in that direction.

Others, who might favor a shift toward lower wages at the bottom of the labor market with those wages supplemented by a tax credit for households, see a practical impediment. In most European countries (France and the Netherlands are exceptions), it is not governments but rather unions that determine the minimum wage level. And unions are resistant to an increase in wage inequality, not to mention an absolute reduction in wage levels at the low end of the distribution.

Might it be useful for Nordic and/or continental countries to introduce a household-based subsidy/credit even if low-end wages do not drop? If the bottom half of the wage distribution is relatively compressed, policy makers may feel compelled to make the subsidy's phase-out (withdrawal) rate fairly steep. Otherwise, a very large share of the population will qualify for the subsidy, which can dramatically increase the program's cost. But as noted earlier, a steep phase-out rate creates work disincentives in the phase-out range.

Yet for a "universal" welfare state such as those in the Nordic countries, a household-based tax credit for which a sizable share of households qualify is not necessarily problematic. Many benefit programs in these countries are structured so that even households well above the low end of the income distribution are potentially eligible. This structure is viewed as creating strong and stable political support for such programs (Korpi and Palme 1998; Rothstein 1998). The cost is held down by taxing a portion of such benefits via the income tax. The same could be done with a household-based employment-conditional earnings subsidy or tax credit.

An additional perceived practical impediment is the difficulty of administering a tax credit directed to households in a country in which the tax system is individualized—that is, in which the tax unit is the individual rather than the household or family. This, however, is not an insurmountable problem. The United Kingdom has had an individualized tax system since 1990 and yet has a household-based earnings subsidy. The default is that the benefit is paid to the mother, though if both spouses agree it can instead be paid to the father.

Each of these considerations is relevant, and some or all of them may continue to discourage the Nordic and continental countries from adopting a US- or UK-style employment-conditional earnings subsidy. The individualized payroll-tax-reduction subsidies currently used in France, Germany, and the Netherlands may be appropriate given the circumstances of those countries. Mark Pearson and Stefano Scarpetta (2000: 19) argue as much in a review of research on policies to "make work pay":

It seems that countries fall into two camps. In those with a low tax-benefit environment and relatively low minimum wages, the essential problem is to encourage labour supply and to provide higher incomes for those in poorly paid jobs. In these circumstances, it seems reasonable to place greater stress on in-work benefits. By contrast, in countries with high levels of taxes and benefits and relatively high wage floors, making work pay schemes are likely to have high fiscal costs and risk reinforcing disincentive effects related to higher marginal effective tax rates. As a result, policy interventions in the second group of countries should probably focus on wage subsidies, as the essential problem is one of increasing labour demand for low-skilled or inexperienced workers.

Then again, analyses of the US labor market have found that a relatively small share of individuals at the low end of the wage distribution in the United States live in households similarly far down in the household income distribution (Dickert-Conlin and Holtz-Eakin 2000: 4; Sawhill and Thomas 2001: 17–18). Though the magnitude of the phenomenon may differ, the same is likely true in other countries. There is, therefore, a compelling argument to be made in favor of households rather than individuals as the unit to which the subsidy should be directed.

An employment-conditional earnings subsidy might also be useful for Australia and Canada. Labor market and social policy in Australia have a very different history than in any of the other countries, including the three other Anglo nations. Until the early 1980s, Australia's economy was structured around commodity exports and a high level of protection of domestic product markets. For approximately a century this was successful at generating high living standards for the population. Social policy worked largely through employment. Product market protection plus Keynesian demand management ensured full employment. Wages set through a centralized arbitration system ensured a decent family wage for those with jobs. Government transfers were minimal but heavily targeted to those whose livelihood was not effectively ensured through the labor market. For the working class, the chief advantage of the minimalistic welfare state was very low taxation.

By the early 1980s it was clear that the old system based around protection of the domestic market and full employment for male breadwinners was no longer feasible. With globalization, higher unemployment, more single-adult families (particularly single mothers), and a need for wage restraint, it was no longer possible to rely so heavily on wages to secure decent incomes for households at the low end of the distribution. Under five successive Labour governments from 1983 to 1996, the system was transformed, in some respects gradually and in others rapidly (Castles 1996; Pierson 2002).

The generosity of some types of benefits has been increased and new programs have been introduced to fill in gaps in the system (Whiteford and Angenent 2002). The heavily targeted character of benefit programs has been maintained, and actually accentuated. Australia is the only one of the four Anglo countries in which government expenditures on transfers directed to working-age households has increased as a share of GDP since the late 1970s, and as of the early 2000s the level of such expenditures was higher than in the other three (Figure 3.9). The country has a statutory minimum wage, and as I noted in Chapter 5 the level of that minimum is high compared to that in other affluent nations. Wage inequality has not increased since the late 1970s (Figure 5.6).

This new system has functioned reasonably effectively up until now. But it is premised on a societal norm of having mothers stay home with their children until formal schooling begins, whether there is an employed father (or other adult in the home) or not. To the extent this changes, due to shifting norms or a need for higher employment, there may be a rationale for allowing the minimum wage to fall a bit and compensating with an employment-conditional subsidy (Dawkins 2001).

As noted in Chapter 5, Canada's statutory minimum wage is only slightly higher than that in the United States, and thus not particularly high by comparative standards. An employment-conditional earnings subsidy could therefore be a useful policy tool. Since 1993 Canada has had a refundable tax credit, the Universal Child Benefit (Myles and Pierson 1997). But it is not conditional on employment; instead it goes to all low-income families with children. Given the economic and political centrality of the child benefit, it may be through the provinces that an employment-conditional subsidy is most likely to be developed. Indeed, Quebec has introduced such a subsidy, the *Prime au travail*. The maximum amount of the benefit is for a couple with two or more children, at 7% of average production worker pay (OECD 2005c: 141).

CONCLUSION

Generous benefits for those with low market incomes are critical to effective redistribution, which in turn is key to successful pursuit of low income
inequality (Figure 7.3 and Chapter 3). A generation ago the chief constraint on
benefit generosity was the level of taxation a country's citizens were willing to
accept. But governments are now more constrained in their ability to raise tax
rates, and in coming decades a larger share of government revenues will have
to be devoted to pensions and health care for a growing elderly population. A
high employment rate can help to fund generous benefits. Affluent countries
thus need to be more attentive than ever to the employment disincentives
created by such benefits.

The macrocomparative evidence examined in this chapter suggests that
benefit generosity may have contributed to cross-country differences in
employment growth since the 1970s. But it also suggests that if so, the magnitude of the effect may not have been very large. Radical reductions in benefit
generosity are therefore unlikely to be necessary to produce reasonably healthy
employment rates.

A benefit package conducive to low inequality and high employment
might usefully include much of what the Nordic countries, and in particular
Denmark and Sweden, have done over the past several decades coupled with
an employment-conditional earnings subsidy.

8

Taxes

Taxes can contribute to reducing income inequality in two ways. First, to the extent they are progressively structured, they reduce inequality directly. Second, taxes provide the chief source of funding for redistributive transfers (as well as for public services). Taxes also affect employment. However, here the main question is not how helpful the tax system is, but rather how much harm it does. There is widespread concern that high levels of taxation, or at least of particular types of taxes, reduce employment. What impact have taxes had on inequality and employment in the twelve countries? What levels and types of taxation have been most effective at facilitating redistribution without impeding employment? What improvements could be made?

TAXES AND INEQUALITY

Inequality Reduction via Taxation

Progressive tax systems—that is, systems in which individuals or households with higher incomes pay a larger share of their income in taxes than do those with lower incomes—can substantially reduce the degree of inequality in the distribution of income. Imagine, for example, a country in which the richest households pay 50% of their income in taxes while the poorest pay none. Even if there were no government transfers to low-income households (all of the tax revenue were spent on services such as education, health care, and policing), there would be considerably less inequality of posttax-posttransfer income than of pretax-pretransfer income.

In practice, however, most of the inequality reduction in affluent countries is achieved via transfers rather than taxes (see also Kesselman and Cheung 2006; Piketty and Saez 2007a; Whiteford 2007). This is shown in Figures 8.1 and 8.2. These data represent the amount of reduction in income inequality achieved by taxes and by transfers in the twelve countries. Unfortunately, in the Luxembourg Income Study data it is not possible to separate out the effect of taxes for France or Italy, so these two countries are not included in

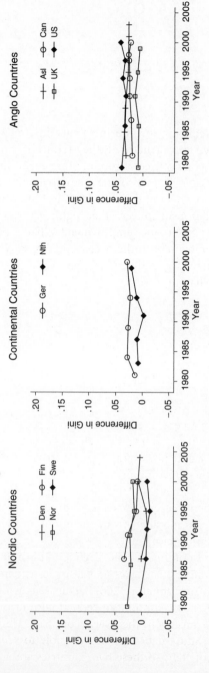

Figure 8.1. Inequality reduction via taxes for working-age households, 1979ff.

Note: Inequality reduction via taxes is calculated as Gini for household pretax-pretransfer income minus Gini for household posttax-pretransfer income. Vertical axis scale is the same as for inequality reduction via transfers in Figure 8.2. France and Italy are not included because it is not possible to measure inequality reduction via taxes for those two countries. For data definitions and sources, see the appendix.

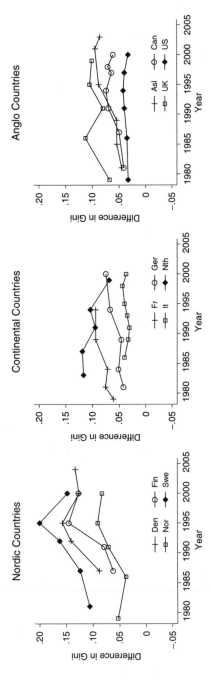

Figure 8.2. Inequality reduction via transfers for working-age households, 1979ff.

Note: Inequality reduction via transfers is calculated as Gini for household pretax-pretransfer income minus Gini for household pretax-posttransfer income. Vertical axis scale is the same as for inequality reduction via taxes in Figure 8.1. For data definitions and sources, see the appendix.

Figure 8.1. As in previous chapters, the data are for households with working-age "heads" only (see Mahler and Jesuit 2006 for similar data that cover the full population).

In the Nordic countries, which are the most redistributive overall, tax systems contribute virtually nothing to inequality reduction. And in some years they have been slightly regressive—increasing, rather than reducing, the degree of income inequality among working-age households. By contrast, in three of the four Anglo countries—Australia, Canada, and the United States— as well as in Germany, the tax system has played a nontrivial role in inequality reduction. Taxes have been particularly important in the United States, where in most years since the late 1970s taxes have contributed roughly the same amount as transfers to reducing household income inequality. This is partly because the US tax system has tended to achieve a bit more inequality reduction than those in other countries. (This is not a function of the Earned Income Tax Credit, which is counted as a transfer in the LIS database.) But it is also because the US transfer system is not especially redistributive.

In most of the countries transfers are responsible for the bulk of inequality reduction. Indeed, the data in Figure 8.1 overstate the degree of inequality reduction achieved by taxes, because they do not account for consumption taxes (sales and value added taxes). Only income taxes and employee payroll taxes are included in the LIS data. Consumption taxes typically are regressive. Those with lower incomes tend to consume a larger share of their income than do those with higher incomes, and the taxes are levied at a flat rate. Hence, low-income households tend to pay a larger share of their income in consumption taxes than do high-income households. If consumption taxes were included, the amount of inequality reduction among working-age households achieved by taxes would be even less than what is suggested by Figure 8.1.

Taxes as the Revenue Source for Inequality Reduction via Transfers

Even if taxes tend to play a circumscribed direct role in reducing inequality in most countries, they nevertheless are vital to redistribution. After all, the level of revenues raised via taxation determines the amount that can be paid out in transfers. (This is true mainly in the long run, as in any given year countries can finance expenditures not only with current revenues but also with borrowing.) Figure 8.3 plots two measures of transfer generosity—government cash social expenditures directed toward the working-age population as a share of GDP and inequality reduction via transfers for working-age households—by tax revenues as a share of GDP. The data are for the year 2000. The associations are positive and fairly strong: $r = .79$ and $.70$. And with the partial exceptions

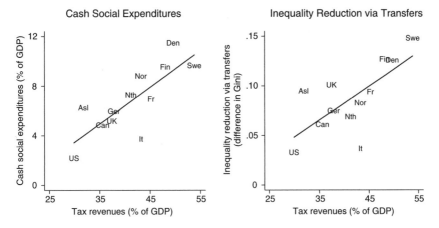

Figure 8.3. Cash social expenditures on the working-age population and inequality reduction via transfers for working-age households by tax revenues, 2000.

Note: Horizontal axes are truncated. For data definitions and sources, see the appendix.

of Australia and the United Kingdom, all of the countries with high levels of cash transfers and inequality reduction via transfers have high tax revenues.

Figure 8.4 shows trends in the level of tax revenues as a share of GDP in the twelve nations since 1979. Revenue levels differ markedly across the three groups: they are highest in the Nordic countries, followed by the continental countries, and lowest in the Anglo countries. There are exceptions. Prior to the mid-1990s, the level in the Netherlands was on par with those of the Nordic countries. As of 2006 Norway and Finland, which are at the low end among the Nordic countries, were similar to France and Italy. And the level in Germany, at the low end of the continental group, was about the same as in Canada and the United Kingdom. Still, the differences between groups are quite marked. As of the mid-2000s, tax revenues averaged 47% of GDP in the Nordic countries, 40% in the continental nations, and 32% in the Anglo countries.

The Tax Mix

We might expect that in countries where labor is strong, leftist parties have been prominent in government, and social programs are comparatively generous, taxation would be focused heavily on capital rather than labor. However, as a number of analysts have noted recently, that is not the case (Becker and Mulligan 1998; Joumard 2002: 126; Steinmo 2002; Wilensky 2002: ch. 10; Kato 2003; Lindert 2004: 235–45; Cusack and Beramendi 2004; Ganghof 2005*a*, 2005*b*,2005*c*; Morgan 2005). Figure 8.5 plots tax revenues as a share of GDP

Jobs with Equality

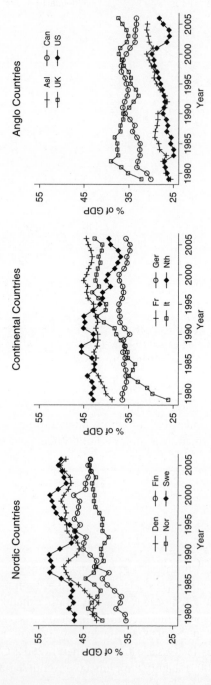

Figure 8.4. Tax revenues as a share of GDP, 1979ff.

Note: Vertical axes are truncated. For data definitions and sources, see the appendix.

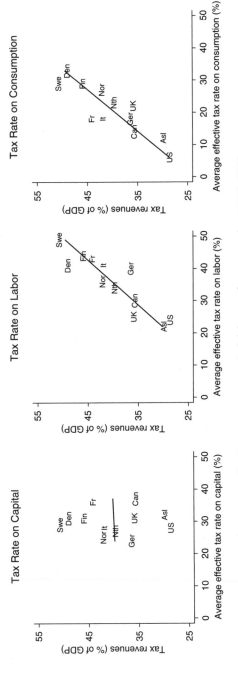

Figure 8.5. Tax revenues by average effective tax rates on capital, labor, and consumption, 1995–2002.

Note: Vertical axes are truncated. For data definitions and sources, see the appendix.

averaged over 1995–2002 by the average effective tax rate on capital (capital income and corporate profits), labor (wage and salary income and payroll taxes), and consumption (goods and services) over the same years. Average effective tax rates take into account not only the statutory rate but also exemptions and deductions. As the chart indicates, there is no association whatsoever between the tax rate on capital and the total amount of tax revenue collected. By contrast, the association between both labor taxation and consumption taxation and tax revenues is quite strong. Countries with high tax revenues and generous social policies tend to rely mainly on taxing labor incomes and consumption rather than capital.

What accounts for this seemingly paradoxical pattern? One hypothesis is that this is a product of political exchange: leftist parties keep capital taxation at low or moderate levels and in return employers and right-of-center parties acquiesce to generous transfer programs (Steinmo 2002; Wilensky 2002: ch. 10).

A second is that leftist parties in strong-labor countries choose not to impose high tax rates on capital in order to enhance economic growth (Lindert 2004: 235–45). In this view, social democrats in Sweden, Denmark, and elsewhere have elected to rely mainly on taxes on wage and salary income, payroll, and consumption in order to promote savings and investment and thereby offset any efficiency reductions stemming from high overall taxes and transfers.

A third is that regardless of preference or political ideology, policy makers no longer have much leeway in choosing the tax rate on capital (Ganghof 2005c). Extensive capital mobility creates a prisoner's dilemma for governments. Each country would be better off (in terms of revenue collection) if policy makers could cooperate to set higher tax rates on capital, but in the absence of an effective enforcement mechanism each has an incentive to reduce its rate in order to attract foreign capital or at least to avoid capital flight.

Whatever the cause(s), the charts in Figure 8.5 indicate that countries with generous transfer programs rely heavily on taxation of labor and consumption to finance them. What does this imply for the progressivity of the tax system? Income taxes typically are progressive, in that the tax rate is higher for those with higher incomes. Deductions and exemptions reduce the degree of progressivity, but by no means fully. To the extent tax systems achieve progressivity, they do so mainly through income taxes (Messere, de Kam, and Heady 2003; Verbist 2004; Ganghof 2005c). Consumption taxes tend to be regressive. They are levied at a flat rate, and since those with lower incomes by necessity spend (rather than save) more of their incomes, a larger portion of their incomes is subject to consumption taxes. The degree of regressivity can be altered by exempting certain types of items, such as housing and basic foods, from the consumption tax. Payroll taxes also tend to be regressive. They too are generally levied at a flat rate. And because there often is a cap on the earnings subject to the tax, the portion of earnings that is taxed tends to be smaller for high earners than for low earners.

Some observers have argued that in the age of capital mobility, countries can maintain a high level of tax revenues only if the bulk of revenues comes from nonincome sources—namely, payroll and consumption taxes (Becker and Mulligan 1998; Wilensky 2002: ch. 10; Kato 2003). However, Steffen Ganghof (2005a, 2005b, 2005c) has pointed out that the pressure for low tax rates applies mainly to a particular type of income: corporate profits and capital income. There is much less pressure on taxation of wage and salary income. Hence, if policy makers are willing to tax wage and salary income at a different rate than capital income and corporate profits (a so-called "dual income tax"), they can choose to rely heavily on income taxes rather than payroll and consumption taxes to finance a large welfare state. The advantage of doing so is that the tax system is likely to be more progressive than it would be if the same quantity of revenues were to be generated from payroll and/or consumption taxes. Denmark pioneered this type of system in the early 1980s, and all of the Nordic countries have made use of it during the past two decades.

Is a High Level of Taxation Sustainable?

In the 1990s, conventional wisdom held that globalization—in particular, capital mobility—would engender a "race to the bottom" in taxation, with countries forced to steadily reduce taxes in order to prevent capital flight. The data in Figure 8.4 (above) suggest that so far this has not occurred (see also Kenworthy 1997; Garrett 1998; Swank 1998, 2002; Kiser and Long 2001; Swank and Steinmo 2002; Messere, de Kam, and Heady 2003; Campbell 2004). In most of the countries, tax revenues around 2000 were at or near their all-time high level. Revenues did tend to drop in the early 2000s, but that is typical in periods of economic downturn. The same thing happened in the early 1980s and the early 1990s.

Yet this does not mean globalization has had no impact on tax systems (Steinmo 1994; Ganghof 2000, 2005c; Genschel 2002; Devereux, Griffith, and Klemm 2002; Messere, de Kam, and Heady 2003; Slemrod 2004; Swank 2005). There has indeed been heightened pressure on governments to reduce tax rates. But thus far that pressure has been confined largely to statutory rates on capital income and corporate profits. These have been lowered. Revenues have not fallen because reduction of statutory tax rates has been offset in various ways: by reducing tax exemptions and deductions on capital income and by increasing rates or broadening the base for taxes on wage and salary income, payroll, and consumption. In addition, there have been countervailing pressures for tax increases, such as higher unemployment, population aging, and formal restrictions on budget deficits. In the absence of capital mobility and tax competition, such pressures very likely would have led to sharp increases in tax revenues.

Globalization is not the only threat to high taxation. Another concern is that a high-tax redistributive strategy might be self-defeating. As countless critics of generous welfare states have noted, one potential impact of high taxes is to reduce economic growth. Taxes may diminish incentives for investment and work, distort the market allocation of resources, and produce deadweight losses in the form of administrative and other costs. If high levels of taxation do indeed reduce economic growth, citizens might eventually press for tax reductions or policy makers might decide on their own that such reductions are needed. As a result, high-tax countries may tend to shift toward a more moderate level of taxation, reducing their redistributive capacity.

Figure 8.6 provides some data relevant to assessing whether or not this hypothetical scenario has played out in any of the twelve countries. The first chart plots the average annual growth rate of real per capita GDP over the period 1970–2005 by tax revenues as a share of GDP averaged over 1965–80. Using tax revenue data for an earlier period helps to reduce the likelihood of reverse causality (1965 is the earliest year for which data are available). Consistent with a variety of earlier findings (Korpi 1985; Kenworthy 1995: ch. 4;

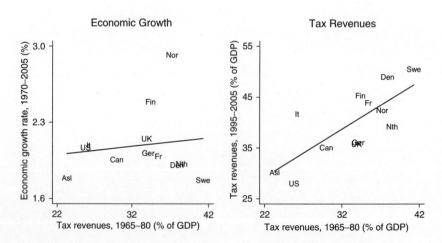

Figure 8.6. Economic growth 1970–2005 and tax revenues 1995–2005 by tax revenues 1965–80.

Note: Chart axes are truncated. For data definitions and sources, see the appendix.

Slemrod 1995; Slemrod and Bakija 2004: ch. 4; though see also Kenworthy 2004*a*: ch. 4), the chart suggests no systematic tendency for high-tax countries to have had slower economic growth. Then again, the three highest-tax countries—Sweden, Denmark, and the Netherlands—are among the four nations with the weakest growth performance over these three and a half decades.

For my purposes here, the key question is whether the experience of comparatively slow growth in these three countries produced a backlash against, and consequent reduction of, high tax levels. The second chart in Figure 8.6 plots tax revenues in 1995–2005 by tax revenues in 1965–80. The association is positive and quite strong, offering little evidence to support the notion that high-tax countries tend to eventually elect to significantly moderate their level of taxation.

In spite of their comparatively low rates of economic growth since the early 1970s, Sweden and Denmark continue to have by far the highest levels of tax revenues. Both of these countries instituted significant tax reforms in the past two decades, but in neither case were the reforms intended to produce sizable reductions in effective tax rates or in revenues. Denmark implemented major reforms in 1985, 1993, and 1998 (Ganghof 2005*b*). The 1985 reform first introduced a dual income tax. The statutory rate on capital income and corporate profits was set at 50%, while various deductions and exemptions were reduced or eliminated. The top marginal tax rate on wage and salary income was set at 68%. The ensuing reforms steadily reduced the tax rates on both types of income while balancing these rate decreases with further reductions in exemptions and deductions.

Sweden's most important tax reform occurred in 1991. Its key features resembled those of the reforms in Denmark, as detailed by Sven Steinmo (2002: 850; see also Norrman and McLure 1997):

With this reform, Sweden took a huge step from a tax system that relied on very high marginal rates softened with very deep tax loopholes to a broader based tax system in which tax rates were reduced substantially for all taxpayers and tax expenditures [exemptions and deductions] were radically scaled back. Not only was the top tax rate on income reduced from more than 80% to 50%, but the tax system was simplified to the point where more than 85% of taxpayers no longer submitted a tax return at all. After this reform, the tax code possessed so few write-offs that the government would simply send a letter to the taxpayer showing the amount of income he or she had earned in the year and asking the taxpayer to confirm that she or he had no extra (not already taxed) income.... Corporate and capital taxation were also radically reformed. Now all capital income faced a flat 30% rate and deductions were substantially rolled back. The Corporate Profits Tax was also reformed. The marginal tax rate was reduced from 57% to 30% at the same time that many of the most generous tax expenditures available in the code were eliminated.

Although tax revenues in Sweden declined following the 1991 reform (Figure 8.4), that was due in large part to the severe economic crisis of the early 1990s.

The Netherlands, on the other hand, did shift from being one of the highest-tax countries to a moderate-tax country in the late 1990s. It dropped from second among the twelve nations in tax revenues' share of GDP in 1965–80 to seventh in 1995–2005. Beginning in the early 1980s, a series of Dutch governments made a commitment to fiscal balance (Seils 2002; Woldendorp 2005). This led to a string of spending decreases and income and payroll-tax reductions, particularly in the 1990s. This trajectory was facilitated and encouraged by the sharp rise in employment that occurred between the mid-1980s and the early 1990s and then again from the mid-1990s through the early 2000s (Figure 3.2), which produced a reduction in government transfer payments to nonelderly households (Figure 3.9). It is possible to interpret the tax reductions in the Netherlands as a response to the country's poor economic performance in the 1970s and early 1980s. But whether that poor performance was a product of high taxation is questionable. And the tax reductions might not have continued had it not been for the health of the Dutch economy since the mid-1980s (Seils 2002).

Taxes and Inequality: Summing Up

Tax systems in the twelve countries do relatively little to reduce inequality directly (Figure 8.1). The bulk of inequality reduction is achieved via transfers (Figure 8.2). What differentiates high-redistribution and low-redistribution countries is mainly the *level* of taxation, rather than the degree of progressivity of the tax system (Figure 8.3). Indeed, tax systems in high-redistribution countries tend to be less progressive than those in low-redistribution countries.

Some analysts have suggested that a high level of tax revenues requires high consumption and/or payroll taxes. It is true that high-tax countries differ from low-tax countries primarily in the degree to which they tax labor rather than capital (Figure 8.5). Yet that difference stems not just from higher payroll and/or consumption taxes but also from higher taxes on wage and salary income.

There are two principal threats to high taxation. One is capital mobility. But while this has led to reduction of statutory tax rates on corporate profits and capital income, countries have been able to maintain revenue levels by base broadening and by increasing revenues from other taxes (Figure 8.4). The second threat is that high taxation will reduce economic growth and thereby engender a tax backlash. However, this has not come to pass to any significant degree (Figure 8.6).

TAXES AND EMPLOYMENT

Taxes may reduce employment for a variety of reasons. On the demand side, taxes on income and corporate profits may diminish job creation by reducing incentives to save, invest, expand output, or start new businesses. Taxes on payroll paid by employers increase nonwage labor costs. Taxes on consumption are likely to raise the price of goods and services, potentially reducing consumer demand and therefore employer revenues. Taxes on income and taxes on payroll paid by employees may lead to employee (or union) demands for higher wages to compensate for the tax payments, thereby increasing labor costs for employers. On the supply side, income taxes and employee-contributed payroll taxes lessen the financial gain from employment, reducing the incentive to work.

Comparative Patterns

A number of recent comparative studies have found empirical support for the notion that high taxes are bad for employment performance (OECD 1994: ch. 9, 1995, 2006*b*; Nickell 1997; Scharpf 1997, 2000; Elmeskov, Martin, and Scarpetta 1998; Nickell and Layard 1999; Esping-Andersen 2000*b*; Daveri and Tabellini 2002; Kenworthy 2004*a*: ch. 5; Kemmerling 2005; Bassanini and Duval 2006). Some, however, do not (Baker et al. 2005). Virtually all of these studies have focused on unemployment.

The first chart in Figure 8.7 shows that there is no association across the twelve countries between taxation levels and employment levels. However, that could be a legacy of the period prior to globalization, heightened domestic competition, declining manufacturing employment, and falling demand for less-skilled workers. If high-tax countries had higher employment rates than low-tax countries prior to the 1980s, adverse effects of high taxation since then might not yet be visible if we examine levels of employment. A more useful test is to examine the impact of taxation on *changes* in employment in recent decades.

The second chart in Figure 8.7 plots change in employment from 1979 to 2000–06 by the average level of tax revenues as a share of GDP over 1979–2006. Employment change is measured as the 2000–06 employment rate minus the

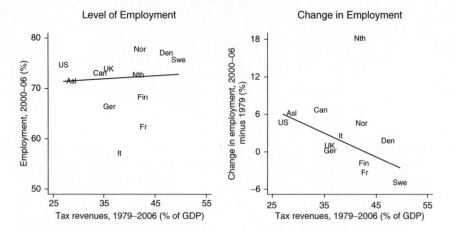

Figure 8.7. Employment levels and employment changes by tax revenues.

Note: Some axes are truncated. Regression line in the first chart is calculated with Italy excluded; the line in the second chart is calculated with the Netherlands excluded. For data definitions and sources, see the appendix.

1979 employment rate. (As noted in Chapter 4, adjusting employment change for countries' employment levels in 1979 does not alter the pattern.) The Netherlands is a distinct outlier; I exclude it in calculating the regression line in the chart. For the other eleven countries there is a strong negative association between tax revenues and employment change: $r = -.71$.

Is the Problem the Level of Taxation or the Type of Taxes?

Some analysts suggest that adverse employment effects are generated by particular types of taxes rather than by the overall level of taxation (OECD 1995: 68, 97; Scharpf 1997, 2000; Kemmerling 2005). In this view, payroll and consumption taxes are especially detrimental to employment in low-productivity services. Fritz Scharpf (1997) puts the argument as follows:

The negative impact on service employment is particularly acute in those countries which, like Germany and France, rely to a large extent on payroll taxes for the financing of the welfare state. In Germany, for instance, 74% of total social expenditures were financed through workers' and employers' contributions to social insurance systems in 1991, and in France that was true of 82%. In Germany, these contributions presently amount to about 42% of the total wage paid by the employer.... If the net wage of the worker cannot fall below a guaranteed minimum [the level of unemployment benefits and social assistance], the consequence is that any social insurance contributions, payroll taxes, and wage taxes that are levied on jobs at the lower end of the pay scale cannot be absorbed by the employee but must be added to the total labor cost borne by the employer. Assuming that additional overhead costs are proportional to total labor cost, the implication is that the minimum productivity that a job must reach in order to be viable in the market is raised by more than 50% above the level of productivity required to pay the worker's net wage. As a consequence, a wide range of perfectly decent jobs, which in the absence of payroll taxes would be commercially viable, are eliminated from the private labor market.

In the United States payroll taxes are comparative low, but a potential off-setting factor is private employer-funded benefits (Hacker 2002). Employers' health insurance contributions and pension commitments can add as much as one-third to their labor costs. These costs appear to have risen substantially in recent years, causing considerable financial strain for some large firms (Freeman and Rodgers 2005). An important difference from countries with heavy payroll taxes, however, is that these costs apply mainly to large firms and chiefly to full-time year-round employees. Many small US employers provide no benefits at all. Most do not provide them, or do so on only a limited scale, for part-time and temporary employees. As of 2004, 56% of private-sector employees in the United States received health care benefits from their employer and 46% received pension benefits (Mishel, Bernstein, and Allegretto 2007: 135, 138).

The first chart in Figure 8.8 plots employment change since the late 1970s by the average level of income tax revenues (wage and salary income, capital

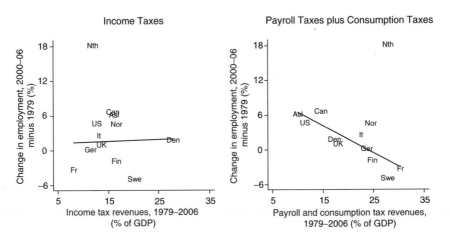

Figure 8.8. Change in employment, 1979 to 2000–06, by type of tax revenues.

Note: Horizontal axes are truncated. Change in employment is calculated as the 2000–06 employment rate minus the 1979 employment rate. The regression lines are calculated with the Netherlands excluded. For data definitions and sources, see the appendix.

income, and corporate profits) as a share of GDP. Consistent with this view, there is no association: $r = .04$.

By contrast, the correlation between employment change and a measure of payroll tax revenues (social security contributions and other payroll taxes paid by employers and employees) plus consumption tax revenues (taxes on goods and services, including general consumption taxes and taxes levied on specific items) is quite strong: $r = -.81$. The second chart in Figure 8.8 shows this association. (Payroll taxes alone and consumption taxes alone are each negatively correlated with employment change. But the magnitude for each is not as strong as that for the combined measure shown in Figure 8.8: $r = -.74$ for payroll tax revenues and $-.40$ for consumption tax revenues.) Coupled with the lack of association between income tax revenues and employment change, this strong correlation suggests that, to the extent taxation has impeded employment growth in these countries since the 1970s, the problem has been the level of payroll and consumption taxes rather than the level of taxation overall.

How Strong Is the Effect?

The magnitude of the effect of payroll and consumption tax revenues appears to be fairly substantial. The coefficient from a regression of employment change on average revenues from payroll and consumption taxes can be used as an upper-bound estimate. It is $-.47$. This suggests that, on average, a difference of 10 percentage points in revenues from payroll and consumption taxes is associated with a difference in employment growth of about 4.5 percentage points since the late 1970s.

Payroll and consumption taxes are presumed to have an adverse employment effect chiefly by impeding employment growth in low-productivity consumer services. Figure 8.9 shows three scatterplots, each with payroll and consumption tax revenues (as a share of GDP) on the horizontal axis and change in employment between 1979 and 2000–06 in a particular sector (or group of sectors) on the vertical axis. The sectors are manufacturing plus agriculture, high-end services (finance, insurance, real estate, and other business services), and low-end services (wholesale and retail trade, restaurants, hotels, and community, social, and personal services).

The strongest negative association is with employment change in manufacturing and agriculture. Yet these are not the sectors that analysts who hypothesize adverse employment effects of payroll and consumption taxes have in mind. And there is little indication that such taxes did in fact play much of a role in influencing employment trends in manufacturing and agriculture. As I noted in Chapter 4, the most important determinant instead was how

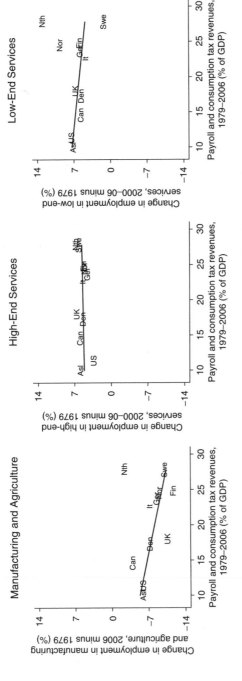

Figure 8.9. Change in employment in various sectors, 1979 to 2000–06, by payroll and consumption tax revenues.

Note: Horizontal axes are truncated. "High-end services" include finance, insurance, real estate, and other business services (ISIC 8). "Low-end services" include wholesale and retail trade, restaurants, and hotels (ISIC 6) and community, social, and personal services (ISIC 9). France is not included due to lack of data on employment by sector. Change in employment is calculated as the 2000–06 employment rate minus the 1979 employment rate. The regression lines are calculated with the Netherlands excluded. For data definitions and sources, see the appendix.

much of a country's employment was in these two sectors at the start of the period. Across the twelve countries, employment change in manufacturing and agriculture from 1979 to 2000–06 correlates at −.86 with the level of employment in these two sectors in 1979. A regression of employment change in manufacturing and agriculture over 1979 to 2000–06 on the 1979 employment rate in these two sectors and the average level of payroll and consumption tax revenues yields a negative but very weak (−.03) coefficient for the tax revenues variable. What does this imply for the association between payroll and consumption tax revenues and employment growth? As noted earlier, a regression of change in total employment over 1979 to 2000–06 on payroll and consumption tax revenues yields a coefficient of −.47. In a similar regression with change in employment outside of manufacturing and agriculture as the dependent variable, the coefficient shrinks to −.17. This suggests a much weaker adverse impact of payroll and consumption taxes.

Finance, insurance, real estate, and other business services are the service jobs least likely to be affected by high payroll and consumption taxes. It is thus not surprising to find, in the second chart in Figure 8.9, no cross-country association between employment change in this sector and the level of such taxes.

The third chart in the figure shows the two service sectors emphasized by analysts who focus on payroll and consumption taxes: wholesale and retail trade, restaurants, and hotels (ISIC 6) and community, social, and personal services (ISIC 9). Productivity in these sectors tends to be low and difficult to increase, and consumption of these services tends to be relatively price-sensitive. It would help to be able to separate private from public employment in these sectors, but unfortunately OECD data do not permit that beyond the mid-1990s.

There is a negative association between payroll and consumption tax revenues and employment growth in these two sectors. But it is weaker than the relationship for overall employment change shown in the second chart in Figure 8.8. While the regression coefficient (excluding the Netherlands) there was −.47, here it is −.14. The difference in the payroll and consumption tax share of GDP between the low and high countries—Australia and Sweden, respectively—is approximately 18 percentage points. If −.14 is the true effect, an 18-percentage-point difference in payroll and consumption tax revenues has yielded, on average, a 2.5-percentage-point difference in employment growth in low-end services since the late 1970s.

Data are available for both payroll and consumption tax revenues and employment change in low-end services for eight other affluent countries: Austria, Belgium, Ireland, Japan, New Zealand, Portugal, Spain, and

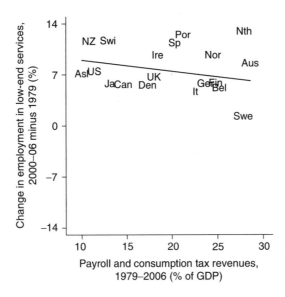

Figure 8.10. Change in employment in low-end services, 1979 to 2000–06, by payroll and consumption tax revenues—19 countries.

Note: France is not included due to lack of data on employment by sector. Change in employment is calculated as the 2000–06 employment rate minus the 1979 employment rate. The regression line is calculated with the Netherlands excluded. For data definitions and sources, see the appendix.

Switzerland. Figure 8.10 replicates the third chart in Figure 8.9 with these countries added. The pattern suggests further reason to believe that the magnitude of the adverse employment impact of payroll and consumption taxation has likely been somewhat modest. Three of the added countries fall more or less in line with the downward-sloping pattern in the third chart in Figure 8.9: New Zealand and Switzerland have had comparatively low tax levels and comparatively high employment growth in low-end services, and Belgium has had relatively high taxes and low employment growth. But Austria, Portugal, and Spain muddy the pattern. These three countries have had moderate-to-high levels of payroll and consumption taxes but have done well in generating job growth in low-productivity services. With all of these countries included, a regression of change in employment in low-end services from 1979 to 2000–06 on the average level of payroll and consumption taxes (excluding the Netherlands) yields a coefficient of −.15—virtually identical to the coefficient for the smaller group of countries.

This is without controlling for other determinants of employment growth. Figure 8.11 shows coefficients for payroll and consumption tax revenues from a variety of regressions with employment change in low-end services over 1979

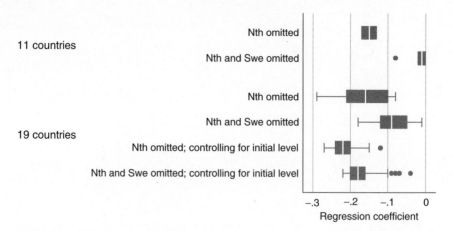

Figure 8.11. Regression results: Estimated effect of payroll and consumption taxes on employment change in low-end services, 1979 to 2000–06.

Note: Unstandardized coefficients for the payroll and consumption tax revenues variable from ordinary least squares (OLS) regressions using all possible combinations of payroll and consumption taxes and one or two of the following additional independent variables: earnings inequality (P50/P10 ratio), government benefit generosity (cash social expenditures on the working-age population as % of GDP), real long-term interest rates (%), imports (% of GDP), change in real unit labor costs (%), and product market regulations (index). Employment protection regulations is not included in any of the regressions due to multicollinearity. The third and fourth sets of regressions for 19 countries include a variable representing the level of employment in low-end services in 1979 to control for "catch-up" effects. The dependent variable is absolute change in the employment rate in low-end services: the employment rate in 2000–06 minus the rate in 1979. For data definitions and sources, see the appendix. France is not included due to lack of data on employment by sector. Finland is missing from regressions that include the real interest rate variable. With 11 countries, there are 6 regressions. For this group of countries the earnings inequality, government benefit generosity, and product market regulations variables are not included due to multicollinearity. With 19 countries, there are 21 regressions. The "whiskers" refer to the minimum and maximum coefficients. The edges of the box indicate the 25th- and 75th-percentile coefficients. The vertical white line is the median coefficient. Separate dots indicate "outliers"—coefficients that are substantially larger or smaller than the others in that set.

to 2000–06 as the dependent variable. As in Chapters 5–7, the figure reports the coefficients for the tax variable in each set of regressions in boxplots. The regressions include the payroll and consumption taxes variable along with all possible combinations of several additional variables highlighted in Chapters 4–7: earnings inequality, government benefit generosity, real long-term interest rates (monetary policy), imports (globalization), change in real unit labor costs (wage restraint), and product market regulations. No more than three independent variables are included in any regression. Because payroll and consumption taxation is very strongly correlated across countries with employment protection regulations, the latter cannot be included in any of the regressions. Earnings inequality, government benefit generosity, and product market regulations can be included only in regressions with the larger set of countries. In measuring government benefit generosity I use cash social expenditures on the working-age population, rather than the benefit employment disincentives index developed in Chapter 7, as the former is available for more countries. As in previous chapters, for the larger group of countries I control for the "catch-up" effect by estimating an additional set of regressions that include a variable representing the 1979 employment level in low-end services.

The coefficient for the payroll and consumption taxes variable in these regressions is consistently negative. Its magnitude, though, turns out to be fairly sensitive to model specification and to the countries included—especially to whether or not Sweden is included. Figures 8.9 and 8.10 suggest that Sweden's record may heavily influence the association between taxation and change in low-end service employment. As I noted in Chapter 5, most of Sweden's employment decline was produced by political choices made during the severe economic crisis of the early 1990s. Also, relative to the other countries Sweden's employment performance is excessively penalized by the fact that it is not possible to adjust the employment measure for work hours (Chapter 4). It thus makes substantive sense to exclude Sweden.

In the 19-country regression with a control for 1979 employment level in low-end services and with Sweden omitted, the median regression coefficient is −.18. This suggests that an 18-percentage-point difference in payroll and consumption taxes as a share of GDP—the difference between the lowest-tax and highest-tax countries—may have produced a difference of about 3.2 percentage points in employment growth in low-end services from 1979 to 2000–06. That is not a huge effect, but nor is it trivial.

Country Experiences

We could gain helpful insight into the impact of taxes on employment growth in low-end services by examining what happens when a country significantly reduces its payroll and/or consumption tax burden. However, none of the affluent countries have done this.

Figure 8.12 shows the tax mix in each of the twelve nations since the late 1970s. The only countries that have reduced the payroll tax burden to any appreciable extent are France and the Netherlands, and in both cases the reduction is quite recent, beginning in the mid-1990s, and relatively small in magnitude. It is therefore difficult to judge the impact. An additional problem is that sector-specific employment data are not available for France. Consumption taxes as a share of GDP have fallen in only three countries: Canada, France, and Norway. Here too the reductions have been fairly marginal. As

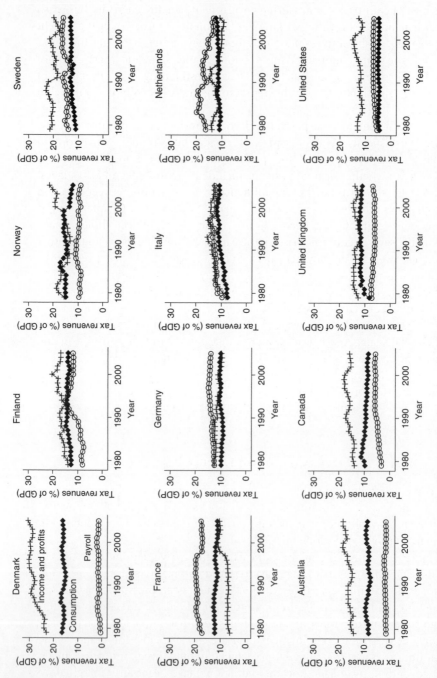

Figure 8.12. Revenues from taxes on income and profits, payroll, and consumption as a share of GDP, 1979ff.

Note: + = taxes on income and profits; o = social security contributions and payroll taxes; ◆ = taxes on consumption (goods and services). For data definitions and sources, see the appendix.

with government benefit generosity (Chapter 7), then, over-time trends in payroll and consumption taxation offer no analytical leverage in assessing impact on employment.

Taxation and Employment: Summing Up

There is a strong negative association between tax levels and employment growth across eleven of the twelve countries since the late 1970s (Figure 8.7, second chart). That association is chiefly a product of payroll and consumption taxes (Figure 8.8, second chart). However, a significant portion of the estimated impact of payroll and consumption taxes may be spurious. The strong negative association between payroll and consumption tax revenues and employment growth owes in part to a strong negative association between these taxes and change in manufacturing and agricultural employment (Figure 8.9, first chart), and the latter association almost certainly is not genuinely causal.

There is a negative association between payroll and consumption tax revenues and employment growth in low-end services since the late 1970s (Figure 8.9, third chart; Figure 8.10). This association holds up in regressions that include a variety of controls and different sets of countries. The precise magnitude of the effect is difficult to pin down, but a seemingly reasonable estimate is that since the 1970s countries with the highest levels of payroll and consumption taxation may have experienced 2 or 3 percentage points less increase in low-end services employment than those with the lowest levels.

TAX POLICY FOR JOBS WITH EQUALITY

A tax policy conducive to low income inequality and high employment should have four principal features:

1. Taxes should generate a high level of revenues, in order to finance generous transfers and services.

2. The tax system should be progressive, or at worst minimally regressive.

3. Payroll and consumption taxes should be moderate, so as not to impede employment growth in low-end services.

4. To encourage investment and entreneurship and prevent capital flight, there should be a relatively low statutory rate and a not-too-high effective tax rate on capital.

These features are not necessarily easy to combine (OECD 1995; Cnossen 2002). A high level of revenues may help with inequality reduction but may require heavy reliance on payroll and/or consumption taxes, which in turn may reduce both employment and tax progressivity.

Some tax systems conform more closely to this ideal than do others. Denmark's is of particular interest. Unlike those of most other European countries, the Danish tax system does not rely heavily on payroll taxes. Instead, it relies principally on income taxes that are focused on wage and salary income (Ganghof 2005*b*). Taxes on corporate profits and capital income are moderate—in line with those in other affluent countries (see Figure 8.5). The tax rate on wage and salary income is high and relatively progressive. Figure 8.12 makes clear the extent to which Denmark, more than the other eleven countries, relies heavily on income taxes and minimally on payroll taxes. Denmark's taxes on consumption are the highest among the twelve countries, but as the third chart in Figure 8.7 indicates, the combined total of payroll and consumption tax revenues nevertheless is considerably lower in Denmark than in the other Nordic countries and the continental countries.

Denmark's tax system generates more revenue (as a share of GDP) than that of any other country except Sweden. Danish employment performance since the late 1970s compares favorably with that of other high-tax countries, and this employment record looks even better if we take into account Denmark's high initial employment rate (second-highest behind Sweden; see Figure 3.2). However, as the charts in Figure 8.9 make clear, the main thing separating Denmark's employment performance from that of other high-tax countries is smaller job losses in manufacturing and agriculture rather than larger gains in services. Hence, we should not be too quick to conclude that Denmark has found the tax system most conducive to a sustainable high-employment, low-inequality society.

This type of tax structure is not without problems (Messere, de Kam, and Heady 2003: 79–80; Ganghof 2005*b*, 2005*c*). It compares unfavorably with other affluent countries in terms of progressivity. As Figure 8.1 indicates, Denmark's tax system does virtually nothing to reduce income inequality among working-age households directly. And bear in mind that the calculations shown in that figure do not include consumption taxes, which are higher in Denmark than in other nations. The Danish strategy has been to offset its regressive tax system with generous transfers and public services. A second potential drawback of a Danish-style tax structure is political. Citizens may perceive a tax structure in which capital income is taxed at a substantially lower rate than labor income as unfair. A third problem is administrative. For owners of unincorporated firms, a differentiated income tax structure creates a strong incentive to count profits as capital income rather than as earnings. This reduces tax revenues and may augment perceptions of inequity.

Perhaps most important, it is unlikely that Denmark's tax system can serve as a blueprint for other affluent nations. Even if they wanted to, policy makers in most countries are not likely to be able to raise tax rates on wage and salary income to Danish levels. Because of the constraints on taxing capital, such countries are forced to rely fairly heavily on consumption and/or payroll taxes if they want to raise large quantities of tax revenue.

Given this, what can such countries do to avoid stifling employment growth? A logical strategy is to exempt or reduce payroll tax payments on low-wage jobs or consumption taxes on items produced in low-productivity sectors. This reduces revenue generated by such taxes. But that may be offset in several ways. Some of those who enter newly created low-wage jobs will move up to higher-paying positions that generate tax revenues. As more people enter employment, government transfer payments should decline. Also, growing employment in low-wage jobs is likely to increase consumption, which should in turn help to boost employment in higher-paying jobs.

As I noted in Chapter 7, several European countries have pursued this strategy recently (Genschel 2002: 264; Joumard 2002: 100; OECD 2003*b*: 124). The Netherlands began doing so in the mid-1990s, helping to sustain the dramatic increase in Dutch employment that began in the mid-1980s. Germany and France have introduced similar exemptions or reductions. In the early 1990s Sweden reduced the consumption tax for restaurant work, contracting services, and tourist services.

The most important lesson regarding tax policy and employment may come from the Netherlands. If high payroll and consumption taxes are a major impediment to employment growth, the Netherlands should have had poor employment performance since the 1970s. As the second chart in Figure 8.8 indicates, the combined payroll and consumption tax burden in the Netherlands has been one of the highest among these countries. Instead, the Netherlands had by far the largest increase in employment during this period. Yes, the starting employment level was comparatively low and most of the increase was in part-time rather than full-time jobs (Figures 3.2 and 3.3). Nonetheless, the employment gain was real and relatively impressive. The Dutch experience suggests that even if low payroll and consumption taxes are conducive to strong employment growth, they are by no means a precondition for it. Austria too has enjoyed rapid employment growth in low-end services despite high payroll and consumption taxes (Figure 8.10).

What is the best route forward for the comparatively low-tax Anglo countries? It is important to recognize the variation *within* this group. As of the most recent year for which data are available, 2005, tax revenues totaled 37% of

GDP in the United Kingdom, 33% in Canada, and 31% in Australia, compared to just 27% in the United States. Transfers and redistribution could be more generous in each of these four countries if tax revenues were greater, but the deficit is particularly pronounced in the United States (Figure 8.3).

Given public opinion, there is little prospect of a sharp expansion of tax revenues in the United States—at least in the near term. But an increase to something like the level in the United Kingdom and Canada (and Germany), around 35% of GDP, is certainly not out of the realm of possibility. There would seem to be three potential openings for an American president and/or Congress committed to higher tax revenues. One is increases in the statutory rates on high wage and salary incomes. The Clinton administration was able to do this in 1993, and opinion polls suggest there might be limited opposition to at least reversing the rate cuts implemented by the Bush administration in the early 2000s (Hacker and Pierson 2005). A second is reduction of income tax exemptions and deductions (Weinstein 2005). A third is creation of a national consumption tax (existing general consumption taxes in the United States are applied at the state and local level). As Figure 8.12 indicates, income and payroll tax revenues in the United States are virtually identical in magnitude to those in the United Kingdom. The difference between the two countries stems almost entirely from the greater consumption tax revenues in the UK.

9

Skills

According to neoclassical economic theory, individuals' employment and earnings are determined by their productivity, which in turn is determined largely by their skills, which consist chiefly of cognitive ability (Mincer 1993; Becker 1993). There is plenty of evidence consistent with this hypothesis. For example, in the United States as of 2005, the employment rate for persons age 25 to 64 was 57% among those with less than a high school degree, 73% among those with a high school degree but less than a four-year college degree, and 83% among those with a college degree or more (OECD 2007b: 260). Among Americans employed full-time, median earnings for those with a four-year college degree or more were about three times the median earnings of those with less than a high school degree and twice the earnings of those with a high school degree but less than a four-year college degree (OECD 2004e: 175). Similar patterns obtain in other countries (OECD 2004e, 2007b).

A way to achieve both low inequality and high employment, therefore, might be to have a high level and equal distribution of cognitive ability across individuals (Reich 1991; Roemer 1999; Blank 2000; Krueger 2003). This is consistent with a prominent policy strategy: improve and equalize schooling.

Can it work? There are several issues here: Can inequality of cognitive ability be reduced? Would reducing inequality of cognitive ability reduce inequality of earnings? Would reducing individual earnings inequality reduce household income inequality? Would increasing cognitive ability increase employment? I consider each of these in turn.

CAN INEQUALITY OF COGNITIVE ABILITY BE REDUCED?

There are reasons to be skeptical about the prospects for substantial equalization of cognitive ability. One is that genetics appears to play a significant role in determining cognitive skills. The best available measure of cognitive ability is IQ (intelligence quotient) test scores. The best resource for examining the genetic contribution to IQ is identical twins raised separately, because identical twins have the exact same genetic makeup. If IQ scores of identical twins raised in different households are similar, then we know genetics matters; if they are different, environment must be the cause. A number of such studies conducted in various countries have found that the IQs of identical twins raised apart are quite similar. A particularly careful one, the Minnesota Study of Twins Reared Apart, looked at 100 pairs of middle-aged identical twins who had been raised separately (Bouchard et al. 1990). It suggested that more than half of the variation in intelligence is due to genetics. This seems likely to be an overestimate, as part of what appears to be genetic could actually be due to similarities in what happens in utero, in early environment (which can be similar even if in different households), and in schooling. Nonetheless, genetic transmission seems likely to have a nontrivial impact on cognitive skills.

Even if genetics plays a sizable role in determining differences in cognitive ability, "environment" in general and schooling in particular could still have a large, and perhaps the dominant, role. A variety of empirical findings suggest that this may well be the case. One is the "Flynn effect." Scores on IQ tests have been rising steadily over the past several generations, in virtually all countries (Flynn 1987; Niesser 1998). Can genetic changes account for this development? If so, they would have to do so via natural selection. But in affluent countries it is no longer the case that being more intelligent gives a person a significantly better chance of survival. If anything, the impact of genetics should have been working in the opposite direction, because people with lower IQ scores tend to have more children. And in any case, natural selection would not have produced this improvement in such a short time span. This trend almost certainly is a product of changes in environment— better nutrition, medical care, living conditions, and schooling.

Another piece of evidence relevant in assessing the influence of genetics and environment on cognitive ability is that in most countries, groups that are economically and/or socially subordinate but genetically similar to the dominant group(s) tend to have lower average IQ scores (Fischer et al. 1996: 188–94). Examples include African Americans in the United States (vs. whites), Irish and Scottish in the United Kingdom (vs. English), Afrikaaners in South Africa (vs. English), Eastern Jews in Israel (vs. Western Jews), Koreans in Japan, and low caste persons in India (vs. upper caste). This too signals a key role for environmental factors.

There is also evidence suggesting that schooling plays an important role in determining cognitive skills. For example, children tend to increase their intellectual performance more during a month in school than during a month of summer vacation (Fischer et al. 1996: 162). IQ test scores correlate more strongly with prior years of schooling than with later years of schooling, which suggests that cognitive ability is more an effect of schooling than a cause of it (Fischer et al. 1996: 63–4). Also, if cognitive ability is heavily genetic in origin, it should correlate more strongly with age than with quantity or quality of schooling. Yet according to one analysis, IQ scores correlate much more closely with years of schooling completed ($r = .54$) and with having been in an academic track in school ($r = .45$) than with age ($r = .16$) (Fischer et al. 1996: 59–62).

The debate about the relative impact of genetic and nongenetic factors in influencing cognitive ability is unlikely to be resolved anytime soon. While those who focus on the genetic basis of intelligence sometimes overstate its importance (e.g., Herrnstein and Murray 1994), it nevertheless seems likely that genetic transmission places nontrivial limits on the degree of skills equalization that a society can achieve.

A second reason to be skeptical about the prospects for substantial equalization of cognitive ability is that individuals have varying "tastes for learning." Some enjoy school, thinking, and learning more than others. Thus, even if genetics played little role in affecting cognitive development and even if school environments were largely equal in the opportunity for learning they provided to students, there likely would be substantial inequality in school completion and in learning.

A third reason for skepticism is that cognitive development is also affected by parents' incomes, personality traits, behavioral patterns, and parenting practices as well as by peers, neighborhoods, and other institutions and experiences (Jencks et al. 1972; Mayer 1997; Jencks and Phillips 1998; Bowles and Gintis 2002; Phillips and Chin 2004). Some of these, such as parental incomes and neighborhood conditions, could potentially be equalized to an extent. But policy makers have very little means of influencing others, particularly parents' personality traits and behavioral patterns.

These considerations, which suggest cause for pessimism about the practical possibility of substantially reducing differences in cognitive ability, are based on studies of individuals within the United States. An examination of cross-country patterns could lead to a different conclusion. Gøsta Esping-Andersen (2004: 308) has suggested that they do. He has examined data from a multicountry study of adult literacy, the International Adult Literacy Survey (IALS), conducted in the mid-1990s by the OECD and Statistics Canada. Individuals were tested on three types of literacy: document, prose, and quantitative. Scores tended to correlate strongly across the three types. Figure 9.1 shows the degree of prose literacy inequality, measured as a P90/P10 ratio, in ten of the twelve countries examined in this book (France and Italy were not included in the IALS). Inequality of literacy was especially low in Denmark and Norway, followed by the Netherlands, Sweden, Germany, and Finland.

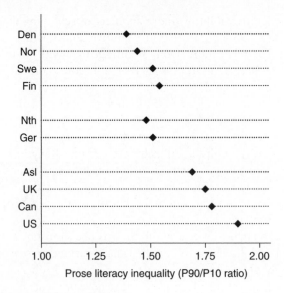

Figure 9.1. Literacy inequality, 1994–98.

Note: Data are not available for France and Italy. For data definitions and sources, see the appendix.

The four Anglo countries, and particularly the United States, had the highest levels of inequality. In the United States, the prose literacy score at the 90th percentile was nearly twice as high as that at the 10th percentile.

Esping-Andersen (2004: 308) argues that the success of the Nordic countries in limiting inequality of cognitive skills is largely a product of extensive high-quality preschool care and education.

Scandinavian day care is basically of uniform, high pedagogical standards, meaning that children from disadvantaged families will benefit disproportionately. Day care in the United States is of extremely uneven quality, and children from disadvantaged families are likely to find themselves concentrated at the low end. Additionally, it is common practice in the Nordic countries for school-age children to remain in schools after classes in organized "after-hours" activities. This implies fewer hours parked in front of the family television.

The upshot is that the uneven distribution of cultural capital among families is greatly neutralized in the Nordic countries, simply because much of the cognitive stimulus has been shifted from the parents to centers that do not replicate social class differences. As Waldfogel's (2002) review of both American and European research shows, childcare programs that are intensive, intervene early, and promote high pedagogical standards contribute very effectively to the raising of the cognitive performance of children from disadvantaged milieux. In turn, this helps children start and

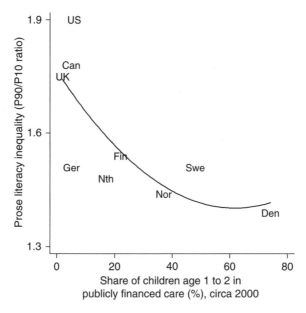

Figure 9.2. Literacy inequality by share of young children in publicly financed child care, 1994–98.

Note: Vertical axis is truncated. For data definitions and sources, see the appendix.

proceed on a much more equal footing once they enter formal education. Although there is precious little longitudinal research, what evidence there is suggests that early quality care continues to exert positive emotional and cognitive results throughout childhood.

This is a plausible hypothesis. But there are two empirical problems. First, across these countries, the association between extensiveness of public childcare and cognitive inequality is not terribly strong. Figure 9.2 shows the pattern for nine of the countries (public childcare data are not available for Australia, and as noted earlier literacy data are not available for France and Italy). The childcare data refer to the share of 1- and 2-year-old children who are in publicly financed (provided or subsidized) care. Consistent with the hypothesis, Denmark, Norway, and Sweden are at one pole with extensive public childcare and low literacy inequality among adults, while the United States, Canada, and the United Kingdom are at the opposite pole with very limited public childcare and high literacy inequality. But Germany, the Netherlands, and Finland also have low literacy inequality despite having very few young children in publicly financed childcare. Second, many things could account for the cross-country differences in cognitive inequality. To adequately assess the Esping-Andersen hypothesis, we need over-time data on cognitive inequality within countries. Unfortunately, to my knowledge such data do not exist.

Then again, the data in Figures 9.1 and 9.2 clearly suggest a lesser degree of cognitive inequality in the Nordic countries, Germany, and the Netherlands than in the Anglo nations. While it is conceivable that the latter group of countries started with more cognitively diverse populations, and that this diversity has simply been passed across generations via genetic transmission, it seems likely that nongenetic factors play a sizable role in the cross-country difference in inequality of cognitive skills. To the extent those factors can be altered, it may be possible for countries to engineer reduced cognitive inequality—whether via public childcare or other means.

WOULD REDUCING INEQUALITY OF COGNITIVE ABILITY REDUCE INEQUALITY OF EARNINGS?

If we want to explain why particular individuals end up at varying positions in the distribution of earnings, skills are a fairly good predictor. But that does not necessarily imply that the degree of skills inequality is a significant determinant of the degree of earnings inequality. To borrow a common metaphor: think of the earnings structure as a building. Even if a person's skill level strongly influences which floor of the building she or he ends up on, the degree of inequality in skills across individuals might have little impact on how many floors the building has (Galbraith 1998: 56).

I consider three types of evidence in assessing the extent to which reducing cognitive inequality would reduce earnings inequality: individual-level data in the United States, within-country over-time trends, and cross-country patterns.

Numerous individual-level studies have attempted to gauge the impact of cognitive skills on earnings, net of other contributing factors. The most common finding is that cognitive ability matters, but that it is merely one among a number of determinants, and probably not the most important. This was the conclusion of one of the first systematic studies on this topic, by Christopher Jencks and colleagues (Jencks et al. 1972: 8): "The primary reason some people end up richer than others is not that they have more adequate cognitive skills. While children who read well, get the right answers to arithmetic problems, and articulate their thoughts clearly are somewhat more likely than others to get ahead, there are many other equally important factors involved. Thus there is almost as much economic inequality among those who score high on standardized tests as in the general population. Equalizing everyone's reading scores would not appreciably reduce the number of economic 'failures'. " Richard Herrnstein and Charles Murray (1994) compared the impact of IQ test scores with that of parental socioeconomic status on a variety of outcomes, including earnings and poverty. Their findings suggested that, of these two factors, cognitive ability is by far the more important. But there are many other potential determinants of earnings, and other analyses have found that cognitive ability tends not to be the most important cause (e.g., Korenman and Winship 2000).

What other factors matter according to these individual-level studies? They include noncognitive traits and abilities, such as motivation, tenacity, perseverance, leadership, discipline, enthusiasm, conscientiousness, agreeableness, aggressiveness, self-confidence, dependability, organization, commitment, and trustworthiness (Bowles and Gintis 1976, 2002; Jencks et al. 1979; MacLeod 1995; Bowles, Gintis, and Osborne 2001; Farkas 2003; Heckman and Rubenstein 2001); preferences for occupation, work versus leisure time, and geographic location (Jencks and Tach 2005); job characteristics and union membership (Wright and Perrone 1977; Kalleberg, Wallace, and Althauser 1981; Baron 1984; Sørensen 1990); the process through which individuals get matched with jobs (Granovetter 1973; Ioannides and Loury 2004); neighborhood conditions (Jencks and Mayer 1990; Jencks and Peterson 1991; Wilson 1996; Brooks-Gunn, Duncan, and Aber 1997; Pebley and Sastry 2004); and ascriptive characteristics such as gender and race (Jencks et al. 1979; England 1992; Fischer et al. 1996; Browne 1999; Blau and Kahn 2000).

Over-time trends within countries may help to shed light on this issue. In particular, we know that in the United States earnings inequality has increased substantially since the late 1970s (see Figure 3.1). Has this been driven by an increase in skills inequality? Although some analysts have suggested that a rise in the number of low-skilled immigrants has been a significant cause, to my knowledge no major study of the rise in US earnings inequality has suggested that it resulted mainly from a jump in skills dispersion.

We do not have reliable time-series data on cognitive ability, but data are available on years of schooling completed (Handel 2003; Wolff 2006). Figure 9.3 shows trends since 1940 in the share of Americans age 25 to 29 with less than a high school degree, the share with a high school degree but less than a four-year college degree, and the share with a four-year college degree or more. Inequality of educational attainment among 25- to 29-year-olds declined somewhat from 1940 through the mid-1970s: the share not

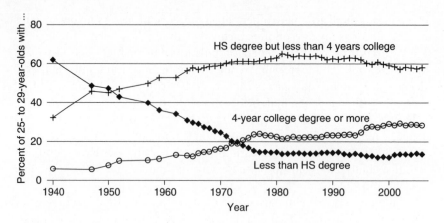

Figure 9.3. Educational attainment in the United States, 1940 ff.

Note: Author's calculations from US Census Bureau data, available at www.census.gov/population/www/socdemo/educ-attn.html.

completing high school decreased steadily while the share with a high school degree but no college degree increased, though this was offset somewhat by the increase in the share with a college degree or better.

By focusing on a narrow age group, the data in Figure 9.3 are effective in showing trends in schooling completed. But for assessing the impact of schooling on earnings inequality the more relevant group is all those age 25 and over, not merely those age 25 to 29. For the former, Edward Wolff (2006: 14) shows that inequality of educational attainment was flat from the mid-1940s to the early 1960s and since then has decreased steadily. Reliable time-series data on earnings inequality begin in 1963 (Katz and Autor 1999: figure 4). They suggest a modest increase between the early 1960s and the late 1970s, followed by a sharp and steady rise since then. These trends are inconsistent with the notion that reducing skills inequality helps to reduce earnings inequality. Wolff (2006: ch. 6) has conducted a multivariate time-series analysis of the association between inequality of educational attainment and inequality of family income in the United States from 1947 to 2000. His results too suggest no beneficial impact of declining schooling inequality.

If policy makers were convinced that reducing inequality of cognitive skills would reduce inequality of earnings, they might well start by reducing inequality of spending (per pupil) across schools. In the United States, where the largest expenditure disparities exist, the dispersion in expenditures in fact has been falling for nearly half a century (Hoxby 2003; Corcoran et al. 2004). What impact has this had on earnings inequality? As noted earlier, earnings inequality increased modestly from the early 1960s through the late 1970s;

since then it has jumped dramatically (Figure 3.1; Katz and Autor 1999)—the opposite of what we would expect given the reduction in school expenditure inequality. Carline Hoxby (2003) has examined state-specific trends in school expenditure inequality and in later individual earnings inequality. She finds only partial and statistically fragile evidence of a weak inequality-reducing impact of reductions in school spending inequality within states. It is unclear whether this apparent lack of impact (or limited impact) is because reducing inequality in school spending fails to reduce inequality in school conditions, reducing inequality in school conditions fails to reduce inequality in cognitive skills, reducing inequality in cognitive skills fails to reduce inequality in earnings, or some combination of these.

What about cross-country patterns? Years of schooling completed is unlikely to be a very helpful measure when comparing across affluent countries due to stark differences in national systems of skill development. The United States relies heavily on formal schooling, whereas Germany and other European countries rely to a much greater extent on apprenticeship systems and other mechanisms of firm-specific training (Crouch, Finegold, and Sako 1999). A more sensible choice is to use the IALS adult literacy data described earlier.

As Figure 9.4 indicates, there is a strong positive association across countries between inequality of literacy (measured using prose literacy) and inequality

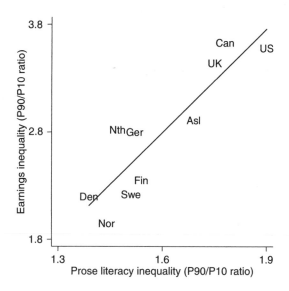

Figure 9.4. Earnings inequality as of 1994–98 by literacy inequality.

Note: Chart axes are truncated. For data definitions and sources, see the appendix.

of earnings. However, as I noted in Chapters 3 and 5, a key determinant of variation in earnings inequality across affluent countries is wage-setting arrangements—specifically, the share of the work force whose wages are determined by collective bargaining and the degree of centralization of the wage-setting process.

How do we sort out the relative impact of literacy inequality and wage-setting arrangements on earnings inequality? Regression analysis will not help because these variables are too highly correlated with one another: across these countries, literacy inequality correlates at $-.78$ with wage centralization and $-.71$ with union wage bargaining coverage. Dan Devroye and Richard Freeman (2002) pursue a useful strategy. Using the IALS data, they first decompose the variation in earnings inequality across four countries: Germany, the Netherlands, Sweden, and the United States. They find that literacy inequality accounts for only 7% of the variation. A much larger portion of the variation, 36%, owes to the larger skill premium in the United States than in the other three countries. In other words, the variation in earnings inequality across these four countries is more a product of the degree to which skills differences translate into earnings differences than of the degree of skills differences per se. Devroye and Freeman then examine earnings inequality among Americans within relatively narrow bands of skills and find that the degree of earnings inequality within such groups tends to exceed the degree of earnings inequality among *all* employed individuals in the other three countries. Francine Blau and Lawrence Kahn (2002*b*) have used the IALS data to examine men and women separately and native-born and immigrant Americans separately, and they reach a similar conclusion.

These findings imply that even if adult literacy were completely equalized in the United States, the US distribution of earnings would remain markedly more unequal than that in Germany, the Netherlands, or Sweden. Like the data on individual-level differences within countries and over-time trends within countries, this suggests that reducing inequality of cognitive ability might do relatively little to reduce inequality of earnings.

On the other hand, this conclusion may miss a key point. Low inequality of cognitive skills may not be the direct cause of comparatively low inequality of earnings in the Nordic countries. Yet Jonas Pontusson has suggested (personal communication) that it might be necessary to the sustainability of an egalitarian earnings distribution, in the sense that high productivity among low-end employees enables employers to afford to pay relatively high wages imposed by strong unions and centralized wage setting. In other words, reducing cognitive inequality in a country might not lead to a reduction in earnings inequality, but low earnings inequality—however achieved—will only be sustainable if cognitive inequality is low.

WOULD REDUCING EARNINGS INEQUALITY REDUCE INCOME INEQUALITY?

Figure 3.6 in Chapter 3 showed that, across the twelve countries, there is a positive association between the level of individual earnings inequality and the level of household pretax-pretransfer income inequality. As of the mid-1990s the correlation (r) was .76. This suggests that, as an upper-bound estimate, a little over half $(r^2 = .58)$ of the variation in market income inequality among households may be a product of earnings inequality among individuals. Other contributing factors include household composition (number of adults, degree of marital homogamy) and employment patterns within households. While reducing individual earnings inequality thus would almost certainly help to reduce income inequality across households, its impact would be somewhat limited.

WOULD INCREASING COGNITIVE ABILITY INCREASE EMPLOYMENT?

Thus far I have focused on the effect of cognitive ability on inequality. The other half of the equation concerns its impact on employment. To what degree would increasing skills for those in the bottom half of the distribution increase employment?

Here too, there is reason for skepticism. It is certainly true that, on average, individuals with better skills—as measured by years of schooling completed or literacy—are more likely to be employed (Pryor and Schaffer 1999: ch. 2). But that does not imply that increasing schooling and/or literacy of those at the low end would increase the employment rate. Whether that happens depends upon whether there is employer demand, at reasonable earnings levels, for the individuals who have improved skill levels (Kuttner 1996: 101–5).

Figure 9.5 shows over-time trends in the United States for the share of 25- to 29 year-olds with less than a high school degree and for the employment rate. Between the mid-1950s and the mid-1970s educational attainment increased steadily and fairly sharply: the share of 25 to 29s without a high school degree declined from 40% to about 15% in those two decades. Yet the employment rate did not increase at all during this period; it stayed at around 65%. In the ensuing three decades, from the mid-1970s to the mid-2000s, the share with less than a high school degree decreased only slightly, yet the employment rate jumped by 10 percentage points. One could argue that the improvement

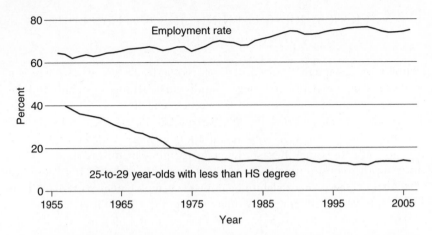

Figure 9.5. Educational attainment and employment in the United States, 1955 ff.

Note: For data definitions and sources, see the appendix and Figure 9.3.

in schooling did have an impact but that there was a substantial time lag. It seems more likely, however, that trends in the employment rate have been driven mainly by other factors.

Cross-country data suggest a similar conclusion. The first chart in Figure 9.6 shows employment rates by mean document literacy as of 1994–98 (the pattern is nearly identical for prose literacy). The Nordic countries have

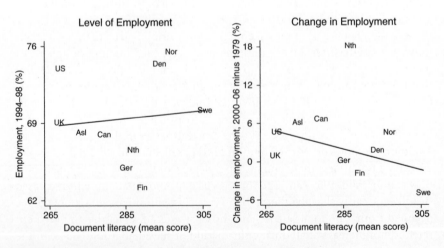

Figure 9.6. Employment levels and employment change by literacy.

Note: Some axes are truncated. Regression line in the second chart is calculated with the Netherlands excluded. For data definitions and sources, see the appendix.

the highest average literacy rates, and as we saw in Chapter 3 they also (with the exception of Finland) tend to have the highest employment rates. But for the continental and Anglo countries the pattern is the opposite of what we would expect to see if high literacy leads to high employment: literacy tends to be higher in the continental countries, but employment rates are higher in the Anglo countries.

The second chart shows employment change over 1979 to 2000–06 by mean document literacy. Here, the pattern is the opposite of what we might expect, with higher-literacy countries tending to have weaker employment growth since the 1970s. This association is almost certainly spurious. As Table 4.1 in Chapter 4 indicates, average literacy is closely correlated across these countries with a variety of labor market institutions and policies, including low-end wage levels, employment protection regulations, government benefit generosity, and taxes. As we have seen in Chapters 5–8, each of these is associated with employment change since the 1970s. Still, the pattern in the chart does not support the notion that skills have helped to boost employment. It would be helpful if data were available on changes over time in literacy levels, but unfortunately they are not.

CONCLUSION

None of the evidence I have examined in this chapter suggests that improving or equalizing cognitive ability would be a bad thing. It may boost job satisfaction for many individuals and help to improve the quality of democratic politics (Wolff 2006). But a focus on skills is unlikely to suffice as a policy strategy for pursuing low inequality and high employment.

10

Women-Friendly Policies

In countries with employment deficits, the problem consists chiefly of a shortage of women's employment. This can be seen in Figure 10.1, which shows employment rates for men and women averaged over 2000–06. Germany's employment rate among men is almost as high as Sweden's, but the employment rate for women in the two countries differs by 13 percentage points. Italy's male employment rate is comparable to that in Finland, but its female rate is more than 20 percentage points lower. The average for men's employment across the twelve countries is 77%, while for women's employment it is 65%. A critical task—perhaps *the* critical task—for low-employment countries, then, is to identify and implement institutional or policy changes that can substantially increase women's employment.

Much of the research on this issue has focused on the impact of "women-friendly" or "family-friendly" policies (Winegarden and Bracy 1995; Ruhm 1998; Meyers, Gornick, and Ross 1999; Plantenga and Hansen 1999; Rubery, Smith, and Fagan 1999; Sainsbury 1999; Daly 2000; Korpi 2000; Dingeldey 2001; OECD 2001; Stier, Lewin-Epstein, and Braun 2001; Esping-Andersen et al. 2002: ch. 3; Orloff 2002; Pettit and Hook 2002; Ferrarini 2003; Gornick and Meyers 2003: ch. 8; Jaumotte 2003; Morgan and Zippel 2003; Mandel and Semyonov 2006; Eliason, Stryker, and Tranby 2008; Hicks and Kenworthy 2008). In this chapter, I examine the link between women-friendly policies and women's employment rates. I conclude that some of these policies very likely have helped to increase female employment, but that no single policy package has been decisive. The countries with high women's employment rates have succeeded via several different paths.

WOMEN'S EMPLOYMENT

Let me make clear that the outcome of interest in this chapter is women's employment, not gender equality. The latter is important (Gornick 1999; Huber et al. 2002; Mandel and Semyonov 2005; Misra et al. 2005), but it is not my concern here.

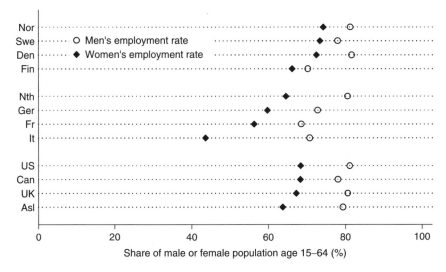

Figure 10.1. Men's and women's employment, 2000–06.

Note: For data definitions and sources, see the appendix.

Should the focus be on women's employment or women's labor force participation? The employment rate refers to the share of working-age women who are employed, while the labor force participation rate refers to the share of working-age women who are either employed or unemployed. The labor force participation rate is a better measure of the share of women who would prefer to be employed. However, my interest is in employment per se rather than in the share of women who desire employment. I therefore focus on the employment rate. As a practical matter, the choice of measure is unlikely to make much difference; across the twelve countries, rates of women's employment and women's labor force participation as of 2000–06 correlate at .98. A recent study by Florence Jaumotte (2003: table 8) uses women's labor force participation as the outcome measure and reaches findings substantively similar to those in this chapter.

Should the female employment rate be measured in the standard way—employed women as a percentage of women age 15 to 64, as in Figure 10.1? Or should the focus be on a narrower age group? Although my chief concern is with the aggregate employment rate, employment patterns vary widely by age group across the twelve countries. Figure 10.2 makes this clear. It shows female employment rates as of 2000–06 among women age 15 to 24, 25 to 54, and 55 to 64. Among "prime-working-age" women, those age 25 to 54, there is some cross-country variation, but less than among all working-age women. Perhaps

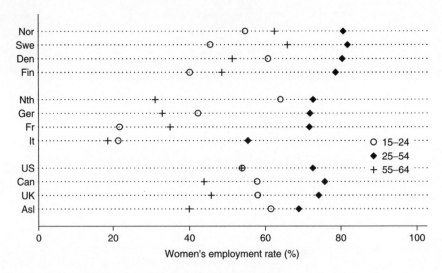

Figure 10.2. Women's employment by age group, 2000–06.

Note: For data definitions and sources, see the appendix.

most noteworthy, female employment rates for this age group are roughly the same in the Netherlands, Germany, and France as in the Anglo countries. Italy's rate is considerably lower, but it is widely suspected that a much larger share of women (and men) work in the underground economy in Italy than in any of the other eleven countries. It is difficult to know the magnitude, but it probably would not be unreasonable to estimate that inclusion of women employed in the informal sector would boost the employment rate for prime-working-age Italian women by 10 percentage points, pulling the country closer to the others.

It is in employment among women age 15–24 and 55–64 that the continental countries lag most severely. There are exceptions: the female employment rate among 15–24s is quite high in the Netherlands, and in Germany it is comparable to the rates in Sweden and Finland. But in France and Italy, very few of this youngest age group are employed. The contrast is even starker for women age 55–64; all four continental countries have female employment rates far below those in the Nordic countries and substantially lower than in the Anglo nations.

Figure 10.3 indicates that patterns of change over time also vary sharply by age group. The chart shows change in women's employment over the past three decades, measured as the female employment rate in 2000–06 minus the rate in 1970–73. Unlike in previous chapters, I include the 1970s in the change measure here. Women's employment increased substantially in the

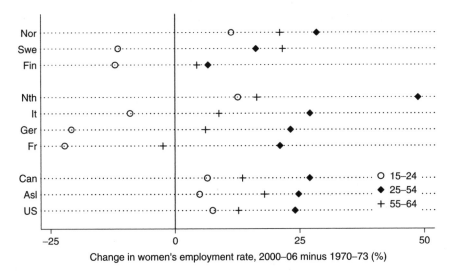

Change in women's employment rate, 2000–06 minus 1970–73 (%)

Figure 10.3. Change in women's employment by age group, 1970–73 to 2000–06

Note: Denmark and the United Kingdom are not included because age-group-specific data are not available prior to 1983 and 1984, respectively. Beginning year for Canada is 1976. Beginning year for 55–64s in Australia is 1978. For data definitions and sources, see the appendix

1970s in some countries, and women-friendly policies are often thought to have played a key role. Age-group-specific data are not available prior to the early 1980s for Denmark and the United Kingdom, so these two countries are not included in the figure. Among 25–54s, women's employment increased most rapidly in the Netherlands, but otherwise there was limited difference between the groups of nations. It is among the 15–24s and the 55–64s that the other three continental countries—Germany, France, and Italy—experienced comparatively poor performance.

Figure 10.4 offers a more detailed picture of over-time developments within each of the twelve countries. The figure includes two charts for each nation. The first shows trends in women's and men's employment rates, with each calculated as a proportion of the female or male population age 15–64. The second shows trends in women's employment rates by age group. The time series begins at different points for the various countries, though for most data are available by the early 1970s. I will discuss the longitudinal patterns shown in Figure 10.4 later in the chapter.

Figures 10.2–10.4 suggest that comparative analysis of women's employment should be disaggregated by age group. The data in Figure 10.4 indicate that within each of these countries employment rates have tended to be very similar among women age 25–34, 35–44, and 45–54. But there are sharp

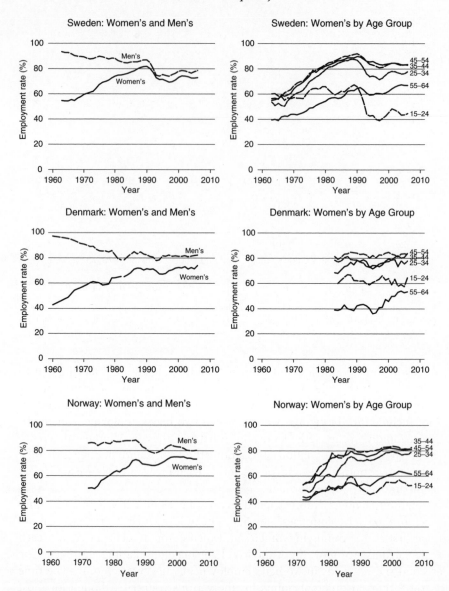

Figure 10.4. Women's and men's employment and women's employment by age group, 1960ff.

Note: The data in the "Women's and Men's" charts are for total female or male employment as a share of the female or male population age 15–64. For Denmark a different time series is used prior to 1983; the same is true for the United Kingdom prior to 1984. In the second chart for the Netherlands, the middle three age groups are combined to enable a lengthier time series. For data definitions and sources, see the appendix.

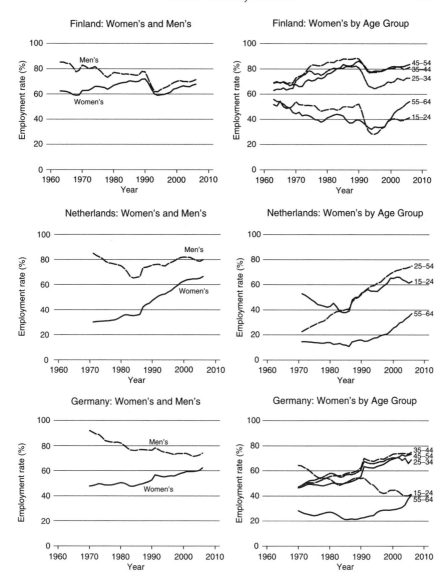

Figure 10.4. (*Continued*)

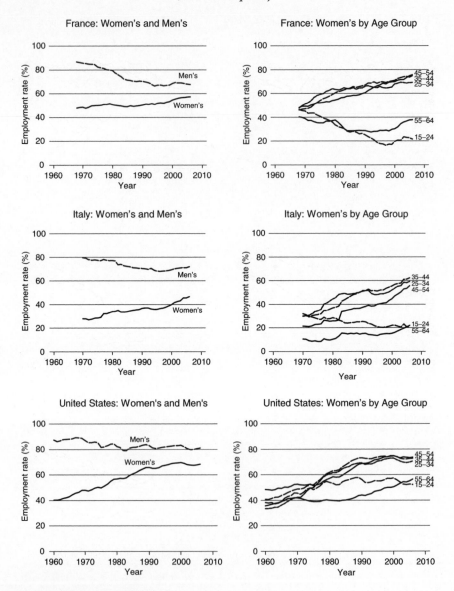

Figure 10.4. (*Continued*)

Figure 10.4. (*Continued*)

differences between those age 15–24, those age 25–54, and those age 55–64. My analyses therefore focus on these three age groups. I concentrate in particular on women age 25–54, as that is the largest group and the one most likely to be affected by women-friendly policies.

WOMEN-FRIENDLY POLICIES

There are six "women-friendly" policies likely to be conducive to women's employment. One is public provision or financing of childcare (Kamerman and Kahn 1995; Sainsbury 1999; OECD 2002*b*: ch. 3; Gornick and Meyers 2003). Lack of affordable childcare can pose a significant obstacle to employment for women with preschool-age children. Many researchers have thus presumed that government-provided or -funded care for young children encourages female employment. This squares with the observation that the Nordic countries, which have been leaders in this area, have the highest rates of women's employment.

In the Nordic countries high-quality and relatively inexpensive childcare is available in public care centers and in the home beginning around six months of age, and a large proportion of parents make use of this option. Denmark is illustrative. In Denmark 64% of children age six months to two years are in formal childcare, commonly between seven and eight hours per day. The high quality stems in part from oversight by both local municipalities and parent boards. It is also a product of the fact that the training requirements and pay levels for childcare teachers are on par with those for schoolteachers. Heavy public subsidies help limit the cost to parents to approximately 10% to 20% of an average production worker's earnings.

Figure 10.5 shows one measure of the generosity of government support for childcare for very young children. The measure is an index ranging from zero to one, compiled by Scott Eliason, Robin Stryker, and Eric Tranby (2008). The data are available as decade averages for the 1960s, 1970s, 1980s, and 1990s for all of the twelve countries except Australia. Consistent with the conventional view, they suggest greater generosity in the Nordic countries, particularly Denmark and Sweden. Among the continental and Anglo countries, only France offers more than a modest level. The difference between the Nordic countries and the others has widened steadily over time, beginning in the 1970s.

Public childcare and/or preschool for children age 3 to 5 may be equally important. Over-time data, again in the form of an index with decade averages, are shown in Figure 10.6. Here too the Nordic countries have been the

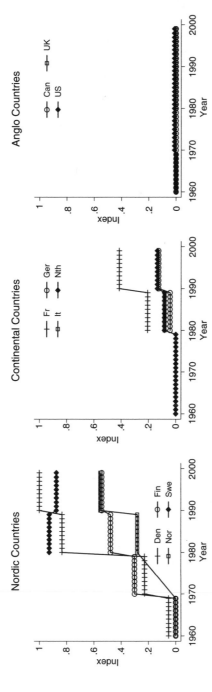

Figure 10.5. Public child care for children age 0 to 2, 1960ff.

Note: Data are decade averages. Missing data: all decades for Australia; 1960s and 1970s for France, Germany, Sweden, and the United Kingdom; 1960s, 1970s, and 1990s for Italy; 1970s for Norway. For data definitions and sources, see the appendix.

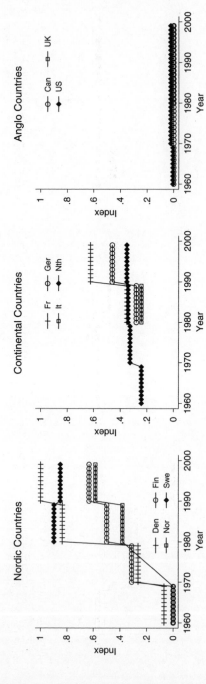

Figure 10.6. Public child care for children age 3 to 5, 1960ff.

Note: Data are decade averages. Missing data: all decades for Australia; 1960s and 1970s for France, Germany, Sweden, and the United Kingdom; 1960s, 1970s, and 1990s for Italy; 1970s for Norway. For data definitions and sources, see the appendix.

leaders, along with France. The other continental countries offer a bit more support for this age group than for the very young.

For women with school-age children (age 6 and older), school hours and the availability of extended-day or after-school services can potentially affect employment opportunities and decisions. Here some of the continental countries have noteworthy roadblocks. For example, most German schools for 6- to 9-year-olds are open for only half days. Schools in France typically are closed on Wednesday afternoons. And in the Netherlands teacher shortages sometimes force schools to close for a half day or full day on short notice (OECD 2002*b*: 22).

A second policy often posited as conducive to women's employment is paid maternity/care leave (Gauthier 1996; Ruhm 1998; Bruning and Plantenga 1999; Daly 2000; OECD 2002*b*: ch. 4; Ferrarini 2003; Gornick and Meyers 2003: ch. 5; Eliason et al. 2008). The expectation is that if women know they can take a reasonably long break from work without losing their job and without forgoing all of their earnings, more will choose to enter the labor market in the first place and more will return after having a child. Here too the Nordic countries have been at the forefront. Each of the four instituted a policy of paid maternity leave by the 1960s, and in the ensuing decades the length and financial generosity of these leaves have gradually been extended.

It is not clear how best to measure the generosity of paid leave. One way is via the replacement rate—the amount of the monetary benefit relative to the forgone earnings. Here again three of the Nordic countries stand out: Denmark, Norway, and Sweden each offer at least a full year of maternity/parental/care leave at a replacement rate of between 80% and 100% (Gornick and Meyers 2003: 124–7). In Sweden, for example, women can take fourteen months of paid leave. The benefit during the first twelve months is set at 80% of the woman's prior earnings, and employers frequently contribute an additional amount so that the replacement rate is nearly 100%. The benefit during the remainder of the leave is a flat rate of approximately US$200 per month. Because replacement rate provisions are so complicated in some countries, it is difficult to create a useful comparative measure of the financial generosity of leave policies. For example, it might be helpful to have a measure of the number of weeks mothers can take a leave with a replacement rate of 75% or better, but in some countries the payment is calculated entirely or partially as a flat rate rather than as a percentage of earnings.

A potentially more relevant measure is the *length* of paid maternity and/or care leave. Data have been compiled by Anne Gauthier and Anita Bortnick (2001). They are shown in Figure 10.7. Unlike the data for public childcare (in Figures 10.5 and 10.6), these data are annual, so they reveal more of the over-time variation. However, they begin only in 1970. Here the countries that

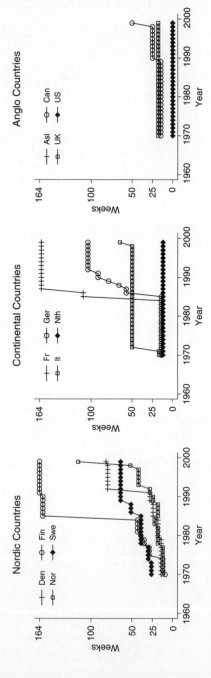

Figure 10.7. Length of paid maternity leave, 1960ff.

Note: Data begin in 1970 and end in 1999. For data definitions and sources, see the appendix.

stand out as most generous are Finland, France, Germany, and Norway, each of which offers a two-to-three-year paid leave. There is reason to expect that leaves of this length reduce women's employment (Rubery et al. 1999: 162; OECD 2001; Gornick and Meyers 2003: 240–1; Morgan and Zippel 2003). And there is some supportive evidence. For example, one recent study finds that a three-year "baby break" has become "a virtually universal phenomenon" among employed German women who have a child (Gottschall and Bird 2003). Among west German mothers with children under age 3, the labor force participation rate fell from 28% to 23% between 1986, when the leave was first implemented, and 2000 (Morgan and Zippel 2003: 67). And for mothers who do return to the work force, the break appears to encourage part-time rather than full-time employment (Ondrich et al. 1999; Gottschall and Bird 2003). France also introduced its long-term care leave in the 1980s. The eligibility criteria for the leave were eased in 1994, and in the ensuing years the rate of women's labor force participation dropped for the first time in several decades (Morgan and Zippel 2003). Marit Rønsen and Marianne Sundstrom (2002) find that Finland's paid care leave has reduced reentry into employment after childbirth among women who had previously been employed, and Rønsen (2001) finds the same to be true in Norway.

A third type of women-friendly policy is government provision of public-sector jobs (Daly 2000; Esping-Andersen et al. 2002: ch. 3; Eliason et al. 2008). Public-sector jobs may be more attractive to women than private-sector jobs because they are more likely to be secure (governments are less likely than private employers to fire employees during economic downturns), to be available at reduced hours (part-time), to not require nonstandard (evening or weekend) hours, and to accommodate family needs such as illness.

Figure 10.8 shows the share of the working-age population (female or male) in public employment from 1960 to 1997 (the most recent available year of data). Once again the Nordic countries have been at the forefront. In the 1960s there was little cross-country variation in rates of public-sector employment. Beginning in the 1970s, public employment in Denmark, Norway, and Sweden—and to a lesser extent Finland—increased sharply and steadily. The only exception has been the decline in Sweden during the 1990s, which was a product of the overall economic crisis. As of the most recent data more than one in five working-age persons, and one in two employed women, worked in the public sector in Denmark, Norway, and Sweden. In the continental and Anglo countries public employment totaled between 10% and 15% of the working-age population.

Fourth, government can promote part-time employment, which women may prefer because the shorter hours facilitate work-family balance (Gornick and Meyers 2003: 163–72). This can be done directly: government can offer

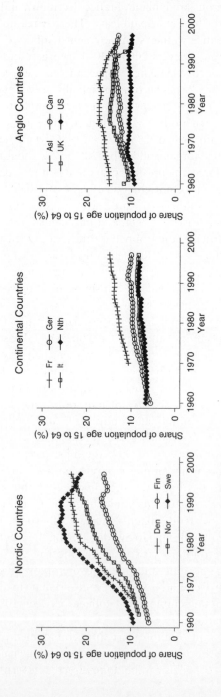

Figure 10.8. Public employment, 1960ff.

Note: The time series for most of the countries ends in 1997. For data definitions and sources, see the appendix.

part-time public-sector jobs. The Swedish and Norwegian governments have actively pursued this strategy, and Finland's government experimented with it in the 1990s (Gornick and Meyers 2003: 166–7). Governments also can encourage part-time hiring by private employers in a variety of ways. One is to make benefits such as health insurance and pensions largely a public responsibility, as is true in most affluent nations aside from the United States. Another is to reduce the length of the standard legal work week. This may make part-time employment (generally defined as less than 30 hours per week) less unappealing to employers, as the typical work week is not too much longer. Governments also can pass laws prohibiting discrimination against part-time employees in pay, working conditions, and opportunity for promotion. The European Union issued a directive to member countries in 1997 requiring such laws, and many European countries have since implemented them. In some countries, parents of young children have a legal right to reduce their work hours without having to change jobs. Sweden was the first to do this in 1978, and the Netherlands and Germany have followed suit more recently (in 2000 and 2001, respectively). Finally, governments can subsidize employers that create part-time jobs. The French government offers a reduction in social security contributions to firms that hire employees for part-time work, provided the hire represents a new job.

I know of no direct measures of policies supporting part-time employment. Figure 10.9 shows the share of the working-age population in part-time work. Unfortunately, these data are available only beginning in the early 1980s for most of the countries. Denmark, Norway, and Sweden had the highest rates of part-time employment as of the early 1980s, but their levels have been more or less constant since then. The Netherlands has experienced by far the sharpest increase, and it had the highest level as of 2006. Together with Finland, the other three continental countries started the 1980s and continued as of the mid-2000s to have the lowest part-time employment rates, though Germany had a nontrivial jump in the late 1990s. Part-time employment in the Anglo countries has increased steadily, aside from the United States, so that by 2006 Australia, Canada, and the United Kingdom had rates of part-time employment similar to those of Denmark, Norway, and Sweden.

These data are potentially a bit misleading, because part-time work is defined by the OECD, the source for the data, as fewer than 30 hours in a typical week. In the Nordic countries it is common for women to work between 30 and 35 hours per week, which many would consider part-time but which is not defined as such in this measure. Then again, average weekly hours among part-time female employees do not differ greatly across most of these countries (Rubery et al. 1999: 258).

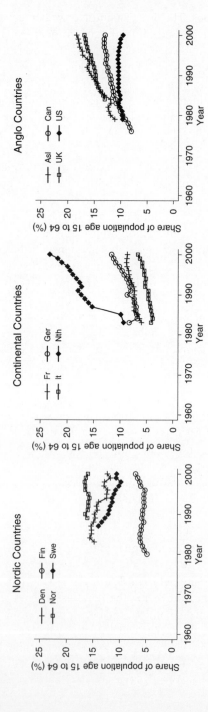

Figure 10.9. Part-time employment, 1960ff.

Note: Part-time is defined here as fewer than 30 hours per week. For data definitions and sources, see the appendix.

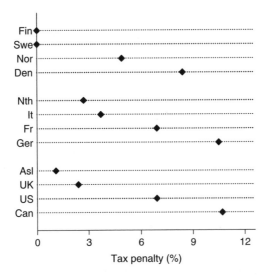

Figure 10.10. Tax penalty for a couple with two earners, *c*.2000.

Note: For data definitions and sources, see the appendix.

A fifth type of policy that may affect women's employment is the structure of the tax system (Plantenga and Hansen 1999; Rubery et al. 1999: 158–9; Sainsbury 1999; Daly 2000; Dingeldey 2001; OECD 2002*b*: ch. 5). Of particular relevance is the degree to which a couple with two earners is penalized relative to a couple with one earner. The greater the tax penalty, the stronger the disincentive for a woman with an employed husband to get a job.

Figure 10.10 shows a measure of the tax penalty for a dual-earner household. It is calculated as the income plus payroll tax rate for a couple with two earners minus the rate for a couple with one earner (at average production worker wage level). The larger the difference between the two rates, the steeper the penalty. Unfortunately, these data are not available over time. Those shown in the chart are for *c*.2000. In Sweden and Finland a couple with two earners faced the same tax rate as a couple with one earner (no penalty), whereas in Germany the tax rate for the former couple was approximately 10 percentage points higher than for the latter.

Finally, a sixth women-friendly policy is antidiscrimination and/or affirmative action laws. To the extent women's employment is impeded by discriminatory action by employers, such policies are likely to help. O'Connor, Orloff, and Shaver (1999) suggest that antidiscrimination and affirmative action policies may help to explain the comparatively high rates of women's employment in the United States and the other Anglo countries, which have relatively limited public childcare, paid maternity leave, and public employment. A useful measure for this type of policy might be the year of introduction of (meaningful) antidiscrimination legislation and/or government-mandated affirmative action. Unfortunately, I have not been able to locate such data for most of the countries.

FINDINGS FROM INDIVIDUAL-LEVEL STUDIES

A variety of studies have examined the link between women-friendly policies and individual behavior. The bulk have analyzed employment behavior of mothers with preschool-age children as a function of the availability and affordability of childcare and/or the duration and generosity of maternity leave. Most studies of childcare have concluded that women with access to affordable care are more likely to reenter employment after childbirth than women without it (Gustafsson and Stafford 1992; Leibowitz, Klerman, and Waite 1992; Barrow 1996; Kimmel 1998; Powell 1998; Anderson and Levine 1999; Michalopoulos and Robins 2000; Chevalier and Viitanen 2002; Del Boca 2002; Rønsen and Sundstrom 2002). Studies of the impact of maternity leave have generally concluded that, up to a point, it both increases women's employment prior to childbirth and increases their propensity to return to the work force afterward, but that very lengthy leaves may discourage such return (Ondrich, Spiess, and Yang 1996; Ilmakunnas 1997; Joesch 1997; Fagnani 1998; Ondrich et al. 1999; Smith, Downs, and O'Connell 2001; Rønsen and Sundstrom 2002; Gottschall and Bird 2003; Pylkkänen and Smith 2003; Hofferth and Curtin 2003).

Is there evidence at the macro (country) level that women-friendly policies affect women's employment?

CROSS-COUNTRY PATTERNS: WOMEN AGE 25 TO 54

Cross-Country Variation in Levels

Figure 10.11 shows a series of scatterplot charts with the employment rate for women age 25–54 as of 2000–06 on the vertical axis and various measures of women-friendly policies around the year 2000 on the horizontal axis.

The first chart shows women's employment rates by the share of children age 1 to 2 that are in publicly financed care. This is a different measure of

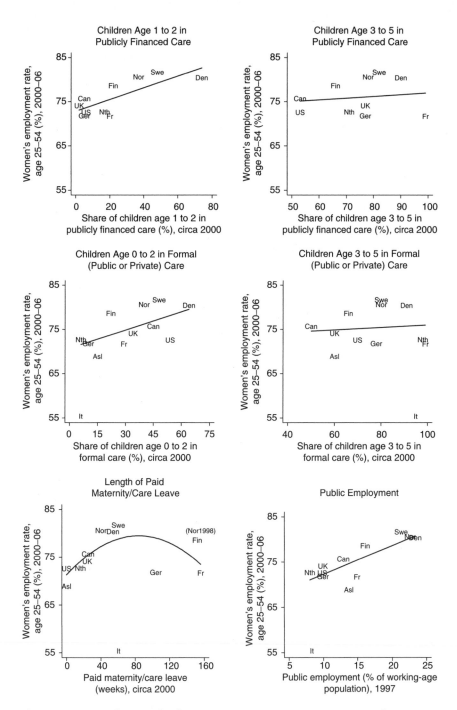

Figure 10.11. Employment levels among women age 25 to 54, 2000–06, by women-friendly policies.

Note: Some axes are truncated. The regression lines and curves are based on data with Italy excluded. For data definitions and sources, see the appendix.

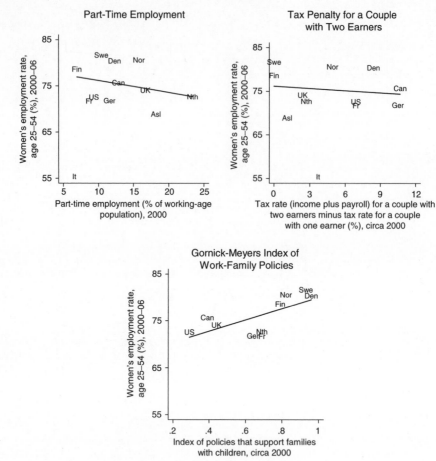

Figure 10.11. (*Continued*)

the generosity of government support for childcare than that shown in Figure 10.5, but it may be a better one (Daly 2000; Gornick and Meyers 2003). Unfortunately, data are not available for Australia or Italy. The regression line suggests some support for the expected positive effect. The fit is not perfect: Denmark, the Netherlands, and France have prime-age women's employment rates a bit lower than the share of very young children in publicly financed care would lead us to expect. However, the pattern is certainly consistent with an interpretation that public provision and/or subsidization of care for very young children helps to boost women's employment.

The second chart shows women's employment rates by the share of children age 3 to 5 in publicly financed care. Here we observe no relationship at all. This is due in part to the anomalous position of France. Almost all 3- to 5-year-old children in France are in public childcare or preschools, yet it has the lowest rate of women's employment among the ten countries in this chart. Even among the other nations, however, there is little evidence of a positive effect.

In principle, what should matter to women is not public provision of childcare per se, but rather the degree to which care is available, affordable, and of sufficiently high quality (Daly 2000: 291; OECD 2001; Orloff 2004). For example, in the United States there is little public support for childcare. Yet 67% of working-age women, including 64% of married mothers with children under age 6, are employed. The country has a well-developed private childcare market; care is widely available and, for many, affordable. As a result, children often are put in nonfamily-based care at a very early age. According to one estimate, nearly half of children less than 1-year-old are in childcare for more than 30 hours per week (Vandell and Wolfe 2000: i). In most of the US states there is little or no publicly provided care prior to age 5, when kindergarten begins (Committee for Economic Development 2002). Affluent parents and more and more middle-class dual-earner couples pay for private childcare and preschool, some of which is of high quality. Many low-income dual-earner couples and single parents also pay for private care, though the care they can afford tends to be of much lower quality (Kamerman and Kahn 1995; Vandell and Wolfe 2000; Blau 2001). Government does help to finance the purchase of private childcare for some families, but its role is very limited. Since 1990 childcare subsidies have been available to low-income parents through the federal Child Care and Development Fund, but the quantity of funds allocated is so small that only 10% of the low-income families formally eligible to receive a subsidy actually do (Helburn and Bergmann 2002: 23; Stoker and Wilson 2006: 135). Most childcare is informal and unregulated; more than two-thirds of preschool-age children of employed women are cared for in homes, rather than in childcare centers (Blau 2001: 13).

The third and fourth charts in Figure 10.11 show women's employment by the share of children age 0 to 2 and age 3 to 5, respectively, in formal childcare—whether public or private. The chart for children age 0 to 2 indicates a positive association. Here and in the other charts in Figure 10.11 I have calculated the regression, or "best-fit," line with Italy excluded, as it is a significant outlier. On the other hand, even discounting Italy the fit is not necessarily any better than for publicly financed childcare. The United States, Canada, the United Kingdom, France, Germany, and the Netherlands differ substantially in the share of children under age 3 that are in formal care arrangements; in the Netherlands fewer than 10% are, while in the United States the share is nearly 60%. Yet these countries differ very little in employment rates among prime-working-age women.

The fourth chart, for children age 3 to 5 in formal care, indicates no association at all. To the extent childcare matters for women's employment, the bivariate patterns suggest it is care in the youngest years that is most relevant.

The fifth chart shows women's employment by the length of paid maternity or care leave. Because Norway's lengthy care leave was introduced so recently, I use the length of paid leave that was in existence in Norway for most of the preceding two decades, though the length beginning in 1998 is noted in the chart in parentheses. The expectation is for a curvilinear relationship: women's employment should increase with the length of paid leave up to a point and then decrease. This is in fact what we observe. Italy plainly is an anomaly, but otherwise the countries more or less conform to the expected hump-shaped pattern.

The sixth chart shows women's employment by the share of the working-age population in public-sector jobs. Here we see a fairly strong association in the expected positive direction. Aside from Italy, the only exceptions to the pattern are Australia and France, where the prime-age women's employment rate is a bit lower than would be expected given their comparatively high levels of public employment.

The seventh chart shows women's employment by the share of the working-age population in part-time employment. There is no indication of the expected positive association. Italy has the lowest share of working-age adults in part-time jobs, and it does have the lowest rate of prime-working-age women's employment among these twelve countries. But the three nations with the largest shares in part-time jobs—the Netherlands, Australia, and the United Kingdom—do not have especially high female employment rates.

The eighth chart shows the rate of women's employment by the tax penalty for a two-earner household. There is no indication of a relationship. Germany and Sweden are at opposite poles in terms of the tax penalty they impose on a dual-earner couple, and the employment rates for women in those two countries are consistent with what we would expect. But the dual-earner tax penalty seems to have little or no predictive utility for the other ten nations. This is consistent with the finding of other recent studies (Sainsbury 1999: 195–6; Dingeldey 2001: 665–6). Denmark is a particularly notable case. It imposes one of the stiffest penalties on two-earner couples among these countries, yet its rate of women's employment is among the highest.

All twelve of the countries have antidiscrimination laws, and most have some sort of affirmative action policy. It is the Anglo countries, particularly the

United States, that were the first to introduce them. Figures 10.1 and 10.2 show that these four countries have rates of women's employment that are higher than an explanation focused on public childcare, paid maternity/care leave, public employment, part-time employment, and/or tax penalties would lead us to predict. Perhaps, then, antidiscrimination laws and affirmative action have indeed helped. I return to this later in the chapter.

Some analysts have suggested that the impact of women-friendly policies is most likely to be observable by examining a composite index rather than individual policies (Plantenga and Hansen 1999; OECD 2001; Gornick and Meyers 2003: ch. 8; Mandel and Semyonov 2006). The last chart in Figure 10.11 shows women's employment by one such index: a measure of policy supports for families with children, created by Janet Gornick and Marcia Meyers (2003). The Nordic countries score highest on the index, followed by the continental countries, with the Anglo countries at the bottom. The overall association with prime-age women's employment rates is positive, but the position of the continental and Anglo countries is the opposite of what the index predicts.

This bivariate examination of cross-country variation in levels of women's employment offers some evidence of a beneficial effect of women-friendly policies. Public childcare for very young children may help. Paid maternity/care leave appears to help, but only up to a point. If available for more than fifteen to eighteen months it may reduce rather than increase women's employment. Public employment also may have a positive impact. There are strong theoretical grounds for suspecting that part-time employment and tax systems should affect women's employment, but at the bivariate level neither appears to be of much use in understanding cross-country patterns.

Are there factors for which we should control? The associations observed in Figure 10.11 might be due to other determinants of women's employment with which the use of women-friendly policies happens to be correlated.

One candidate is women's preferences regarding employment (Hakim 2000; Bielenski, Bosch, and Wagner 2002). Unfortunately, available data on this cover only a subset of the twelve countries. The first two charts in Figure 10.12 show employment among prime-working-age women by two measures of preferences. The preference data in the first chart are from the 1995–97 World Values Survey. They represent the share of women age 25–59 strongly agreeing that "both husband and wife should contribute to household income." The data in the second chart are from the 1994 International Social Survey Program (ISSP). They represent the share of women responding that mothers with preschool children should work part-time or full-time rather than stay home.

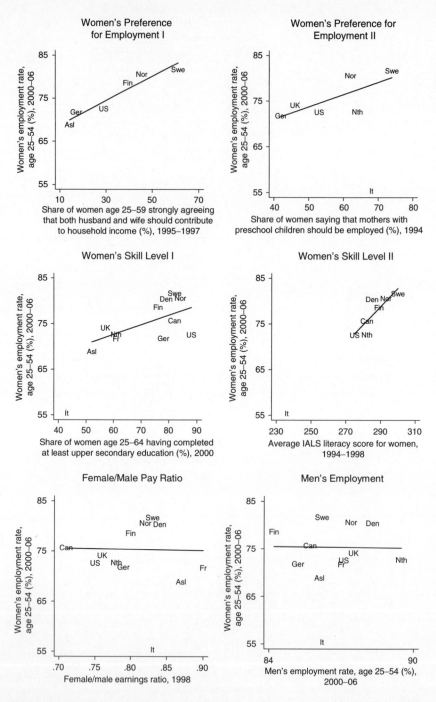

Figure 10.12. Employment levels among women age 25 to 54, 2000–06, by potential control variables.

Note: Chart axes are truncated. The regression lines are based on data with Italy excluded. For data definitions and sources, see the appendix.

Both charts suggest a strong positive association across countries between women's preference for employment and women's actual employment rate. There are only two notable puzzles, both in the second chart. One is Italy, in which a relatively large share of women responded that a mother with preschool children should be employed and yet comparatively few prime-working-age women actually are employed. The other is the Netherlands, which has a somewhat (but not terribly) lower female employment rate than would be predicted given the apparent preference of women for employment. Otherwise, the patterns suggest that women's preferences may be an important factor driving women's employment.

On the other hand, it could be that the causality runs in the opposite direction: preferences may have responded to employment patterns that were generated by women-friendly policies. If that is the case, we would not want to control for preferences in a multivariate analysis. In any event, doing so is not possible because of the limited number of countries covered by the preference data.

A second potentially important control is women's skills. The higher women's skill levels, the greater the opportunity cost of nonemployment and thus the stronger the incentive to be employed. And from employers' point of view, better skills make it more attractive to hire women. Within each of the twelve countries there is a strong positive association between women's educational attainment and women's employment (Figure 10.21; Rubery et al. 1999: 87–93). In Sweden, for example, the employment rate among women age 25–64 is 61% for those with less than upper secondary education, 80% for those having completed upper secondary education, and 86% for those having completed tertiary education. In Germany the comparable figures are 50%, 71%, and 83%. In the United States they are 45%, 65%, and 78%.

The third and fourth charts in Figure 10.12 show women's employment by two measures of women's skills. In the third chart the skills measure is the share of women age 25–64 who have completed at least upper secondary education. In the fourth chart the measure is women's average literacy score in the 1994–98 International Assessment of Literacy Skills (IALS). This second measure is available for only nine of the twelve countries. Both charts suggest a relatively strong positive correlation between women's skills and women's employment. Perhaps most noteworthy, the very low average educational attainment and literacy level among Italian women may help to account for Italy's low female employment rate.

Like preferences for employment, women's skills may be endogenous; it may be that supportive policies lure more women into the work force, which in turn encourages younger women to stay in school longer. But reverse causality seems less likely for skills than for preferences.

Third, it may be helpful to control for the gender pay gap. This can be considered an indicator of the payoff to women from entering the work force. The smaller the gender pay gap, the stronger the incentive for women to choose paid work over domestic work. The measure I use here is the ratio (rather than the gap) of median earnings among full-time employed women to median earnings among full-time employed men. The fifth chart in Figure 10.12 shows women's employment by the female/male pay ratio as of 1998 (the most recent year for which data are available for the full group of countries). As it turns out, there is no association across these twelve countries.

Fourth, it may be that countries in which women's employment is low are those in which employment is low in general. If so, this would suggest that the key determinants of cross-country variation in women's employment are not women-friendly policies, or indeed anything specific to women, but rather factors that affect employment for both men and women. One way to examine this possibility is to look at the cross-country pattern for levels of female and male employment. This is shown in the sixth chart in Figure 10.12. There is no apparent association across the countries between women's and men's employment rates.

Among these possible controls, then, only women's preference for employment and women's skill level are correlated with prime-working-age women's employment rates, and the former seems very likely to be endogenous. Do the associations in the bivariate scatterplots in Figure 10.11 hold up if women's skills are controlled for?

I first regressed the prime-age women's employment rate in 2000–06 on women's educational attainment (secondary school completion). The residuals from this regression represent women's employment rates adjusted for women's educational attainment. I used these residuals as the dependent variable in a series of regressions that included all possible combinations of three or fewer of the women-friendly policies as independent variables. Some of the policies could not be included together in the same regressions, because they are too strongly correlated with one another ($r > \pm .65$). Both public childcare and formal (public or private) childcare for very young children could not be included together with public employment. I transformed ("linearized") the paid care leave measure so that high scores represent paid leaves of moderate length and low scores represent leaves of short or long duration. A positive coefficient is therefore expected for this variable.

Figure 10.13 shows the results for the women-friendly policy variables from the various regressions in which each was included. The coefficients reported

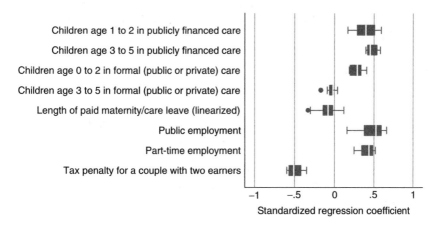

Figure 10.13. Regression results: Estimated effect of women-friendly policies on education-adjusted levels of employment among women age 25 to 54, 2000–06.

Note: Standardized coefficients from ordinary least squares (OLS) regressions using all possible combinations of three or fewer of the independent variables. Dependent variable is the residuals from a regression of employment rates among women age 25–54 on the share of women age 25–64 having completed at least upper secondary education. $N = 10$ or 12, depending on which combination of variables is included. The number of regressions ranges from 11 to 25 for the variables. For data definitions and sources, see the appendix. The "whiskers" refer to the minimum and maximum coefficients. The edges of the box indicate the 25th- and 75th-percentile coefficients. The vertical white line is the median coefficient. Separate dots indicate "outliers"—coefficients that are substantially larger or smaller than the others in that set.

are standardized; they estimate the amount of change, in standard deviations, that occurs in the dependent variable given a one-standard-deviation increase in the independent variable. As in previous chapters, the coefficients are reported in boxplots—one for each women-friendly policy.

These regressions suggest more support for several of the women-friendly policies than do the bivariate patterns in Figure 10.11. The variables representing share of children in publicly financed childcare, both those age 1 to 2 and those age 3 to 5, yield consistently positive signs. The same is true for the share of children age 0 to 2 (but not 3 to 5) in formal care, for public employment, and for part-time employment. And the tax penalty variable consistently yields the expected negative sign.

On the other hand, one of the variables for which there seems to be clear support in the bivariate patterns—the length of paid maternity/care leave— receives no support in these regressions. Most of its coefficients are close to zero. This is partly a function of Italy and Germany, which have moderately lengthy leaves but low (raw and adjusted) employment rates among prime-working-age women. It also is because Australia, Finland, and France, which have very short or very lengthy paid maternity/care leaves and comparatively low employment rates among prime-age women, score better when employment is adjusted for women's education.

Cross-Country Variation in Over-Time Trends

Figure 10.14 shows a set of scatterplots with (adjusted) change in employment among women age 25–54 on the vertical axis and various measures of women-friendly policies on the horizontal axis. Data for women's employment in Denmark and the United Kingdom are not available prior to the mid-1980s (see Figure 10.4), so these two countries are not in any of the charts.

I include only the women-friendly policies for which there are longitudinal data going back to 1970: publicly financed childcare, paid maternity/care leave, and public employment. The policies are measured in two ways: as levels and as change scores. The level measures are calculated as averages over the period 1970 to 2000 (1970 to 1997 for public employment). The change score measures are calculated in two different ways. Because the data for publicly financed childcare for 0–2s and 3–5s are available only as decade averages, the change scores for these policies are calculated as the average for the 1990s minus the average for the 1970s. For paid maternity leave and public employment, the change scores are calculated as the 2000 (or nearest available year) value minus the 1970 value. For reasons noted earlier, I use 1998 rather than 2000 as the end point in calculating change scores for paid maternity/care leave in Norway.

Change in women's employment is measured as the age 25–54 female employment rate in 2000–06 minus the rate in 1970–73. The measure of change shown in the charts is adjusted for two things. One is the 1970–73 level of women's employment. There has been a very strong "catch-up" pattern across the countries for which data are available; those with low rates of employment among women age 25–54 in the early 1970s have tended to experience faster growth since then. The correlation between 1970–73 levels and change from 1970–73 to 2000–06 is -.87. The second is change in women's educational attainment. Here I use the only longitudinal data of which I am aware: average years of schooling completed among the female population age 25 and over, from a data set compiled by Robert Barro and Jong-Wha Lee (n.d.). The measure used in the charts is the residuals from a regression of change in women's age 25–54 employment on the 1970–73 level and change in women's educational attainment. Italy and the Netherlands are outliers, and they are not included in calculating the regression lines and curves.

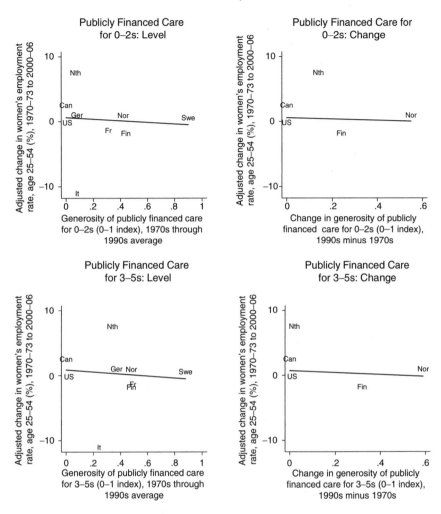

Figure 10.14. Adjusted change in employment among women age 25 to 54 by women-friendly policies, 1970–73 to 2000–06.

Note: Denmark and the United Kingdom are not included because age-group-specific data are not available prior to 1983 and 1984, respectively. The regression lines and curves are based on data with Italy and the Netherlands excluded. For data definitions and sources, see the appendix.

Unlike the patterns in Figures 10.11 and 10.13, the patterns in the eight scatterplots in Figure 10.14 suggest little support for the notion that women-friendly policies boost female employment. In none of the eight charts do we observe a strong positive—or hump-shaped for paid care leave—association between women-friendly policies and adjusted change in employment rates

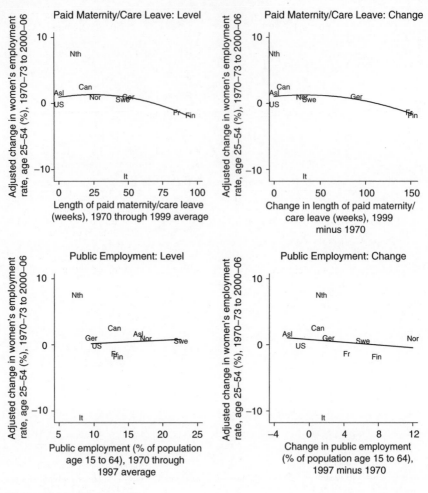

Figure 10.14. (*Continued*)

among prime-working-age women. Most of the regression lines are flat, or nearly so.

One qualification is worth noting. Two countries with comparatively generous women-friendly policies, Sweden and Finland, experienced severe economic crises in the first half of the 1990s that dramatically reduced employment rates among both women and men. These crises were not a product of women-friendly policies, but they substantially reduced the amount of increase in women's employment in those two nations.

CROSS-COUNTRY PATTERNS: WOMEN AGE 15 TO 24

As the data in Figure 10.2 make clear, the variation in the overall women's employment rates among the twelve countries owes heavily to large differences in employment rates among the youngest and oldest groups of working-age women. Among women age 15–24, the Nordic and Anglo countries (Sweden and Finland are exceptions) have employment rates around 50% to 60%, compared to just 20% to 40% in Germany, France, and Italy. Among women age 55–64, the Nordic countries have employment rates around 40% to 50%, compared to 20% to 30% in Germany, France, and Italy. What accounts for the very low female employment rates among these two age groups in Germany, France, and Italy?

Let's begin with the 15–24s. We would hope for a relatively large share of women in this age group, especially those age 15–19, to be in school. But like work and family, work and school need not be mutually exclusive. Figure 10.15 shows school and work activity among women age 15–24 in the twelve countries. I have separated this group into two subgroups: 15–19s and 20–24s. In the charts each of these age subgroups is further divided into four groups: those in school and also employed, those in school and not employed, those not in school and employed, and those not in school and not employed. Among women age 15–19, between 80% and 95% are in school in each of the twelve countries. The key difference across the countries is in the share of women who are in school and also employed. In France and Italy, virtually none of the women who are enrolled in school also engage in paid work. Among women age 20–24, a much larger share in all of the countries is out of school. Here too, however, France and Italy stand apart in their low shares of women that are simultaneously in school and employed. In every other country aside from Finland, 60% or more of women age 20–24 are employed, whether they are also in school or not. In France and Italy, by contrast, fewer than 40% are employed.

This suggests that opportunities for part-time work may be an important determinant of the cross-country variation in employment rates among women age 15–24. Although some women enrolled in school work full-time, that is very difficult to pull off. Figure 10.16 plots the employment rate among women age 15–24 by the share of the working-age population employed part-time. The latter can be treated as an indicator of the availability of part-time jobs. Although there are some exceptions, countries in which there is greater opportunity for part-time employment tend to have higher employment levels among the youngest group of working-age women. The time-series data for the Netherlands in Figure 10.4 offer additional grounds for pointing to part-time employment as the key. As the availability of part-time work increased

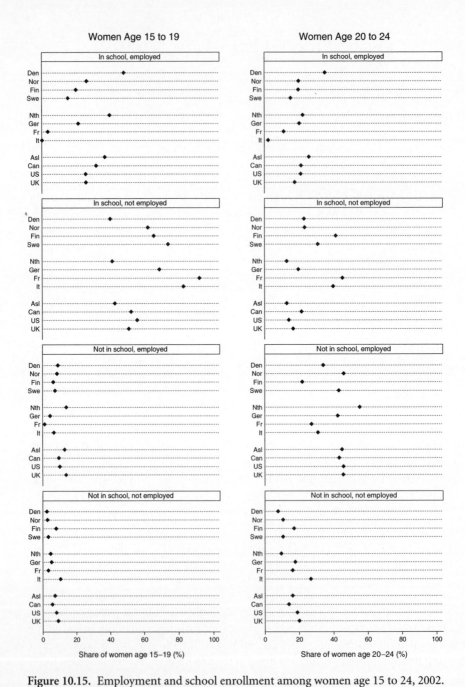

Figure 10.15. Employment and school enrollment among women age 15 to 24, 2002.

Note: Within each group, the countries are ordered according to the share in school and employed. For data definitions and sources, see the appendix.

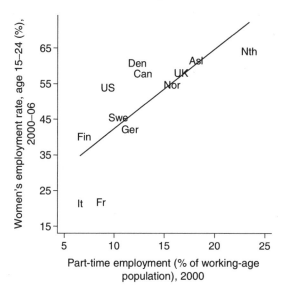

Figure 10.16. Employment levels among women age 15 to 24, 2000–06, by part-time employment.

Note: Chart axes are truncated. For data definitions and sources, see the appendix.

rapidly in the Netherlands in the 1980s and 1990s, employment rates among Dutch women age 15–24 increased at the same pace as among women age 25–54. That did not happen in any other country.

Is it a good thing for large numbers of young women to be simultaneously in school and in employment? There are two ways in which this can be beneficial. First, employment experience helps to build human capital. Even a part-time job sweeping floors or working a cash register can be helpful in instilling discipline and developing work habits. An employment history also signals the presence of traits such as reliability and perseverance. These may be even more important to employers than cognitive skills (Bowles and Gintis 2002; Heckman and Rubinstein 2002; Farkas 2003). For students at top universities on their way to professional careers as doctors, lawyers, and professors, working part-time as a waitress to help pay the rent or to earn some discretionary spending money contributes little or nothing to future employment prospects. But most women in these twelve countries do not obtain a college degree, and for those women it may help a great deal. The second benefit stems from the fact that more women in employment, even if only part-time and at relatively low wages, reduces government expenditures on social assistance and other similar programs and broadens the tax base. It thereby enlarges the scope for government efforts to limit inequality via redistribution to the truly needy.

CROSS-COUNTRY PATTERNS: WOMEN AGE 55 TO 64

What accounts for the very low employment rates among women age 55–64 in Germany, France, and Italy? One possibility is that this is a cohort effect. In this interpretation, these countries began the shift from low to high employment rates for prime-working-age women later than the Nordic and Anglo countries and the high-employment cohorts have yet to reach age 55–64, or have done so only very recently. When they do, female employment rates for this age group will begin to catch up.

This is not implausible, but the employment patterns shown in Figure 10.4 offer tepid support at best. The OECD age-group-specific employment data for Germany, France, and Italy are available beginning in 1970. They are shown in Figure 10.4. Employment rates among women age 25–34 began to increase in the early 1970s, though we cannot tell if this increase had begun earlier. If it in fact began right at that moment, then the cohort interpretation may hold water. The cohort that was 25–34 in 1970 was 55–64 in 2000, and the 55–64 female employment rates in these three countries did start increasing in the late 1990s. However, employment rates among women age 35–44 and 45–54 were also increasing in the 1970s in these countries, and these groups reached age 55–64 prior to the 1990s. This suggests reason for skepticism about a cohort effect. Then again, it could be the case that there is something different about the cohort that was 25–34 in the 1970s. Because of the cultural changes occurring in the late 1960s and through the 1970s, this group may well have a different orientation toward employment that will keep them in the work force during their late working-age years to a greater extent than was true of their predecessors.

An alternative explanation for the very low rates of employment among German, French, and Italian women age 55–64 is the more general condition of the labor market in those three countries. Figure 10.17 shows employment rates for women age 55–64 by employment rates for men age 55–64 as of 2000–06. Unlike for 25–54s (see Figure 10.12), the data suggest a strong positive association across the twelve countries. Employment rates are low in Germany, France, and Italy not only among older women but also among older men. In response to heightened competition, high labor costs, strict employment protection rules, and other factors, firms and governments in these countries have encouraged early retirement for many workers over

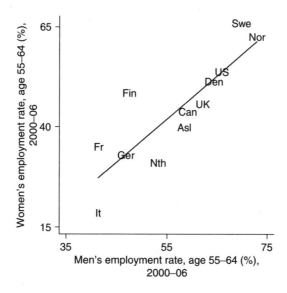

Figure 10.17. Employment among women age 55 to 64 by employment among men age 55 to 64, 2000–06.

Note: Chart axes are truncated. For data definitions and sources, see the appendix.

age 50 (Ebbinghaus 2000). Although this development has affected men to a greater extent than women, plenty of women have retired early too. Some utilize an early retirement offer for themselves, and others take advantage of the early pension offered to their husband to leave the work force.

DEVELOPMENTS IN INDIVIDUAL COUNTRIES

I turn now to a more detailed examination of developments within the individual countries. Here I draw heavily on the time-series data for women's employment rates shown in Figure 10.4 and for women-friendly policies shown in Figures 10.5 through 10.9.

Nordic Countries

With the exception of Finland, each of the Nordic countries has experienced a substantial increase in women's employment—between 20 and 30 percentage points—over the past four decades. Almost all of this occurred in the 1960s, 1970s, and 1980s. There has been little further rise since then. In Finland the women's employment rate was very high already by the early 1960s, but it has increased relatively little since then.

As of the mid-2000s, the employment rate among women age 25–54 was around 80% in all four Nordic countries. As Figure 10.2 indicated, this is higher than in the continental or Anglo nations. But the Nordic countries also tend to have high rates of employment among women age 15–24 and women age 55–64. With the exception of the younger group in Sweden and both groups in Finland, the employment rates for both the youngest and oldest groups of working-age women are around 60%. Among the continental and Anglo countries, only the United States comes close to matching these levels.

Sweden

Sweden has been at the forefront in introducing and extending women-friendly policies. It was among the first to introduce public childcare for preschool-age children, paid maternity/care leave, large-scale public employment, a right for parents to reduce work hours, and individualized taxation with no penalty for a couple's second earner.

Plainly, Sweden's high women's employment rate is "overdetermined"; there are a large number of factors that seem likely to have contributed. Not only have policies been very supportive, but women's preferences are strongly oriented toward employment, female educational attainment and literacy levels are high, the gender pay gap is comparatively low, and the employment rate for men has tended to be relatively high.

The 1970s was the decade in which Sweden began or most significantly expanded many of these policies (OECD 2005a). The share of children age 0 to 6 in public childcare increased from 10% in 1970 to 30% in 1980. Paid maternity leave was gradually expanded from six months in 1970 to a year in 1980, and between 1970 and 1975 the replacement rate jumped from 65% to 90%. In 1971 the tax penalty for a second household earner was substantially reduced. And in 1978 parents with preschool-age children were given the right to reduce their work hours from eight per day to six. We would expect, therefore, to observe an acceleration in the rate of increase in women's employment in the 1970s and/or the 1980s. But the time-series data shown in Figure 10.4 are not clear on this. The overall women's employment rate as well as the rates for women age 25 to 34 and age 35 to 44 were flat in the mid-1960s but then began to increase rapidly in the late 1960s. This continued through the 1970s and 1980s, but with no apparent acceleration. If we presume that the late-1960s' acceleration would have continued of its own accord, we must wonder why the female employment rate did not accelerate in the 1970s and/or 1980s following the 1970s boom in introduction and expansion of women-friendly policies.

One possibility is that the women-friendly policies that have mattered most in boosting women's employment in Sweden have been the extensive provision of public-sector jobs and/or the availability of paid maternity leave. These began in the 1950s and 1960s and were already fairly well-developed by 1970. Yet as Figures 10.7 and 10.8 indicate, these too were expanded considerably after 1970. Public employment increased from 15% of the working-age population in 1970 to 25% in 1990, and paid maternity/parental leave was gradually extended from 26 weeks in 1970 to 64 weeks in 1990. A second possibility is that had it not been for the expansion of various women-friendly policies during the 1970s, the rate of increase in women's employment would have slowed in the 1970s and 1980s. However, it is not clear why that should be expected. GDP growth did slow during those two decades, but it was nevertheless reasonably healthy, and the employment rate for men remained at a very high level (more than 85%). A third possibility is that the women-friendly policy enhancements in the 1970s did produce an acceleration in employment rates among women with young children but that this is hidden in the aggregate women's employment data because birth rates declined beginning in the mid-to-late 1960s. Unfortunately, I am not aware of time-series data on employment rates specifically for women with young children, women with older children, and women with no children, so I am unable to assess this.

The over-time data thus offer somewhat lukewarm support for the notion that women-friendly policies have had a significant impact on women's employment in Sweden. They may well have played an important role, but the evidence in favor of this conclusion is by no means overwhelming.

The other striking feature of the time-series for women's employment in Sweden is the sharp drop that occurred in the early 1990s. This is a product of the early 1990s economic crisis, as indicated by the equally sharp fall in the male employment rate. Among women, the employment rate decreased most dramatically for those age 15 to 24. As employment opportunities declined during the crisis years, young women became more likely to stay in school for longer periods of time.

Denmark

Denmark followed Sweden in implementing a number of women-friendly policies, and today it is perhaps the most generous affluent country (it receives the highest score on the Gornick-Meyers index shown in Figure 10.11). It has the largest share of preschool-age children, especially children under 3, in publicly financed care, it has a very generous but not too lengthy paid parental leave policy, and it has high levels of public employment. The one exception to Denmark's otherwise very women-friendly policy package is the tax system, which imposes a comparatively severe penalty on a couple's second earner.

Like Sweden, Denmark significantly expanded its array of family-friendly policies in the 1970s. For example, the share of children age 0 to 3 in publicly financed care nearly doubled from 20% to close to 40% (OECD 2002*b*: 60). And like in Sweden, the overall rate of women's employment in Denmark increased fairly steadily during the 1960s, 1970s, and 1980s. Here too, then, there is a puzzle as to why the rate of increase did not accelerate in response to implementation and expansion of women-friendly policies in the 1970s. Unfortunately, age-group-specific employment data for Denmark are available only since the early 1980s, so they provide no help on this question. A recent report by the OECD offers a skeptical view of the causal role of women-friendly policies: "In fact, universal Danish childcare coverage, extensive leave rights, individual benefits, etc., did *not* precede the achievement of high participation rates in that country. Rather, these were the demands made by women who found that they had entered the labour market as desired by government, but who faced great demands on their time" (OECD 2002*b*: 23).

Norway

Norway is close behind Sweden and Denmark in the generosity and comprehensiveness of its women-friendly policies. A large share of Norwegian preschool-age children are in publicly financed care, and there is extensive public and part-time employment. In the 1980s and 1990s Norway also had a paid maternity leave policy similar to those of Sweden and Denmark, but that was altered with the introduction of a three-year paid care leave in 1998. The care benefit can be used either to support a stay-at-home parent or to purchase childcare. Because it was enacted so recently, however, it could not have had an impact on the bulk of the over-time trend shown in Figure 10.4.

Unfortunately, comparable data on women's and men's employment rates in Norway are not available prior to the 1970s. Like Sweden and Denmark, Norway increased the generosity of its women-friendly policies in the 1970s, and there was rapid growth in the female employment rate during that decade and through most of the 1980s. But we cannot tell if the increase was faster in the 1970s and 1980s than it had been previously.

Finland

Among the four Nordic countries, Finland has the least generous women-friendly policies (OECD 2005*a*). It has a far smaller share of young children in publicly financed care, it offers an extended maternity/care leave policy that encourages mothers to take long breaks from the work force, and it has a comparatively small share of its working-age population in public employment and in part-time employment. The only exception is its tax system, which is on par with Sweden's in imposing no penalty on two-earner households.

Despite its laggard status with respect to women-friendly policies, prior to the economic crisis of the early 1990s Finland's female employment rate, at around 70%, was approximately the same as those of Denmark and Norway and not far behind that of Sweden. What accounts for this?

One hypothesis might be that it is not the policies that have mattered in the Nordic countries. Instead, perhaps egalitarian gender attitudes have been the key factor encouraging women to enter paid employment in these countries. But the first chart on women's attitudes toward work in Figure 10.12 suggests that women are less employment-oriented in Finland than in Sweden and Norway (there are no data for Denmark). As of the mid-1990s the share of Finnish women strongly agreeing that both husband and wife should contribute to household income was some 20 percentage points lower than in Sweden.

Another possibility is that high skill levels have been the key to high Nordic rates of women's employment. Some support for this is suggested by the two "women's skills" charts in Figure 10.12. As of the late-1990s Finnish women were comparable to those in Sweden, Norway, and Denmark in secondary educational completion and in adult literacy. Yet because we lack good time-series data for both of these measures of skills, we do not know whether this apparent skill comparability has been true for some time or is a more recent phenomenon.

The simplest explanation of the Finnish anomaly lies in the fact that its rate of women's employment was already very high in the mid-1960s—60% at a time when the rate in the other eleven countries ranged from 30% to 50%. The rate of increase in women's employment during the 1960s, 1970s, and 1980s was slower in Finland than in the other three Nordic countries, which is consistent with what we would expect given its less generous set of women-friendly policies. What accounts for Finland's high rate of female employment in the 1960s? Rønsen and Sundstrom (2002: 129) suggest the following: "The longer tradition of gainful, and mainly full-time, employment among Finnish women may be a result in part of the for long lower per capita income in Finland after the Second World War, and in part of differences in country-specific cultural norms and values, generated for example by the way industrialization took place."

Continental Countries

In all four continental countries the overall women's employment rate—that is, among women age 15 to 64—is comparatively low. Although it has increased substantially in the Netherlands since the mid-1980s, there has been more limited progress in Germany, France, and Italy. This suggests both reason for worry about these three continental countries and reason to think that women-friendly policies may have played a critical role in accounting for the cross-country differences.

However, the data in Figures 10.2–10.4, which show women's employment broken down by age group, suggest a somewhat different conclusion. If we focus on employment rates for women age 25 to 54, Germany, France, and Italy do not look nearly as bad in comparative terms. As of 2000–06, the average employment rate among women age 25–54 was around 80% in the Nordic countries, 73% in the Anglo countries, and a little above 70% in Germany and France. That is a difference, to be sure, but it is not an enormous one. In Italy, the rate is approximately 55%, or 65% if we add 10 percentage points to account for the high level of informal (unmeasured) employment. There also is similarity in growth of women's employment. Since 1980 the employment rate for women age 25–54 has increased by approximately 15% to 20% in the Anglo countries. Germany and Italy, and to a lesser degree France, have done nearly as well. It is among the 15–24s and 55–64s that Germany, France, and Italy lag most severely.

The Netherlands

The Netherlands is the one continental country that has succeeded in significantly increasing women's employment. The rate jumped from around 30% in 1970 to more than 65% by the mid-2000s, with most of that increase occurring since the mid-1980s. This dramatic rise must be placed in context: women's employment in the Netherlands was extremely low at the beginning of this period, so it was in principle easier to increase than in countries where the rate was already fairly high. Still, the increase was sizable, especially when compared to the relative stagnation of women's employment in the other three continental nations.

What explains this development? As indicated by the charts in Figures 10.5–10.8, and 10.11, the Netherlands has not relied on the Nordic strategy of extensive government commitment to childcare, paid maternity/care leave, and public employment. There is only one women-friendly policy area in which the Netherlands is on the high end: part-time work. As shown in Figure 10.9, the share of the working-age population in part-time jobs is higher in the Netherlands than in any of the other eleven nations, and it increased markedly in the 1980s and 1990s. Indeed, at least two-thirds of all new jobs created in the Netherlands in those two decades were part-time (Salverda 1998; Hartog 1999; Visser 2002).

In my view, Jelle Visser (2002) has offered the most compelling account of the dramatic increase in women's employment in the Netherlands. Due to rising educational attainment and pay opportunities along with shifting cultural norms, beginning in the mid-to-late 1970s Dutch women became more interested in paid work. Because of limited availability of affordable childcare and irregular school hours, many such women came to view part-time employment as an attractive means of reconciling work and family obligations. Employers viewed part-time jobs as a useful way to attract educated women into the work force. In the Wassenaar Accord reached in the early 1980s, unions agreed to wage restraint in exchange for a reduction in the work week for full-time employees. Soon after, employers reneged and offered increased part-time employment instead. Within a relatively short period of time, part-time work became a norm for women entering the labor market—especially young women—leading to further acceleration in its use.

In the ensuing years, particularly since the late 1990s, Dutch policy makers have eased restrictions on part-time employment and indeed encouraged it. Most notably, the Work Hours Adjustment Act of 2000 requires employers to permit employees to reduce their work hours unless there are "specific conflicting business interests" to justify denying the request. The intent behind this policy is to encourage fathers to reduce work hours, so that in couples with young children both parents work three-quarters time and share equally in childcare duties.

There are two important points to emphasize regarding the Dutch experience with women's employment. First, it is too early to pronounce the Dutch case a success. Though the rate of women's employment has increased dramatically since the early 1980s, it currently is not too much higher than in Germany and France. And since a far larger share of Dutch women work part-time—including some at well below 20 hours per week—the overall volume of work among Dutch women is similar to that in Germany and France. On the other hand, women's employment in the Netherlands clearly has been on an upward trajectory, and to the extent this continues the country's performance will indeed qualify as successful.

Second, the increase in Dutch women's employment since the early 1980s is not a product of the women-friendly policies that have received the most attention from researchers. This suggests that there are multiple ways to boost female employment.

Germany

Like the successful records of Sweden, Denmark, and Norway in generating high women's employment, Germany's comparatively poor record is overdetermined. Childcare for children under 3 is undersupplied: as of the early 2000s there were spaces for only 6% of such children (Appelbaum et al. 2003: 30). Public preschool is available for children age 3 to 6, and approximately 80% of such children attend. But this schooling is half day, which poses a problem for parents in full-time jobs. Half-day schooling for 6- to 9-year-olds forces many couples with even school-age children to keep one parent home during the heart of the working day. The maternity/care leave is too long. It encourages mothers to take a three-year break from employment, which increases the number who never return or who return only part-time (Ondrich, Spiess, and Yang 1996; Ondrich et al. 1999; Gottschall and Bird 2003). Moreover, eligibility for the leave is not conditional on prior employment, so there is no incentive for women who wish to make use of the leave to enter the labor market beforehand. There is little public employment and not much part-time employment. The tax system imposes a comparatively stiff penalty on households with two earners. The German pension system further reinforces the male breadwinner model: if a husband qualifies for a pension, the wife automatically does too. In addition, the survey data shown in Figure 10.12 suggest that German women are less favorably disposed toward employment than their counterparts in most other affluent nations.

Given this array of obstacles to women's employment, it is perhaps surprising that the rate of employment among prime-working-age women is so high. As Figure 10.2 indicates, employment among German women age 25–54 is nearly as high as in the Netherlands and in the Anglo countries. However, this is somewhat artificial—inflated by unification with the east. Employment rates among women in the former East Germany tended to be much higher than in the west. The "Women's by Age Group" chart for Germany in Figure 10.4 shows that the employment rate for women age 25–54 jumped by 7 percentage points between 1990 and 1991, when unification occurred.

Then again, after a temporary dip in the early 1990s, the employment rate for prime-working-age women in unified Germany has increased steadily.

This is not a product of women-friendly policies. Instead, it seems to be the result of a combination of other factors: improvements in women's educational attainment, increases in pay, changes in attitudes toward work among German women, and higher unemployment among men.

German women's employment is lowest among those age 55–64. The rate for this age group has been increasing since the late 1970s. As I suggested earlier, the fact that the employment rate among German men in this age group is also comparatively low suggests problems in the labor market that are not necessarily gender-specific.

France

Aside from Italy, France has the lowest rate of women's employment among the twelve countries. And it has increased by only 15 percentage points since the mid-1960s. This is somewhat puzzling, as France has been far ahead of the other three continental countries in providing women-friendly policies (Belgium, which I do not include here, is similar). Most notably, France has for several decades had a strong commitment to publicly financed childcare for preschool-age children. The government provides care services directly and subsidizes the purchase of childcare from private care providers in the home or outside it (Fagnani 1998; Gornick and Meyers 2003). The second chart in Figure 10.11 shows that although only one in five children age 1 to 2 is in publicly financed care, virtually all children age 3 to 5 are. The latter share is higher in France than in any of the other eleven countries, including the Nordic ones. This policy orientation is supported by public opinion that, at least according to surveys, is largely supportive of women's employment, even for mothers with young children (Fagnani 1998: 59).

Why, then, is the women's employment rate in France so low? As noted earlier, among French women age 25–54 the employment rate is on par with that of the Netherlands and only slightly below those of the Anglo countries. The chief source of its comparatively low overall women's employment is its exceptionally low rates among women age 15–24 and, to a lesser extent, among women age 55–64. I discussed the causes of low employment in these two age groups earlier.

Yet even though the prime-age women's employment rate is not especially low relative to some of the other countries, it is nevertheless too low. One possible culprit is France's three-year paid parental care leave. The policy, introduced in 1985, provides a flat-rate benefit for up to three years. Although the leave can be used by either the mother or the father, 99% of those who use it are mothers. This policy has almost certainly had the effect of increasing the number of French mothers who drop out of the work force temporarily

or permanently. Indeed, that was one of the aims. The care leave was introduced and expanded in a context of high unemployment. According to Jeanne
Fagnani (1998: 62), "the implicit objective of these measures has been to
encourage women to retire from the labour market, thereby leaving their jobs
open for others." Then again, the rate of women's employment in France was
low prior to the leave's introduction in the mid-1980s, and it had not been
increasingly particularly rapidly. Moreover, between 1985 and 1994 the benefit
was available only beginning with a family's third child, and since 1994 only
starting with a second child. Another problem is the French practice of school-
free Wednesday afternoons, though this too is likely to be only part of the story.
Lastly, Figure 10.12 indicates that only 60% of working-age French women
have completed secondary education. This is one of the lowest levels among
the twelve countries.

Italy

Among the twelve countries, the rate of women's employment in Italy is by
far the lowest. Even if we assume that informal-sector jobs add 10 percentage
points to the employment rate among prime-working-age Italian women,
the rate is still well below those of Germany and France. As with France
and to a lesser degree Germany, a key source of Italy's low level of women's
employment is the lack of employment among those age 15–24 and 55–64
(Figure 10.2). But in Italy the rate among women age 25–54 is comparatively
low too (Figure 10.2).

Attitudes toward employment among Italian women do not appear to be
the chief barrier. The "Women's Preferences for Employment II" chart in
Figure 10.12 shows that as of the mid-1990s nearly 70% of Italian women—
more than in Norway or the United States and only slightly less than in
Sweden—said that mothers with preschool-age children should work.

The employment rate for Italian men is low, but it is not exceptionally low
(Figure 10.1). And among men age 25–54, the employment rate in Italy is
similar to those in Sweden, Finland, Canada, Australia, and Germany.

The country's paid maternity leave is moderate in generosity and duration,
and the tax penalty facing two-earner couples is not terribly severe, but otherwise Italy, like the other continental nations, has done very little in the way
of offering women-friendly policies to encourage women to enter the labor
market (Figures 10.5 through 10.11). There is very limited public commitment
to childcare for children under age 3, especially in the south. The little formal
care that is available is mostly oriented toward part-time employment, but
there are relatively few part-time jobs in Italy (Del Boca 2002).

The level of educational attainment among Italian women is very low. As of 2005, 63% of Italian women age 25 to 64 who had completed secondary education, and 75% of those with tertiary education, were employed (OECD 2004*e*: 307). But only 43% of working-age Italian women have a secondary education degree or better, which is the lowest among the twelve countries (Figure 10.12). Even more striking, the "Women's Skill Level II" chart in Figure 10.12 shows that average literacy among Italian women, as measured in the 1994–98 International Adult Literacy Survey, is far below the level in the other eleven countries. This is largely a function of the bifurcated distribution in Italy, with women at the low end scoring particularly low in comparative terms (Blau and Kahn 2002*b*: table 1). This perhaps helps to account for why the (official) employment rate among Italian women with less than a secondary education is just 30%. Educational attainment is improving, but there is considerable room for further improvement. Among Italian women age 25 to 34, 60% have completed secondary education. But this is well below the share in most of the other twelve countries, which ranges from 75% to 95% (OECD 2004*e*).

Anglo Countries

All four of the Anglo nations had women's employment rates around 40% in the early to mid-1960s, and they have increased those rates by 20 to 30 percentage points since then. The growth pattern for each of these countries has been relatively steady during this period.

The employment rates of women age 25–54 in the four Anglo countries are, on average, about 5 percentage points lower than those in the Nordic countries. On the one hand, this calls into question the importance of women-friendly policies in promoting women's employment, as the Anglo countries have tended to be the least generous in providing policy supports such as publicly financed childcare, paid maternity/care leave, public employment, and support for part-time employment. On the other hand, perhaps the conclusion to draw is that women-friendly policies do help to encourage female employment, but their impact is limited. A difference of 5 percentage points is not huge, but it is not trivial either.

Another interpretation is that the Anglo countries *have* been somewhat active in provision of women-friendly policies, but they have focused on antidiscrimination and affirmative action measures rather than the types of supports favored by the Nordic countries (O'Connor, Orloff, and Shaver 1999; Orloff 2004).

United States

As the charts in Figures 10.5–10.8 and 10.11 make clear, the moderately high women's employment rate in the United States is not due to generous government provision of childcare, paid maternity/care leave, or public employment. Nor is it a product of government encouragement of part-time work or a tax system supportive of dual-earner couples. Instead, the most likely influence of women-friendly policies has to do with antidiscrimination and affirmative action policy. The United States was the first country with an antidiscrimination law and the first to make extensive use of affirmative action programs for university admissions and employment. The Civil Rights Act took effect in 1965 and affirmative action became widespread in the 1970s.

The time series in the US chart in Figure 10.4 begins in 1960, as this is when the OECD data begin. But this sheds only limited light on the impact of antidiscrimination legislation, which began in the mid-1960s. Data from the US Census Bureau for women's labor force participation are available going back to the beginning of the twentieth century. Figure 10.18 shows these data. There is no observable impact of the Civil Rights Act and affirmative action. The rate of female labor force participation was increasing just as rapidly before the implementation of these policies as afterward.

This does not mean these policies have been irrelevant. But clearly there is more to the story. The key question for the US case is why a growing and comparatively large share of women are employed despite an almost complete

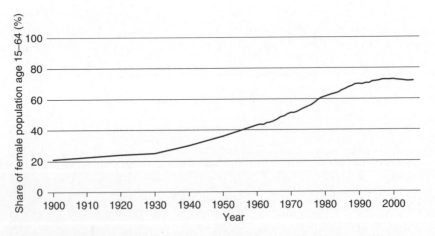

Figure 10.18. Women's labor force participation in the United States, 1900ff.

Note: Data are every ten years until 1960 and annual thereafter.

Source: US Census Bureau and OECD.

lack of Nordic-style policy supports. The answer seems to have two components.

First, women's educational attainment in the United States has been increasing steadily over the past century (Bergmann 2005), and wage levels for well-educated Americans are relatively high. This creates a large opportunity cost for choosing to stay home. There is a large group of highly educated American women earning fairly high wages and salaries. Their high wages are due in part to the fact that women have had significant success in entering high-paying professions that formerly were male-dominated. Figure 10.19 shows one indicator of this: women's share of managers, legislators, and senior officials. Among the twelve countries, the share is highest in the United States. Here antidiscrimination law and affirmative action may well have played an important role.

Second, American women with low education have been increasingly pushed into the labor market. This is due in part to stagnant or declining wage levels for less-educated men. Reduced marriage rates among these women have also played a role; many single women, particularly those without children, need employment for income and for health insurance. Since the mid-1990s, the enactment of welfare time limits has been an additional force pushing US women into employment. On the demand side, low wages

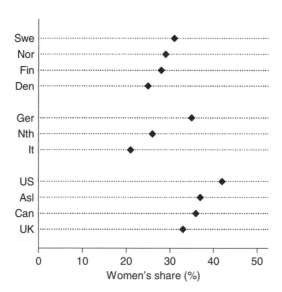

Figure 10.19. Women's share of managers, legislators, and senior officials, mid-2000s.

Note: Data are not available for France. For data definitions and sources, see the appendix.

have made it attractive to firms, especially in consumer services, to hire these women. Women's employment is facilitated by the private childcare market. Childcare is widely available and, for many, affordable—even if not always of high quality. The extensiveness of the private childcare market is due, in turn, to the fact that it is subject to very limited government regulation. An important part of the women's employment story in the United States, then, is the absence of regulation, both of wages and of childcare. The US route to high women's employment is thus in part what might be called a "low road" route. Low wages push less-educated women into the labor market— because it is difficult for a couple to survive on the earnings of a man who has limited education—and make it attractive for employers to hire such women despite their low skill level. Inexpensive childcare makes it possible for less-educated women to purchase such care despite their low incomes. A high rate of women's employment in turn increases demand for consumer services such as restaurants, cleaning, and laundry, which further heightens employer demand for less-educated women (Esping-Andersen 1999; Freeman 2007: 28).

In summary, there are two parts to an explanation of the comparatively high rate of women's employment in the United States. One has to do with relatively high women's educational attainment and policy supports that have helped make it possible for well-educated women to enter high-paying occupations. The other has to do with low wages encouraging less-educated women to work and employers to hire them, facilitated by a virtually unregulated childcare market. The former appears to have been the more important of the two. Figure 10.20 shows labor force participation rates for US women by educational attainment since 1969. The rate increased substantially for women with some college and those with a college degree in the 1970s and 1980s before flattening out in the 1990s. The same was true for women with a high school degree but no college. The rate increased for women without a high school degree too, but to a much lesser extent.

Canada

Like the United States, Canada's commitment to public support for childcare has been very limited (Quebec is an exception), and consequently a very small share of preschool-age children are in publicly funded care (OECD 2005*a*). Canada has a paid maternity leave and slightly higher levels of both public employment and part-time employment than the United States, but the difference is not large. On the Gornick-Meyers composite index of work-family support policies, Canada scores only slightly higher than the United States.

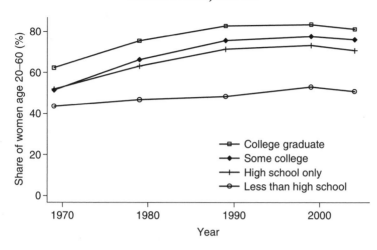

Figure 10.20. Women's labor force participation in the United States by education, 1969ff.

Source: Juhn and Potter (2006: table 2, using current population survey data).

Like its southern neighbor, Canada has implemented both antidiscrimination legislation and affirmative action. These policies were begun in 1977. Unfortunately, a consistent employment time series for Canada is not available prior to 1976, so it is not possible to know whether there was an acceleration in female employment growth following the introduction of these policies.

As in the United States, wage levels in Canada are comparatively low at the bottom end and comparatively high at the top, a large share of women have completed secondary schooling or more, and private childcare is widely available and not too expensive. The key in Canada too, therefore, seems most likely to have been rising women's educational attainment and high wages for those at the top along with low wages for men and women at the bottom coupled with a well-developed private childcare market.

United Kingdom

The United Kingdom has a larger share of children age 3 to 5 in publicly financed care and a smaller tax penalty for a two-earner couple than do the United States or Canada. But otherwise it is similar with respect to women-friendly policies. On the Gornick-Meyers composite index, the UK is scored only slightly above the United States and Canada. It too has antidiscrimination legislation, though no affirmative action. The antidiscrimination law took effect in 1975. Once again, however, the time-series data offer no evidence of a response in the women's employment rate to this policy change. The rate of increase in female employment did not accelerate at any point after the mid-1970s (Figure 10.4).

The explanation for relatively high women's employment in the United Kingdom appears to be similar to that in the United States and Canada. It centers on wage inequality, rising educational attainment for women, and expansion of the private childcare market.

But there also are noteworthy differences. First, educational attainment among British women is, on average, significantly lower than in the United States or Canada (Figure 10.12). All else being equal, this would lead us to expect a lower rate of women's employment in the UK. But employment rates among better-educated women are higher in the United Kingdom. The employment rate in both the United States and Canada is 67% among women with secondary education and 78% among women with tertiary education. The figures for comparably educated British women are 74% and 86%, respectively (OECD 2004: 306–8).

Second, a smaller share of very young children are in formal childcare in the UK than in the United States or Canada: 35% versus 45% and 54%, respectively. This seems to be due largely to lesser availability of affordable childcare in Britain (Paxton, Pearce, and Reed 2005). To get around this constraint, a larger share of employed British women work part-time than is the case in the United States or Canada: 40% versus 18% and 28%, respectively (OECD 2004: 310; see also O'Connor, Orloff, and Shaver 1999). Recent reforms by the New Labour government may help (Lister 2004; OECD 2005a; Stewart 2005). "Sure Start" programs in poor areas were given funding to provide a variety of services, including childcare, for children age 0 to 4. And recipients of the Working Tax Credit, a subsidy for households with low earnings, now receive a tax credit of up to 70% of childcare costs, depending on the number of children. This is surely a key part of the reason why the employment rate for single mothers increased from 45% in 1997 to 54% in 2004 (OECD 2005a: 75).

Australia

Australia differs from the United States and Canada in having a much larger portion of its working-age population in part-time jobs and a smaller tax penalty for a second household earner. But otherwise it too has made limited use of the women-friendly policies pursued by the Nordic countries. Like the United States and Canada, it has antidiscrimination and affirmative action policies. These began in 1985. As with the other Anglo countries, however, the time-series data in Figure 10.4 fail to suggest any impact of these policies on the female employment rate. There was an acceleration in the rate of increase in women's employment in the 1980s, but it began prior to 1985. And after that the rate of increase returned to its pre-1980s level.

Australia's rate of women's employment is below that of the other three Anglo countries, even though part-time jobs are plentiful and there is less of a tax penalty for a second household earner. This would appear to be a function of two factors. First, the private childcare market is less developed than in the United States and Canada. Limited capacity has posed a significant barrier to women seeking to purchase childcare, though this seems to have lessened somewhat in recent years (OECD 2002*b*: ch. 3). Second, Australian women express a much stronger preference than their American and Canadian counterparts in favor of staying home with children, at least during the preschool years. The data in the "Women's Preference for Employment I" chart in Figure 10.12 suggest that a comparatively small share of Australian women feel that both the husband and the wife should contribute to household income. And according to an OECD (2002*b*: 103) study, "In 1999 54% of Australian women of working age citing childcare as the main reason they were not looking for work said that they preferred to look after the child at home (for other than financial reasons)."

HAVE WOMEN-FRIENDLY POLICIES MATTERED?

The macro-level evidence surveyed in this chapter offers some reason to think that each of the women-friendly policies I have considered have helped to boost women's employment. Examination of cross-country variation in levels of prime-working-age women's employment suggests that availability and affordability of childcare and paid maternity/care leaves of somewhere between three months and eighteen months are beneficial. Multivariate analysis of cross-country variation in levels, with a control for women's educational attainment, suggests that public childcare, public employment, part-time employment, and tax systems with little or no disincentive for a second household earner are helpful. Examination of the over-time developments within countries suggests that part-time employment has played an important role in the Netherlands, and to a lesser extent in the United Kingdom and Australia. Analysis of employment patterns for women age 15–24 suggests that the availability of part-time work is especially important for this group. And the experience of the United States, and perhaps the other three Anglo countries as well, suggests a role for antidiscrimination and/or affirmative action policies.

On the other hand, some of the evidence suggests grounds for skepticism about the role of women-friendly policies. There is little indication of a positive association between the generosity of women-friendly policies (whether measured as average level or as change over time) and changes in prime-working-age women's employment between the early 1970s and the 2000s (Figure 10.14). Over-time trends within individual nations—particularly the Nordic and Anglo countries—do not suggest a noticeable response in female employment rates to introduction or expansion of women-friendly policies. And the dramatic increase in part-time employment in the Netherlands was not to any significant degree a product of government policy.

I conclude that women-friendly policies have mattered, but the evidence in favor of this conclusion is less decisive than I expected it to be.

MULTIPLE PATHS TO HIGH WOMEN'S EMPLOYMENT

One thing that emerges clearly from the evidence is that there have been multiple paths to high women's employment (see also Orloff 2002). Sweden, Denmark, and Norway appear to have succeeded through a combination of high women's educational attainment, extensive public employment, generous public funding of childcare, paid maternity/care leave, and availability of part-time employment. The Anglo countries, by contrast, seem to have succeeded via a combination of low wages, private childcare, moderate-to-high women's educational attainment, and antidiscrimination laws and affirmative action programs. The Netherlands has succeeded, or at least moved decisively in the direction of success, largely via improved women's educational attainment and widespread availability of part-time employment.

None of these models is without drawbacks. The weak spot in the Nordic route is a high degree of occupational sex segregation. Women have disproportionately entered traditionally female jobs in social and personal services. As a result, the degree of occupational sex segregation in these countries exceeds that in the Anglo nations. The gender pay gap is lower in the Nordic countries, mainly because there is less inequality in the overall wage distribution (Blau and Kahn 1992). But the crowding into female-dominated jobs appears to have limited upward mobility for many women (Rubery et al. 1999: ch. 5).

In the Anglo model, too, there is reason for concern about the quality of the jobs many women have entered. Although well-educated women have increasingly obtained high-status, high-paying positions, less-educated women frequently end up in low-paying jobs with no benefits and limited opportunity for advancement (Edin and Lein 1997; Ehrenreich 2001). The gender pay gap in the United States has narrowed since 1980, but it remains comparatively large, in part because women are overrepresented in low-paying service sector jobs (Figure 10.12).

One way to potentially improve this situation is via more and better education for women. In Australia and the United Kingdom the rate of secondary school completion among women is far too low (Figure 10.12). In the United States and Canada the completion rate is much higher, but women still lag in learning, as suggested by the lower average literacy rates among American and Canadian women than among their counterparts in Sweden, Norway, Finland, and Denmark (Figure 10.12). This is mainly a function of differences at the low end, where female literacy levels in the United States and Canada are much lower than in the Nordic countries (Blau and Kahn 2002*b*: table 1).

Another concern about the Anglo model has to do with the quality of childcare. Research suggests that the care received by a nontrivial share of children in the United States is of mediocre or poor quality (Kamerman and Kahn 1995; Vandell and Wolfe 2000; Blau 2001). Even in formal childcare centers, two-thirds of the staff have no more than a high school degree and staff turnover is very high (Vandell and Wolfe 2000). This has potentially worrisome effects on economic and social opportunities for such children, as there is compelling evidence that childcare quality at early ages affects cognitive development (Buchinal 1999; Vandell and Wolfe 2000; Blau 2001: ch. 7; Waldfogel 2006).

In the English-speaking countries the private market for childcare is so developed that it is difficult to imagine it being replaced by public facilities. In the United States, a strategy for improving childcare might feature a voucher to help parents defray the cost of paid childcare for children under age 3. Suzanne Helburn and Barbara Bergmann (2002) suggest that the cost of childcare should be fully subsidized for families with incomes below the poverty line, and that for others the subsidy should cover care expenses in excess of 20% of family income. To encourage high quality, David Blau (2001: 219) recommends that the value of the voucher vary according to the quality of the childcare it is used to purchase: "For example, a low-income family might receive a subsidy of 30 percent of the average cost of unaccredited child care if they use unaccredited care, 60 percent of the average cost of care if they use a provider accredited as of good quality, and 100 percent of the average cost of care if they use care accredited as of excellent quality. This gives families an incentive to seek care of high quality, and it gives providers an incentive to offer high-quality care in order to attract consumers." Care for 3-, 4-, and 5-year-olds could be provided via full-day year-round public preschool.

Concerns about the Dutch route center on its heavy reliance on part-time employment. First, some worry that part-time jobs do little to reduce gender inequality, because they produce limited earnings and offer limited upward mobility. Policy changes in the past decade in the Netherlands have focused on ensuring that part-time employees have rights and benefits similar to those of full-time workers and encouraging Dutch fathers to reduce work hours in order to foster more gender equality in parental childcare practices. These steps do not, however, address the limited earnings and promotion prospects of female part-timers.

A second concern has to do with the quantity of employment. Not only are too few women in the Netherlands employed, but many of those that are employed work too few hours. By "too few" I do not mean with respect to how much those women would prefer to work; many Dutch women appear to be satisfied with employment of between 10 and 30 hours per week. Instead, I mean with respect to meeting the needs of a generous welfare state that aims to hold income inequality at bay and to cover its pension obligations to a growing elderly population.

Of course, these criticisms of the Dutch path presuppose that the relevant counterfactual scenario is a similar overall female employment rate with more full-time and less part-time employment. In practice, that may not be realistic; in the absence of extensive part-time jobs more women might remain outside the paid labor force altogether. Still, from the point of view of improving gender equality and increasing the volume of employment it would be better if more Dutch women worked longer hours. The 2000 work hours legislation allows employees not only to reduce their work hours but also to increase them. It will be interesting to see if this helps to promote a rise in working time among employed Dutch women.

WHICH WAY FORWARD?

What should be the goal for women's employment? The Lisbon European Council in 2000 set 60% as the women's employment rate target for member countries to reach by 2010. For the countries on which I focus here, this is far too low. As a rough guideline I would suggest the following: 75% of women age 15–64 in employment at an average of at least 30 hours per week, or 1,380 hours per year. (I assume six weeks of vacation. Multiplying the remaining 46 weeks by 30 hours per week yields 1,380 hours.) Of course, by choice or necessity some women will work a good bit more than 30 hours and others less. But 30 hours on average seems a reasonable goal. For men, the employment rates in the Nordic and Anglo countries currently are between 75% and 80%, with average weekly work hours well above 30 (Figure 10.1; Rubery et al. 1999: 258; OECD 2002*b*: 49).

It may help to break this down by age group. If we assume, to make the calculation simple, cohorts of approximately equal size, one way to reach the goal of an overall 75% employment rate would be the following: 85% employment among women age 25–54, 70% among women age 55–64, and 50% among women age 15–24.

None of the twelve countries currently meets this aim. Denmark, Norway, and Sweden come close. As of 2006 their overall women's employment rates were 74%, 73%, and 73%, respectively. Typical hours worked by women are relatively high in these countries. In Denmark and Sweden, for example, 80% of employed women work more than 30 hours per week, and in Denmark 65% work more than 35 hours (OECD 2002*b*: 49; European Commission 2004: 63).

In all four of the Nordic countries, especially in Sweden and Finland, the rate of employment among women is virtually the same as among men. This suggests limited room for further increases via women-friendly policies. Denmark and Finland could boost their rates among women age 55–64, and Finland and Norway might be able to increase employment among prime-working-age women by reducing the length of their paid home-care leaves. But otherwise the main source of further increases in women's employment is likely to be policies or institutions that contribute to increased employment in general.

The Anglo countries, and particularly Australia, have farther to go. As of 2003, female employment rates among this group ranged from 66% to 70%. Average work hours, on the other hand, tend to be relatively high. Australia has the largest share of female part-timers among the four English-speaking countries, yet 60% of employed Australian women work 30 or more hours per week and 30% work 40 or more (OECD 2002*b*: 49).

There are three areas in which policy reforms might be of significant help in the Anglo countries. First, each of these countries might be able to increase women's employment by increasing the availability of affordable, high-quality childcare. Second, in the United States and Australia introduction of paid maternity/care leave would likely help. With the exception of a few states, such as California, there is no paid maternity (or parental) leave in the United States. The current federal policy merely requires that employers with 50 or more employees allow twelve weeks of unpaid leave. Although the absence of paid maternity/care leave has not proved a debilitating barrier to employment by American women, it is unjustly stingy from the point of view of helping parents balance work and family concerns and ensuring that children are cared for full-time by a parent in the months immediately following birth. Twelve weeks of paid leave seems a sensible minimum to provide, and something closer to forty weeks might be even better. Third, the employment rate among women age 55–64 is just 46–56% in the four English-speaking countries. Finding ways to boost female employment in this age group would be helpful.

All four of the continental countries are a long way from the goal of a 75% women's employment rate. The female employment rate in 2006 was 47% in Italy, 57% in France, 62% in Germany, and 67% in the Netherlands. Although the rate of female employment in the Netherlands is higher than in Germany or France, hours worked tend to be lower. Sixty percent of employed Dutch women work part-time versus just 38% of German women and 23% of French women. And women employed part-time in the Netherlands tend to work fewer hours than do their counterparts in Germany and France (Rubery et al. 1999: 258). Overall, only 30% of employed Dutch women work 30 hours or more per week, and nearly 30% work fewer than 20 hours (OECD 2002b: 49).

What is the best way forward for the continental countries? As I noted earlier, there is evidence to suggest that each of the women-friendly policies I have considered may help. Are any of them *necessary* for high women's employment? This may be the case for childcare. If women are in paid employment, someone has to take care of preschool-age children. The only ways to evade the need for childcare for preschool children are to have an additional family member, perhaps a grandparent, handle it or to have two half-time-employed parents. The latter may be possible for some couples, but it seems unlikely to be either a viable or a desirable strategy on a large scale. Even the aim in the Netherlands for two three-quarters-time parents presumes childcare by someone other than the parents for part of the work week (see Gornick and Meyers 2003: ch. 4). And the notion of two three-quarters-time or half-time parents is of no relevance for single parents.

The 2002 Barcelona European Council set a target of making formal childcare spaces available for at least 33% of children under age 3 by 2010. A number of the twelve countries considered here already exceed this goal, but the Netherlands, Germany, and Italy have a long way to go.

If childcare is a necessary ingredient for high women's employment, what is the best strategy for getting it? The Nordic and Anglo countries each rely mainly on childcare outside the home. The Nordic countries utilize both public provision and public funding of private care centers, while the Anglo countries rely chiefly on private provision that is privately funded.

Germany and France have chosen a different route. The three-year parental/care leaves that have been in place in both countries since the 1980s effectively allocate childcare responsibility for the first three years of life to the parent(s). To a large extent this is consistent with the dominant view about childcare in Germany and France, and indeed that is a key reason why these policies were put in place (Morgan and Zippel 2003). But not only do extended care leave programs create work disincentives for mothers; they also very likely inhibit both public provision and funding of formal childcare services and the development of a private childcare market. If many mothers of young children are home providing the childcare, there will be limited demand—both economic and political—for provision of care outside the home. As a result, little formal childcare will be available, which strengthens the incentive for mothers to make use of the care leave. Although France has more childcare slots than Germany, there is a shortage of availability in both countries (Gornick and Meyers 2003: ch. 7). In Germany, an early-2000s survey found that 89% of nonemployed mothers with preschool-age children cited insufficient childcare facilities as the reason for not being employed (Spiess and Wagner 2003: 307).

One possible way around this is to get more fathers to make use of the leave. If fathers were to increasingly take a year or so of the paid leave and then go back to work, the employment-reducing impact of the leave on women might be lessened, without much reduction in men's employment. But that seems a long-term hope at best, as fathers are likely to resist both for cultural and for economic reasons. The take-up rate among fathers currently is very low (Gottschall and Bird 2003; Morgan and Zippel 2003).

Another possibility is to reduce the length of the leaves. Yet that will be difficult. Long paid leaves have a distinct political advantage in terms of rhetoric: they can be justified on grounds of choice (Morgan 2004; Kenworthy 2008c). Advocates can argue that public provision or subsidization of care outside the home benefits only those who wish to use it, and is of no help to mothers (or fathers) who prefer to stay home with their children. In part for this reason, extended leave measures may well be introduced in other countries in the near future. Finland and Norway each have one. Sweden had one briefly in the 1990s, though it was quickly abandoned when the social democrats returned to power. The issue has been debated in Denmark (OECD 2002b).

Of course, a care leave only truly provides choice if the benefit can either be kept by the parent(s) *or* used to purchase childcare. That is the case in Finland and Norway, but not in France or Germany (Morgan and Zippel 2003: 53). Hence, if the care leaves in France and Germany cannot be shortened, changing them to permit the money to be used for purchase of childcare could be a way to enhance availability of childcare outside the home.

A continental country government committed to significantly boosting women's employment in the space of a decade would do well to start by substantially increasing the number of affordable childcare spaces, via public provision and/or subsidization of private care. In Germany and France this ideally would be combined either with a shortening of the three-year parental/care leave or introduction of an option to use the money to purchase childcare.

Closely related to this, France, Germany, and the Netherlands should close the existing gaps in their school schedules. The German federal government announced in 2002 that it would allocate 4 billion euros to fund expansion of full-day childcare (Spiess and Wagner 2003: 310), and several regions have moved in recent years to institute full-day schooling. Also of considerable importance is improving women's educational attainment. This clearly is a barrier in Italy, as I noted earlier. Among the continental countries, it is a problem in the Netherlands and France too, although as in Italy significant progress has been made with recent cohorts. In Germany it would be helpful to reduce the sizable tax disincentive for a second household earner and to try to begin to alter, perhaps via a publicity campaign, the view of many Germans that it is best if mothers of young children stay home to care for them well into their preschool years.

Perhaps most important for Germany, France, and Italy is to increase employment rates among women age 15–24 and 55–64. For the younger group, widespread availability of part-time work appears to be key (Figure 10.16). For the older group, the evidence points to a more general problem facing the German, French, and Italian labor markets, as male employment among this age group also is very low (Figure 10.17).

WOMEN'S EMPLOYMENT AND INCOME INEQUALITY

My objective in this book is to assess policy strategies in terms of their effect on both employment and equality. Women's employment is likely to have a significant effect on gender equality, and that should be central to any overall assessment of it. But my concern is instead with household income inequality. Does the level of female employment affect the distribution of income among households?

The most likely effect is to increase household income inequality as a country moves from a low to a moderate level of women's employment, and then to decrease inequality as it moves to high women's employment. Better-educated women are more likely to be in the work force in all affluent nations. This is clear from Figure 10.21, which shows women's employment rates among those with less than secondary education, those having completed secondary but not tertiary schooling, and those with a tertiary degree. As a country shifts from low to moderate women's employment, a disproportionate share of the women entering the labor force will be those with greater education. Because they are more likely to be partnered with a man with higher educational attainment and therefore higher earnings, this tends to increase household

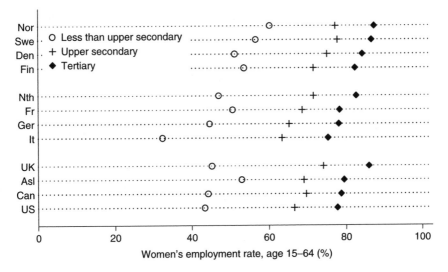

Figure 10.21. Women's employment by educational attainment, 2005.

Source: OECD (2007*b*: 258–60).

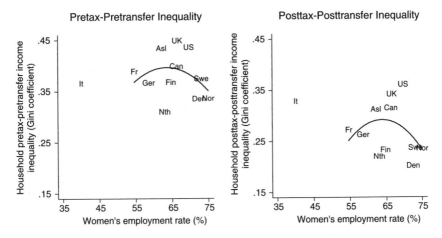

Figure 10.22. Income inequality among working-age households by women's employment, 2000.

Note: Chart axes are truncated. Regression curves are based on data with Italy excluded. For data definitions and sources, see the appendix.

incomes more in households that already had high earnings than in households with low earnings, thereby increasing income inequality across households. Eventually, however, as women's employment continues to increase, the effect will tilt in the other direction. Employment of highly educated women will push toward its ceiling, so a disproportionate share of women entering employment will be less-educated. This should help to reduce household income inequality.

The first chart in Figure 10.22 shows the relationship between women's employment and pretax-pretransfer income inequality across the twelve countries as of 2000. The pattern corresponds to some degree to what we might expect, but only loosely at best. The Netherlands and Finland are notable exceptions to the hump-shaped pattern: both have moderately high levels of women's employment but relatively low levels of household income inequality. Of course, many things affect the distribution of market income, and there is no reason to presume that the rate of women's employment is among the most important (see Chapter 3).

Heightened rates of women's employment also increase the tax base. As a country moves from low to moderate rates of women's employment, governments committed to holding income inequality in check could use the increase in revenues to offset the likely increase in inequality of market incomes across households via greater redistribution. That is a political decision, of course; some countries may do this, while others will not. The second chart in Figure 10.22 shows a similar hump-shaped relationship between levels of women's employment and the degree of inequality in the posttax-posttransfer distribution of income among households. But again the relationship is quite weak. Here too there are a large number of contributing factors, among which the female employment rate is likely to be of only secondary importance.

At the very least, it seems safe to say that high women's employment is not incompatible with low income inequality. And in all likelihood it contributes to that aim.

11

Toward a High-Employment, High-Equality Society

Income inequality is of concern for reasons of fairness and because it has adverse effects on other socioeconomic goods. The principal determinants of income inequality are the distribution of earnings among employed individuals, the distribution of employment across households, and government redistribution. Market inequality has risen in almost all affluent countries in recent decades. This trend seems likely to continue: wage compression is increasingly difficult to achieve, and both single-adult households and highly educated dual-earner couples are increasing, leading to widening earnings inequality among households. Redistribution, which has always been a critical component of egalitarian strategies, is therefore likely to increase in importance.

As populations age, an increasing share of government revenues will need to be allocated to the elderly. If so, and if greater redistribution is needed for working-age households in order to offset inegalitarian changes in the wage distribution and in household composition, where will the money come from? As welfare states expanded steadily in the 1950s, 1960s, and 1970s, the additional funds were generated by rapid productivity growth and higher tax rates. But productivity growth has slowed, and capital mobility has made it difficult to raise tax rates.

A potentially useful strategy is to increase employment. Doing so enlarges the tax base, allowing tax revenues to rise without an increase in tax rates. It also reduces welfare state costs by decreasing the amount of government benefits going to individuals and households.

What policies and institutions can help? I have focused on six: high wages at the low end of the distribution, strong employment protection regulations, generous government benefits, high taxes, high and/or equal skills, and generous "women-friendly" policies. My aim has been to investigate the impact of these institutions and policies on employment. I have concentrated on variation in employment growth across countries since the late 1970s, with some attention to individual country experiences. The focus has been on twelve countries: Australia, Canada, Denmark, Finland, France, Germany, Italy, the Netherlands, Norway, Sweden, the United Kingdom, and the United States.

What have I found? What should affluent countries do?

FINDINGS: A SUMMARY AND SYNTHESIS

In Chapters 5–8, I examined the employment impact of low-end wages, employment protection regulations, government benefits, and tax levels. For each of these, the bivariate pattern suggests an adverse impact on employment growth (growth in the employment rate) since the late 1970s, if we set aside the Netherlands. However, the magnitude of these estimated effects shrinks considerably, sometimes to zero, when we do any or all of the following: (*a*) disaggregate by sector and focus on employment growth in "low-end" services—wholesale and retail trade, restaurants, hotels, and community, social, and personal services; (*b*) control for other potential determinants of employment change, such as macroeconomic policy, imports, wage changes, and product market regulations; (*c*) omit countries that are substantive and statistical outliers, especially Sweden (Figures 5.5, 6.8, 7.8, 8.11). I do not think these findings should lead us to feel confident that high low-end wages, stiff employment protection rules, generous government benefits, and high payroll and consumption taxation have had no impact on employment growth in these countries. But they do suggest reason to suspect that, to the extent there has been an adverse effect, its magnitude probably has been relatively small.

In Chapter 9 I considered skills. Equalization of skills may or may not result in low income inequality. While there is a strong association across countries between low inequality of adult literacy and low earnings inequality, several studies suggest that this association may be largely spurious. Countries with a less unequal distribution of cognitive skills also tend to have strong unions and centralized wage setting, and the latter appear to be the main determinants of earnings dispersion (Figure 9.4). Furthermore, the distribution of earnings among employed individuals is just one determinant, albeit an important one, of the distribution of market income among households. What effect would an increase in skills have on employment? Theoretically, it is not clear, as much depends on employer demand. Across countries, we do not observe the expected positive association between adult literacy and either employment rates or employment growth (Figure 9.6).

Chapter 10 examined "women-friendly" policies. Such policies may initially increase income inequality among households, as a larger share of the new female labor force entrants come from households that have a moderate- or high-earning male. Eventually, however, employment growth must come from the low end of the distribution, and thereby is likely to reduce income inequality across households. The chief impact of women-friendly policies is expected to be on employment. Most of the variation across affluent countries in employment rates and in employment growth over the past several decades has been concentrated among women. There are strong cross-sectional associations between several of the key types of women-friendly policies—public provision or subsidization of childcare and preschool, generous but not-too-lengthy paid parental leaves, extensive public employment, support for part-time employment, and favorable tax treatment of two-earner households—and high rates of employment among 25- to 54-year-old women (Figure 10.11). This is true even controlling for women's educational attainment (Figure 10.13). But there is limited evidence of a connection between these policies and *growth* of prime-working-age women's employment over the past several decades (Figure 10.14). Furthermore, the bulk of the cross-country variation in levels and changes in female employment is among younger and older women—those age 15–24 and 55–64. For the former, the availability of part-time work appears to be crucial, though it is not clear how much of a role policy has played in national differences in part-time employment among the young. For the latter, the key source of national variation appears to be non-gender-specific, as differences in female employment rates among 55–64s mirror those for males.

Figure 11.1 offers some summary evidence to help provide insight into what conclusions can be drawn from the analyses in Chapters 5–10. The twelve countries are listed along the horizontal axis. They are ordered from worst to best employment performance. Employment performance is measured as an average of the country's rank-order position on employment change from 1979 to 2000–06 and employment level as of 2000–06.

The figure includes scores for eight policies and institutions that I examined in Chapters 5 through 10. One is low-end wage levels, measured as P50/P10 earnings inequality among full-time employed individuals (Chapter 5). The second is employment protection regulations, measured with an index (Chapter 6). The third is government benefit generosity, measured as cash social expenditures on the working-age population as a share of GDP (Chapter 7). The fourth is payroll and consumption taxes as a share of GDP (Chapter 8). The fifth is a measure of skills: average document literacy score on the 1994–98 International Adult Literacy Survey (Chapter 9). The sixth is the women-friendly policy that appears to have had the most sizable impact on female employment (Chapter 10): public support for childcare and preschool, measured as government expenditures on childcare and preprimary education as a share of GDP. The seventh and eighth are two other factors (control

Jobs with Equality

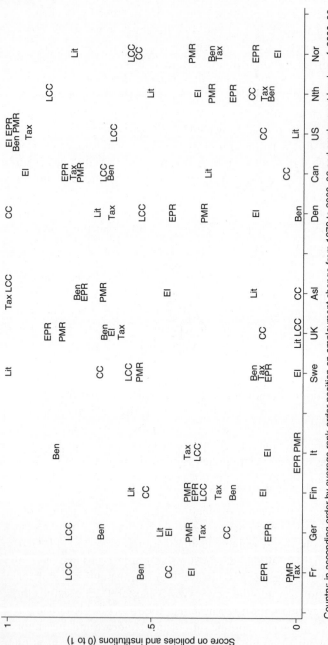

Country: in ascending order by average rank-order position on employment change from 1979 to 2000–06 and employment level as of 2000–06

Figure 11.1. Policies, institutions, and employment performance by country.

Note: Scores for the policies and institutions represent 1979–2006 averages, adjusted to vary from zero to one. Each is coded such that levels of the policy or institution expected to promote employment are scored high and levels expected to impede employment are scored low. EI = earnings inequality (P50/P10 ratio) among full-time employed persons (high coded 0, low coded 1); see Chapter 5. EPR = employment protection regulations (strict coded 0, lenient coded 1); see Chapter 6. Ben = cash social expenditures on the working-age population as % of GDP (high coded 0, low coded 1); see Chapter 7. Tax = payroll and consumption taxes as % of GDP (high coded 0, low coded 1); see Chapter 8. Lit = mean document literacy score on International Adult Literacy Survey (low coded 0, high coded 1); see Chapter 9. CC = public expenditures on childcare and preprimary education as % of GDP (low coded 0, high coded 1); see Chapter 10. LCC = average annual real unit labor cost change (high coded 0, low coded 1); see Chapter 4. PMR = product market regulations (strict coded 0, lenient coded 1); see Chapter 4.

variables in the analyses in prior chapters) that appear likely to have had an impact on employment growth: wage increases, measured as average annual change in real unit labor costs, and product market regulations, measured with an index.

I rescored the measures for each of these eight policies and institutions to a common metric: a scale of zero to one ([raw score − minimum]/range). I then inverted the scores for some of them so that for each policy or institution a high score is expected to be conducive to good employment performance. For example, high government expenditures on childcare and preschool are thought to promote employment. It was therefore rescored to a zero–one scale and then left as is. But high levels of payroll and consumption taxes as a share of GDP are expected to impede employment, so after rescoring this indicator to a zero–one scale I inverted the scores. Countries with high payroll and consumption taxes end up with scores near zero and those with low taxes have scores closer to one. The score for each policy and institution in each country is shown on the vertical axis in the figure.

What do we learn from the chart? The main conclusion is that there is no parsimonious set of policies and/or institutions that can be identified as the key to good or bad employment performance.

Five countries rank among the top seven on both employment change and employment levels: Norway, the Netherlands, the United States, Canada, and Denmark. These five nations have widely varying configurations of institutions and policies. They suggest that there are *multiple paths to employment success*.

The United States and Canada feature high earnings inequality, limited government benefits, low payroll and consumption taxes, low employment protection and product market regulations, and low-to-moderate labor cost growth. On the other hand, they score low on adult literacy and public support for childcare. Norway and Denmark are in some respects the mirror image of Canada and the United States. They score high, or at least moderately high, on public support for childcare and adult literacy, and they have low earnings inequality (high low-end wages) and relatively generous government benefits. Of course, Norway's oil wealth mandates considerable caution in drawing inferences about the impact of its policies and institutions. Denmark differs from the other Nordic countries in having moderate levels of payroll and consumption taxes and employment protection.

The Netherlands is a particularly interesting case. It has achieved by far the fastest employment growth of the twelve countries. As I have pointed out several times, this is tempered by the fact that the country's employment rate was comparatively low at the start of the 1980s and a large share of the new jobs have been part-time. Nonetheless, the Dutch case is a genuine employment success story. Yet the charts reveal that the Netherlands scores *moderate or low on all but one* of the eight indicators. The only institution or policy it has featured that is expected to be conducive to healthy employment performance is wage restraint.

What about employment failure? Four countries rank among the bottom five on both employment change and employment levels: France, Germany, Finland, and Italy. In contrast to the successful cases, these four have rather similar institutional and policy configurations. Each scores moderate to low on most of the policies and institutions in Figure 11.1.

This is true even of Finland, which unlike the other three Nordic countries has only moderate public childcare support (largely a function of its lengthy home care allowance). Of course, Finland's employment performance was heavily influenced by the deep economic crisis it suffered in the first half of the 1990s, which owed mainly to the collapse of its main export market, the Soviet Union. Still, Finland's employment rate was already the lowest among the four Nordic countries coming into the 1990s.

France, Germany, and Italy are characterized (to varying degrees) by a mix of policies and institutions that is very conducive—both theoretically and empirically—to low employment. The problem is that, because each of the countries has a relatively similar mix, it is difficult to extract from their experiences much useful information about how best to break out of the low-employment equilibrium. From the Netherlands we can draw the conclusion that this configuration does not guarantee failure. But the records of these countries since the 1970s does not point clearly to one or two policies or institutions at which reform efforts might best be targeted.

RECOMMENDATIONS

In this section I offer a set of suggestions for reform in affluent nations. Let me preface these recommendations with three general points (for kindred views, see Hemerijck 2005; Rodrik 2007).

First, based on the findings in earlier chapters and on the summary portrait provided by Figure 11.1, one of the key lessons to draw is that there is *no silver bullet*. The experiences of these twelve countries since the late 1970s do not reveal a particular policy or institution that is the obvious choice to focus upon for a country wishing to be a high-equality, high-employment society. Improvement may require changes to multiple policies and/or institutions.

Table 11.1. Summary of recommendations

Anglo Countries
    Increase the generosity of the statutory minimum wage
    Increase the generosity of some government benefits, including
        employment-conditional earnings subsidy, social assistance, and social insurance
    Increase tax rates
Anglo and Continental Countries
    Increase support for high-quality childcare and preschool
    Increase support for activation: active labor market programs and (as "last resort")
        public employment
Continental and Nordic Countries
    Soften employment protection regulations
    Shift tax revenues away from payroll and consumption taxes
    Reduce lengthy maternity/home care leaves (Fr, Ger, Fin, Nor)
    Allow wages to fall a bit at the low end of the distribution and tighten eligibility/reduce
        duration for some benefits
    Add an employment-conditional earnings subsidy and perhaps a statutory minimum
        wage

Note: This table simplifies in order to organize the recommendations by country group. The text provides a more nuanced discussion.

Second, each country is different in its existing configuration of institutions and policies and in its citizens' preferences about equality and employment. Thus, there is *no one-size-fits-all reform package* that will yield optimal results for every nation.

Third, because there is, inevitably, considerable uncertainty regarding the best course of action for any particular country, governments and other economic actors have little option but to experiment. Success requires learning from the experiences of other countries, learning from one's own past, and *continuous experimentation and adjustment*.

My recommendations are as follows. They are summarized in Table 11.1.

Government Benefit Generosity

In the Anglo countries, particularly the United States, reducing inequality is the key priority from a jobs-with-equality perspective. There are various ways to do this. Raising wages at the low end of the distribution would help, as would reducing the number of zero-earner households. But getting to moderate or low inequality is not possible on the pretax-pretransfer side alone. It also will be necessary to increase the generosity of government benefits. The key benefits for working-age households are employment-conditional earnings subsidies, social insurance programs (unemployment, sickness, and disability insurance), and social assistance. The empirical distribution of posttax-posttransfer incomes among low-earning single-adult households shown in Figures 7.1 and 7.2 indicates that benefit levels in the Anglo countries have tended to be comparatively low.

Italy also has a comparatively high level of posttax-posttransfer income inequality. This is despite extensive wage compression. As the data in Chapter 3 indicate, inequality in Italy is mainly a product of low employment (manifested partly in a large number of zero-earner households) and of limited and inefficient redistributive policies. Historically, Italy's transfers have been targeted to particular demographic groups—the elderly, the disabled, and so on—rather than to those with low incomes per se. As a result, too much of the money that is transferred, which by comparative standards is itself low, goes to individuals or households with moderate or high incomes (Ferrera 1996; Gough 1996; Baldini, Bosi, and Toso 2002; Matsaganis et al. 2003; Sacchi and Bastagli 2005). In the late 1990s and early 2000s several reforms were introduced to try to remedy this deficiency. The most important of these was a social assistance benefit, the "minimum insertion income" (RMI), modeled on that introduced in France a decade earlier to fill a similar gap in its welfare state. The RMI was experimented with in a small number of regions beginning in 1998 and in a larger number starting in 2001. But the Berlusconi government elected in 2001 discontinued the program (Sacchi and Bastagli 2005).

The concern with raising benefit levels is that doing so will reduce work incentives. The best way to mitigate this problem is to ensure that employment pays. The most effective tools are a reasonably high minimum wage and an employment-conditional earnings subsidy (discussed below).

Support for Childcare and Preschool

I concluded in Chapter 10 that government provision and/or subsidization of childcare probably has boosted employment among prime-working-age women across these twelve countries, but that the evidence is by no means conclusive. Still, if large numbers of parents, and particularly mothers, are to be employed full-time, childcare is a necessity. The Netherlands has achieved substantial growth of female employment with limited childcare, but its rate of employment among prime-age women is still no higher than in Germany and France (Figure 10.2), and many Dutch women work part-time. Having extensive childcare does not require a large government investment. After all, a larger share of children under age 2 are in formal care in the United States than in Sweden (Figure 10.11). But having extensive, affordable, *and high-quality* childcare and preschool almost certainly does require public funding. That does not necessarily imply public provision of care. Government can subsidize high-quality care by providing vouchers that shoulder a larger portion of the cost if parents choose better care centers (Blau 2001; Helburn and Bergmann 2002).

Government support for quality childcare and preschool is good policy in two respects. One is promotion of women's employment. The other, as I discussed in Chapter 9, is equalization of cognitive skills (Esping-Andersen 2004). We have little empirical evidence to look to here, but it is encouraging that the two countries in which a fairly large share of young children have been in formal care over the past generation, Denmark and Sweden, have among the lowest levels of measured cognitive inequality among adults (Figure 9.2). And this does not appear to come at a sacrifice of the average level of cognitive ability. The countries with less cognitive inequality also tend to have the highest average levels of cognitive ability (Figure 9.6). It is unclear to what degree, if any, low inequality of cognitive ability reduces inequality of earnings and incomes; the evidence we currently have is too thin to judge (Chapter 9). But it surely does not hurt.

A third respect in which childcare and preschool is helpful is in allowing citizens to feel comfortable about imposing a work obligation on single parents. Some have no qualms about imposing such an obligation regardless of whether or not there are adequate supports in place. But for many this is a difficult issue, and sentiments are divided. With affordable high-quality childcare, concerns about children's well-being when their lone parent is in paid work, even full-time paid work, are surely lessened. A work obligation is, in turn, helpful in ensuring political support for an adequate level of social assistance benefits (Gilens 1999).

Parental/Home Care Leaves

Paid parental leaves appear to promote women's employment. But leaves of very long duration reduce such employment by discouraging return to the work force. Four of the twelve countries—Finland, France, Germany, and Norway—currently have maternity or "home care" leaves that last up to three years, much and in some cases all of which is paid. The evidence examined in Chapter 10 suggests an adverse impact on employment among prime-working-age women. It would help to reduce the length of these leaves, to perhaps no more than sixteen months.

Politically, this is tricky. Proponents of home care leaves can utilize the rhetoric of choice, which often has considerable political resonance (Morgan

2004; Kenworthy 2008c). The argument is that mothers (and fathers) who choose to stay home with their children are not helped by government provision or subsidization of out-of-home childcare, so there should be a benefit that permits parental choice during the first few years of a child's life. Still, from the point of view of promoting women's employment, lengthy home care leaves almost certainly are detrimental. Sweden offers an encouraging precedent. A center-right coalition government introduced a home care leave in 1994, but when the Social Democrats were elected the following year they eliminated this program (Duvander, Ferrarini, and Thalberg 2005).

Employment Protection Regulations

Employment protection has been a key labor market institution in a number of affluent countries for several decades. It provides security to the employed. And in so doing it likely heightens cooperation between labor and management, which can contribute to higher productivity (Brown, Stern, and Ulman 1993; Buechtemann 1993; Levine and Parkin 1994; Hicks and Kenworthy 1998). It also encourages investments by both employers and employees in firm- or industry-specific skills (Estevez-Abe, Iversen, and Soskice 2001; Hall and Soskice 2001).

The worry is that strong employment protection rules may discourage hiring and thereby reduce employment. However, the comparative evidence offers little support for this hypothesis. The multivariate analyses in Chapter 6 suggested a relatively weak and fragile association between employment protection regulations and employment growth across the affluent countries.

I suggested in Chapter 6 that relaxing employment protection may nevertheless be a wise course of action for countries in which they currently are strong. Doing so *may* help to increase employment. And it seems very likely that looser employment protection facilitates economic adjustment—that is, rapid movement of employees between firms and industries. Employment protection probably contributes relatively little, if at all, to lower household income inequality. And to the extent it does contribute, it likely does so mainly by excluding some people from jobs (see Chapter 6), which is not a particularly desirable means of achieving inequality reduction.

Loosening employment protection regulations for regular employees would reduce job security for many workers. That, however, does not inherently imply less employment security. While people may no longer be able to feel confident about the likelihood of remaining in their *current* job, public policy can ensure that they have confidence they will always have *some* job. This has been the guiding labor market philosophy in Sweden for many years, though it is Denmark that has been the clearest practitioner of this approach (Egger and Sengenberger 2003; EC 2006; Madsen 2006; Campbell and Pedersen 2007). The key policy tools are active labor market programs and public employment as a last resort.

Payroll and Consumption Taxes

To the extent high taxes impede employment growth, the experiences of these twelve countries since the 1970s suggest it is mainly, and perhaps exclusively, high payroll and consumption taxes that do so. Thus, shifting revenue collection from either or both of these to income taxes may be helpful. One of the most attractive features of doing so is that it is likely to have little or no impact on earnings or income inequality. If anything, it may help to reduce inequality, as income taxes generally are less regressive than payroll and consumption taxes.

This is not an easy thing to do politically. The issue was part of the discussion in Germany's "Alliance for Jobs" in the late 1990s, but agreement to reform the tax system was not reached (Streeck 2005). However, it is not impossible. In 1990 France introduced a new tax on personal income (the CSG) in order to shift taxation away from payroll taxes. This was only a partial step; payroll taxes still account for four-fifths of the revenues that support social policy in France (Palier 2000). But it was a step in the right direction.

A complimentary initiative is to fully or partially exempt employers in some low-end services from payroll taxes and/or to exempt some low-end goods and services from consumption taxes. Several continental countries and Sweden have experimented with doing so since the mid-1990s.

Social Insurance Benefit Eligibility and Duration

The evidence I examined in Chapter 7 suggests uncertainty about the impact of the generosity of government benefits on employment performance across the twelve countries. It may be that benefit generosity accounts for a sizable amount of the cross-country variation in employment growth (Figure 7.6). But some estimates—for example, if we control for labor cost changes and leave out Sweden—suggest no effect at all.

If there is an element of benefits that is most likely to have an impact, it is their duration. Provided sufficient supports exist to help people back into paid work, then, this is an aspect of benefit generosity that can, in some countries, usefully be reduced.

By most accounts, part of the reason for Denmark's strong employment performance since the mid-1990s has been the fact that it significantly reduced the duration of unemployment compensation (Benner and Vad 2000; Björklund 2000; Goul Andersen 2002; Madsen 2006). Prior to that time eligibility lasted seven or nine years, depending on the person's circumstances. In 1995 it was shortened to five years and in 1998 to four. Eligibility rules were stiffened. Persons under age 25 with limited education were required to enroll in school or training or to find a job within six months. Monitoring was intensified. At the same time, heightened funding was allocated to job retraining and job placement and more individualized support was provided to the unemployed.

Reducing duration is a key component of "Hartz Commission" reforms in Germany that took effect in 2003, 2004, and 2005 (Kemmerling and Bruttel 2005; Siebert 2004; Streeck and Trampusch 2005). Formerly, an unemployed German received unemployment insurance for up to 32 months, depending on age and length of prior employment. The benefit was 60% of former earnings (67% for those with children). After the person reached the end of the eligibility period, she or he could receive means-tested "unemployment assistance." The replacement rate was 53% of former earnings (57% with children), and the duration was indefinite. Nonemployed adults not eligible for unemployment insurance or unemployment assistance could receive social assistance. In the new system, unemployment insurance can be received for 12 months (18 months for those over age 55). After this, the benefit level no longer depends on prior earnings; it is reduced to the level of social assistance, which is approximately 340 euros per month plus housing assistance. For many, this is much less generous than the previous unemployment assistance benefit. In addition, after the first year of unemployment benefits a person is in principle obligated to accept any available job, even if the skill requirements and/or wage level are far below that of his or her previous job. It will be some time before it is possible to reasonably assess the impact of these reforms.

Low-End Wage Levels

There is reason to suspect that high wages at the low end of the distribution reduce employer demand for labor in low-productivity services. But as we discovered in Chapter 5, the macrocomparative evidence is not clear. There may be a fairly significant impact, but there might be no impact at all. My best guess is that there is an effect but that it is relatively small in magnitude. Still, even if it is indeed a small effect, allowing wages to drop a bit at the low end in countries where they currently are high might help to stimulate some employment growth.

A key obstacle is that wages in many countries are determined via collective bargaining, so this choice is outside the reach of policy. Policy makers may need to exchange tax relief or benefit increases to get unions to agree to such a reduction.

On the other hand, even in many countries with extensive collective bargaining there are jobs that are outside the framework of the bargaining system. The highest level of bargaining coverage—the share of the employed whose wages are determined by collective bargaining—is 95%, and in many countries it is around 80% (OECD 2004*h*). This is why two recent studies have found that wages for at least some low-end service jobs are as low relative to average wages in countries such as France and Germany as they are in the United States (Freeman and Schettkat 2000; Glyn et al. 2005). Paradoxically, then, there is a danger that wages in low-end services in some European countries could drop too much. A statutory minimum wage is one way to ensure that does not happen.

In Denmark, no jobs at the low end of the wage distribution are outside the reach of the collectively bargained minimum wage. As of 2006 that wage was 87.5 Danish kroner per hour, which converts to approximately 15.00 per hour in US dollars. From the employer's point of view that may be quite high for a low-end service job. But the combined tax package paid by the employee is close to 50%. In other words, the net pay is just $7.50 per hour. Thus, the wage cannot be lowered much, if at all, without posing a financial burden for low-skilled workers and their families. One way to address this might be in the form of a tax credit for low-earning individuals or households. This would facilitate a decrease in the minimum wage without reducing net earnings or income for those at the low end of the distribution.

In the United States, low-end wages need to be raised. The most direct way to accomplish this is to increase the statutory minimum. By how much? It is currently scheduled to rise to $7.25 per hour by 2009. I would recommend it be set at a slightly higher level, around $7.50, and indexed for inflation. If there is no adverse impact on employment, it could of course be raised further a few years later.

Employment-Conditional Earnings Subsidy

Low wages may help to boost employment rates, but they are problematic from the point of view of equality. As I suggested in Chapter 7, if there is to be a low-wage segment of the labor market, the most useful policy mechanism to ensure that this does not produce excessively high income inequality among households is an employment-conditional earnings subsidy—best exemplified currently by the Earned Income Tax Credit in the United States and the Working Tax Credit in the United Kingdom. This is a type of benefit particularly well-suited to achievement of the dual goals of low income inequality and high employment: it creates pro-employment incentives and it boosts the incomes of low-end households rather than individuals.

There are limits to how generous such a subsidy can be. As the amount of the subsidy is increased, either the phase-out rate must increase, which can begin to create work disincentives, or eligibility for the subsidy must extend fairly far up the income distribution, which may not only increase political support for the program but also raise its cost substantially. There are two ways to avoid having to make the subsidy excessively generous. One, which I described in Chapter 7, is to increase the statutory minimum wage in concert with the subsidy. Another is to expand government support for low-income households in other (noncash) ways, for example through increased subsidization of childcare and/or housing costs.

Support for Activation

The continental and Anglo countries could usefully increase public support for training and job placement. Most countries have moved in this direction in the past decade, with a particular emphasis on individualized support (OECD 2006*b*).

Supply-side programs—retraining, job placement assistance, and the like—may be insufficient to ensure employment for some at the low end of the labor market. Timothy Bartik (2001) offers a compelling argument for government activism on the demand side, particularly in the form of subsidies to employers to encourage hiring. If need be, government should provide jobs to ensure that individuals are not out of work for too long.

Special Attention to the Young and the Elderly

In Italy and France, an important aspect of low overall employment rates is very limited employment among those age 15 to 24, especially women in this age group. As I suggested in Chapter 10, a key to this story appears to be the fact that hardly any young women in these two countries combine schooling with paid work. This in turn is strongly correlated with the frequency of part-time employment (Figure 10.16). Facilitating and encouraging part-time work is likely to pay off not only in higher employment rates among this age group but also stronger attachment to the labor force later in life.

All four of the continental countries, including the Netherlands, have comparatively low employment rates among persons age 55 to 64. This is true both for women and for men (Figure 10.17). Part of this is a cohort effect, and part of it is a product of more general labor market problems, which can be addressed via the suggestions offered earlier in this section. But there are also steps countries can take to directly encourage employment among persons in this older age group: retraining and job placement support specially targeted to older workers, reforming pension systems and disability benefit programs, eliminating mandatory retirement policies in the public sector and discouraging their use in private firms, implementing anti-age-discrimination legislation, using information campaigns to raise awareness among employers of the potential value of older workers, facilitating access to part-time jobs, promoting flexible hours, and providing employer subsidies to encourage hiring (OECD 2006*a*).

Product Market Regulations

The strictness of product market regulations is negatively correlated with employment growth since the late 1970s (Figure 4.8). Given the large number of other potential causes of the cross-national variation, it is difficult to be certain that this relationship is causal. Still, because relaxing such regulations is likely to have little if any adverse impact on the distribution of income, this too is a useful candidate for action.

On the other hand, all twelve countries have in fact steadily relaxed product market regulations, particularly since the late 1980s. In many of those countries there has been little or no rise in the employment rate since then. This suggests that either the employment payoff takes a while to play out or there is in fact no noteworthy payoff to speak of.

OBJECTIONS AND ALTERNATIVES

An array of objections might plausibly be raised to my view of the problem, the solution, the lessons that can be drawn from recent comparative experience, and the best course of action for affluent countries. I attempt to address these here.

Is Market Inequality Really Rising?

I have suggested that a key part of the challenge for countries wishing to maintain or move toward low income inequality is rising market inequality. Yet in Chapter 5 I noted that in most affluent countries there has been relatively little change in the P50/P10 ratio for individual earnings. Is this contradictory?

No. I used the P50/P10 earnings ratio for employed individuals in Chapter 5 because it is the best available measure of wage levels at the low end of the distribution relative to the country norm (the country median). And it is indeed true that earnings inequality among employed individuals in the bottom half of the distribution has not increased in most countries. However, earnings inequality *has* risen in the overall distribution—that is, including the top half—in a number of nations since the mid-1990s. This is shown in Figure 3.1 in Chapter 3.

More important, of chief concern is market inequality among *households*. This is determined not only by earnings dispersion among employed individuals but also, as I emphasized in Chapter 3, by the distribution of employment and earnings across households. The latter is heavily influenced by aspects of household composition such as the prevalence of single-adult households and marital homogamy. Figure 3.5 shows that market income inequality among households has increased not only in the United States and the United Kingdom but also in every country except the Netherlands. And in many of these countries the degree of increase was rather large.

It is impossible to be certain that this trend will continue. But ongoing declines in unionization, increases in competition in domestic and international markets, delays in age of marriage, and increases in assortative mating suggest reason for worry.

Why Not Productivity Growth or Population Growth Instead of Employment Growth?

I have argued that increases in employment rates can help to finance generous redistributive programs for working-age households, which in turn are likely to play an increasingly critical role in holding income inequality at bay. But in principle a country could rely on productivity growth, rather than employment growth, to achieve this aim. Instead of increasing taxable income by raising the share of adults in employment, the country would increase it by raising the amount of output per employed person (or per work hour).

This is a perfectly reasonable suggestion, and I would hardly want to encourage policy makers to ignore productivity growth. The problem is that we know even less about what causes differences in productivity growth across the affluent countries and over time than we do about employment growth (for some recent attempts, see Amable 2003; Hall and Gingerich 2004; Sapir et al. 2004; Kenworthy 2006; Baumol, Litan, and Schramm 2007). As I noted in Chapter 1, productivity growth in the past several decades has been slower, rather than faster, than in the decades immediately following World War II. And there is no convincing evidence to suggest that this pattern will soon reverse. Trying to increase employment is therefore probably the wiser course.

An additional concern with relying mainly on productivity growth is the potential for tax resistance. The smaller the share of the population that is employed, the larger the share of total tax revenues each employed person provides, and therefore the greater the likelihood for political division between taxpayers and benefit recipients.

Another alternative to raising the employment rate is to increase the size of the population, whether via higher immigration or higher fertility. This too can help, but only if the additional people are employed.

Why Not Increase Tax Rates?

I have suggested that increasing the employment rate is desirable because it enables an increase in tax revenues, which can be used to maintain or increase redistributive generosity without requiring an increase in tax rates. Raising tax rates was a common strategy for funding increases in redistribution in the 1960s and 1970s, but I have argued that this is now more difficult because of capital mobility. Is that really true? Is there no room for further hikes in tax rates?

Surely the Anglo countries and Italy, in which the tax take is around 25–35% of GDP, could increase tax rates somewhat without provoking significant capital flight (Glyn 2006). These countries, especially the United States, need to do so—not merely to solve the problem of pension commitments for an aging population, but to reduce income inequality. The question, however, is whether countries with tax levels at 45–50% of GDP can increase revenues via higher rates. I do not want to dismiss the possibility, but current and likely future pressures push in the opposite direction.

Can Higher Employment in Low-End Services Really Help to Fund Generous Redistributive Programs?

Much of my discussion and analysis of employment has focused on low-end services. This is because jobs in these sectors have been, and seem likely to continue to be, a key part of employment growth in affluent countries. They also are the source of most of the cross-country variation in employment growth over the past several decades. (Loss of employment in manufacturing and agriculture also has varied sharply across countries. As I noted in Chapter 4, that variation is almost entirely a function of the amount of employment that remained in these sectors at the beginning of the 1980s.) But if the aim of employment increases is to raise tax revenues in order to fund generous redistributive programs, will low-paying service jobs really help?

It is impossible to guarantee that they will. Much depends on the degree of employment increase and on what the new employees were doing formerly. But there is reason for optimism.

Even low-wage employees tend to contribute to tax revenues. Depending on the structure and level of the tax system, they are likely to pay income and/or payroll taxes on their earnings. A generous employment-conditional earnings subsidy, which I advocate, may offset these tax payments for some households. (The US Earned Income Tax Credit was originally conceived as a way to refund payroll tax payments for low-earning households.) But to the extent those households spend some of their earnings and government transfers, they will add to government revenues via consumption-tax payments.

Rising employment also may reduce government expenses. Transfer payments for households on social assistance tend to be much greater than for those receiving an employment-conditional earnings subsidy.

Another consideration is underground employment. One of the reasons for making low-wage jobs financially viable—for both employers and employees—is to bring them into the formal sector. If high minimum wage levels or generous social assistance benefits or high payroll taxes raise the cost of employment in certain low-end service areas, such as restaurants or home cleaning, one result will be a growing amount of off-the-books work in such jobs. From a jobs-with-equality perspective, this is a particularly unfortunate outcome. The earnings are not taxed, the people in such jobs are not eligible for an employment-conditional earnings subsidy, and they are not protected by rules governing working conditions.

A final consideration on this issue is upward mobility. As I suggest below, it is probably too optimistic to hope that a large share of those in low-end service jobs will succeed in moving up to a middle-earnings position. But certainly some will. And as they do, the tax revenues they generate will increase.

Consider a case in which employment seems least likely to add to government revenues: the government hires a woman to provide childcare which is heavily subsidized. In other words, the government is paying her, so any tax revenues generated by her earnings are merely recycling prior government revenues rather than generating new ones. Moreover, because the government is subsidizing the service she provides, it is losing money on that end. Will this add to government revenues? Possibly not in this situation. Clearly it is preferable from a revenue-enhancing standpoint to create jobs in the private sector. But even in this scenario there may be payoffs due to spillover effects. Because she is in the labor force, this woman is likely to outsource some of her second-shift work (e.g., cleaning or cooking). That helps to provide a job for someone else, who may leave social assistance (saving the government money) or add to her household's income and thus to their tax payments.

How Will Rising Employment Affect Market Inequality?

Suppose a country succeeds in raising its employment rate and that this increases its tax revenues, allowing it to maintain or even increase the generosity of its redistributive programs for working-age households and their children. Presumably this is good for equality. But what if the rise in employment contributes to *greater market* inequality? Won't that offset any gains achieved via redistribution?

Here again it is critical to keep in mind the distinction between two types of "market" inequality—earnings inequality among employed individuals and pretax-pretransfer income inequality among households. The latter is more important. If much of the added employment is in relatively low-wage jobs, earnings inequality among employed individuals will rise. The question, though, is what effect this will have on the distribution of earnings and income among *households*.

Where the newly employed are in households that formerly had no earner, the effect will be to reduce market inequality across households. This is a key part of the reason why market income inequality has declined in the Netherlands since the late 1970s (Chapter 3). If many of the newly employed are in households that formerly had a low-wage worker, the impact again will almost certainly be to diminish market inequality among households.

The problematic scenario is where a sizable share of the newly employed are in households that already had a moderate-to-high earner. If this occurs, the rise in employment will increase market inequality. As I discussed in Chapter 10, this is a realistic possibility, particularly for countries in which most of those moving into employment will be women. Women with more education are likely to have an advantage over less-educated women in obtaining employment and a stronger preference for doing so. Because they tend to be partnered with someone who is similarly educated and thus in the top half of the earnings distribution, their entrance into employment will tend to increase interhousehold earnings inequality. But this is not the end of the story. If employment continues to rise, eventually many of those moving into the work force will be less-educated women. Eventually, therefore, rising employment will *reduce* market inequality among households.

Am I Recommending a Modified Social Democratic Model?

As of the mid-2000s, Denmark, Norway, and Sweden have the highest employment rates among the twelve countries. Along with Finland and the Netherlands, they also, as of the most recent available data, have the lowest levels of posttax-posttransfer household income inequality. Perhaps, then, there is no mystery about how best to achieve a high-employment, high-equality society: the solution is "the Nordic way."

Although the Nordic countries vary somewhat in their policies and institutions, there is a common core. It might usefully be termed the "social democratic model," as most of it was put in place by or with the support of social democratic parties (Esping-Andersen 1990; Björklund and Freeman 1997; Korpi and Palme 1998; Huber and Stephens 2001; Pontusson 2005, 2007).

High employment is pursued through various means. Some are no different from those used in all affluent countries—fiscal and monetary policy, special tax incentives, adjustment of the exchange rate (prior to the 1990s). Several particular policy strategies set the model apart. A strong schooling system provides a moderate-to-high level of education and learning to the bulk of the population (Figure 9.6). Active labor market programs such as retraining and job placement assistance improve the efficiency of the private-sector labor market, and the public sector employs a comparatively large share of the population (Figure 7.10). The Nordic countries also have been committed to generous women-friendly policies such as government support for childcare, paid maternity leave, support for part-time employment, and individualized taxation (Figure 10.11).

Income inequality is contained in the social democratic model in several ways. Strong unions and relatively centralized wage bargaining generate wage compression, so earnings inequality among those in paid work is relatively low (Figure 3.1). High employment ensures that there are comparatively few zero-earner households (Figure 3.4). And generous social policies redistribute income from high-earning to low-earning households (Figures 3.9 and 3.10).

There is no question but that the social-democratic model has been successful at generating both high employment and low inequality in the Nordic countries. Is there any need for modification? In my view, there are two chief concerns for these nations.

One is whether levels of taxation around 50% of GDP will continue to be sustainable. (The tax level is lower in Norway, largely due to government oil

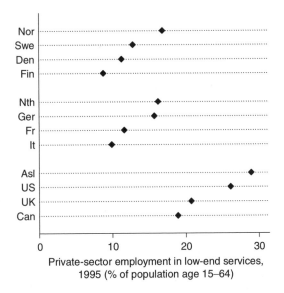

Figure 11.2. Private-sector employment in low-end services, 1995.

Note: For data definitions and sources, see the appendix. 1995 is the most recent year for which low-end service employment data can be disaggregated into private and public.

revenues.) There is little sign of public support for significant tax reduction (Svallfors and Taylor-Gooby 1999), but that could of course change. If it does, the Nordic countries may have to shift somewhat away from universalism and in favor of greater use of targeting in their transfer programs (Kenworthy 2008*b*).

The second concern is whether these countries can continue to sustain high employment rates without extensive private-sector employment in low-end services. Figure 11.2 shows that, as of the mid-1990s (which unfortunately is the most recent year for which data are available), private-sector employment levels in low-end services tended to be comparatively low in the Nordic countries, with the partial exception of Norway. They have compensated for these low rates with extensive public sector employment. But that strategy may have reached its limit (Esping-Andersen 1999; Iversen 1999; Ferrera, Hemerijck, and Rhodes 2000). Further increases in the employment rate, which can help to maintain redistributive generosity, may have to come in the private sector. If so, some of the reforms I suggest in the "Recommendations" section— in particular, lower wages at the low end of the distribution, less stringent employment protection (not a concern in Denmark), less reliance on payroll taxes (also not an issue in Denmark)—may prove useful complements to the social democratic approach to jobs with equality.

The most problematic of these possible reforms is likely to be allowing a drop in wages at the low end of the earnings distribution. Here introduction of an employment-conditional earnings subsidy would help. As I argue above and at greater length in Chapter 7, this type of program compensates at the household level for widening inequality in the distribution of individual earnings. In doing so it better targets the aspect of monetary inequality about which egalitarians should be most concerned—inequality of income (rather than earnings) among households (rather than individuals).

What about the continental and Anglo countries? Is my recommendation essentially that they aim for a modified version of the social democratic model? As a practical matter, that is unlikely to be possible. Even if left parties in the continental and Anglo countries were committed to such a vision, ingrained public opinion, institutional inertia, and the realities of global financial markets would make it very difficult to implement.

The most important obstacle, in my view, is the difficulty that most of these countries, especially the Anglo ones, would have in increasing their tax share to around half of GDP. The continental countries certainly could shift revenues from payroll to income taxes. And the Anglo countries, particularly the United States, could very likely increase revenues to perhaps 40% of GDP. But governments aiming to increase tax rates face a more daunting set of impediments now than the Nordic countries did when they sharply increased taxation levels in the 1960s and 1970s (Chapter 8).

In part because of the constraints on taxation, it also seems unlikely that most of the continental and Anglo countries could reach the levels of public employment that exist in Denmark and Sweden. As Figure 7.10 in Chapter 7 shows, the public sector employs nearly 25% of the working-age population in those two countries. In the Anglo and continental nations, the figure is 10–15%. I suggested a few paragraphs ago that the Nordic countries may have to rely more on private-sector jobs for future employment growth. Certainly that is true for their continental and Anglo counterparts.

The continental countries are relatively egalitarian but suffer from low employment. The Anglo countries have done comparatively well in increasing employment but have high inequality. In spite of these commonalities, each of the nations within these groups is different. Each, therefore, may need to find a somewhat different strategy, or path, for improvement. And the most important reforms may not always be in the direction of the social democratic model. For example, in my estimation the single most productive reform for Germany would be to shift tax revenues from payroll to income taxes. That is not a Nordic or social democratic reform per se. For the United States, my top recommendations for reform would be universal health care, an increase in the minimum wage and expansion of the Earned Income Tax Credit, and support for high-quality childcare. Only the third of these is a feature closely identified with the social democratic model.

The underlying point is that there is no one-size-fits-all recipe for success. Each country will have to find its own way. While certain movements in the direction of the social democratic model would clearly be beneficial for a number of the continental and Anglo nations, positing that model as the end goal is too simplistic.

The Third Way?

The term "third way" is identified variously with the 1983–96 Hawke and Keating Labour governments in Australia, Bill Clinton's 1993–2000 Democratic Party administration in the United States, the Chretien and Martin Liberal Party governments in Canada from 1993 to 2006, Tony Blair and Gordon Brown's New Labour government in the United Kingdom since 1997, and Gerhard Schroeder's Social Democratic government in Germany from 1997 to 2005. Christoffer Green-Pedersen, Kees van Kersbergen, and Anton Hemerijck (2001) argue that the social democrat-led coalition governments in Denmark and the Netherlands in the mid-to-late 1990s also pursued a third way approach to social and economic policy.

Many descriptions of third way principles and policies have been offered (Giddens 1998, 2000; Blair and Schroeder 1999; Reich 1999; Streeck 1999; Myles and Quadagno 2000; Rhodes 2000; Green-Pedersen, van Kersbergen, and Hemerijck 2001; Pierson and Castles 2002; Jensen and Saint-Martin 2003; Lewis and Surrender 2004; Taylor-Gooby and Larsen 2004). Green-Pedersen, van Kersbergen, and Hemerijck (2001: 312–13, 320) identify the main characteristics of a third way policy strategy as the following: "A tax policy that promotes growth, implying the reduction of taxation of hard work and enterprise.... A macroeconomic policy that emphasizes sound public finances.... It is essential that high levels of government borrowing decrease and not increase. Reforms of welfare schemes that limit an individual's ability to find a job, i.e. schemes that encourage passivity and inactivity.... Active labor market policies that stress personal responsibility. Policies that promote flexibilization of the labor market and promote labor market participation.... Altogether, the 'third way' is about the creation of good jobs and the promotion of high rates of labor force participation, and the means to achieve these goals is both the market and state intervention."

In many respects, the third way approach has been successful both in political/electoral terms and as judged by economic and social results (Green-Pedersen, van Kersbergen, and Hemerijck 2001; Blank and Ellwood 2002;

Card, Blundell, and Freeman 2004; Hills and Stewart 2005; Jencks 2005; Pearce and Paxton 2005; Mishel, Bernstein, and Allegretto 2007). A number of third way policy orientations are consistent with those I suggest in the "Recommendations" section of this chapter. But a key element is absent: an emphasis on the importance of redistribution as a means of securing low inequality. Indeed, for many third way proponents, low income inequality is not a central aim at all. As one description puts it: "Greater egalitarianism is to be achieved not through the income distribution but by action to affect the initial distribution of skills, capacities, and productive endowments" (Surender 2004: 4). In the third way approach, the aim is to reduce inequality of opportunities, not of outcomes.

I suggested in Chapter 2 that the goal of equalizing opportunities is desirable but not sufficient. One problem is that parental income and assets influence children's development and later opportunities, so unequal outcomes among parents interfere with equality of opportunity. A second is that it is impossible to truly equalize opportunities. Even if parents' assets and incomes as well as schooling and access to job placement assistance and retraining were equalized, society can have little if any impact on differences in genetic endowments, parents' dispositions and behaviors, peer influence, and the myriad chance events that occur throughout childhood and adolescence.

Though it is seldom articulated explicitly, there is an implicit third way stance on what should be considered a fair distribution of income. It is the "maximize average income subject to a floor" view that I described in Chapter 2 (White 2004b). In the third way approach there are three principal mechanisms for setting and lifting the income floor. One is a societal minimum wage. This is set by the government in the United Kingdom and United States and by collective bargaining in most other affluent countries. The second is low unemployment, achieved via human capital development and activation obligations and supports. A low unemployment rate helps to push up wages (Blanchflower and Oswald 1994; Bernstein and Baker 2003). The third is an employment-conditional earnings subsidy. This is perhaps the most important of the three, because it targets low-income households (rather than low-earning individuals) directly.

How effective is this approach in practice? If it were effective, we might expect to find something like the following in comparing the household income distribution in a country with an avowedly third way government with the distribution in a more egalitarian country such as Sweden: there will be greater income inequality in the third way country, but absolute low-end income levels in the two countries will be similar.

Figure 11.3 provides some empirical insight. It shows levels of posttax-posttransfer household income at various percentiles of the distribution as of

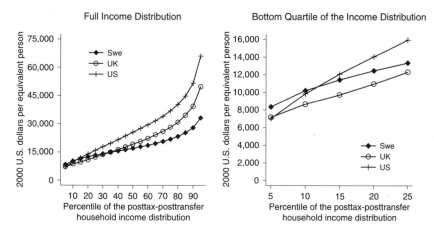

Figure 11.3. Absolute income levels in Sweden, the United Kingdom, and the United States, 2000.

Note: For data definitions and sources, see the appendix.

2000 for Sweden and the United States and 1999 for the United Kingdom. This is the most recent year for which comparable data are available. It was the final year of the Clinton presidency but very early in the Blair-Brown government's term. There are two charts. The first chart shows the full distribution, from the 5th percentile to the 95th. The second shows the same data, but only for the bottom quarter of the distribution (the 5th percentile through the 25th), because the magnitude of the country differences at the low end is difficult to gauge in the first chart. Incomes in the United Kingdom and Sweden have been converted into US dollars using purchasing power parities (and with an inflation adjustment for the 1999 UK data). Following common practice, I adjust for household size by dividing each household's income by the square root of the number of persons in the household (see Chapter 3). This means the incomes are expressed "per equivalent person." The incomes shown in the charts can be read as approximating those for single-person households. For four-person households, the incomes in the chart must be multiplied by two. For example, the first chart shows a median (50th percentile) income in the United States of approximately $25,000 per equivalent person. The median for a four-person household was thus $25,000 × 2 = $50,000.

The patterns in the first chart indicate that, as we saw in Chapter 3, income inequality was indeed much greater in the United Kingdom and the United States than in Sweden. There was a much larger gap between the bottom and the top in the former countries than in the latter. Are the patterns consistent with what a proponent of "maximize average income subject to a floor" would hope to see for the UK and US? At first glance, the answer would appear to be yes: absolute incomes at the low end in these two countries were roughly similar to those in Sweden.

But that conclusion would be too hasty. As can be seen more clearly in the second chart, in the lower part of the income distribution—from the 5th to the 25th percentile—incomes in the United Kingdom were in fact about $1,500 to $2,000 per person ($3,000 to $4,000 for four-person households) lower than in Sweden. Incomes at the low end in the United States were similar to those in Sweden at the 10th and 15th percentiles, and higher at the 20th and 25th. But this picture is misleading, as it fails to take into account differences in the provision of public services. Many Americans in this income range must either purchase health insurance or pay directly for health care. Some receive a health insurance subsidy from their employer, and some qualify for Medicaid. But most do not. Also, for many Americans with low incomes, public primary and secondary schools are underfunded and/or of low quality.

This kind of comparison of absolute income levels is by no means unproblematic. Purchasing power parities, which are designed to reflect differences in average living costs across countries, may do so more accurately for households in the middle of the income distribution than for those at the low end. Another concern is uncertainty regarding how much income matters relative to the cost and quality of services. The latter are difficult to compare across countries. Still, what the data suggest is that, to the extent the third way position on income distribution is a "maximize average income subject to a floor" view, as of 2000 the approach may have been less effective than supporters would have hoped. If we consider low-end incomes in Sweden to be a reasonable floor for an affluent country, the United Kingdom and United States have a considerable way to go—in additional income and/or more and better public services—to satisfy the floor component of the "maximize average income subject to a floor" criterion.

Bringing up the floor is likely to require additional public resources and redistribution. But as I suggested above, the need for such has tended to be downplayed by third way proponents. Of course, the countries in which third way policies have been put in place have had very different starting points. In Denmark and the Netherlands there was no need in the 1990s for an emphasis on redistribution, as these countries already were highly redistributive. Indeed, some of their programs—unemployment insurance in Denmark and disability compensation in the Netherlands—arguably were *too* generous. In the United States and United Kingdom, on the other hand, the generosity of government benefits was considerably lower as the Clinton and Blair-Brown governments began in 1992 and 1997. As an electoral strategy, the commitment made by both governments to not substantially increase taxes was probably wise. And the emphasis on increasing employment (activation) is, in my view, entirely salutary. The Clinton and Blair-Brown governments have by and large done an admirable job of improving employment opportunities and helping to boost the incomes of those in low-wage jobs.

Yet there is a limit to what a government can do when tax revenues total 28% of GDP, as they do in the United States, and perhaps even 38%, as in the United Kingdom. Yes, services can be delivered more efficiently, administration can be streamlined, and transfers can be better targeted to those most in need. But these improvements can only go so far. To provide universal health care, a first-class educational system, extensive support for childcare and preschool, effective crime prevention, active labor market programs, public-sector jobs for those unable to find work in the private sector, generous pensions and other social insurance programs, a generous employment-conditional earnings subsidy, along with the many other things government must do—this requires considerable resources.

From the perspective of attaining jobs with equality, the limitation of the third way approach is this underestimation of the quantity of redistribution required and of the tax revenues needed to finance that redistribution. The third way emphasis on promoting employment holds the potential to facilitate an increase in tax revenues and therefore in redistribution. But in low-tax countries, funding a serious effort to reduce income inequality probably will require an increase in tax rates. The Blair-Schroeder (1999) conclusion that "public expenditure as a proportion of national income has more or less reached the limits of acceptability" will need to be reconsidered—not in Denmark, but probably so in the United Kingdom and certainly in the United States.

There is, of course, a political problem: in countries with comparatively low taxation, public opinion tends to lean heavily against tax increases. Is taxation low because of public opinion, or is public opposition to taxes largely an adaptation to the low-tax regime? In all likelihood the causality runs in both directions. Unfortunately, we do not have comparative data on public attitudes toward taxation far enough back in time to be able to sort this out.

Even where the public opposes higher taxation, citizens tend to express considerable support for higher spending on particular transfer programs and services (Gilens 1999; Hills 2004; Taylor-Gooby 2005; McCall and Kenworthy 2008). A strategy for generating public support for increased taxation, therefore, is to earmark tax revenues to particular programs. For example, one proposal to pay for providing universal health insurance in the United States is to create a national consumption tax (at 3–4%, with exemptions) earmarked specifically to pay for it (Lambrew, Podesta, and Shaw 2005). In the United

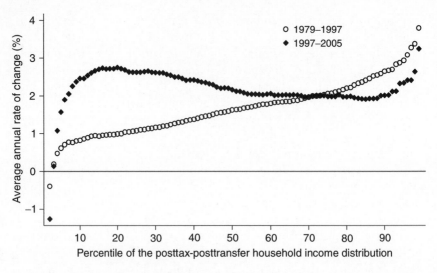

Figure 11.4. Real income growth in the United Kingdom, 1979–97 and 1997–2005.

Note: The data are for size-adjusted households.

Source: Brewer et al. (2006: Figure 2.8, p. 21).

Kingdom, an increase in income tax or consumption tax could be earmarked for public subsidization of childcare. Earmarking should perhaps be a last resort, as it constrains policy makers in a way that can turn out to be problematic years down the road (Hills 2004: 178–80). But in a political climate in which public opposition to increased taxation is especially strong, there may be no useful alternative.

In fairness to the New Labour government in the United Kingdom, the data in Figure 11.3 are for 1999, which is before the main thrust of its policy reforms had taken full effect. Indeed, it was in 1999 that the statutory minimum wage was introduced and the employment-conditional tax credit was substantially expanded. In ensuing years social assistance benefit levels for families with young children and public funding for childcare were increased substantially (Lister 2004; Hills and Stewart 2005). Figure 11.4 shows rates of increase in inflation-adjusted posttax-posttransfer household income at each percentile of the UK income distribution over the periods 1979–97 and 1997–2005. The data suggest a very respectable rate of increase among those between the 5th and the 25th percentiles during the New Labour years. Perhaps, then, a comparison similar to that in Figure 11.3 with data for the mid-2000s, rather than for 1999, will tell a different story. Unfortunately, such a comparison will not be possible until the next wave of LIS data is available.

The other side of inequality is the high end of the distribution. In some countries, dramatic increases in pay and/or investment income among those at the very top of the distribution have been a key driver of recent increases in household income inequality (Atkinson and Piketty 2007; Brewer et al. 2006; Mishel, Bernstein, and Allegretto 2007). In the second half of the 1990s, an explosion in compensation for corporate executives and top entertainers and athletes coupled with a sharp rise in stock share values led to soaring incomes for a small segment of households.

Third way proponents tend not to worry about this as a problem in its own right. Despite the considerable media attention devoted to skyrocketing CEO compensation in the early and mid-1990s, Bill Clinton said little about the issue. And Tony Blair once remarked that "The issue isn't in fact whether the very richest person ends up becoming richer.... It's not a burning ambition of mine to make sure that David Beckham earns less money" (quoted in Sefton and Sutherland 2005: 233). Yet as I suggested in Chapter 2, there is a compelling rationale on fairness grounds to be concerned about incomes at the top pulling farther away from the rest of society.

What should be done? One proposal is to impose a "maximum wage" (Pizzigati 1992; Ramsay 2005). The idea is in effect to tax earnings or income above a certain amount at a rate of 100%. The problem is that this would likely reduce the amount of income that is subject to taxation, as high earners would shift their compensation to nonmonetary forms—a new home, vacations at expensive resorts, payment for children's schooling, and so on. This would reduce the quantity of government revenues available for redistribution. And depending on how low the maximum allowable level were set at, 100% taxation might also create severe work disincentives for a nontrivial share of the labor force.

A seemingly wiser course of action is to impose a relatively high, but far from confiscatory, rate of income taxation on very high incomes. Exactly what that rate should be can only be determined by trial and error. Also useful in this respect is an asset tax—an annual tax on household wealth. Some European nations already have an asset tax (Wolff 2002). Other countries, including the United Kingdom and the United States, instead have only an "estate tax," which is imposed at death. An estate tax tends to be far less effective than a regular asset tax at redistributing money, because an estate tax makes it easier to draw down assets, via consumption and/or gifting, before they become subject to taxation.

Life-Course Equality?

Another alternative is to aim for what might be termed "life course equality." Gøsta Esping-Andersen has argued that affluent countries should forsake the goal of contemporaneous equality in favor of equality over the life course:

Substantial service employment growth outside the public sector depends on flexibility and low wages, something that social democracy cannot easily accept. The social democratic strategy will therefore not escape the fundamental "equality-jobs" tradeoff....

There is in truth only one way out of the impasse, namely to refine what kind of equality we desire. *Homo socialdemocraticus* must be convinced that we cannot aspire for all kinds of equality at once, that some inequalities can be made compatible with some equalities.

The principle of equality that must go is ... equality for all "here-and-now". In practice, this may not be so difficult a task. *Homo socialdemocraticus*, like many of his rivals, has surely held any number of lousy jobs in his youth. Like all Scandinavians, he left the parental home very early and lived for years on bread and water (this is what he tells his children). Yet, he is now a respectable citizen with a respectable career. Temporary deprivation is unimportant if it does not affect our life chances.

We can return to Schumpeter's omnibus: always full, but always with different people. Everybody gets off at the next stop, or at least where desired. If, like *Homo socialdemocraticus*, we cling to a notion of equality for all, here and now, we shall never resolve the fundamental dilemma of our times. The kinds of inequalities that are inevitable in the world of *Homo liberalismus* can become acceptable, even welcomed, if they coincide with a welfare regime capable of guaranteeing all citizens against entrapment: no one should find him- or herself in an omnibus with locked doors.

Our search for a postindustrial welfare optimum requires, therefore, some kind of a mobility guarantee. (Esping-Andersen 1999: 179–80, 182–3; see also Esping-Andersen 2001; Esping-Andersen et al. 2002; Diamond and Giddens 2005)

Esping-Andersen suggests that eradication of child poverty, provision of high-quality public childcare and schooling beginning very early in life, and opportunity for skill development throughout the life course will enable people to move up the occupational ladder over time. An individual may start in a low-paying job, but with a strong educational foundation, continued opportunity for training, and perhaps assistance with job placement, she or he will be able to advance into a more lucrative and fulfilling position.

Note that the life-course equality vision is not that of the industrial period, when a young male would begin work on an assembly line in a manufacturing firm at age 16 or so, starting with a low wage but eventually, via regular pay raises and some seniority bonuses, ending up with "middle-class" earnings. In the life-course equality scenario, a young person starts in a low-paying service job. This job, because its productivity is relatively low and difficult to increase, will continue to be relatively low-paying. The person's earnings increase because she or he moves to a different, higher-paying job.

The life-course equality approach is closely related to, but nevertheless distinguishable from, that of third wayers. The chief aim of third way proponents is equality of opportunity—not in the simplistic sense of an absence of discriminatory barriers, but rather in the fuller sense of providing public support for skill development at the early stages and throughout the life course. Life-course equality favors this too, but the aim is not just equal opportunity but extensive intragenerational occupational mobility. To achieve low income inequality over the life course, a society needs for those who start in low-paying positions to move into better-paying ones at some point. Equality of opportunity is a means to this end, rather than an end in itself.

Is this feasible? One potential problem is the scale of mobility that would be required. Consider the United States. In the contemporary American labor market nearly one out of five employed persons (approximately 25 million people) works in the following low-productivity, low-paying occupations: farm worker, food preparation (low level), health care aide/orderly/attendant, household childcare worker, household cleaner, janitor/maid, laborer (assembler, fabricator, hand packer), mail sorter, messenger, receptionist, retail sales cashier, secretary, teachers' aide/assistant, telephone operator, truck driver, typist, waiter/waitress, or assistant (US Bureau of the Census, various years). Even if cognitive and other skills were substantially equalized, is it realistic to expect that a large proportion of those who begin their adult lives in these types of occupations will move into higher-skill, higher-paying ones? I am not optimistic. While mobility would almost certainly increase, achieving it on a very large scale seems likely to require a fairly extensive degree of regulation—either self-imposed by employers or imposed by government.

Is there evidence that bears on the life-course equality strategy? Studies in the United States, the United Kingdom, and the Nordic countries suggest that high-quality childcare and preschool can improve cognitive ability, and to a larger degree for children from disadvantaged backgrounds (Waldfogel 2002, 2006; Carneiro and Heckman 2003; Clarke-Stewart and Allhusen 2005; Karoly, Kilburn, and Cannon 2005; OECD 2005a: 116). In a variety of affluent countries, individuals with greater cognitive ability tend to have higher-paying jobs (OECD and Statistics Canada 2000). And two recent studies in the United States have found that low-paid workers who change employers are more likely to increase their pay and earnings. One such study, by Heather Boushey (2005), used panel data from the Survey of Income and Program Participation (SIPP) to examine mobility patterns among low-wage employees over three-year periods in the 1990s and early 2000s. Another, by Fredrik Andersson, Harry Holzer, and Julia Lane (2005), used panel data from administrative records to analyze mobility among low-wage workers over a six-year period in the late 1990s. All of this is consistent with the life-course equality vision.

For the life-course equality vision to be viable, a key institution is organized intra-firm and inter-firm career ladders. These are programs that facilitate transitions from low-skill, low-paying jobs in an industry into higher-skill, better-paying ones. Joan Fitzgerald (2006) has examined organized career ladders in the United States in health care, childcare, and a variety of other industries. In health care, for example, career ladder programs provide training and classroom education at low cost and feasible schedules to help transitions from aide to nursing assistant to registered nurse. Many of the programs Fitzgerald surveys are small-scale and have thus far had limited impact. But they are promising.

What can we learn from cross-national comparison? Denmark and Sweden have low levels of child poverty, offer high-quality public childcare beginning less than a year after birth, and provide substantial opportunity for retraining or new skill development via their active labor market programs. The United States, by contrast, features high child poverty, little or no public childcare prior to age 5, and limited opportunity for "lifelong learning" (Martin 2000; OECD 2002b, 2005a; Gornick and Meyers 2003; Rainwater and Smeeding 2003). A particularly noteworthy difference between these countries is in childcare and preschool institutions. Parents in Denmark and Sweden are granted paid parental leave for up to a year, so having one parent take a considerable period of time off from work is attractive. But after the first year, formal childcare tends to be the option of choice. High-quality and relatively inexpensive childcare is available in the home and in public centers beginning around 6 months of age, and a large proportion of parents make use of this option. As a result, according to Esping-Andersen (2004: 308), in the Nordic countries "much of the cognitive stimulus has been shifted from the parents to centers that do not replicate social class differences." As noted in Chapter 9, data from the mid-1990s International Adult Literacy Survey (IALS) suggest that inequality of cognitive ability is much lower in Denmark and Sweden than in the United States.

If the life-course equality proposal is plausible, we might therefore expect to find greater intragenerational earnings and occupational mobility in Denmark and Sweden than in the United States. (Here we must assume that the cross-country variation in cognitive ability has existed for some time, as there are no good comparative data on cognitive inequality for earlier years.) Robert Erikson and John Goldthorpe (1993: 331) found that rates of intragenerational occupational mobility in Sweden and the United States were similar. For example, the share of men who began their occupational careers as skilled blue-collar workers and ended up as professionals, managers, or technicians was 22% in Sweden and 20% in the United States. An OECD (1996a) study found that the degree of overall earnings mobility among employed workers was similar across Denmark, Sweden, and the United States (as well as France, Germany, Italy, and the United Kingdom) between 1986 and 1991. However, it also found that there was more upward mobility among low-paid workers in Denmark and Sweden than in the United States. In a more recent study, Rolf Aaberge et al. (2002) found that Denmark, Sweden, and the United States (and also Norway) had similar levels of earnings mobility between 1980 and 1990.

These studies perhaps suggest cause for skepticism about the life-course equality strategy, as Denmark and Sweden do not appear to have markedly more intragenerational mobility of occupation or earnings than the United States. Then again, these studies examined relatively short periods of time and used data that preceded the 1990s. A fairer assessment would utilize data from more recent years and examine mobility over a longer period.

As I suggested earlier in this chapter, there is good reason to favor public support for high-quality childcare and for opportunities for education and training throughout the life course. I am skeptical, however, about the prospects for a society characterized by sufficiently extensive intragenerational occupational mobility, and therefore sufficiently low income inequality over the life course, that contemporaneous inequality could become a secondary concern for egalitarians.

"High-Road" Employment?

For some, what I have suggested here will seem a "low-road" approach to high employment. In a low-road approach the aim is job creation, no matter the quality of the jobs. That is too simplistic an interpretation. Although I have suggested that wages might usefully be reduced at the low end in some European countries, I have said they ought to be increased (via a hike in the statutory minimum) in the United States and Canada. Further, I favor an array of policy supports to enhance cognitive ability (early childcare and preschool), to facilitate upward job mobility (retraining and job placement assistance), and to boost the incomes of low earners (employment-conditional earnings subsidy). Still, the "high-employment, high-equality" society I envision does include a low-wage sector, and some view that is undesirable.

There are (at least) two distinct high-road visions. To my knowledge neither has been spelled out clearly in print. Rather, they are visions expressed implicitly or explicitly in various conversations I have had with academic colleagues and policy analysts.

The first, which I call the "utopian" high-road vision, extrapolates from the success of large and medium-size manufacturing firms in Germany and other European countries. These firms use skilled employees and continuous process and product innovation to produce high-quality goods that command a premium price in domestic and international markets. They are therefore able to pay their employees high wages. This competitive strategy is facilitated by an array of supportive institutions: an apprenticeship system that trains workers in specialized tasks; research collaboration among firms and with universities; well-organized employer associations that ensure firms do not opt out of the high road; cohesive unions that force firms to adhere to the high road by pushing wages up; decision-making procedures within firms, such as works councils and codetermination (employee representation on company boards), that force continuous dialogue between labor and management about firm strategy; and policy makers who recognize the merits of this system and engage in efforts to keep it going, by facilitating cooperation among various actors and rewarding such cooperation with targeted subsidies or tax breaks (Hansen and Burton 1992; Streeck 1992; Herrigel 1994).

Of course, manufacturing now accounts for a relatively small share of employment in all affluent countries (see Figure 4.6), and there is little prospect of that reversing. Even in Germany fewer than 15% of working-age persons are now employed in manufacturing. (For a "high-road" argument meant to pertain to manufacturing firms in urban areas, see Luria and Rogers 1999.) But in a high-road utopia high-productivity, high-paying manufacturing jobs would be complemented by large numbers of service-sector counterparts. These would be professional and managerial jobs: researcher, designer, engineer, architect, accountant, physician, lawyer, teacher, strategist, and so on. Because these types of jobs contribute a significant amount to firms' value-added, they can command relatively high pay. These are jobs Robert Reich has referred to as "symbolic analysts." In an early-1990s book, *The Workers of Nations*, Reich advised countries to invest heavily in skill-development in order to maximize the number of such jobs (Reich 1991). It is not clear whether Reich himself envisioned a scenario in which most or all of a country's workers could have such jobs, but optimists can certainly draw on his discussion to imagine this.

The problem with the utopian high-road vision is that it ignores the large number of relatively low-skill tasks that are required to keep a modern society functioning—sweeping floors, cleaning bathrooms, collecting trash, serving food, stocking retail store shelves, and many others. It is very unlikely that these types of services can be automated. While I favor increasing the number, and the share, of high-skill analytical jobs, it is not realistic to imagine that they could somehow account for all, or even most, of a country's employment. And although there is room for some employers to upgrade the skills of their service employees and to pay them higher wages, there are real limits (Appelbaum, Bernhardt, and Murnane 2003; Ferguson 2005).

A second, less fanciful, high-road vision suggests that tax revenues generated by high-productivity, high-paying jobs can be used to create public sector positions for low-end services and to pay such workers above-productivity wages. This is, to an extent, what Sweden, Denmark, and Norway have been doing for the past four decades. These countries have relatively high employment rates in low-end service sectors, with many of those workers employed by the government. Wages for these jobs are high relative to productivity. This is made possible by heavy taxation of the profits and incomes generated in the high-road sectors of the economy.

Then again, low-end public service employment in the Nordic countries consists heavily of teachers, childcare workers, and medical employees. Few retail store clerks, waiters and waitresses, and hotel room cleaners are employed by the government. Nor are they likely to be. There is a limit, in other words, to how far even a highly egalitarian society is likely to go in pursuing this version of the high-road approach. Even in Sweden and Denmark, the public sector has never employed more than one-quarter of the working-age population. And if anything, the opportunity for pursuing this strategy is diminishing as manufacturing declines and pressure to keep a lid on tax rates intensifies.

Here is a "back-of-the-envelope" calculation: Suppose we assume an employment rate of 80% of the working-age population (the population age 15 to 64) as a target. And suppose we treat 25% as an upper-bound estimate of the share that can be employed by the government. The other 55% would need to be a combination of symbolic analysts and lower-level workers in high-road private sector manufacturing and service firms. Let's assume that to become a symbolic analyst, one needs a four-year university degree. In the country with the largest share of college graduates, the United States, approximately 28% of those age 25 and over currently have such a degree. That could perhaps be increased to 40%. This leaves another 15% to work in less-skilled jobs in private-sector high-road companies.

This is not impossible. But it is a tall order. And my guess is that it would take at least a generation to put this arrangement in place.

We come back to the question I raised earlier about the future of the "social democratic model": Will it hold up, or will the Nordic countries need to turn to low-end private-sector service jobs in order to increase or perhaps even just maintain their high employment rates?

Another question should be asked about the Nordic route and the "realistic" high-road vision I am discussing here: Is it a good idea to stifle the creation of certain types of low-end service jobs? Most home cleaners, waiters and waitresses, retail sales clerks, and the like are unlikely to be employed by the government. Nor are most of them likely to be employed by firms that have high enough profit margins to pay them moderate or high wages—aside from some special exceptions such as the Las Vegas hotels discussed in Chapter 5. One option, therefore, is to effectively decide as a society that there will be few, if any, such jobs—in other words, that they should be priced out of the market. But if these are useful tasks, if some people are willing to pay for them and others to perform them, and if low wages can be topped up by an employment-conditional earnings subsidy, is it a bad idea to permit these jobs? In my view, the answer is no.

To some, the chief benefit of a "high-road" employment strategy would lie not only in the better pay but also in the superior quality of *working conditions*. The concern is that low-end jobs are more likely to offer limited opportunity for mental stimulation or participation in decision-making and to be highly intense and stressful. According to Duncan Gallie, among those responding to a mid-1990s survey in various European Union countries, semi-skilled and nonskilled workers were less likely than higher-skilled workers to report being in jobs in which they could "definitely learn new things or exercise significant influence over the way things are done" (Gallie 2002: 100). Surveys from a variety of affluent countries suggest an increase in work intensity and work effort in the 1980s and 1990s (Gallie 2002; Green 2006; Kalleberg forthcoming). Interestingly, in the mid-1990s EU survey there was no difference across skill groupings in the likelihood of experiencing heightened work pressure. But Gallie points out that "there is now a wide body of research that points to the fact that the long-term health effects of increased pressure are likely to be particularly severe among the low-skilled. This is because the impact of work pressure is mediated by the degree of control that employees can exercise over the work task. Where people are allowed initiative to take decisions themselves about how to plan and carry out their work, they prove to be substantially more resilient in the face of high levels of work pressure. It is jobs that combine high demand with low control that pose the highest health risks."

This suggests reason for concern about trends in the quality of work life for those in low-end jobs. However, if we accept that there will continue to be a relatively large low-skill sector of the labor market, especially in services, the question is whether there is a way to improve working conditions in those jobs. Gallie (2002: 120–2) suggests an auditing procedure, whereby government leaves it up to firms to decide *how* to improve work conditions but monitors their efforts to do so and the outcomes for employees. He describes this as

...a system of periodic 'health audits' in organizations, which will provide for an external evaluation of an organization's strategy in relationship to both physical and psychological health, of the internal system for monitoring working conditions, and of the internal procedures for acting upon issues that are likely to be detrimental to the health (in the broad sense of the term) of employees. Such audits would require organizations to develop systematic risk assessments, which would clearly need to take account of employees' reports of their jobs and working conditions, as part of the evidence collected. As well as providing a strong incentive to organizations to improve their practices, such audits would provide a means for the diffusion of best practice information to individual work organizations. Such a system would require the development of specialized health-audit organizations that would be licensed to assess and approve company policies.

There is some evidence that efforts by government, unions, and employers to improve working conditions and to increase employee participation in decision-making can yield the intended effects. Denmark and Sweden are the countries in which the most concerted such efforts have been made, and survey evidence suggests that these two countries stand out among European nations as the ones in which job quality and employee participation are highest (Gallie 2003). Although not to quite the same extent, Finland's government and interest group organizations also have encouraged greater attention to these issues among employers (Gallie 2003). Francis Green (2006: ch. 5) has examined survey data on employee discretion and influence over their work tasks in the United Kingdom and Finland, the only two countries for which there are comparable data over a number of years. He finds evidence of decreased worker discretion in the UK but increased discretion in Finland.

There is a limit to the amount of stimulation that some low-end jobs will ever be able to provide. Still, most could do better, and efforts to figure out how and to push firms in that direction are well worth undertaking. Indeed, there is good reason to favor direct action to improve working conditions in *all* jobs, rather than merely assuming that higher-skilled, better-paying positions will automatically have decent work quality (O'Toole and Lawler 2006).

One final consideration with respect to low-road jobs: In a recent study of the US economy, Harriett Presser (2003) found that about two-fifths of the American labor force works primarily at nonstandard times—during the evening or at night, on a rotating shift, or on the weekend. For some in a dual-earner couple, this is by choice; it helps accommodate childcare needs. But most of those working nonstandard schedules said they did so out of necessity. Many of these jobs are low-end service positions, accepted (rather than chosen) by the employee because she or he could not get a decent-paying job with a typical schedule. This suggests an additional reason for concern about proliferation of low-end service positions.

Here too, however, it is not clear that the interests of the less-skilled would be best served by reducing the number of such jobs. A better solution might be to increase the availability of high-quality affordable childcare, so that those with children have more options, and to improve pay levels for employees working nonstandard hours (Presser 2003: ch. 9).

THE POLITICS OF THE HIGH-EMPLOYMENT ROUTE TO LOW INEQUALITY

Is pursuing low inequality via high employment and generous redistribution a politically viable strategy? The answer is likely to vary somewhat depending on the national context.

In the Nordic countries there is, and has been for some time, considerable sentiment in favor of high employment, generous redistribution, and low income inequality. Each has been a key element of social democratic ideology and policy orientation for half a century. And social democrats in each of the Nordic countries recognize the need for modifications of various social programs; indeed, adjustments have been ongoing since the early 1990s.

The suggestion I have made that would represent the sharpest departure from traditional social democratic strategy is to permit lower wage levels at the bottom of the distribution and compensate for this with an employment-conditional earnings subsidy. To my knowledge, none of the Social Democratic parties in the Nordic countries has embraced either idea.

In these countries there are very few, if any, low-end service jobs to which the collectively bargained minimum wage level does not apply. But that does not mean no one works for below-minimum pay. There are indications of a relatively substantial and growing number of jobs in the underground economy. From the perspective of financing a generous welfare state, this is especially problematic. Not only do some of the people working in those jobs end up with low incomes, but the revenue generated by the work is not taxed. Sometimes the household does not have a low income, as the worker may be coupled with a moderate earner, or she or he may be receiving government benefits and working "under the table" to supplement those benefits. Even so, inability to tax the earnings is a problem for governments increasingly strained by the cost of pensions and health care and constrained in their capacity to raise tax rates. Also, a large underground economy is unlikely to be conducive to social harmony.

The Nordic countries already have an earnings subsidy to ensure that households with low earnings end up with a decent posttax-posttransfer income. It is social assistance. Most households with a market income below a designated "minimum" receive social assistance to bring the household's income up to that level. Sometimes this cash benefit is supplemented by housing assistance or other forms of near-cash support. The amount and form of the assistance is determined by the local caseworker. Social assistance thus functions as an earnings subsidy that is *not* conditional on employment. In principle, those who are able are expected to search for and take a paying job, and both supports and pressures are exercised to encourage this. Even so, this arrangement creates a nontrivial work disincentive for some people. Introducing an earnings subsidy that is explicitly conditioned on employment, and that increases with earnings (up to a point), would represent a significant departure from this practice. But it would be consistent with the longstanding "productivist" orientation in the Nordic countries, which places a priority on paid work and which features a wide array of supports—high-quality primary and secondary education, government support for childcare and preschool, active labor market policy, extensive public employment, and others—to facilitate it. In this respect, an employment-conditional earnings subsidy is perfectly consistent with a key element of the "social democratic model."

Allowing a somewhat lower wage level at the bottom of the distribution and instituting an employment-conditional earnings subsidy would not be much more radical than several other changes implemented by social democratic governments in the recent past, such as the changes to Denmark's unemployment benefits and active labor market policy in the 1990s and Sweden's pension reform in the late 1990s. Neither of these has turned out to be politically problematic for social democrats.

Another important policy concern in the Nordic countries is the extended paid parental/home care leaves that currently exist in Finland and Norway. These appear to reduce women's employment. They also have adverse effects on the public childcare system, by reducing demand for it and creating greater uncertainty about the level of that demand. The home care leave has been in existence for a decade in Norway and longer in Finland. These will be difficult to remove or even reform, not only for reasons of path dependency but also because, as I noted earlier, they can be justified on grounds of parental choice. Indeed, there likely will be considerable pressure on policy makers in Denmark and Sweden to follow this course. Doing so would clearly represent a setback for gender equality and women's employment, and therefore possibly for redistribution and inequality reduction as well.

I have recommended a number of potentially helpful changes to current labor market and social policies in France, Germany, and Italy. But as I stressed above, the fact that there are many reforms which might help boost employment in these countries does not imply that *all* of them need to be implemented. It may be that one or two reforms will be enough to generate substantial progress. The Dutch example is instructive. Although the volume of employment in the Netherlands is still only moderate in comparative terms, the country has made substantial progress in the past three decades, and it has done so without massive change in its institutional and policy configuration. The main contributing factors appear to have been sustained declines in labor costs and growing availability of part-time employment.

Political reform in the continental countries is complicated by the role of organized interest groups in policy discussion and decision-making, in Germany also by the federal structure of the government, and in Italy also by the limited administrative capability of the state (Palier 2000; Matsaganis et al. 2003; Streeck 2005). Still, reform does happen. Since the early 1990s France has shifted part of the funding of social policy from payroll taxes to a new income tax, introduced payroll tax exemptions for low earners, and implemented an employment-conditional earnings subsidy for low-income households. Each of these reforms was minor, but they suggest the possibility for moving further. On the other hand, the failed attempt in 2006 to reduce employment protection regulations for young workers highlights the obstacles reform efforts can encounter. As I write (January 2008), it is unclear how far the Sarkozy government will get with its intended reforms. In Germany the Schroeder government was unsuccessful in its attempt to get the social partners to come to agreement on reforming taxes and social policy, but then to the surprise of many it was able to push significant reforms through the parliament. Italy is the country where reform is most needed but faces the largest obstacles: fragile coalition governments, an entrenched tradition of male breadwinner employment patterns and reliance on the family as a substitute for social policy, limited government administrative capacity, and extensive regional division. A pessimistic view of Italy's near-term future is that political inaction will yield a slow deterioration of living standards and rising inequality, which eventually will produce support for a Thatcher-style full-scale deregulatory solution. Without appropriate supports, including more developed unemployment insurance and social assistance programs and some kind of active labor market policy, that kind of reform could have a devastating impact on those at the low end of, or excluded altogether from, the Italian labor market.

Will center-left parties in the continental countries pay an electoral price for instituting reforms? In the short run, quite possibly yes. But it is far better that the reforms be instituted by governments committed not only to high employment but also to low inequality.

In the Anglo countries, third way-oriented approaches have been successful electorally over the past two decades. As of early 2008, parties of the right hold the government in Canada and the United States, and New Labour appears to be barely holding on in the United Kingdom. But there is no indication that center-left parties' emphasis on employment creation precipitated a loss of political support. There *is* a danger that in embracing labor market flexibility and activation, these parties will alienate their political base in the working class (Reich 1999). But it is no longer feasible to rely on this shrinking base for electoral success in any case, so the risk is probably worth taking.

The larger question is whether center-left parties in the Anglo countries will try to put inequality reduction back on their political agenda. As I suggested earlier, this will require frank discussion about redistribution and higher taxes. Blair's New Labour government proved fairly successful in boosting redistribution by stealth—that is, without saying much about it. But there are likely to be profound limits to how much can be accomplished with that strategy.

What, over the long run, are the probable political consequences of pursuing a high employment route to low inequality? In my view, they are almost certainly positive. As a larger share of the able-bodied population is engaged in paid labor, the space for a politics of division between the employed and the nonemployed—between those perceived as pulling their weight and those not—is likely to diminish. It can increasingly be replaced by a politics of reciprocity. This, in turn, should enhance the possibility for an electorally saleable politics of fairness. Society gives everyone as fair a chance as possible, all those able to contribute do so, and society helps those who for one reason or another do not fare well. Reciprocity and fairness: high employment and high equality.

Data Definitions and Sources

The data used in this book are available on my webpage: www.u.arizona.edu/~
lkenwor.

Active labor market policy. Expenditures on active labor market programs as a share of
GDP. *Source*: OECD (2004g).

Childcare: children age 0 to 2 in formal care. Share of children age 0 to 2 in formal
(public or private) care. *Source*: OECD (2001: 144).

Childcare: children age 3 to 5 in formal care. Share of children age 3 to 5 in formal
(public or private) care. *Source*: OECD (2001: 144).

Childcare: children age 1 to 2 in publicly financed care. Share of children age 1 to 2 in
publicly financed care. *Source*: Gornick and Meyers (2003: 204–5).

Childcare: children age 3 to 5 in publicly financed care. Share of children age 3 to 5 in
publicly financed care. *Source*: Gornick and Meyers (2003: 204–5).

Childcare: public child care for children age 0 to 2. Index of the generosity of government
provision and subsidization. *Source*: Eliason, Stryker, and Tranby (2008).

Childcare: public child care for children age 3 to 5. Index of the generosity of government
provision and subsidization. *Source*: Eliason, Stryker, and Tranby (2008).

Collective bargaining coverage. Share of the employed work force whose wage or salary
is determined by a collectively bargained agreement. *Source*: Traxler, Blaschke, and
Kittel (2001).

Earnings. Inflation-adjusted earnings levels at the various percentiles (e.g., tenth,
fiftieth, ninetieth) of the distribution. Full-time employed individuals only. *Source*:
Author's calculations from data in OECD (2007a).

Economic growth. See growth of real GDP per capita.

Educational attainment. Share of population age 25 to 64 having completed at least
upper secondary education. *Source*: OECD (2004e: 58, table A2.2).

Employment. Employed persons as a share of the population age 15 to 64. *Source*:
Author's calculations from data in OECD (2006c, 2008).

Employment: agriculture. Employment in agriculture, hunting, forestry, and fishing
(ISIC 1) as a share of the population age 15 to 64. *Source*: OECD (2006c, 2008).

Employment: community, social, and personal services. Employment in community,
social, and personal services (ISIC 9) as a share of the population age 15 to 64. *Source*:
Author's calculations from data in OECD (2006c, 2008).

Employment: construction. Employment in construction (ISIC 5) as a share of the
population age 15 to 64. *Source*: Author's calculations from data in OECD (2006c,
2008).

Employment: electricity, gas, and water. Employment in electricity, gas, and water (ISIC 4) as a share of the population age 15 to 64. *Source:* Author's calculations from data in OECD (2006*c*, 2008).

Employment: finance, insurance, real estate, and business services. Employment in finance, insurance, real estate, and business services (ISIC 8) as a share of the population age 15 to 64. *Source:* Author's calculations from data in OECD (2006*c*, 2008).

Employment: high-end services. Employment in finance, insurance, real estate, and business services (ISIC 8) as a share of the population age 15 to 64. *Source:* Author's calculations from data in OECD (2006*c*, 2008).

Employment: low-end services. Employment in wholesale and retail trade, restaurants, and hotels (ISIC 6) and community, social, and personal services (ISIC 9) as a share of the population age 15 to 64. *Source:* Author's calculations from data in OECD (2006*c*, 2008).

Employment: manufacturing. Employment in manufacturing (ISIC 3) as a share of the population age 15 to 64. *Source:* Author's calculations from data in OECD (2006*c*, 2008).

Employment: men's. Employed men as a share of the male population age 15 to 64 (or other age groups). *Source:* Author's calculations from data in OECD (2006*c*, 2008).

Employment: mining. Employment in mining (ISIC 2) as a share of the population age 15 to 64. *Source:* Author's calculations from data in OECD (2006*c*, 2008).

Employment: part-time. Persons employed part-time as a share of the population age 15 to 64 (or as a share of total employment). Defined as usually working less than 30 hours per week. *Source:* Author's calculations from data in OECD (2006*c*, 2008).

Employment: private-sector low-end services. Employment in private-sector consumer-oriented services—wholesale and retail trade, restaurants and hotels, and community/social/personal services (ISIC 6 and 9; ISIC revision3 50–52, 55, 90–93)—as a percentage of the population age 15 to 64. Unfortunately, private-sector employment can be distinguished from public-sector employment in these industries only through 1995, so the time series for this variable ends in that year. *Source:* Torben Iversen, Department of Government, Harvard University, calculated from OECD data; see Iversen and Wren (1998) for discussion.

Employment: transport, storage, and communication. Employment in transport, storage, and communication (ISIC 7) as a share of the population age 15 to 64. *Source:* Author's calculations from data in OECD (2006*c*, 2008).

Employment: wholesale and retail trade, restaurants, hotels. Employment in wholesale and retail trade, restaurants, and hotels (ISIC 6) as a share of the population age 15 to 64. *Source:* Author's calculations from data in OECD (2006*c*, 2008).

Employment: women's. Employed women as a share of the female population age 15 to 64 (or other age groups). *Source:* Author's calculations from data in OECD (2006*c*, 2008).

Employment and school enrollment among women age 15–24. *Source:* Author's calculations from data in OECD (2004*e*: 334–5, table C4.2b).

Employment protection regulations. Index representing the strictness of employment protection regulations—both legislation and collective agreements. Range is 0 to 3.5, with higher scores indicating greater strictness. *Source:* Bassanini and Duval (2006) update of data in OECD (2004 *f*).

Female/male pay ratio. Median earnings among full-time employed women divided by median earnings among full-time employed men. *Source:* Author's calculations from data in OECD (2006*c*).

GDP per capita. Adjusted for inflation. Currencies converted using OECD purchasing power parities (PPPs). *Source:* Author's calculations from data in OECD (2008).

Gornick-Meyers index of work-family policies. Index of policies that support families with children, focusing on childcare, maternity/parental leave, and flexible working time. *Source:* Gornick and Meyers (2003: 258, "Index C").

Government benefit generosity: average minimum income. Average posttax-posttransfer income when pretax-pretransfer income is zero, expressed as a percentage of the country's median pretax-pretransfer household income. Calculated for single-adult households with no children, one child, and two children. Households with heads age 25 to 59 only. Income adjusted for household size using the square root of the number of persons in the household as the equivalence scale. Incomes top-coded at 10 times the unequivalized median and bottom-coded at 1% of the equivalized mean. *Source:* Author's calculations from Luxembourg Income Study data (variables: MI, DPI). Another version of this measure, which I refer to as the "income floor" in Figure 7.4, is calculated as the average minimum income across all three types of households and over all years for which LIS data are available.

Government benefit generosity: benefit employment disincentives. Composite measure that combines the average minimum income and the payoff to additional earnings. The measure is calculated by first standardizing both the income floor and earnings payoff measures. I then reverse the sign for the earnings payoff standardized scores, so that higher scores represent a smaller earnings payoff. I then average the two standardized scores for each country. This yields a measure of benefit employment disincentives that ranges from approximately −1.5 to +1.5, with positive values indicating stronger work disincentives.

Government benefit generosity: payoff to additional earnings. Average amount that posttax-posttransfer income increases per unit (dollar, euro, kronor) increase in market income, expressed as a percentage of the country's median pretax-pretransfer household income. Calculated for single-adult households with no children, one child, and two children. Households with heads age 25 to 59 only. Income adjusted for household size using the square root of the number of persons in the household as the equivalence scale. Incomes top-coded at 10 times the unequivalized median and bottom-coded at 1% of the equivalized mean. *Source:* Author's calculations from Luxembourg Income Study data (variables: MI, DPI).

Government cash social expenditures on the working-age population. Sum of family benefits and benefits for incapacity (disability, occupational injury and disease, sickness), unemployment, and "other contingencies" (mainly low income) as a share of

GDP. The categories of public social expenditures that I do *not* include in this measure are old age, survivors, health, active labor market programs, and housing assistance. *Source*: Author's calculations from data in OECD (2004*g*).

Growth of real GDP. Average annual rate of change of real gross domestic product. *Source*: Author's calculations from data in OECD (2008).

Growth of real GDP per capita. Average annual rate of change of real gross domestic product per capita. *Source*: Author's calculations from data in OECD (2008).

Hours worked. Average annual hours worked per employed person. *Source*: OECD (2006*c*).

Imports. Imports as a share of gross domestic product. *Source*: Author's calculations from data in OECD (2008).

Income: households. Households with heads age 25 to 59 only. Income adjusted for household size using the square root of the number of persons in the house- hold as the equivalence scale. Incomes top-coded at 10 times the unequivalized median and bottom-coded at 1% of the equivalized mean. For France and Italy, the pretax-pretransfer income data actually are posttax-pretransfer. Where over-time data are shown, incomes are adjusted for inflation. *Source*: Author's calculations from Luxembourg Income Study data (variables: MI, DPI).

Inequality of earnings among full-time employed individuals. Ratio of pretax earnings of a person at the 50th percentile of the earnings distribution to a person at the 10th percentile. Or the 90th to the 10th; or the 75th to the 25th. Annual earnings for Canada, Finland, France (posttax), the Netherlands, and Sweden. Monthly earnings for Germany and Italy. Weekly earnings for Australia, the United Kingdom, and the United States. Hourly earnings for Denmark and Norway. The P75/P25 ratios used in Chapter 3 are estimated for Denmark, France, Italy, and Sweden. *Source*: Author's calculations from data in OECD (2007*a*).

Inequality of income among households. Gini coefficient for pretax-pretransfer or posttax-posttransfer household income. Households with heads age 25 to 59 only. Income adjusted for household size using the square root of the number of persons in the household as the equivalence scale. Incomes top-coded at 10 times the unequiv- alized median and bottom-coded at 1% of the equivalized mean. For France and Italy, the pretax-pretransfer income data actually are posttax-pretransfer. *Source*: Author's calculations from Luxembourg Income Study data (variables: MI, DPI).

Interest rates: real long-term. Long-term nominal interest rate (yield on long-term government bonds) minus current rate of inflation. *Source*: Author's calculations from interest rate data in IMF (n.d.) and OECD (2008) and inflation data in OECD (2008).

Labor force participation. Persons in the labor force (employed or unemployed) as a share of the population age 15 to 64. *Source*: Author's calculations from data in OECD (2006*c*). Additional historical data for women's labor force participation in the United States are from US Bureau of the Census (various years).

Literacy. Shares of the adult population scoring at levels 1, 2, 3, and 4/5 on "document literacy." *Source*: OECD and Statistics Canada (2000: 137).

Marital homogamy. Pearson correlation between earnings of household "heads" and earnings of household "spouses." Households with heads age 25 to 59 only. *Source*: Author's calculations from Luxembourg Income Study data (variables: v39, v41).

Market income. Pretax-pretransfer household income. For France and Italy, the data are posttax-pretransfer. *Source*: Author's calculations from Luxembourg Income Study data (variable: MI).

Net government transfers. Cash and near-cash government transfers minus payroll and income taxes. *Source*: Author's calculations from Luxembourg Income Study data.

Paid maternity/care leave. Length of paid maternity or care leave, in weeks. In France the paid leave applies only to the second and subsequent child. *Source*: Gauthier and Bortnik (2001); Gornick and Meyers (2003: 123–7); Morgan and Zippel (2003: 52, 54–5).

Product market regulations. Index representing regulatory impediments to competition in seven industries: gas, electricity, post, telecommunications, passenger air transportation, rail transportation (freight and passenger), and road freight. Range is 0 to 6, with higher scores indicating greater strictness. *Source*: Bassanini and Duval (2006).

Prose literacy inequality. Ratio of prose literacy at the 90th percentile of the distribution to prose literacy at the 10th percentile. *Source*: OECD and Statistics Canada (2000: table 4.13, p. 176).

Public employment. Persons employed in the public sector as a share of the population age 15 to 64. These data are not available beyond 1997. *Source*: Author's calculations from data in OECD (2008).

Public expenditures on services for education, health care, families, the disabled, and the elderly. As a share of GDP. Education expenditures include those on primary, secondary, and postsecondary nontertiary schooling. *Source*: Author's calculation from data in OECD (2002c: 171, table B2.1b; 2004g).

Public health care expenditures. As a share of GDP. *Source*: Author's calculation from data in OECD (2004g).

Real unit labor cost index. Index of employee compensation, adjusted for productivity and for inflation. *Source*: Author's calculations from nominal unit labor cost and consumer price index data in OECD (2008).

Real unit labor cost changes. Year-to-year percentage change in employee compensation, adjusted for changes in productivity and for inflation. *Source*: Author's calculations from nominal unit labor cost and consumer price index data in OECD (2008).

Redistribution via taxes. Gini coefficient for pretax-pretransfer household income minus Gini coefficient for posttax-pretransfer household income. Households with heads age 25–59 only. *Source*: Author's calculations from Luxembourg Income Study data.

Redistribution via transfers. Gini coefficient for pretax-pretransfer household income minus Gini coefficient for pretax-posttransfer household income. Households with heads age 25–59 only. *Source*: Author's calculations from Luxembourg Income Study data.

Sickness decommodification. Decommodification index for sickness insurance. *Source*: Scruggs (2005*a*).

Single-adult households. Single-adult households as a share of all households. Households with heads age 25 to 59 only. *Source*: Author's calculations from Luxembourg Income Study data (variables: D4, D27).

Tax penalty for a couple with two earners. Tax rate (income plus payroll) for a couple with two earners minus tax rate for a couple with one earner. *Source*: Daly (2000: 496); Dingeldey (2001: 659).

Tax rates on capital, labor, and consumption: average effective tax rates. Source: Ganghof (2005*c*: table 1, using Eurostat and OECD data).

Tax revenues. Government tax revenues as a share of GDP. *Source*: OECD (2008); see also OECD (2007*c*).

Tax revenues: taxes on income and profits. Government revenues from taxes on income and profits as a share of GDP. *Source*: OECD (2008).

Tax revenues: payroll taxes. Government revenues from social security contributions and payroll taxes as a share of GDP. *Source*: OECD (2008).

Tax revenues: consumption taxes. Government revenues from taxes on goods and services (consumption). *Source*: OECD (2008).

Unemployment decommodification. Decommodification index for unemployment insurance. *Source*: Scruggs (2005*a*).

Wage centralization. Index of centralization of bargaining level, with ranking based on the most important level and special scores in case of equally important levels. Range is 1 to 12, with higher scores indicating greater centralization. *Source*: Traxler, Blaschke, and Kittel (2001: 114, 307, variable = BCEN).

Women's preferences for employment I. Share of women age 25 to 59 strongly agreeing that both husband and wife should contribute to household income. *Source*: Author's calculations from data in World Values Survey (1995–97).

Women's preferences for employment II. Share of women saying that mothers with preschool-age children should be employed. *Source*: Morgan (2004), using data from the 1994 International Social Survey Programme (ISSP).

Women's share of managers, legislators, and senior officials. Share of administrative and managerial positions held by women. *Source*: UNDP (2006: 367).

Women's skill level I. Share of women age 25–64 having completed at least upper secondary education. *Source*: OECD (2002: 55, table A3.1c).

Women's skill level II. Average literacy score of women on the 1994–98 International Adult Literacy Survey (IALS). *Source*: Blau and Kahn (2002*b*: table 1).

Working-age population. Population age 15 to 64. *Source*: Author's calculations from data in OECD (2008).

Zero-earner households. Share of households with heads age 25 to 59 that have no earners. *Source*: Author's calculations from Luxembourg Income Study data (variable: D6).

References

Aaberge, Rolf, Anders Björklund, Markus Jänti, Mårten Palme, Peder J. Pedersen, Nina Smith, and Tom Wennemo. 2002. "Income Inequality and Income Mobility in the Scandinavian Countries Compared to the United States." *Review of Income and Wealth* 48: 443–69.

Abrahamson, Peter. 2006. "Welfare Reform: Renewal or Deviation?" Pp. 356–74 in *National Identity and the Varieties of Capitalism: The Danish Experience*, edited by John L. Campbell, John A. Hall, and Ove K. Pedersen. Montreal: McGill-Queen's University Press.

Achen, Christopher H. 2002. "Toward a New Political Methodology: Microfoundations and ART." *Annual Review of Political Science* 5: 423–50.

Agell, Jonas. 1996. "Why Sweden's Welfare State Needed Reform." *Economic Journal* 106: 1760–71.

—— 1999. "On the Benefits from Rigid Labour Markets: Norms, Market Failures, and Social Insurance." *Economic Journal* 109: F143–64.

Akerlof, George and Janet Yellen, eds. 1986. *Efficiency Wage Models of the Labor Market*. Cambridge: Cambridge University Press.

—— —— 1990. "The Fair Wage-Effort Hypothesis and Unemployment." *Quarterly Journal of Economics* 55: 255–83.

Alesina, Alberto and Francesco Giavazzi. 2006. *The Future of Europe: Reform or Decline?* Cambridge, MA: MIT Press.

—— and Dani Rodrik. 1994. "Distributive Politics and Economic Growth." *Quarterly Journal of Economics* 109: 465–90.

Amable, Bruno. 2003. *The Diversity of Modern Capitalism*. Oxford: Oxford University Press.

Andersen, Torben M. 2004. "Challenges to the Scandinavian Welfare Model." *European Journal of Political Economy* 20: 743–54.

Anderson, Patricia M. and Andrew Levine. 1999. "Child Care and Mother's Employment Decisions." Working Paper 7058. National Bureau of Economic Research. Cambridge, MA.

Andersson, Fredrik, Harry J. Holzer, and Julia I. Lane. 2005. *Moving Up or Moving On: Who Advances in the Low-Wage Labor Market*. New York: Russell Sage Foundation.

Aoki, Masahiko. 1988. *Information, Incentives, and Bargaining in the Japanese Economy*. Cambridge: Cambridge University Press.

Appelbaum, Eileen, Annette Bernhardt, and Richard J. Murnane, eds. 2003. *Low-Wage America*. New York: Russell Sage Foundation.

—— Peter Berg, Ann Frost, and Gil Preuss. 2003. "The Effects of Work Restructuring on Low-Wage, Low-Skilled Workers in U.S. Hospitals." Pp. 77–117 in *Low-Wage America*, edited by Eileen Appelbaum, Annette Bernhardt, and Richard J. Murnane. New York: Russell Sage Foundation.

Ashenfelter, Orley and Cecilia Rouse. 2000. "Schooling, Intelligence, and Income in America." Pp. 89–117 in *Meritocracy and Economic Inequality*, edited by Kenneth Arrow, Samuel Bowles, and Steven Durlauf. Princeton, NJ: Princeton University Press.

Atkinson, Anthony B. and Andrea Brandolini. 2001. "Promise and Pitfalls in the Use of 'Secondary' Data-Sets: Income Inequality in OECD Countries as a Case Study." *Journal of Economic Literature* 39: 771–99.

—— and Thomas Piketty. 2007. *Top Incomes over the Twentieth Century*. Oxford: Oxford University Press.

—— Lee Rainwater, and Timothy M. Smeeding. 1995. *Income Distribution in OECD Countries*. Paris: Organization for Economic Cooperation and Development.

Baccaro, Lucio and Diego Rei. 2007. "Institutional Determinants of Unemployment in OECD Countries: Does the Deregulatory View Hold Water?" *International Organization* 61: 527–69.

Baker, Dean, Andrew Glyn, David R. Howell, and John Schmitt. 2005. "Labor Market Institutions and Unemployment: Assessment of the Cross-Country Evidence." Pp. 72–118 in *Fighting Unemployment: The Limits of Free Market Orthodoxy*, edited by David R. Howell. Oxford: Oxford University Press.

Baldini, Massimo, Paolo Bosi, and Stefano Toso. 2002. "Targeting Welfare in Italy: Old Problems and Perspectives on Reform." *Fiscal Studies* 23: 51–75.

Ball, Lawrence. 1999. "Aggregate Demand and Long-Run Unemployment." *Brookings Papers on Economic Activity* 2: 189–251.

Baron, James N. 1984. "Organizational Perspectives on Stratification." *Annual Review of Sociology* 10: 37–69.

Barr, Nicholas. 1992 "Economic Theory and the Welfare State: A Survey and Interpretation." *Journal of Economic Literature* 30: 741–803.

Barro, Robert J. 2000. "Inequality and Growth in a Panel of Countries." *Journal of Economic Growth* 5: 5–32.

—— and Jong-Wha Lee. N.d. "International Data on Educational Attainment." Available at: www.cid.harvard.edu/ciddata/ciddata.html.

Barrow, Lisa. 1996. "An Analysis of Women's Labor Force Participation Following First Birth." Working Paper 363. Industrial Relations Section, Princeton University.

Bartik, Timothy J. 2001. *Jobs for the Poor: Can Labor Demand Policies Help?* New York and Kalamazoo, MI: Russell Sage Foundation and Upjohn Institute for Employment Research.

Bassanini, Andrea and Romain Duval. 2006. "Employment Patterns in OECD Countries: Reassessing the Role of Policies and Institutions." OECD Social, Employment, and Migration Working Paper 35. Organization for Economic Cooperation and Development. Available at: www.oecd.org.

Baumol, William J., Sue Anne Bately Blackmun, and Edward N. Wolff. 1989. *Productivity and American Leadership: The Long View*. Cambridge, MA: MIT Press.

—— Robert E. Litan, and Carl J. Schramm. 2007. *Good Capitalism, Bad Capitalism, and the Economics of Growth and Prosperity*. New Haven, CT: Yale University Press.

Bazen, Stephen. 2000. "The Impact of the Regulation of Low Wages on Inequality and Labour-Market Adjustment: A Comparative Analysis." *Oxford Review of Economic Policy* 16(1): 57–69.

Becker, Gary. 1993. *Human Capital*. 3rd edition. Chicago: University of Chicago Press.

—— 1996. "Why Europe is Drowning in Joblessness." *Business Week*, April 8, p. 22.

—— and Casey Mulligan. 1998. "Deadweight Costs and the Size of Government." Working Paper 6789. National Bureau of Economic Research. Available at: www.nber.org.

Beckfield, Jason. 2004. "Does Inequality Harm Health? New Cross-National Evidence." *Journal of Health and Social Behavior* 45: 231–48.

Belot, Michèle and Jan C. van Ours. 2000. "Does the Recent Success of Some OECD Countries in Lowering Their Unemployment Rates Lie in the Clever Design of Their Labour Market Reforms?" Discussion Paper 147. Institute for the Study of Labor (IZA). Bonn, Germany.

Bénabou, Roland. 1996. "Inequality and Growth." Pp. 11–74 in *NBER Macroeconomics Annual 1996*, edited by Ben S. Bernanke and Julio J. Rotemberg. Cambridge, MA: MIT Press.

Benner, Mats and Torben Bundgaard Vad. 2000. "Sweden and Denmark: Defending the Welfare State." Pp. 399–466 in *Welfare and Work in the Open Economy. Volume II: Diverse Responses to Common Challenges*, edited by Fritz W. Scharpf and Vivien A. Schmidt. Oxford: Oxford University Press.

Beramendi, Pablo and Thomas R. Cusack. 2007. "Diverse Disparities: The Politics and Economics of Wage, Market, and Disposable Income Inequalities." Unpublished.

Bergmann, Barbara R. 2005. *The Economic Emergence of Women*. Second edition. New York: Palgrave Macmillan.

Berk, Richard. 2004. *Regression Analysis: A Constructive Critique*. Thousand Oaks, CA: Sage.

Bernstein, Jared and Dean Baker. 2003. *The Benefits of Full Employment*. Washington, DC: Economic Policy Institute.

—— and John Schmitt. 1998. *Making Work Pay: The Impact of the 1996–97 Minimum Wage Increase*. Washington, DC: Economic Policy Institute.

Bertola, Giuseppe. 2000. "Policy Choices and Interactions with Existing Instruments." *OECD Economic Studies* 31: 185–98

—— and Andrea Ichino. 1995. "Wage Inequality and Unemployment: United Sates vs. Europe." Pp. 13–54 in *NBER Macroeconomics Annual 1995*, edited by Ben S. Bernanke and Julio J. Rotemberg. Cambridge, MA: MIT Press.

—— Francine D. Blau, and Lawrence M. Kahn. 2001. "Comparative Analysis of Labor Market Outcomes: Lessons for the United States from International Long-Run Evidence." Working Paper 8526. National Bureau of Economic Research. Available at: www.nber.org.

—— Tito Boeri, and Sandrine Cazes. 1999. "Employment Protection and Labour Market Adjustment in OECD Countries: Evolving Institutions and Variable Enforcement." Employment and Training Papers 48. International Labour Organization. Geneva.

Bielenski, Harald, Gerhard Bosch, and Alexandra Wagner. 2002. *Working Time Preferences in Sixteen European Countries.* Dublin: European Foundation for the Improvement of Living and Working Conditions.

Birdsall, Nancy, David Ross, and Richard Sabot. 1995. "Inequality and Growth Reconsidered." *World Bank Economic Review* 9: 477–508.

Björklund, Anders. 1998. "Income Distribution in Sweden: What Is the Achievement of the Welfare State?" *Swedish Economic Policy Review* 5: 39–80.

—— 2000. "Going Different Ways: Labour Market Policy in Denmark and Sweden." Pp. 148–80 in *Why Deregulate Labour Markets?* edited by Gøsta Esping-Andersen and Marino Regini. Oxford: Oxford University Press.

—— and Richard B. Freeman. 1997. "Generating Equality and Eliminating Poverty, the Swedish Way." Pp. 33–78 in *The Welfare State in Transition: Reforming the Swedish Model,* edited by Richard B. Freeman, Robert Topel, and Birgitta Swedenborg. Chicago: University of Chicago Press.

Blair, Tony and Gerhard Schroeder. 1999. "Europe: The Third Way." Available at www.labour.org.uk.

Blanchard, Olivier. 2006. "European Unemployment: The Evolution of Facts and Ideas." *Economic Policy* 1–54.

—— and Justin Wolfers. 2000. "Shocks and Institutions and the Rise of European Unemployment: The Aggregate Evidence." *Economic Journal* 100: 1–33.

Blanchflower, David G. and Andrew J. Oswald. 1994. *The Wage Curve.* Cambridge, MA: MIT Press.

Blank, Rebecca M. 1997. *It Takes a Nation: A New Agenda for Fighting Poverty.* New York and Princeton, NJ: Russell Sage Foundation and Princeton University Press.

—— 2000. "Enhancing the Opportunities, Skills, and Security of American Workers." Pp. 105–23 in *A Working Nation,* edited by David T. Ellwood et al. New York: Russell Sage Foundation.

—— 2001. "Economics of Welfare Programs." Pp. 16426–32 in *International Encyclopedia of the Social and Behavioral Sciences.* Amsterdam: Elsevier.

—— 2003. "Evaluating Welfare Reform in the United States." *Journal of Economic Literature* 40: 1105–166.

—— David Card, and Philip K. Robbins. 2000. "Financial Incentives for Increasing Work and Income Among Low-Income Families." In *Finding Jobs: Work and Welfare Reform,* edited by Rebecca M. Blank and David Card. New York: Russell Sage Foundation.

—— and David T. Ellwood. 2002. "The Clinton Legacy for America's Poor." Pp. 749–800 in *American Economic Policy in the 1990s,* edited by Jeffrey A. Frankel and Peter R. Orszag. Cambridge, MA: MIT Press.

Blau, David M. 2001. *The Child Care Problem: An Economic Analysis.* New York: Russell Sage Foundation.

Blau, Francine D. and Lawrence M. Kahn. 1992. "The Gender Earnings Gap: Learning from International Comparisons." *American Economic Review* 82: 533–8.

Blau, Francine D. and Lawrence M. Kahn. 2000. "Gender Differences in Pay." *Journal of Economic Perspectives* 14(4): 75–99.

—— —— 2002a. *At Home and Abroad: U.S. Labor Market Performance in International Perspective*. New York: Russell Sage Foundation.

—— —— 2002b. "Do Cognitive Test Scores Explain Higher U.S. Wage Inequality?" Unpublished. Department of Economics, Cornell University.

Blundell, Richard, Alan Duncan, Julian McCrae, and Costas Meghir. 2000. "The Labor Market Impact of the Working Families Tax Credit." *Fiscal Studies* 21: 75–104.

Bouchard, Thomas J., Jr., David T. Lykken, Matthew McGue, Nancy Segal, and Auke Tellegen. 1990. "Source of Human Psychological Differences: The Minnesota Study of Twins Reared Apart." *Science* 250: 223–8.

Boushey, Heather. 2005. "No Way Out: How Prime-Age Workers Get Trapped in Minimum Wage Jobs." Briefing Paper. Center for Economic and Policy Research. Available at: www.cepr.net.

—— Chauna Brocht, Bethney Gundersen, and Jared Bernstein. 2001. *Hardships in America: The Real Story of Working Families*. Washington, DC: Economic Policy Institute.

Bowles, Samuel and Herbert Gintis. 1976. *Schooling in Capitalist America*. New York: Basic Books.

—— —— 1998–99. "Is Equality Passé? Homo Reciprocans and the Future of Egalitarian Politics." *Boston Review*, December–January. Available at: bostonreview.net.

—— —— 2002. "The Inheritance of Inequality." Unpublished.

—— —— and Melissa Osborne. 2001. "The Determinants of Earnings: A Behavioral Approach." *Journal of Economic Literature* 39: 1137–76.

—— —— —— eds. 2004. *Unequal Chances: Family Background and Economic Success*. New York and Princeton, NJ: Russell Sage Foundation and Princeton University Press.

Bradley, David. 2002. *The Political Economy of Employment Performance: Testing the Deregulation Thesis*. Ph.D. dissertation. Department of Political Science, University of North Carolina.

—— Evelyne Huber, Stephanie Moller, François Nielsen, and John Stephens. 2003. "Distribution and Redistribution in Postindustrial Democracies." *World Politics* 55: 193–228.

—— and John Stephens. 2007. "Employment Performance in OECD Countries." *Comparative Political Studies* 40: 1486–510.

Brady, David. 2003. "Rethinking the Sociological Measurement of Poverty." *Social Forces* 81: 715–52.

Brady, Henry E. 2004. "An Analytical Perspective on Participatory Inequality and Income Inequality." Pp. 667–702 in *Social Inequality*, edited by Kathryn M. Neckerman. New York: Russell Sage Foundation.

—— Kay Lehman Schlozman, Sidney Verba, and Laurel Elms. 2002. "Who Bowls? Class, Race, and Participatory Inequality—1973–1994." In *Understanding Public Opinion*, edited by Barbara Norrander and Clyde Wilcox. Washington, DC: CQ Press.

Brewer, Mike. 2001. "Comparing In-Work Benefits and the Reward to Work for Families with Children in the US and the UK." *Fiscal Studies* 22: 41–77.

—— Alissa Goodman, Jonathan Shaw, and Luke Sibieta. 2006. "Poverty and Inequality in Britain: 2006." Institute for Fiscal Studies. London. Available at: www.ifs.org.uk.

Brooks-Gunn, Jeanne, Greg J. Duncan, and J. Lawrence Aber, eds. 1997. *Neighborhood Poverty. Volume I: Context and Consequences for Children*. New York: Russell Sage Foundation.

Brown, C., M. Reich, D. Stern, and L. Ulman. 1993. "Conflict and Cooperation in Labor-Management Relations in Japan and the United States." Industrial Relations Research Association Series, Proceedings of the Forty-Fifth Annual Meeting: 426–36.

Browne, Irene, ed. 1999. *Latinas and African American Women at Work*. New York: Russell Sage Foundation.

Bruning, Gwennaelle and Janneke Plantenga. 1999. "Parental Leave and Equal Opportunities Experiences in Eight European Countries." *Journal of European Social Policy* 9: 195–209.

Buchinal, Margaret. 1999. "Child Care Experiences and Developmental Outcomes." *Annals of the American Academy of Political and Social Science* 563: 73–97.

Buechtemann, C. F., ed. 1993. *Employment Security and Labor Market Behavior*. Ithaca, NY: ILR Press.

Burtless, Gary. 1999. "Effects of Growing Wage Disparities and Changing Family Composition on the U.S. Income Distribution." *European Economic Review* 43: 853–65.

—— and Christopher Jencks. 2003. "American Inequality and Its Consequences." Pp. 61–108 in *Agenda for the Nation*, edited by Henry Aaron, Pietro S. Nivola, and James M. Lindsay. Washington, DC: Brookings Institution.

Campbell, John L. 2004. *Institutional Change and Globalization*. Princeton, NJ: Princeton University Press.

—— and Ove K. Pedersen. 2007. "The Varieties of Capitalism and Hybrid Success: Denmark in the Global Economy." *Comparative Political Studies* 40: 307–32.

Canberra Group (Canberra International Expert Group on Household Income Statistics). 2001. *Final Report and Recommendations*. Ottawa: Canberra Group.

Card, David, Richard Blundell, and Richard B. Freeman, eds. 2004. *Seeking a Premier Economy: The Economic Effects of British Economic Reforms, 1980–2000*. Chicago: University of Chicago Press.

—— and Alan B. Krueger. 1995. *Myth and Measurement: The New Economics of the Minimum Wage*. Princeton, NJ: Princeton University Press.

—— —— 2000. "Minimum Wages and Employment: A Case Study of the Fast-Food Industry in New Jersey and Pennsylvania: Reply." *American Economic Review* 90: 1397–1420.

Carneiro, Pedro and James J. Heckman. 2003. "Human Capital Policy." Pp. 77–239 in *Inequality in America: What Role for Human Capital Policies*, edited by Benjamin M. Friedman. Cambridge, MA: MIT Press.

Castles, Francis G. 1996. "Needs-Based Strategies of Social Protection in Australia and New Zealand." Pp. 88–115 in *Welfare States in Transition*, edited by Gøsta Esping-Andersen. London: Sage.

Center for American Progress. 2005. "A Fair and Simple Tax System for Our Future: A Progressive Approach to Tax Reform." Available at: www.americanprogress.org.

Center on Budget and Policy Priorities. 2002. "Facts About the Earned Income Credit." Available at: www.cbpp.org.

—— 2006. "Earned Income Credit Benefits for Tax Year 2006 at Various Income Levels." Available at: www.cbpp.org.

Chapman, Jeff. 2004. "Employment and the Minimum Wage: Evidence from Recent State Labor Market Trends." Briefing Paper 150. Economic Policy Institute. Available at: www.epinet.org/briefingpapers/150/bp150.pdf.

Chevalier, A. and T. Viitanen. 2002. "The Causality Between Female Labour Force Participation and the Availability of Childcare." *Applied Economics Letters* 9: 915–18.

Clarke, George R. G. 1995. "More Evidence on Income Distribution and Growth." *Journal of Development Economics* 47: 403–27.

Clarke-Stewart, Alison and Virginia D. Allhusen. 2005. *What We Know About Childcare*. Cambridge, MA: Harvard University Press.

Cleveland, William S. 1994. *The Elements of Graphing Data*. Summit, NJ: Hobart Press.

Cnossen, Sijbren. 2002. "Tax Policy in the European Union: A Review of Issues and Options." Working Paper 758. CESifo. Available at: www.cesifo.de.

Cohn, Jonathan 2007. "Great Danes." *The New Republic*, January 1–15: 13–17.

Collier, David, Henry E. Brady, and Jason Seawright. 2004. "Sources of Leverage in Causal Inference: Toward an Alternative View of Methodology." Pp. 229–66 in *Rethinking Social Theory*, edited by Henry E. Brady and David Collier. Lanham, MD: Rowman and Littlefield.

Corcoran, Mary. 1995. "Rags to Rags: Poverty and Mobility in the United States." *Annual Review of Sociology* 21: 213–67.

—— 2001. "Mobility, Persistence, and the Consequences of Poverty for Children: Child and Adult Outcomes." Pp. 127–89 in *Understanding Poverty*, edited by Sheldon H. Danziger and Robert H. Haveman. New York and Cambridge, MA: Russell Sage Foundation and Harvard University Press.

Corcoran, Sean, William N. Evans, Jennifer Godwin, Sheila E. Murray, and Robert M. Schwab. 2004. "The Changing Distribution of Education Finance, 1972 to 1997." Pp. 433–65 in *Social Inequality*, edited by Kathryn M. Neckerman. New York: Russell Sage Foundation.

Corak, Miles, ed. 2004. *Generational Income Mobility in North America and Europe*. Cambridge: Cambridge University Press.

Costa, Dora L. and Matthew E. Kahn. 2003*a*. "Civic Engagement and Community Heterogeneity: An Economist's Perspective." *Perspectives on Politics* 1: 103–11.

—— —— 2003*b*. "Understanding the American Decline in Social Capital, 1952 to 1998." *Kyklos* 56: 17–46.

Crouch, Colin, David Finegold, and Mari Sako. 1999. *Are Skills the Answer? The Political Economy of Skill Creation in Advanced Industrial Countries.* Oxford: Oxford University Press.

Cusack, Thomas R. and Pablo Beramendi. 2004. "Taxing Work: Some Political and Economic Aspects of Labor Income Taxation." Unpublished. Wissenschaftszentrum Berlin für Sozialforschung (WZB). Berlin, Germany.

Daly, Mary. 2000. "A Fine Balance: Women's Labor Market Participation in International Comparison." Pp. 467–510 in *Welfare and Work in the Open Economy, Volume II: Diverse Responses to Common Challenges,* edited by Fritz W. Scharpf and Vivien A. Schmidt. Oxford: Oxford University Press.

Daveri, Francesco and Guido Tabellini. 2002. "Unemployment, Growth, and Taxation in Industrial Countries." *Economic Policy* 30: 48–104.

Dawkins, Peter. 2001. "The Five Economists' Plan: The Original Ideas and Subsequent Developments." Unpublished.

Deaton, Angus. 2003. "Health, Inequality, and Economic Development." *Journal of Economic Literature* 41: 113–58.

DeFina, Robert H. and Kishor Thanawala. 2004. "International Evidence on the Impact of Transfers and Taxes on Alternative Poverty Indexes." *Social Science Research* 33: 322–38.

Del Boca, Daniela. 2002. "Low Fertility and Labour Force Participation of Italian Women: Evidence and Interpretations." Labour Market and Social Policy Occasional Paper 61. Organization for Economic Cooperation and Development. Available at: www.oecd.org.

Devereux, Michael P., Rachel Griffith, and Alexander Klemm. 2002. "Corporate Income Tax Reforms and International Tax Competition." *Economic Policy* 450–95.

Devroye, Dan and Richard Freeman. 2002. "Does Inequality in Skills Explain Inequality of Earnings Across Advanced Countries?" CEP Discussion Paper 0552. Centre for Economic Performance.

Diamond, Patrick and Anthony Giddens. 2005. "The New Egalitarianism: Economic Inequality in the UK." Pp. 101–19 in *The New Egalitarianism: Opportunity and Prosperity in Modern Societies,* edited by Anthony Giddens and Patrick Diamond. London: Polity.

Dickens, Richard and David Ellwood. 2001. "Welfare to Work: Poverty in Britain and the US." *New Economy* 8: 98–103.

Dickert-Conlin, Stacy and Douglas Holtz-Eakin. 2000. "Employee-Based Versus Employer-Based Subsidies to Low-Wage Workers: A Public Finance Perspective." Pp. 262–98 in *Finding Jobs: Work and Welfare Reform,* edited by David Card and Rebecca M. Blank. New York: Russell Sage Foundation.

Dilnot, Andrew and Julian McCrae. 2000. "The Family Credit System and the Working Families Tax Credit in the United Kingdom." *OECD Economic Studies* 31: 69–84.

Dingeldey, Irene. 2001. "European Tax Systems and Their Impact on Family Employment Patterns." *Journal of Social Policy* 30: 653–72.

DiPrete, Thomas A. 2005. "Labor Markets, Inequality, and Change: A European Perspective." *Work and Occupations* 32: 110–30.

DiPrete, Thomas A., Dominique Goux, Eric Maurin, and Amelie Quesnel-Vallee. 2006. "Work and Pay in Flexible and Regulated Labor Markets: A Generalized Perspective on Institutional Evolution and Inequality Trends in Europe and the U.S." *Research in Social Stratification and Mobility* 24: 311–32.

Dore, Ronald. 1986. *Flexible Rigidities*. Stanford, CA: Stanford University Press.

—— 1987. *Taking Japan Seriously*. Stanford, CA: Stanford University Press.

Dornbusch, Rudiger. 1986. "Unemployment: Europe's Challenge of the '80s." *Challenge*, September–October: 11–18.

Draka, Mirko, Richard Dickens, and Romesh Vaitilingam. 2005. "The National Minimum Wage: The Evidence of its Impact on Jobs and Inequality." Policy Analysis. Centre for Economic Performance, London School of Economics and Political Science.

Duncan, Greg J. and Jeanne Brooks-Gunn, eds. 1997. *Consequences of Growing Up Poor*. New York: Russell Sage Foundation.

Duvander, Ann-Zofie, Tommy Ferrarini, and Sara Thalberg. 2005. "Swedish Parental Leave and Gender Equality." Working Paper. Institute for Futures Studies. Stockholm.

Dworkin, Ronald. 1985. *A Matter of Principle*. Oxford: Oxford University Press.

Ebbinghaus, Bernhard. 2000. "Any Way Out of 'Exit from Work'? Reversing the Entrenched Pathways of Early Retirement." Pp. 511–53 in *Welfare and Work in the Open Economy, Volume II: Diverse Responses to Common Challenges*, edited by Fritz W. Scharpf and Vivien A. Schmidt. Oxford: Oxford University Press.

EC (European Commission: Directorate-General for Employment, Social Affairs, and Equal Opportunities). 2004. "Employment Structures in Europe and the US: The Role of Skills, Wages, and Final Demand." Pp. 97–157 in *Employment in Europe 2004*. Brussels: European Commission.

—— 2005. "Earnings Disparities and Determinants of the Earnings Distribution in the EU." Pp. 163–209 in *Employment in Europe 2005*. Brussels: European Commission.

—— 2006. "Flexibility and Security in the EU Labour Markets." Pp. 75–118 in *Employment in Europe 2006*. Brussels: European Commission.

The Economist. 1997. "Europe Hits a Brick Wall." April 5, pp. 21–3.

—— 2007. "Rich Man, Poor Man." 20 January: 15–16.

Edin, Kathryn and Laura Lein. 1997. *Making Ends Meet: How Single Women Survive Work and Welfare*. New York: Russell Sage Foundation.

Egger, Philippe and Werner Sengenberger, eds. 2003. *Decent Work in Denmark*. Geneva: International Labour Organization.

Ehrenreich, Barbara. 2001. *Nickel and Dimed: On (Not) Getting By in America*. New York: Henry Holt and Company.

Eliason, Scott, Robin Stryker, and Eric Tranby. 2008. "The Welfare State, Family Policies, and Women's Labor Market Participation: Combining Fuzzy-Set and Statistical Methods to Assess Causal Relations and Estimate Causal Effects." In *Method and Substance in Macrocomparative Analysis*, edited by Lane Kenworthy and Alexander Hicks. Basingstoke, UK: Palgrave Macmillan.

Ellwood, David. 1996. "Welfare Reform as I Knew It." *The American Prospect*, May–June: 26.

Elmeskov, Jørgen, John P. Martin, and Stefano Scarpetta. 1998. "Key Lessons for Labour Market Reforms: Evidence from OECD Countries' Experiences." *Swedish Economic Policy Review* 5: 205–52.

England, Paula. 1992. *Comparable Worth: Theories and Evidence*. New York: Aldine de Gruyter.

Epstein, Jessica, Daniel Duerr, Lane Kenworthy, and Charles Ragin. 2008. "Comparative Employment Performance: A Fuzzy-Set Analysis." In *Method and Substance in Macrocomparative Analysis*, edited by Lane Kenworthy and Alexander Hicks. Basingstoke, UK: Palgrave Macmillan.

Erikson, Robert and John H. Goldthorpe. 1993. *The Constant Flux: A Study of Class Mobility in Industrial Societies*. Oxford: Oxford University Press.

Esping-Andersen, Gøsta. 1990. *The Three Worlds of Welfare Capitalism*. Princeton, NJ: Princeton University Press.

—— 1999. *Social Foundations of Postindustrial Economies*. Oxford: Oxford University Press.

—— 2000*a*. "Regulation and Context: Reconsidering the Correlates of Unemployment." Pp. 99–112 in *Why Deregulate Labour Markets?* edited by Gøsta Esping-Andersen and Marino Regini. Oxford: Oxford University Press.

—— 2000*b*. "Who Is Harmed by Labour Market Regulations? Quantitative Evidence." Pp. 66–98 in *Why Deregulate Labour Markets?* edited by Gøsta Esping-Andersen and Marino Regini. Oxford: Oxford University Press.

—— 2001. "A Welfare State for the 21st Century." Pp. 134–56 in *The Global Third Way Debate*, edited by Anthony Giddens. Cambridge: Polity Press.

—— 2004. "Unequal Opportunities and the Mechanisms of Social Inheritance." Pp. 289–314 in *Generational Income Mobility in North America and Europe*, edited by Miles Corak. Cambridge: Cambridge University Press.

—— 2007. "Equal Opportunities and the Welfare State." *Contexts* 6(3): 23–7.

—— with Duncan Gallie, Anton Hemerijck, and John Myles. 2002. *Why We Need a New Welfare State*. Oxford: Oxford University Press.

—— and Marino Regini, eds. 2000. *Why Deregulate Labour Markets?* Oxford: Oxford University Press.

Estevez-Abe, Margarita, Torben Iversen, and David Soskice. 2001. "Social Protection and the Formation of Skills: A Reinterpretation of the Welfare State." Pp. 145–83 in *Varieties of Capitalism*, edited by Peter A. Hall and David Soskice. Oxford: Oxford University Press.

European Commission, Directorate-General for Employment and Social Affairs. 2004. *Industrial Relations in Europe 2004*. Available at: europa.eu.int.

Eyraud, François and Catherine Saget. 2005. *Fundamentals of Minimum Wage Fixing*. Geneva: International Labour Office.

Fagnani, J. 1998. "Recent Changes in Family Policy in France: Political Tradeoffs and Economic Constraints." Pp. 58–65 in *Women, Work, and Family in Europe*, edited by Eileen P. Drew, Ruth Emerek, and Evelyn Mahon. London: Routledge.

Farkas, George. 2003. "Cognitive Skills and Noncognitive Traits and Behaviors in Stratification Processes." *Annual Review of Sociology* 29: 541–62.

Feldstein, Martin. 1999. "Reducing Poverty, Not Inequality." *The Public Interest*, Fall: 33–41.

Ferguson, Ronald F. 2005. "The Working-Poverty Trap." *The Public Interest*, Winter: 71–82.

Ferrarini, Tommy. 2003. *Parental Leave Institutions in Eighteen Post-War Welfare States*. Swedish Institute for Social Research Dissertation Series, No. 58.

—— and Kenneth Nelson. 2003. "Taxation of Social Insurance and Redistribution: A Comparative Analysis of Ten Welfare States." *Journal of European Social Policy* 13: 21–33.

Ferrera, Maurizio. 1996. "The 'Southern Model' of Welfare in Social Europe." *Journal of European Social Policy* 6: 17–37.

—— Anton Hemerijck, and Martin Rhodes. 2000. "The Future of Social Europe: Recasting Work and Welfare in the New Economy." Report prepared for the Portuguese Presidency of the European Union.

Fischer, Claude, Michael Hout, Martin Sanchez Jankowski, Samuel R. Lucas, Ann Swidler, and Kim Voss. 1996. *Inequality by Design: Cracking the Bell Curve Myth*. Princeton, NJ: Princeton University Press.

Fitzgerald, Joan. 2006. *Moving Up in the New Economy: Career Ladders for U.S. Workers*. Ithaca, NY: ILR Press.

Flynn, James. 1987. "Massive IQ Gains in 14 Nations: What IQ Tests Really Measure." *Psychological Bulletin* 101(2): 171–91.

Forbes, Kristin J. 2000. "A Reassessment of the Relationship Between Inequality and Growth." *American Economic Review* 90: 869–87.

Förster, Michael and Marco Mira d'Ercole. 2005. "Income Distribution and Poverty in OECD Countries in the Second Half of the 1990s." OECD Social, Employment, and Migration Working Paper 22. Organization for Economic Cooperation and Development. Available at: www.oecd.org.

—— and Mark Pearson. 2002. "Income Distribution and Poverty in the OECD Area: Trends and Driving Forces." *OECD Economic Studies* 34: 7–39.

Frank, Robert H. 1999. *Luxury Fever*. New York: Free Press.

—— 2005. "Positional Externalities Cause Large and Preventable Welfare Losses." *American Economic Review* 95 (Papers and Proceedings): 137–41.

Freeman, Richard B. 1996. "Why Do So Many Young American Men Commit Crimes and What Might We Do About It?" *Journal of Economic Perspectives* 10(1): 22–45.

—— 2004. "What, Me Vote?" Pp. 703–28 in *Social Inequality*, edited by Kathryn M. Neckerman. New York: Russell Sage Foundation.

—— 2005. "Labour Market Institutions Without Blinders: The Debate over Flexibility and Labour Market Performance." Working Paper 11286. National Bureau of Economic Research. Available at: www.nber.org.

—— 2007. *America Works: The Exceptional U.S. Labor Market*. New York: Russell Sage Foundation.

—— and William M. Rodgers III. 2005. "The Weak Jobs Recovery: Whatever Happened to 'the Great American Jobs Machine'?" Federal Reserve Bank of New York *Economic Policy Review*, August: 3–18.

—— and Ronald Schettkat. 2000. "Low-Wage Services: Interpreting the US-German Difference." Pp. 157–76 in *Labour Market Inequalities*, edited by Mary Gregory, Wiemer Salverda, and Stephen Bazen. Oxford: Oxford University Press.

Frohlich, Norman, Joe A. Oppenheimer, and Cheryl L. Eavey. 1987. "Laboratory Results on Rawls's Distributive Justice." *British Journal of Political Science* 17: 1–21.

Furåker, Bengt. 2002. "Is High Unemployment Due to Welfare State Protection? Lessons from the Swedish Experience." Pp. 123–42 in *Europe's New State of Welfare: Unemployment, Employment Policies, and Citizenship*, edited by Jørgen Goul Andersen, Jochen Clasen, Wim van Oorschot, and Knut Halvorsen. Bristol, UK: The Policy Press.

Galbraith, James K. 1998. *Created Unequal: The Crisis in American Pay*. A Century Foundation book. Chicago: University of Chicago Press.

—— Pedro Conceição, and Pedro Ferreira. 1999. "Inequality and Unemployment in Europe: The American Cure." *New Left Review* 237: 28–51.

Gallie, Duncan. 2002. "The Quality of Working Life in Welfare Strategy." Pp. 96–129 in Gøsta Esping-Andersen et al., *Why We Need a New Welfare State*. Oxford: Oxford University Press.

—— 2003. "The Quality of Working Life: Is Scandinavia Different?" *European Sociological Review* 19: 61–79.

Galston, William A. 2001. "What About Reciprocity?" Pp. 29–33 in *What's Wrong with a Free Lunch?* edited by Joshua Cohen and Joel Rogers. Boston: Beacon Press.

Ganghof, Steffen. 2000. "Adjusting National Tax Policy to Economic Internationalization: Strategies and Outcomes." Pp. 597–645 in *Welfare and Work in the Open Economy. Volume II: Diverse Responses to Common Challenges*, edited by Fritz W. Scharpf and Vivien A. Schmidt. Oxford: Oxford University Press.

—— 2005*a*. "Globalization, Tax Reform Ideals, and Social Policy Financing." *Global Social Policy* 5: 77–95.

—— 2005*b*. "High Taxes in Hard Times: How Denmark Built and Maintained a Huge Income Tax." Unpublished. Max Planck Institute for the Study of Societies. Cologne, Germany.

—— 2005*c*. "The Politics of (Income) Tax Structure." Unpublished. Max Planck Institute for the Study of Societies. Cologne, Germany.

Gangl, Markus. 2005. "Income Inequality, Permanent Incomes, and Income Dynamics: Comparing Europe to the United States." *Work and Occupations* 32: 140–62.

—— Joakim Palme, and Lane Kenworthy. 2008. "Is High Inequality Offset by Mobility?" Unpublished.

Garrett, Geoffrey. 1998. *Partisan Politics in the Global Economy*. Cambridge: Cambridge University Press.

Gauthier, Anne H. 1996. *The State and the Family: A Comparative Analysis of Family Policies in Industrialized Countries*. Oxford: Clarendon Press.

Gauthier, Anne H. and Anita Bortnik. 2001. "Comparative Maternity, Parental, and Childcare Database." Data set. Version dated February 2001. University of Calgary. Available at: soci.ucalgary.ca/fyppfamily_policy_databases.htm.

Genschel, Philipp. 2002. "Globalization, Tax Competition, and Welfare State." *Politics and Society* 30: 245–75.

George, Alexander L. and Andrew Bennett. 2004. *Case Studies and Theory Development in the Social Sciences*. Cambridge, MA: MIT Press.

Gerring, John. 2004. "What Is a Case Study and What Is It Good For?" *American Political Science Review* 98: 341–54.

Giddens, Anthony. 1998. *The Third Way*. Cambridge: Polity Press.

—— 2000. *The Third Way and Its Critics*. Cambridge: Polity Press.

Gilens, Martin. 1999. *Why Americans Hate Welfare*. Chicago: University of Chicago Press.

Ginsburg, Helen. 1983. *Full Employment and Public Policy: The United States and Sweden*. Lexington, MA: D.C. Heath.

Glyn, Andrew. 2006. *Capitalism Unleashed*. Oxford: Oxford University Press.

—— Wiemer Salverda, Joachim Möller, John Schmitt, and Michel Sollogoub. 2005. "Employment Differences in Services: The Role of Wages, Productivity, and Demand." Working Paper 12 (revised version). DEMPATEM. Available at: www.uva-aias.net.

Gomez, Rafael and Noah Meltz. 2001. "The Zero Sum Illusion: Industrial Relations and Modern Economic Approaches to Growth and Income Distribution." Paper presented at the conference on Linkages between Economic Growth and Inequality, Institute for Research on Public Policy—Centre for the Study of Living Standards, Ottawa, CA. Available at: www.irpp.org/events/index.htm.

Goodin, Robert E., Bruce Headey, Ruud Muffels, and Henk-Jan Dirven. 1999. *The Real Worlds of Welfare Capitalism*. Cambridge: Cambridge University Press.

Gornick, Janet C. 1999. "Gender Equality in the Labour Market." Pp. 210–42 in *Gender and Welfare State Regimes*, edited by Diane Sainsbury. Oxford: Oxford University Press.

—— and Marcia K. Meyers. 2003. *Families That Work: Policies for Reconciling Parenthood and Employment*. New York: Russell Sage Foundation.

Gorter, Cees. 2000. "The Dutch Miracle?" Pp. 181–210 in *Why Deregulate Labour Markets?* edited by Gøsta Esping-Andersen and Marino Regini. Oxford: Oxford University Press.

Gottschalk, Peter and Sheldon Danziger. 2005. "Inequality of Wage Rates, Earnings, and Family Income in the United States, 1975–2002." *Review of Income and Wealth* 51: 231–54.

Gottschall, Karin and Katherine Bird. 2003. "Family Leave Policies and Labor Market Segregation in Germany: Reinvention or Reform of the Male Breadwinner Model?" *Review of Policy Research* 20: 115–34.

Gough, Ian. 1996. "Social Assistance in Southern Europe." *Southern European Society and Politics* 1: 1–13.

Goul Andersen, Jørgen. 2002. "Denmark: From the Edge of the Abyss to a Sustainable Welfare State." Pp. 143–62 in *Europe's New State of Welfare: Unemployment, Employment Policies, and Citizenship*, edited by Jørgen Goul Andersen, Jochen Clasen, Wim van Oorschot, and Knut Halvorsen. Bristol, UK: Policy Press.

Granovetter, Mark. 1973. *The Strength of Weak Ties*. Cambridge, MA: Harvard University Press.

Green, Francis. 2006. *Demanding Work: The Paradox of Job Quality in the Affluent Economy*. Princeton, NJ: Princeton University Press.

Green-Pedersen, Christoffer, Kees van Kersbergen, and Anton Hemerijck. 2001. "Neo-Liberalism, the 'Third Way', or What? Recent Social Democratic Welfare Policies in Denmark and the Netherlands." *Journal of European Public Policy* 8: 307–25.

Greenstein, Robert. 2003. "What Is the Magnitude of EITC Overpayments?" Center on Budget and Policy Priorities. Available at: www.cbpp.org.

Gregg, Paul. 1996. "It Takes Two: Employment Polarisation in the OECD." Discussion Paper 304. Centre for Economic Performance. Available at: cep.lse.acuk/pubs.

—— 2000. "The Use of Wage Floors as Policy Tools." *OECD Economic Studies* 31: 133–46.

Griffin, Larry J., Pamela Barnhouse Walters, Phillip O'Connell, and Edward Moor. 1986. "Methodological Innovations in the Analysis of Welfare-State Development: Pooling Cross Sections and Time Series." Pp. 101–38 in *Futures for the Welfare State*, edited by Norman Furniss. Bloomington: Indiana University Press.

Gregory, Mary and Giovanni Russo. 2004. "The Employment Impact of Differences in Demand and Production Structures." Working Paper 10. DEMPATEM. Available at: www.uva-aias.net.

Gustafsson, Siv and Frank Stafford. 1992. "Child Care Subsidies and Labor Supply in Sweden." *Journal of Human Resources* 27: 204–30.

Hacker, Jacob S. 2002. *The Divided Welfare State: The Battle over Public and Private Social Benefits in the United States*. Cambridge: Cambridge University Press.

—— and Paul Pierson. 2005. "Abandoning the Middle: The Bush Tax Cuts and the Limits of Democratic Control." *Perspectives on Politics* 3: 33–53.

Hakim, Catherine. 2000. *Work-Lifestyle Choices in the 21st Century: Preference Theory*. Oxford: Oxford University Press.

Hall, Peter A. 2003. "Aligning Ontology and Methodology in Comparative Research." Pp. 373–404 in *Comparative Historical Analysis in the Social Sciences*, edited by James Mahoney and Dietrich Rueschemeyer. Cambridge: Cambridge University Press.

—— and Daniel W. Gingerich. 2004. "Varieties of Capitalism and Institutional Complementarities in the Macroeconomy: An Empirical Analysis." Discussion Paper 04/5. Max Planck Institute for the Study of Societies. Cologne, Germany. Available at: www.mpi-fg-koeln.mpg.de.

—— and David Soskice. 2001. "An Introduction to Varieties of Capitalism." Pp. 1–68 in *Varieties of Capitalism*, edited by Peter A. Hall and David Soskice. Oxford: Oxford University Press.

Hall, Peter V. 2005. "Review of Egalitarian Capitalism." *Perspectives on Politics* 3: 691–2.

Handel, Michael. 2003. "Skills Mismatch in the Labor Market." *Annual Review of Sociology* 29: 135–65.

Hansen, Kathleen M. and Daniel F. Burton. 1992. *German Technology Policy: Incentive for Industrial Innovation*. Washington, DC: Council on Competitiveness.

Harding, David J., Christopher Jencks, Leonard M. Lopoo, and Susan E. Mayer. 2005. "The Changing Effect of Family Background on the Incomes of American Adults." Pp. 100–44 in *Unequal Chances: Family Background and Economic Success*, edited by Samuel Bowles, Herbert Gintis, and Melissa Osborne Groves. New York and Princeton, NJ: Russell Sage Foundation and Princeton University Press.

Hartog, Joop. 1999. "The Netherlands: So What's So Special About the Dutch Model?" Employment and Training Paper 54. International Labour Organization. Available at: www.ilo.org.

Haveman, Robert H. 1997. "Equity with Employment." *Boston Review*. Available at: bostonreview.net/ndf.html.

Heckman, James J. and Yona Rubinstein. 2001. "The Importance of Noncognitive Skills: Lessons from the GED Testing Program." *American Economic Review* (Papers and Proceedings) 91: 145–9.

Helburn, Suzanne and Barbara R. Bergmann. 2002. *America's Child Care Problem: The Way Out*. New York: Palgrave.

Hemerijck, Anton. 2005. "Linking Welfare Recalibration and Social Learning." Unpublished. Netherlands Scientific Council for Government Policy.

—— 2007. "Towards Developmental Welfare Recalibration in Europe." Unpublished. Netherlands Scientific Council for Government Policy.

—— and Martin Schludi. 2000. "Sequences of Policy Failures and Effective Policy Responses." Pp. 125–228 in *Welfare and Work in the Open Economy. Volume 1: From Vulnerability to Competitiveness*, edited by Fritz W. Scharpf and Vivien A. Schmidt. Oxford: Oxford University Press.

—— Brigitte Unger, and Jelle Visser. 2000. "How Small Countries Negotiate Change: Twenty-Five Years of Policy Adjustment in Austria, the Netherlands, and Belgium." Pp. 175–263 in *Welfare and Work in the Open Economy, Volume II: Diverse Responses to Common Challenges*, edited by Fritz W. Scharpf and Vivien A. Schmidt. Oxford: Oxford University Press.

Herrigel, Gary. 1994. "Industry as a Form of Order: A Comparison of the Historical Development of the Machine Tool Industries in the United States and Germany." In *Governing Capitalist Economies: Performance and Control of Economic Sectors*, edited by J. Rogers Hollingsworth, Philippe C. Schmitter, and Wolfgang Streeck. Oxford: Oxford University Press.

Herrnstein, Richard and Charles Murray. 1994. *The Bell Curve: Intelligence and Class Structure in American Life*. New York: Free Press.

Herzenberg, Stephen A., John A. Alic, and Howard Wial. 1998. *New Rules for a New Economy*. A Century Fund book. Ithaca, NY: ILR Press.

Hicks, Alexander. 1999. *Social Democracy and Welfare Capitalism*. Ithaca, NY: Cornell University Press.

—— and Lane Kenworthy. 1998. "Cooperation and Political Economic Performance in Affluent Democratic Capitalism." *American Journal of Sociology* 103: 1631–72.

————— 2003. "Varieties of Welfare Capitalism." *Socio-Economic Review* 1: 27–61.

————— 2008. "Family Policies and Women's Employment: A Regression Analysis." In *Method and Substance in Macrocomparative Analysis*, edited by Lane Kenworthy and Alexander Hicks. Basingstoke, UK: Palgrave Macmillan.

—— and Duane Swank. 1984. "Governmental Redistribution in Rich Capitalist Democracies." *Policy Studies Journal* 13: 265–86.

—— and Christopher Zorn. 2005. "Economic Globalization, the Macro Economy, and Reversals of Welfare: Expansion in Affluent Democracies, 1978–94." *International Organization* 59: 631–62.

Hills, John. 2004. *Inequality and the State*. Oxford: Oxford University Press.

—— and Kitty Stewart, eds. 2005. *A More Equal Society? New Labour, Poverty, Inequality, and Exclusion*. Bristol, UK: Policy Press.

Hofferth, Sandra L. and Sally C. Curtin. 2003. "The Impact of Parental Leave on Maternal Return to Work After Childbirth in the United States." OECD Social, Employment, and Migration Working Paper 7. Organization for Economic Cooperation and Development. Available at: www.oecd.org/dataoecd/26/45/2955849.pdf.

Hoffman, Saul D. and Laurence S. Seidman. 2003. *Helping Working Families: The Earned Income Tax Credit*. Kalamazoo, MI: Upjohn Institute for Employment Research.

Holmes, Stanley and Wendy Zellner. 2004. "The Costco Way." *Business Week*, April 12: 76–7.

Hotz, V. Joseph and John Karl Scholz. 2000. "Not Perfect, but Still Pretty Good: The EITC and Other Policies to Support the US Low-Wage Labour Market." *OECD Economic Studies* 31: 25–42.

————— 2004. "The Earned Income Tax Credit." Pp. 141–97 in *Means-Tested Transfer Programs in the United States*, edited by Robert Moffitt. Chicago: University of Chicago Press.

Hoxby, Caroline. 2003. "Our Favorite Method of Redistribution: School Spending Equality, Income Inequality, and Growth." Unpublished. Department of Economics, Harvard University.

Howell, David R. 2002. "Increasing Earnings Inequality and Unemployment in Developed Countries: Markets, Institutions, and the 'Unified Theory'." *Politics and Society* 30: 193–243.

—— 2005. "Unemployment and Labor Market Institutions: An Assessment." Pp. 310–43 in *Fighting Unemployment: The Limits of Free Market Orthodoxy*, edited by David R. Howell. Oxford: Oxford University Press.

—— and Friedrich Huebler. 2005. "Wage Compression and the Unemployment Crisis: Labor Market Institutions, Skills, and Inequality-Unemployment Tradeoffs." Pp. 35–71 in *Fighting Unemployment: The Limits of Free Market Orthodoxy*, edited by David R. Howell. Oxford: Oxford University Press.

Howell, David R., Dean Baker, Andrew Glyn, and John Schmitt. 2006. "Are Protective Labor Market Institutions Really at the Root of Unemployment? A Critical Perspective on the Statistical Evidence." Unpublished.

Huber, Evelyne and John D. Stephens. 2001. *Development and Crisis of the Welfare State*. Chicago: University of Chicago Press.

—— John D. Stephens, David Bradley, Stephanie Moller, and François Nielsen. 2002. "The Welfare State and Women's Economic Independence." Paper presented at the Conference of Europeanists, Chicago.

Iceland, John. 2003. *Poverty in America*. Berkeley: University of California Press.

Ilmakunnas, S. 1997. "Public Policy and Child Care Choice." Pp. 178–93 in *Economics of Family and Family Policy*, edited by I. Persson and C. Jonung. London: Routledge.

IMF. 2003. "Unemployment and Labor Market Institutions: Why Reforms Pay Off." Pp. 129–50 in *World Economic Outlook*. Washington, DC: IMF.

—— N.d. International Financial Statistics database. Available at: www imfstatistics. org.

Institute for Futures Studies. 2006. *Sustainable Policies in an Ageing Europe: A Human Capital Response*. Stockholm: Institute for Futures Studies.

Ioannides, Yannis M. and Linda Datcher Loury. 2004. "Job Information Networks, Neighborhood Effects, and Inequality." *Journal of Economic Literature* 42: 1056–93.

ISSP (International Social Survey Programme). 1999. Cross-National Survey on "Social Inequality." Available at: www.issp.org.

Iversen, Torben. 1999. *Contested Economic Institutions*. Cambridge: Cambridge University Press.

—— 2005. *Capitalism, Democracy, and Welfare*. Cambridge: Cambridge University Press.

—— and Anne Wren. 1998. "Equality, Employment, and Budgetary Restraint: The Trilemma of the Service Economy." *World Politics* 50: 507–46.

Jahoda, Marie. 1982. *Employment and Unemployment: A Social Psychological Analysis*. Cambridge: Cambridge University Press.

Jacobs, Lawrence et al. 2004. "American Democracy in an Age of Rising Inequality." *Perspectives on Politics* 2: 651–66.

Jäntti, Markus, Knut Røed, Robin Naylor, Anders Björklund, Bernt Bratsberg, Oddbjørn Raaum, Eva Österbacka, and Tor Eriksson 2006. "American Exceptionalism in a New Light: A Comparison of Intergenerational Earnings Mobility in the Nordic Countries, the United Kingdom, and the United States." Discussion Paper 1938. Institute for the Study of Labor (IZA). Bonn, Germany.

Jaumotte, Florence. 2003. "Female Labour Force Participation: Past Trends and Main Determinants in OECD Countries." Working Paper 376. OECD Economics Department. Paris: OECD.

Jencks, Christopher. 2005. "What Happened to Welfare?" *New York Review of Books*, December 15: 76–81, 86.

—— Marshall Smith, Henry Acland, Mary Jo Bane, David Cohen, Herbert Gintis, Barbara Heyns, and Stephan Michelson. 1972. *Inequality: A Reassessment of the Effect of Family and Schooling in America*. New York: Basic Books.

—— Susan Bartlett, Mary Corcoran, James Crouse, David Eaglesfield, Gregory Jackson, Kent McClelland, Peter Mueser, Michael Olneck, Joseph Schwartz, Sherry Ward, and Jill Williams. 1979. *Who Gets Ahead? The Determinants of Economic Success in America*. New York: Basic Books.

—— and Susan E. Mayer. 1990. "The Social Consequences of Growing Up in a Poor Neighborhood." Pp. 111–86 in *Inner-City Poverty in the United States*, edited by L. E. Lynn and M. G. H. McGeary. Washington, DC: National Academy Press.

Jencks, Christopher and Meredith Phillips. 1998. "The Black-White Test Score Gap: An Introduction." Pp. 1–51 in *The Black-White Test Score Gap*, edited by Christopher Jencks and Meredith Phillips. Washington, DC: Brookings Institution.

—— and Paul E. Peterson, eds. 1991. *The Urban Underclass*. Washington, DC: Brookings Institution.

—— and Laura Tach. 2005. "Would Equal Opportunity Mean More Mobility?" Pp. 25–38 in *Mobility and Inequality: Frontiers of Research in Sociology and Economics*, edited by Stephen Morgan, David Grusky, and Gary Fields. Stanford, CA: Stanford University Press.

Jensen, Jane and Denis Saint-Martin. 2003. "Building Blocks for a New Welfare Architecture: Is LEGO the Model for an Active Society?" Unpublished. University of Montreal.

Joesch, Jutta M. 1997. "Paid Leave and the Timing of Women's Employment Before and After Childbirth." *Journal of Marriage and the Family* 59: 1008–21.

Joumard, Isabelle. 2002. "Tax Systems in European Union Countries." *OECD Economic Studies* 34: 91–151.

Juhn, Chinhui and Simon Potter. 2006. "Changes in Labor Force Participation in the United States." *Journal of Economic Perspectives* 20(3): 27–46.

Kalleberg, Arne L. Forthcoming. *Good Jobs, Bad Jobs, No Jobs: Changing Work and Workers in America*. New York: Russell Sage Foundation.

—— Michael Wallace, and Robert P. Althauser. 1981. "Economic Segmentation, Worker Power, and Income Inequality." *American Journal of Sociology* 87: 651–83.

Kamerman, Sheila B. and Alfred J. Kahn. 1995. *Starting Right: How America Neglects Its Youngest Children and What We Can Do About It*. Oxford: Oxford University Press.

Kane, Thomas J. 2004. "College-Going and Inequality." Pp. 319–53 in *Social Inequality*, edited by Kathryn M. Neckerman. New York: Russell Sage Foundation.

Karoly, Lynn A., M. Rebecca Kilburn, and Jill S. Cannon. 2005. *Early Childhood Interventions: Proven Results, Future Promise*. Santa Monica, CA: RAND Corporation.

Kato, Junko. 2003. *Regressive Taxation and the Welfare State*. Cambridge: Cambridge University Press.

Katz, Lawrence F. and David Autor. 1999. "Changes in the Wage Structure and Earnings Inequality." In *Handbook of Labor Economics*, vol. 3A, edited by Orley Ashenfelter and David Card. Amsterdam: Elsevier.

Kawachi, Ichiro, Richard G. Wilkinson, and Bruce P. Kennedy. 1999. "Introduction." Pp. xi–xxxiv in *The Society and Population Health Reader. Volume 1: Income*

Inequality and Health, edited by Ichiro Kawachi, Bruce P. Kennedy, and Richard G. Wilkinson. New York: Free Press.

Keil, Manfred, Donald Robertson, and James Symons. 2001. "Minimum Wages and Employment." Centre for Economic Performance, London School of Economics and Political Science.

Kemmerling, Achim. 2005. "Tax Mixes, Welfare States, and Employment: Tracking Diverging Vulnerabilities." *Journal of European Public Policy* 12: 1–22.

—— and Oliver Bruttel. 2005. "New Politics in Germany Labour Market Policy? The Implications of the Recent Hartz Reforms for the German Welfare State." Discussion Paper. Wizzenschaftszentrum Berlin (WZB).

Kenworthy, Lane. 1995. *In Search of National Economic Success: Balancing Competition and Cooperation*. Thousand Oaks, CA: Sage.

—— 1997. "Globalization and Economic Convergence." *Competition and Change* 2: 1–64.

—— 1999. "Do Social-Welfare Policies Reduce Poverty? A Cross-National Assessment." *Social Forces* 77: 1119–39.

—— 2001. "Wage-Setting Measures: A Survey and Assessment." *World Politics* 54: 57–98.

—— 2002 "Corporatism and Unemployment in the 1980s and 1990s." *American Sociological Review* 67: 367–88.

—— 2003. "Do Affluent Countries Face an Incomes–Jobs Tradeoff?" *Comparative Political Studies* 36: 1180–209.

—— 2004a. *Egalitarian Capitalism*. New York: Russell Sage Foundation.

—— 2004b. "Rising Inequality Not a Surge at the Top." *Challenge*, September–October: 51–5.

—— 2006. "Institutional Coherence and Macroeconomic Performance." *Socio-Economic Review* 4: 69–91.

—— 2007a. "Reconsidering the Effect of Public Opinion on Social Policy Generosity." Unpublished.

—— 2007b. "Toward Improved Use of Regression in Macro-Comparative Analysis." *Comparative Social Research* 24: 343–50.

—— 2008a (forthcoming). "Institutions, Wealth, and Inequality." In *The Oxford Handbook of Comparative Institutional Analysis*, edited by Glenn Morgan, John Campbell, Colin Crouch, Peer Hull Kristensen, Ove Kai Pedersen, and Richard Whitley. Oxford: Oxford University Press.

—— 2008b. "Is Targeting Inferior?" Unpublished.

—— 2008c. "Who Should Care for Under-Threes?" In *Institutions for Gender Egalitarianism: Creating the Conditions for Egalitarian Dual-Earner/Dual-Caregiver Families*, Janet Gornick and Marcia Meyers et al. London: Verso.

—— and Alexander Hicks. 2008. "Introduction." In *Method and Substance in Macrocomparative Analysis*, edited by Lane Kenworthy and Alexander Hicks. Basingstoke, UK: Palgrave Macmillan.

—— and Jonas Pontusson. 2005. "Rising Inequality and the Politics of Redistribution in Affluent Countries." *Perspectives on Politics* 3: 449–71.

Kesselman, Jonathan R. and Ron Cheung. 2006. "Taxation Impacts on Inequality in Canada: Methodologies and Findings." Pp. 347–415 in *Dimensions of Inequality in Canada*, edited by David A. Green and Jonathan R. Kesselman. Vancouver: UBC Press.

Kimmel, Jean. 1998. "Child Care Costs as a Barrier to Employment for Single and Married Mothers." *Review of Economics and Statistics* 2: 287–99.

Kiser, Edgar and Aaron Matthew Long. 2001. "Have We Overestimated the Effects of Neoliberalism and Globalization? Some Speculations on the Anomalous Stability of Taxes on Business." Pp. 51–68 in *The Rise of Neoliberalism and Institutional Analysis*, edited by John L. Campbell and Ove K. Pedersen. Princeton, NJ: Princeton University Press.

Kittel, Bernhard. 1999. "Sense and Sensitivity in Pooled Analysis of Political Data." *European Journal of Political Research* 35: 225–53.

Kok, Wim, Carlos Dell'Aringa, Federico Duran Lopez, Anna Eckström, Marta João Rodrigues, Christopher Pissarides, Annette Roux, and Günther Schmid. 2003. *Jobs, Jobs, Jobs: Creating More Employment in Europe*. Report of the European Commission's Employment Taskforce. Brussels: European Commission.

Konow, James. 2003. "Which Is the Fairest One of All? A Positive Analysis of Justice Theories." *Journal of Economic Literature* 41: 1188–239.

Korenman, Sanders and Christopher Winship. 2000. "A Reanalysis of *The Bell Curve*: Intelligence, Family Background, and Schooling." Pp. 136–78 in *Meritocracy and Economic Inequality*, edited by Kenneth Arrow, Samuel Bowles, and Steven Durlauf. Princeton, NJ: Princeton University Press.

Korpi, Walter. 1985. "Economic Growth and the Welfare State: Leaky Bucket or Irrigation System?" *European Sociological Review* 1: 97–118.

——— 2000. "Faces of Inequality: Gender, Class, and Patterns of Inequalities in Different Types of Welfare States." *Social Politics* 7: 127–91.

——— and Joakim Palme. 1998. "The Paradox of Redistribution and Strategies of Equality: Welfare State Institutions, Inequality, and Poverty in the Western Countries." *American Sociological Review* 63: 661–87.

——— ——— 2003. "New Politics and Class Politics in the Context of Austerity and Globalization: Welfare State Regress in 18 Countries, 1975–95." *American Political Science Review* 97: 425–46.

Krueger, Alan B. 2003. "Inequality, Too Much of a Good Thing." Pp. 1–75 in *Inequality in America: What Role for Human Capital Policies*, edited by Benjamin M. Friedman. Cambridge, MA: MIT Press.

Krueger, A. and B. Meyer. 2002. "Labor Supply Effects of Social Insurance." *Handbook of Public Economics*, vol. 3, edited by A. Auerback and M. Feldstein. Amsterdam: Elsevier.

Krugman, Paul. 1996. "The Causes of High Unemployment." *Policy Options*, July–August: 20–4.

——— 2007. *The Conscience of a Liberal*. New York: W. W. Norton.

Kuttner, Robert. 1996. *Everything for Sale*. New York: Knopf.

Kvist, Jon and Niels Ploug. 2003. "Active Labour Market Policies: When Do They Work? And Where Do They Fail?" Paper presented at the annual meeting of Research Committee 19 of the International Sociological Association, Toronto, August.

Lambrew, Jeanne M., John D. Podesta, and Tereas L. Shaw. 2005. "Change in Challenging Times: A Plan for Extending and Improving Health Coverage." *Health Affairs*, 23 March: 119–32.

Layard, Richard and Stephen Nickell. 2003. "Full Employment Is Not Just a Dream." *CentrePiece*, Winter: 10–17.

—— —— and Richard Jackman. 1991. *Unemployment*. Oxford: Oxford University Press.

Lazear, Edward P. 1989. "Pay Equality and Industrial Politics." *Journal of Political Economy* 97: 561–80.

Leibowitz, A., J. A. Klerman, and L. J. Waite. 1992. "Employment of New Mothers and Child Care Choice." *Journal of Human Resources* 27: 112–33.

Leigh, Andrew. 2005. "Optimal Design of Earned Income Tax Credits: Evidence from a British Natural Experiment." Discussion Paper 488. Economics Program, Australian National University.

Levine, David I. 1991. "Cohesiveness, Productivity, and Wage Dispersion." *Journal of Economic Behavior and Organization* 15: 237–55.

—— and R. J. Parkin. 1994. "Work Organization, Employment Security, and Macro-economic Stability." *Journal of Economic Behavior and Organization* 24: 251–71.

Lewis, Jane and Rebecca Surender, eds. 2004. *Welfare State Change: Towards a Third Way?* Oxford: Oxford University Press.

Lieberman, Evan S. 2005. "Nested Analysis as a Mixed-Method Strategy for Comparative Research." *American Political Science Review* 99: 435–52.

Lindert, Peter. 2004. *Growing Public: Social Spending and Economic Growth Since the Eighteenth Century, Volume 1*. Cambridge: Cambridge University Press.

Lister, Ruth. 2004. "The Third Way's Social Investment State." Pp. 157–81 in *Welfare State Change: Towards a Third Way?* edited by Jane Lewis and Rebecca Surender. Oxford: Oxford University Press.

Living Wage Resource Center. 2006. "Living Wage Wins." Available at: www.livingwagecampaign.org.

Low Pay Commission. 2006. *National Minimum Wage: Low Pay Commission Report 2006*. Available at: www.lowpay.gov.uk.

Lucifora, Claudio, Abigail McKnight, and Wiemer Salverda. 2005. "Low-Wage Employment in Europe: A Review of the Evidence." *Socio-Economic Review* 3: 259–92.

Luria, Daniel D. and Joel Rogers. 1999. *Metro Futures: Economic Solutions for Cities and Their Suburbs*. Boston: Beacon Press.

Lynch, John W. and George A. Kaplan. 1997. "Understanding How Inequality in the Distribution of Income Affects Health." *Journal of Health Psychology* 2: 297–14.

MacLeod, Jay. 1995. *Ain't No Makin' It: Aspirations and Attainment in a Low-Income Neighborhood*. Second edition. Boulder, CO: Westview Press.

Maddison, Angus. 2001. *The World Economy: A Millennial Perspective*. Paris: OECD.

Madsen, Per Kongshøj. 2001. "Employment Protection and Labour Market Policies: Tradeoffs and Complementarities. The Case of Denmark." Employment Papers 2001/21. Geneva. International Labour Organization.

—— 2006. "How Can It Possibly Fly? The Paradox of a Dynamic Labour Market in a Scandinavian Welfare State." Pp. 323–55 in *National Identity and the Varieties of Capitalism: The Danish Experience*, edited by John L. Campbell, John A. Hall, and Ove K. Pedersen. Montreal: McGill-Queen's University Press.

Mahler, Vincent and David Jesuit. 2006. "Fiscal Redistribution in the Developed Countries." *Socio-Economic Review* 4: 483–511.

Mahoney, James. 2000. "Strategies of Causal Inference in Small-N Analysis." *Sociological Methods and Research* 28: 387–424.

Mandel, Hadas and Moshe Semyonov. 2005. "Family Policies, Wage Structures, and Gender Gaps: Sources of Earnings Inequality in 20 Countries." *American Sociological Review* 70: 949–67.

—— 2006. "A Welfare State Paradox: State Interventions and Women's Employment Opportunities in 22 Countries." *American Journal of Sociology* 111: 1910–46.

Manning, Alan. 2003. *Monopsony in Motion: Imperfect Competition in Labor Markets*. Princeton, NJ: Princeton University Press.

Martin, Andrew. 2004. "The EMU Macroeconomic Policy Regime and the European Social Model." Pp. 20–50 in *Euros and Europeans: Monetary Integration and the European Model of Society*, edited by Andrew Martin and George Ross. Cambridge: Cambridge University Press.

Martin, John P. 2000. "What Works Among Active Labour Market Policies: Evidence from OECD Countries' Experiences." *OECD Economic Studies* 30: 79–113.

Matsaganis, Manos, Maurizio Ferrera, Luíz Capucha, and Luis Moreno. 2003. "Mending Nets in the South: Anti-Poverty Policies in Greece, Italy, Portugal, and Spain." *Social Policy and Administration* 37: 639–55.

Maxwell Poll. 2007. "The Maxwell Poll: Civic Engagement and Inequality." Available at: http://www.maxwell.syr.edu/campbell/Poll/PollHome.htm.

Mayer, Susan E. 1997. *What Money Can't Buy: Family Income and Children's Life Chances*. Cambridge, MA: Harvard University Press.

—— and Christopher Jencks 1989. "Poverty and the Distribution of Material Hardship." *Journal of Human Resources* 24: 88–114.

McCall, Leslie and Lane Kenworthy. 2008. "Has Rising Inequality Affected Social Policy Preferences?" Unpublished.

McCarty, Nolan, Keith T. Poole, and Howard Rosenthal. 2006. *Polarized America: The Dance of Ideology and Unequal Riches*. Cambridge, MA: MIT Press.

Merton, Robert K. 1968. *Social Theory and Social Structure*. New York: Free Press.

Messere, Ken, Flip de Kam, and Christopher Heady. 2003. *Tax Policy: Theory and Practice in OECD Countries*. Oxford: Oxford University Press.

Meyer, Bruce D. 1995. "Lessons from the U.S. Unemployment Insurance Experiments." *Journal of Economic Literature* 33: 91–131.

Meyer, Bruce D. and Dan T. Rosenbaum. 2002. "Making Single Mothers Work: Recent Tax and Welfare Policy and Its Effects." Pp. 69–115 in *Making Work Pay: The Earned Income Tax Credit and Its Impact on America's Families*, edited by Bruce D. Meyer and Douglas Holtz-Eakin. New York: Russell Sage Foundation.

Meyers, Marcia K., Janet C. Gornick, and Katherin E. Ross. 1999. "Public Childcare, Parental Leave, and Employment." Pp. 117–46 in *Gender and Welfare State Regimes*, edited by Diane Sainsbury. Oxford: Oxford University Press.

—— Dan Rosenbaum, Christopher Ruhm, and Jane Waldfogel. 2004. "Inequality in Early Childhood Education and Care: What Do We Know?" Pp. 223–69 in *Social Inequality*, edited by Kathryn M. Neckerman. New York: Russell Sage Foundation.

Meyerson, Harold. 2004. "Las Vegas as a Workers' Paradise." *The American Prospect*, January: 38–41.

Michalopoulos, Charles and Philip K. Robins. 2000. "Employment and Child Care Choices in Canada and the United States." *Canadian Journal of Economics* 33: 435–70.

Milanovic, Branko. 2003. "Why We All Do Care About Inequality (But Are Loath to Admit It)." Unpublished. Available at: papers.ssrn.com.

Miller, David. 2005. "What Is Social Justice?" Pp. 3–20 in *Social Justice: Building a Fairer Britain*, edited by Nick Pearce and Will Paxton. London: Institute for Public Policy Research.

Miller, Matthew. 2003. *The Two Percent Solution*. New York: PublicAffairs.

Mincer, Jacob. 1993 (1979). "Human Capital and Earnings." Pp. 69–97 in *Studies in Human Capital: Collected Essays of Jacob Mincer*. London: Edward Elgar.

Mishel, Lawrence, Jared Bernstein, and Sylvia Allegretto. 2007. *The State of Working America, 2006–07*. An Economic Policy Institute book. Ithaca, NY: Cornell University Press.

Misra, Joya, Midhelle Budig, and Stephanie Moller. 2005. "Employment, Wages, and Poverty: Reconciliation Policies and Gender Equity." Unpublished.

Mitchell, Deborah. 1991. *Income Transfers in Ten Welfare States*. Brookfield: Avebury.

Moffitt, Robert A. 1992. "Incentive Effects of the U.S. Welfare System: A Review." *Journal of Economic Literature* 30: 1–61.

Morgan, Kimberly. 2004. "Caring Time Policies in Western Europe: Trends and Implications." Paper presented at the annual meeting of the Research Committee on Poverty, Social Welfare, and Social Policy (RC 19), International Sociological Association, Paris.

—— 2005. "Taxation and the Politics of Poverty and Inequality in America: 1945 to the Present." Unpublished. Department of Political Science, George Washington University.

—— and Kathrina Zippel. 2003. "Paid to Care: The Origins and Effects of Care Leave Policies in Western Europe." *Social Politics* 10: 49–85.

Morris, Martina and Bruce Western. 1999. "Inequality in Earnings at the Close of the Twentieth Century." *Annual Review of Sociology* 25: 623–57.

Mullahy, John, Stephanie Robert, and Barbara Wolfe. 2004. "Health, Income, and Inequality." Pp. 523–44 in *Social Inequality*, edited by Kathryn M. Neckerman. New York: Russell Sage Foundation.

Murray, Charles. 1984. *Losing Ground: American Social Policy, 1950–1980*. New York: Basic Books.

Myles, John and Paul Pierson. 1997. "Friedman's Revenge: The Reform of 'Liberal' Welfare States in Canada and the United States." *Politics and Society* 25: 443–72.

—— and Jill Quadagno. 2000. "Envisioning a *Third Way*: The Welfare State in the Twenty-First Century." *Contemporary Sociology* 29: 156–67.

Neumark, David. 2002. *How Living Wage Laws Affect Low-Wage Workers and Low-Income Families*. San Francisco, CA: Public Policy Institute of California.

—— Mark Schweitzer, and William Wascher. 2004. "Minimum Wage Effects Throughout the Wage Distribution." *Journal of Human Resources* 39: 425–50.

—— and William Wascher. 2000. "Minimum Wages and Employment: A Case Study of the Fast-Food Industry in New Jersey and Pennsylvania: Comment." *American Economic Review* 90: 1362–96.

—— —— 2000. "Using the EITC to Help Poor Families: New Evidence and a Comparison with the Minimum Wage." Working Paper 7599. National Bureau of Economic Research. Available at: www.nber.org.

Nickell, Stephen. 1997. "Unemployment and Labor Market Rigidities: Europe Versus North America." *Journal of Economic Perspectives* 11(3): 55–74.

—— and Richard Layard. 1999. "Labor Market Institutions and Economic Performance." Pp. 3029–84 in *Handbook of Labor Economics*, volume 3C, edited by Orley Ashenfelter and David Card. Amsterdam: Elsevier.

—— Luca Nunziata, and Wolfgang Ochel. 2005. "Unemployment in the OECD Since the 1960s: What Do We Know?" *Economic Journal* 115: 1–27.

Niesser, Ulrich, ed. 1998. *The Rising Curve: Long-Term Gains in IQ and Related Measures*. Washington, DC: American Psychological Association.

Norrman, Erik and Charles E. McLure, Jr. 1997. "Tax Policy in Sweden." Pp. 109–53 in *The Welfare State in Transition*, edited by Richard B. Freeman et al. Chicago: University of Chicago Press.

O'Connor, Julia S., Ann Orloff, and Sheila Shaver 1999. *States, Markets, and Families*. Cambridge: Cambridge University Press.

OECD (Organization for Economic Cooperation and Development). 1994. *The OECD Jobs Study*. Paris: OECD.

—— 1995. *Taxation, Employment, and Unemployment*. Paris: OECD.

—— 1996*a*. "Earnings Inequality, Low-Paid Employment, and Earnings Mobility." Pp. 59–108 in *OECD Employment Outlook*. Paris: OECD.

—— 1996*b*. "Making Work Pay." Pp. 25–8 in *OECD Employment Outlook*. Paris: OECD.

—— 1998. "Recent Labour Market Developments and Prospects." Pp. 1–30 in *OECD Employment Outlook*. Paris: OECD.

—— 1999*a*. *A Caring World: The New Social Policy Agenda*. Paris: OECD.

OECD 1999*b*. "Employment Protection and Labour Market Performance." Pp. 48–132 in *OECD Employment Outlook*. Paris: OECD.

—— 2001. "Balancing Work and Family Life: Helping Parents into Paid Employment." Pp. 129–66 in *OECD Employment Outlook*. Paris: OECD.

—— 2002*a*. "And the Twain Shall Meet: Cross-Market Effects of Labour and Product Market Policies." Pp. 245–300 in *OECD Employment Outlook*. Paris: OECD.

—— 2002*b*. *Babies and Bosses: Reconciling Work and Family Life. Volume 1: Australia, Denmark, and the Netherlands.* Paris: OECD.

—— 2002*c*. *Education at a Glance.* Paris: OECD.

—— 2003*a*. "Benefits and Employment, Friend or Foe? Interactions Between Passive and Active Social Programmes." Pp. 171–235 in *OECD Employment Outlook*. Paris: OECD.

—— 2003*b*. "Making Work Pay, Making Work Possible." Pp. 113–170 in *OECD Employment Outlook*. Paris: OECD.

—— 2004*a*. *Benefits and Wages.* Paris: OECD.

—— 2004*b*. "Benefits and Wages Country Chapter: Germany, 2004." Available at: www.oecd.org.

—— 2004*c*. "Benefits and Wages Country Chapter: Sweden, 2004." Available at: www.oecd.org.

—— 2004*d*. "Benefits and Wages Country Chapter: United States, 2004." Available at: www.oecd.org.

—— 2004*e*. *Education at a Glance.* Paris: OECD.

—— 2004*f*. "Employment Protection Regulation and Labour Market Performance." Pp. 61–125 in *OECD Employment Outlook*. Paris: OECD.

—— 2004*g*. "Social Expenditure Database." Unpublished. Paris: OECD.

—— 2004*h*. "Wage-Setting Institutions and Outcomes." Pp. 127–81 in *OECD Employment Outlook*. Paris: OECD.

—— 2005*a*. *Babies and Bosses: Reconciling Work and Family Life. Volume 4: Canada, Finland, Sweden, and the United Kingdom.* Paris: OECD.

—— 2005*b*. *Extending Opportunities: How Active Social Policy Can Benefit Us All.* Paris: OECD.

—— 2005*c*. "Increasing Financial Incentives to Work: The Role of In-Work Benefits." Pp. 125–71 in *OECD Employment Outlook*. Paris: OECD.

—— 2006*a*. *Live Longer, Work Longer.* Paris: OECD.

—— 2006*b*. *OECD Employment Outlook: Boosting Jobs and Incomes.* Paris: OECD.

—— 2006*c*. *OECD Labour Force Statistics Database.* Formerly available at: www.oecd.org/scripts/cde/members/lfsdataauthenticate.asp. Now discontinued; replaced by OECD (2008).

—— 2007*a*. "Earnings Database." Unpublished. Available at: www.oecd.org/els/employment/data.

—— 2007*b*. *OECD Employment Outlook.* Paris: OECD.

—— 2007*c*. *Revenue Statistics, 1965–2006.* Paris: OECD.

—— 2008. *OECD.Stat.* Online database. Available at: stats.oecd.org.

OECD and Statistics Canada. 2000. *Literacy in the Information Age: Final Report of the International Adult Literacy Survey*. Paris and Ottowa: OECD and Statistics Canada.

Ondrich, Jan, C. Katherina Spiess, and Qing Yang. 1996. "Barefoot in a German Kitchen: Federal Parental Leave and Benefit Policy and the Return to Work After Childbirth in Germany." *Journal of Population Economics* 9: 247–66.

————— and G. G. Wagner. 1999. "Full Time or Part Time? German Parental Leave Policy and the Return to Work After Childbirth in Germany." *Research in Labor Economics* 18: 41–74.

Orloff, Ann. 2002. "Women's Employment and Welfare Regimes." Social Policy and Development Programme Paper 12. United Nations Research Institute for Social Development.

————— 2004. "Farewell to Maternalism: State Policies and Mothers' Employment." Paper presented at the annual meeting of the Research Committee on Poverty, Social Welfare, and Social Policy (RC 19), International Sociological Association, Paris.

Oskarsson, Sven. 2005. "Divergent Trends and Different Causal Logics: The Importance of Bargaining Centralization When Explaining Earnings Inequality across Advanced Democratic Societies." *Politics and Society* 33: 359–85.

Osterman, Paul. 1999. *Securing Prosperity*. Princeton, NJ: Princeton University Press.

O'Toole, James and Edward E. Lawler III. 2006. *The New American Workplace*. New York: Palgrave Macmillan.

Palier, Bruno. 2000. " 'Defrosting' the French Welfare State." *West European Politics* 23: 113–36.

Palme, Joakim, Åke Bergmark, Olof Bäckman, Felipe Estrada, Johan Fritzell, Olle Lundberg, Ola Sjöberg, Lena Sommestad, and Marta Szebehely. 2002. *Welfare in Sweden: The Balance Sheet for the 1990s*. Stockholm: Ministry of Health and Social Affairs.

Paxton, Will, Nick Pearce, and Howard Reed. 2005. "Foundations for a Progressive Century." Pp. 355–401 in *Social Justice: Building a Fairer Britain*, edited by Nick Pearce and Will Paxton. London: Institute for Public Policy Research.

Pearce, Nick and Will Paxton, eds. 2005. *Social Justice: Building a Fairer Britain*. London: Institute for Public Policy Research.

Pearson, Mark and Stafano Scarpetta. 2000. "What Do We Know About Policies to Make Work Pay?" *OECD Economic Studies* 31: 11–24.

Pebley, Anne R. and Narayan Sastry. 2004. "Neighborhoods, Poverty, and Children's Well-Being." Pp. 119–45 in *Social Inequality*, edited by Kathryn M. Neckerman. New York: Russell Sage Foundation.

Perotti, Roberto. 1996. "Growth, Income Distribution, and Democracy: What the Data Say." *Journal of Economic Growth* 1: 149–87.

Persson, Torsten and Guido Tabellini. 1994. "Is Inequality Harmful for Growth?" *American Economic Review* 84: 600–21.

Peter, Waltraut. 2004. "The Earned Income Tax Credit: A Model for Germany?" Unpublished. American Institute for Contemporary German Studies. Washington, DC.

Pettit, Becky and Jennifer Hook. 2002. "The Structure of Women's Employment in Comparative Perspective." Working Paper 330. Luxembourg Income Study. Available at: www.lisproject.org.

Pew Research Center for the People and the Press. 2007. "Trends in Political Values and Core Attitudes: 1987–2007." Available at: people-press.org.

Phelps, Edmund S. 1997. *Rewarding Work*. Cambridge, MA: Harvard University Press.

Phillips, Kevin. 2002. *Wealth and Democracy: A Political History of the American Rich*. New York: Broadway Books.

Phillips, Meredith and Tiffani Chin. 2004. "School Inequality: What Do We Know?" Pp. 467–518 in *Social Inequality*, edited by Kathryn M. Neckerman. New York: Russell Sage Foundation.

Pierson, Chris. 2002. "'Social Democracy on the Back Foot': The ALP and the 'New' Australian Model." *New Political Economy* 7: 179–97.

—— and Francis G. Castles. 2002. "Australian Antecedents of the Third Way." *Political Studies* 50: 683–702.

Pierson, Paul. 2001. *The New Politics of the Welfare State*. Oxford: Oxford University Press.

Piketty, Thomas and Emmanuel Saez. 2007*a*. "How Progressive is the U.S. Federal Tax System? A Historical and International Perspective." *Journal of Economic Perspectives* 21(1): 3–24.

————2007*b*. "Income and Wage Inequality in the United States, 1913–2002." Pp. 141–225 in *Top Incomes over the Twentieth Century*, edited by Anthony B. Atkinson and Thomas Piketty. Oxford: Oxford University Press.

Pizzigati, Sam. 1992. *The Maximum Wage*. New York: Apex Press.

Plantenga, Janneke and Johan Hansen. 1999. "Assessing Equal Opportunities in the European Union." *International Labour Review* 138: 351–79.

Ploug, Niels. 1999. "Cuts in and Reform of the Nordic Cash Benefit Systems." Pp. 79–103 in *Nordic Social Policy*, edited by Mikko Kautto, Matti Heikkilä, Bjørn Hvinden, Staffan Marklund, and Niels Ploug. London: Routledge.

Pontusson, Jonas. 2005. *Inequality and Prosperity: Social Europe Versus Liberal America*. Ithaca, NY: Cornell University Press.

——2006. "Whither Social Europe? Which Social Europe?" *Challenge* 49(6): 35–54.

Powell, Lisa M. 1998. "Part-Time Versus Full-Time Work and Child Care Costs: Evidence for Married Mothers." *Applied Economics* 30: 503–11.

Prais, S. J., Valerie Jarvis, and Karin Wagner. 1989. "Productivity and Vocational Skills in Services in Britain and Germany: Hotels." *National Institute Economic Review*, November: 52–74.

Presser, Harriet B. 2003. *Working in a 24/7 Economy*. New York: Russell Sage Foundation.

Pryor, Frederic L. and David L. Schaffer. 1999. *Who's Not Working and Why*. Cambridge: Cambridge University Press.

Putnam, Robert D. 1993. *Making Democracy Work: Civic Traditions in Modern Italy*. Princeton, NJ: Princeton University Press.

—— 2000. *Bowling Alone: The Collapse and Revival of American Community*. New York: Simon & Schuster.

Pylkkänen, Elina and Nina Smith. 2003. "Career Interruptions Due to Parental Leave: A Comparative Study of Denmark and Sweden." Social, Employment, and Migration Working Paper 1. Organization for Economic Cooperation and Development. Available at: www.oecd.org.

Ragin, Charles C. 1987. *The Comparative Method: Moving Beyond Qualitative and Quantitative Strategies*. Berkeley: University of California Press.

Rainwater, Lee and Timothy M. Smeeding. 2003. *Poor Kids in a Rich Country: America's Children in Comparative Perspective*. New York: Russell Sage Foundation.

Ramsay, Maureen. 2005. "A Modest Proposal: The Maximum Wage." *Contemporary Politics* 11: 201–15.

Rawls, John. 1971. *A Theory of Justice*. Cambridge, MA: Harvard University Press.

—— 2001. *Justice as Fairness: A Restatement*, edited by Erin Kelly. Cambridge, MA: Harvard University Press.

Reed, Deborah and Maria Cancian. 2001. "Sources of Inequality: Measuring the Contributions of Income Sources to Rising Family Income Inequality." *Review of Income and Wealth* 47: 321–33.

Rehn, Gosta. 1985. "Swedish Active Labor Market Policy: Retrospect and Prospect." *Industrial Relations* 24: 62–89.

Reich, Robert B. 1991. *The Work of Nations*. New York: Vintage.

—— 1999. "We Are All Third Wayers Now." *The American Prospect*, March–April. Available at: www.prospect.org/print/V10/43/reich-r.html.

Rhodes, Martin. 1996. "Globalization and West European Welfare States: A Critical Review of Recent Debates." *Journal of European Social Policy* 6: 305–27.

—— 2000. "Desperately Seeking a Solution: Social Democracy, Thatcherism, and the 'Third Way' in British Welfare." *West European Politics* 23: 2.

Rodrik, Dani. 2007. *One Economics, Many Recipes*. Princeton, NJ: Princeton University Press.

Roemer, John E. 1998. *Equality of Opportunity*. Cambridge, MA: Harvard University Press.

—— 1999. "Egalitarian Strategies." *Dissent*, Summer: 64–74.

Rønsen, Marit. 2001. "Market Work, Child Care, and the Division of Household Labour: Adaptations of Norwegian Mothers Before and After the Cash-for-Care Reform." Report 2001/3. Statistics Norway.

—— and Marianne Sundstrom. 2002. "Family Policy and After-Birth Employment Among New Mothers: A Comparison of Finland, Norway, and Sweden." *European Journal of Population* 18: 121–52.

Rothstein, Bo. 1998. *Just Institutions Matter: The Moral and Political Logic of the Universal Welfare State*. Cambridge: Cambridge University Press.

Rubery, Jill, Mark Smith, and Colette Fagan. 1999. *Women's Employment in Europe*. London: Routledge.

Rueda, David and Jonas Pontusson. 2000. "Wage Inequality and Varieties of Capitalism." *World Politics* 52: 350–83.

Ruhm, Christopher J. 1998. "The Economic Consequences of Parental Leave Mandates: Lessons from Europe." *Quarterly Journal of Economics* 113: 285–317.

Sacchi, Stefano and Francesca Bastagli. 2005. "Italy: Striving Uphill but Stopping Halfway; the Troubled Journey of the Experimental Minimum Insertion Income." In *Welfare State Reform in Southern Europe*, edited by Maurizio Ferrera. London: Routledge.

Sainsbury, Diane. 1999. "Taxation, Family Responsibilities, and Employment." Pp. 185–209 in *Gender and Welfare State Regimes*, edited by Diane Sainsbury. Oxford: Oxford University Press.

Salverda, Wiemer. 1998. "Incidence and Evolution of Low-Wage Employment in the Netherlands and the United States, 1979–1989." Pp. 25–62 in *Low-Wage Employment in Europe*, edited by Stephen Bazen, Mary Gregory, and Wiemer Salverda. Northampton, MA: Edward Elgar.

Samuelson, Robert J. 1996. "Why America Creates Jobs." *Newsweek*, July 29, p. 49.

Sapir, André, Philippe Aghion, Guiseppe Bertola, Martin Hellwig, Jean Pisanni-Ferry, Dariusz Rosati, Jose Viñals, and Helen Wallace, with Marco Buti, Mario Nava, and Peter M. Smith. 2004. *An Agenda for a Growing Europe: The Sapir Report*. Oxford: Oxford University Press.

Sawhill, Isabel and Adam Thomas. 2001. "A Hand Up for the Bottom Third." Unpublished. Brookings Institution. Available at: www.brook.edu/views/papers/sawhill/20010522.pdf.

Scharpf, Fritz W. 1997. "Employment and the Welfare State: A Continental Dilemma." Working Paper 97/7. Max Planck Institute for the Study of Societies. Available at: www.mpi-fg-koeln.mpg.de.

—— 2000. "Economic Changes, Vulnerabilities, and Institutional Capabilities." Pp. 21–124 in *Welfare and Work in the Open Economy. Volume 1: From Vulnerability to Competitiveness*, edited by Fritz W. Scharpf and Vivien A. Schmidt. Oxford: Oxford University Press.

—— and Vivien A. Schmidt. 2000. "Conclusions." Pp. 310–36 in *Welfare and Work in the Open Economy. Volume 1: From Vulnerability to Competitiveness*, edited by Fritz W. Scharpf and Vivien A. Schmidt. Oxford: Oxford University Press.

Schettkat, Ronald. 2004. "U.S. Sclerosis?" *Challenge*, May–June, 52.

—— 2005. "Is Labor Market Regulation at the Root of European Unemployment? The Case of Germany and the Netherlands." Pp. 262–83 in *Fighting Unemployment: The Limits of Free Market Orthodoxy*, edited by David R. Howell. Oxford: Oxford University Press.

Schiller, Bradley R. 2001. *The Economics of Poverty and Discrimination*. 8th edition. Upper Saddle River, NJ: Prentice-Hall.

Scruggs, Lyle. 2004. "Welfare State Entitlements Data Set: A Comparative Institutional Analysis of Eighteen Welfare States." Data set. Version 1.0. Available at: sp.uconn.edu/~scruggs/wp.htm.

—— 2005a. "Revised Decommodification Scores." Data set. Unpublished. Department of Political Science, University of Connecticut.

—— 2005*b*. "Welfare State Generosity Across Space and Time." Unpublished. Department of Political Science, University of Connecticut.

—— and James P. Allan. 2005. "The Material Consequences of Welfare States: Benefit Generosity and Absolute Poverty in 16 OECD Countries." Working Paper 409. Luxembourg Income Study. Available at: www.lisproject.org.

Seils, Eric. 2002. "Financial Policy in the Netherlands, 1977–2002: The Effects of Fiscal Contracts." Discussion Paper 04/2. Max Planck Institute for the Study of Societies. Available at: www.mpi-fg-koeln.mpg.de.

Sefton, Tom and Holly Sutherland. 2005. "Inequality and Poverty under New Labour." Pp. 231–49 in *A More Equal Society? New Labour, Poverty, Inequality, and Exclusion*, edited by John Hills and Kitty Stewart. Bristol: Policy Press.

Sen, Amartya. 1983. "Poor, Relatively Speaking." *Oxford Economic Papers* 35: 153–69.

Shalev, Michael. 2007. "Limits and Alternatives to Multiple Regression in Comparative Research." *Comparative Social Research* 24: 261–308.

Shulman, Beth. 2003. *The Betrayal of Work: How Low-Wage Jobs Fail 30 Million Americans*. New York: New Press.

Siebert, Horst. 1997. "Labor Market Rigidities: At the Root of Unemployment in Europe." *Journal of Economic Perspectives* 11(3): 37–54.

—— 2004. *The German Economy*. Princeton, NJ: Princeton University Press.

Skocpol, Theda. 2004. "Civic Transformation and Inequality in the Contemporary United States." Pp. 729–67 in *Social Inequality*, edited Kathryn M. Neckerman. New York: Russell Sage Foundation.

Slemrod, Joel. 1995. "What Do Cross-Country Studies Teach About Government Involvement, Prosperity, and Economic Growth?" *Brookings Papers on Economic Activity* 1995: 373–431.

—— 2004. "Are Corporate Tax Rates, or Countries, Converging?" *Journal of Public Economics* 88: 1169–86.

—— and Jon Bakija. 2004. *Taxing Ourselves*. Third edition. Cambridge, MA: MIT Press.

Smeeding, Timothy M. 2004. "Public Policy and Economic Inequality: The United States in Comparative Perspective." Working Paper 367. Luxembourg Income Study. Available at: www.lisproject.org.

Smith, Kristen, Barbara Downs, and Martin O'Connell. 2001. "Maternity Leave and Employment Patterns: 1961–1995." Household Economic Studies Report P70-79. Washington, DC: U.S. Bureau of the Census.

Sørensen, Aage B. 1990. "Throwing the Sociologists Out? A Reply to Smith." *American Sociological Review* 55: 842–5.

Spiess, C. Katharina and Gert G. Wagner. 2003. "Why Are Day Care Vouchers an Effective and Efficient Instrument to Combat Child Poverty in Germany?" Pp. 305–16 in *Combating Poverty in Europe: The German Welfare Regime in Practice*, edited by Peter Krause, Gerhard Bäcker, and Walter Hanesch. Aldershot, UK.: Ashgate.

Steinmo, Sven. 1994. "The End of Redistribution? International Pressures and Domestic Tax Policy Choices." *Challenge*, November–December: 9–17.

Steinmo, Sven. 2002. "Globalization and Taxation: Challenges to the Swedish Welfare State." *Comparative Political Studies* 35: 839–62.

Stewart, Kitty. 2005. "Towards an Equal Start? Addressing Childhood Poverty and Deprivation." Pp. 143–166 in *A More Equal Society? New Labour, Poverty, Inequality and Exclusion*, edited by John Hills and Kitty Steward. Bristol, UK: Policy Press.

Stier, Haya, Noah Lewin-Epstein, and Michael Braun. 2001. "Welfare Regimes, Family-Supportive Policies, and Women's Employment Along the Life-Course." *American Journal of Sociology* 106: 1731–60.

Stoker, Robert P. and Laura A. Wilson. 2006. *When Work Is Not Enough: State and Federal Policies to Support Needy Workers*. Washington, DC: Brookings Institution.

Streeck, Wolfgang. 1992. *Social Institutions and Economic Performance*. London: Sage.

—— 1999. "Competitive Solidarity: Rethinking the 'European Social Model.'" Working Paper 99/8. Max Planck Institute for the Study of Societies. Available at: www.mpi-fg-koeln.mpg.de.

—— 2005. "From State Weakness as Strength to State Weakness as Weakness: Welfare Corporatism and the Private Use of Public Interest." Pp. 38–164 in *Governance in Contemporary Germany: The Semisovereign State Revisited*, edited by Simon Green and William E. Paterson. Cambridge: Cambridge University Press.

—— and Christina Trampusch. 2005. "Economic Reform and the Political Economy of the German Welfare State." Working Paper 05/2. Max Planck Institute for the Study of Societies. Available at: www.mpi-fg-koeln.mpg.de.

Surender, Rebecca. 2004. "Modern Challenges to the Welfare State and the Antecedents of the Third Way." Pp. 3–24 in *Welfare State Change: Towards a Third Way?* edited by Jane Lewis and Rebecca Surender. Oxford: Oxford University Press.

Svallfors, Stefan and Peter Taylor-Gooby, eds. 1999. *The End of the Welfare State?* London: Routledge.

Swank, Duane. 1998. "Funding the Welfare State: Globalization and the Taxation of Business in Advanced Market Economies." *Political Studies* 46: 671–92.

—— 2002. *Global Capital, Political Institutions, and Policy Change in Developed Welfare States*. Cambridge: Cambridge University Press.

—— 2005. "Tax Policy in an Era of Internationalization: An Assessment of a Conditional Diffusion Model of the Spread of Neoliberalism." Unpublished. Department of Political Science, Marquette University.

—— and Sven Steinmo. 2002. "The New Political Economy of Taxation in Advanced Capitalist Democracies." *American Journal of Political Science* 46: 642–55.

Swenson, Peter. 1989. *Fair Shares: Unions, Pay, and Politics in Sweden and West Germany*. Ithaca, NY: Cornell University Press.

Taylor-Gooby, Peter. 2005. "Attitudes to Social Justice." Pp. 106–30 in *Social Justice: Building a Fairer Britain*, edited by Nick Pearce and Will Paxton. London: Institute for Public Policy Research.

—— and Trine Larsen. 2004. "The Genuinely Liberal Genuine Welfare State." In *New Risks, New Welfare: The Transformation of the European Welfare State*, edited by Peter Taylor-Gooby. Oxford: Oxford University Press.

Townsend, Peter. 1979. *Poverty in the United Kingdom: A Survey of Household Resources and Standards of Living.* Berkeley: University of California Press.

Traxler, Franz, Sabine Blaschke, and Bernhard Kittel. 2001. *National Labour Relations in Internationalized Markets.* Oxford: Oxford University Press.

Uchitelle, Louis. 2006. *The Disposable American: Layoffs and Their Consequences.* New York: Knopf.

UNDP (United Nations Development Programme). 2006. *Human Development Report.* Available at: www.undp.org.

U.S. Bureau of the Census. 2002. "Financing the Future: Postsecondary Students, Costs, and Financial Aid, 1996–1997." P70-83. Available at: www.census.gov/population/www/socdemo/sch_cost.html.

——Various years. *Statistical Abstract of the United States.* Washington, DC: Government Printing Office.

U.S. Department of Labor. 2008. "Minimum Wage Laws in the States." Available at: www.dol.gov/esa/minwage/america.htm.

Vandell, Deborah Lowe and Barbara Wolfe. 2000. "Child Care Quality: Does It Matter and Does It Need to Be Improved?" Special Report 78. Institute for Research on Poverty, University of Wisconsin-Madison. Available at: www.ssc.wisc.edu/irp.

Verba, Sidney, Kay Lehman Schlozman, and Henry E. Brady. 2004. "Political Equality: What Do We Know About It?" Pp. 635–66 in *Social Inequality*, edited by Kathryn M. Neckerman. New York: Russell Sage Foundation.

Verbist, Gerlinde. 2004. "Redistributive Effect and Progressivity of Taxes: An International Comparison Across the EU Using EUROMOD." Working Paper EM5/04. EUROMOD.

Visser, Jelle. 2002. "The First Part-Time Economy in the World: A Model to Be Followed?" *Journal of European Social Policy* 12: 23–42.

Visser, Jelle and Anton Hemerijck. 1997. *"A Dutch Miracle": Job Growth, Welfare Reform, and Corporatism in the Netherlands.* Amsterdam: Amsterdam University Press.

Voitchovsky, Sarah. 2003. "Does the Profile of Income Inequality Matter for Economic Growth?" Working Paper 354. Luxembourg Income Study. Available at: www.lisproject.org.

Waldfogel, Jane. 2002. "Child Care, Women's Employment, and Child Outcomes." *Journal of Population Economics* 15: 527–48.

——2006. *What Children Need.* Cambridge, MA: Harvard University Press.

Wallerstein, Michael. 1999. "Wage-Setting Institutions and Pay Inequality in Advanced Industrial Societies." *American Journal of Political Science* 43: 649–80.

Warren, Elizabeth and Amelia Warren Tyagi. 2003. *The Two-Income Trap: Why Middle-Class Parents Are Going Broke.* New York: Basic Books.

Wasow, Bernard. 2000. "Expanding the Earned Income Tax Credit for Working Families." Idea Brief 11. The Century Foundation. Available at: www.tcf.org.

Weinstein, Paul, Jr. 2005. "Family-Friendly Tax Reform." Policy Report. Progressive Policy Institute. Washington, DC.

Wessel, David and Daniel Benjamin. 1994. "Looking for Work: In Employment Policy, America and Europe Make a Sharp Contrast." *Wall Street Journal*, March 14, pp. A1, A6.

Western, Bruce. 1996. "Vague Theory and Model Uncertainty in Macrosociology." *Sociological Methodology* 6: 165–92.

——Meredith Kleykamp, and Jake Rosenfeld. 2004. "Crime, Punishment, and American Inequality." Pp. 771–96 in *Social Inequality*, edited by Kathryn M. Neckerman. New York: Russell Sage Foundation.

White, Stuart. 2004*a*. "A Social Democratic Framework for Benefit Conditionality." In Kate Stanley and Liane Asta Lohde with Stuart White, *Sanctions and Sweeteners: Rights and Responsibilities in the Benefits System*. London: Institute for Public Policy Research.

——2004*b*. "Welfare Philosophy and the Third Way." Pp. 25–46 in *Welfare State Change: Towards a Third Way?* edited by Jane Lewis and Rebecca Surender. Oxford: Oxford University Press.

Whiteford, Peter. 2007. "Targeting, Redistribution, and Poverty Reduction in OECD Countries." Unpublished.

——and Gregory Angenent. 2002. "The Australian System of Social Protection: An Overview." Occasional Paper 6. Department of Family and Community Services. Available at: www.facs.gov.au.

Wilensky, Harold L. 2002. *Rich Democracies*. Berkeley: University of California Press.

Wilkinson, Richard G. 1996. *Unhealthy Societies: the Afflications of Inequality*. London: Routledge.

Wilson, William Julius. 1987. *The Truly Disadvantaged*. Chicago: University of Chicago Press.

——1996. *When Work Disappears*. New York: Knopf.

Winegarden, C. R. and Paula M. Bracy. 1995. "Demographic Consequences of Maternal-Leave Programs in Industrial Countries: Evidence from Fixed-Effects Models." *Southern Economic Journal* 6: 1020–35.

Woldendorp, Jaap. 2005. *The Polder Model: From Disease to Miracle? Dutch Neo-Corporatism, 1965–2000*. Amsterdam: Vrije Universiteit.

Wolff, Edward N. 2002. *Top Heavy*. Updated edition. New York: New Press.

——2006. *Does Education Really Help?* Oxford: Oxford University Press.

World Values Survey. 1995–97. Available at: www.icpsr.org.

Wright, Erik Olin and Rachel Dwyer. 2003. "The Patterns of Job Expansions in the United States: A Comparison of the 1960s and 1990s." *Socio-Economic Review* 1: 289–325.

——and Luca Perrone. 1977. "Marxist Class Categories and Income Inequality." *American Sociological Review* 42: 32–55.

Wuthnow, Robert. 2002. "United States: Bridging the Privileged and the Marginalized?" In *Democracies in Flux: The Evolution of Social Capital in Contemporary Society*, edited by Robert D. Putnam. Oxford: Oxford University Press.

Index